ABOVE THE AMERICAN RENAISSANCE

ABOVE THE AMERICAN RENAISSANCE

David S. Reynolds and the Spiritual Imagination in American Literary Studies

EDITED BY
Harold K. Bush
and
Brian Yothers

University of Massachusetts Press
AMHERST AND BOSTON

Copyright © 2018 by University of Massachusetts Press
All rights reserved
Printed in the United States of America

ISBN 978-1-62534-360-4 (paper); 359-8 (hardcover)

Designed by Sally Nichols
Set in Monotype Dante Std
Printed and bound by Maple Press, Inc.

Cover design by Sally Nichols
Cover art: S. J. Ferris., *Washington & Lincoln (Apotheosis)*, c. 1865.
Courtesy of Library of Congress.

Library of Congress Cataloging-in-Publication Data

Names: Bush, Harold K. (Harold Karl), 1956– editor. | Yothers, Brian, 1975– editor.
Title: Above the American renaissance : David S. Reynolds and the spiritual imagination in American literary studies / edited by Harold K. Bush, Saint Louis University, and Brian Yothers, University of Texas at El Paso.
Other titles: Spiritual imagination in American literary studies
Description: Amherst : University of Massachusetts Press, 2018. | Includes bibliographical references and index. |
Identifiers: LCCN 2017050263 (print) | LCCN 2017055748 (ebook) | ISBN 9781613766002 (e-book) | ISBN 9781613766019 (e-book) | ISBN 9781625343598 (hardcover) | ISBN 9781625343604 (pbk.)
Subjects: LCSH: American literature—19th century—History and criticism. | Spirituality in literature. | Religion in literature. | Religion and literature—United States—History—19th century. | Reynolds, David S., 1948– Beneath the American Renaissance.
Classification: LCC PS166 (ebook) | LCC PS166 .A26 2018 (print) | DDC 810.9/382—dc23
LC record available at https://lccn.loc.gov/2017050263

British Library Cataloguing-in-Publication Data
A catalog record for this book is available from the British Library.

CONTENTS

Preface ix
Brian Yothers

Introduction. Above the American Renaissance
Tracking and Theorizing the Spiritual Turn in American Literary Studies
Harold K. Bush 1

Part I
Reconstructing the Spiritual and the Secular

Chapter 1. Haunted America
Reading the Spiritual Turn
Tracy Fessenden 21

Chapter 2. "The Spirit of Instructive Investigation"
Bronson Alcott, Transcendental Childhood, and the Search for Divinity
John Matteson 37

Chapter 3. Secular Melancholy
Religious Skepticism and the "Literature of Misery"
Dawn Coleman 52

Chapter 4. Whittier and the Mormons
From Folk Magic to Freedom and Back Again
Zachary McLeod Hutchins   69

Chapter 5. "Will He Perish?"
Moby-Dick *and Nineteenth-Century Extinction Discourse*
Timothy Sweet   87

Part II
Reconstructing the Scriptures

Chapter 6. Higher Reading
Uncle Tom's Cabin *and Biblical Higher Criticism*
Gail K. Smith   107

Chapter 7. The "Art of Attaining Truth" in *Moby-Dick*
Print Technologies, Hermeneutics, and Castaway Readers
Jeffrey Bilbro   125

Chapter 8. "New-born Bard[s] of the Holy Ghost"
The American Bibles of Walt Whitman and Joseph Smith
Michael Robertson   140

Chapter 9. The Other *Traditions of Palestine*
An 1863 Novel by Ebenezer Wheelwright
Richard Kopley   161

Chapter 10. The Millennial Impulse above the American Renaissance
From Jonathan Edwards to Charles Grandison Finney and the Second Great Awakening
Mason I. Lowance, Jr.   175

Part III
Reconstructing Popular Religion

Chapter 11. Hymns by the Fireside
Religious Verse and the Rise and the Fall of the Fireside Poets
Claudia Stokes   195

Chapter 12. Keeping the Sabbath at Home
Emily Dickinson and the Rise of Private Hymnody
Christopher N. Phillips   211

Chapter 13. "The Nearest Dream Recedes – Unrealized"
Emily Dickinson, Thomas Wentworth Higginson, and Fascicle 14
Vivian R. Pollak   227

Chapter 14. Harriet Beecher Stowe and Martyrdom
Protestant Missions in Uncle Tom's Cabin *and*
Uncle Tom's Cabin *in Protestant Missions*
Brian Yothers   245

Chapter 15. "God Will Give Him Blood to Drink"
Unholy Dying in The House of the Seven Gables
Jonathan A. Cook   259

Afterword. God Above, America Beneath
Abraham Lincoln and Religion
David S. Reynolds   275

Contributors   293
Index   297

PREFACE

Brian Yothers

SOME SCHOLARLY books alter scholarly lives. My first encounter with David S. Reynolds's *Beneath the American Renaissance* was the stimulus for such an alteration. I first read the book in the spring before starting my doctoral studies in American literature, and his idea that the texts I was supposed to feel good about reading and the texts I felt duty-bound to scorn could be mutually illuminating in ways that shed equal light on cultural and aesthetic questions struck me with the force of revelation. Reynolds showed me that Edgar Allan Poe's work could be newly viewed by the lurid light of George Lippard's and George Thompson's sexually explicit "male Subversive fiction"; Herman Melville's *Moby-Dick* could become freshly revelatory in the light of New England sermonic traditions; Ralph Waldo Emerson and Henry David Thoreau lived in the midst of the populist culture of their times rather than being dreamily abstracted from it. As I learned that reading sermons, pamphlets, popular fiction, and advice books was necessary to understanding one of American literature's most vibrant periods, I became increasingly certain that nineteenth-century American literature was a field I could study without fear of boredom or exhaustion.

Beneath the American Renaissance suggests that it is not only permissible but beneficial to scan the nineteenth-century literary archive with abandon. Indeed, it is practically mandatory in order to understand the most frequently assigned and discussed works of the period, both those that F. O. Matthiessen canonized decades ago in *American Renaissance* (Emerson, Melville, Thoreau, Nathaniel Hawthorne, and Walt Whitman) and those that have since been resurrected (Poe, Emily Dickinson, and, more recently, Harriet Beecher Stowe). For the young scholar looking to explore mid-nineteenth-century American literary culture more widely, the sky is the limit, and we owe much of this fervor and ferment to Reynolds's work in *Beneath the American Renaissance*.

The essays in this book, as our title *Above the American Renaissance* implies, take *Beneath the American Renaissance* as both a model and a provocation. In his introduction, Harold K. Bush notes that Reynolds's scholarship in the 1980s helped to reinvigorate investigations of religious culture; and since then, for reasons ranging from a rising respect for interdisciplinarity to the trauma of the 9/11 attacks and their aftermath, religion in literature has gone from a sideshow to a major area of inquiry for many nineteenth-century Americanists. The essays in our book seek to capture a moment in which questions related to religion and spirituality are being investigated with increasing urgency and skill. They both acknowledge the vibrancy of what is already happening in the intersection of literary and religious studies and point toward sustaining and extending those investigations.

Reynolds's *Beneath the American Renaissance*, first published in 1989, transformed Americanist literary studies by demonstrating the interconnections of popular and canonical literary cultures. Its topics range from race to poetics, and it considers both well-known authors such as Melville, Hawthorne, Dickinson, Whitman, and Stowe and more neglected figures such as Ebenezer Wheelwright, Augusta Jane Evans, Elizabeth Stoddard, and John Greenleaf Whittier. As the essays in our own book show, Reynolds's reconstructive methodology, which excavates previously unknown connections between popular and canonical literary cultures, meshes beautifully with the current emphasis among religious studies scholars on the lived experience of religion.

Our book is divided into three sections that highlight interlocking aspects of Reynolds's legacy. Part 1, which includes essays by Tracy Fessenden, John Matteson, Dawn Coleman, Zachary McLeod Hutchins, and Timothy Sweet, makes reference to Reynolds's reconstructive method of literary and cultural criticism as the contributors consider how to redraw the lines between the spiritual and the secular. Part 2, with essays by Gail K. Smith, Jeffrey Bilbro, Michael Robertson, Richard Kopley, and Mason I. Lowance, Jr., shows how scriptures are reconfigured in nineteenth-century American literature and culture. Part 3, including pieces by Claudia Stokes, Christopher N. Phillips, Vivian R. Pollak, Brian Yothers, and Jonathan A. Cook, illustrates the shifting boundaries of popular religious phenomena from hymns to missionary activity. Bush's introduction and David S. Reynolds's afterword demonstrate how these impulses interact in American literary scholarship and in the literary legacy of Abraham Lincoln.

We are grateful to Saint Louis University, the University of Texas at El Paso, the HSI-Pathways to the Professoriate Program, and the Frances Spatz Leighton Endowed Distinguished Professorship for their financial support of this project. David Goldfield, Judith Madera, Megan Marshall, and John Matteson answered many questions about the significance of cultural biography, and David S. Reynolds was unfailingly generous and supportive of our efforts. At the University of Massachusetts Press, Mary Dougherty has been an insightful and supportive editor at every step along the way. Finally, we thank our spouses, Hiroko Hara Bush and Maryse Jayasuriya, for their wisdom and encouragement.

ABOVE THE AMERICAN RENAISSANCE

INTRODUCTION

ABOVE THE AMERICAN RENAISSANCE

Tracking and Theorizing the Spiritual Turn in American Literary Studies

Harold K. Bush

SCHOLARS IN literary studies often turn to this or that new way of theorizing a topic or period or author: the linguistic turn, the object turn, the cognitive turn, the constructivist turn, the affective turn, and so on. Early in my career I wrote about the term *repentance* in this regard, noting that the Hebrew root of the biblical concept refers to, among other things, a 180-degree turn in a dance. Thus, when one repents, one figuratively turns completely and forcefully around in a different direction. My major interest in those days was noting how America's many cultural declarations (including the Declaration of Independence) were in certain ways radical acts of repentance. In New Testament ideology, such a successful and wholehearted turn allows and empowers a thoroughly reimagined way of looking at the world—for instance, through the lens of the Kingdom of God.[1]

However we might conceive of it, a turn suggests a sudden awakening or reawakening, a fresh interpretive strategy that has been overlooked, a sensibility that has not been fully perceived. A turn may well be seen as a renaissance—the experience of being born again—and it may be steeped in the heightened language of surprised revelation, a critical repentance of shocked rediscovery. Throughout the reign of high theory, critics have frequently turned to face new ideas, driven by this wind or that. There is a certain irony, then, to the constant invocation of turning within what has often been thought of as the highly secularized profession of literary and cultural studies.

The essays in *Above the American Renaissance* celebrate the legacy of a particular turn in cultural studies, one spearheaded almost thirty years ago by a group of literary scholars who came to be known as the New Americanists.[2] The impact of their deeply contextualized studies of the various discursive formations that lay beneath major authors set the bar for my own graduate studies agenda. This collection had its origins in the celebration of the twenty-fifth anniversary of the publication of what was possibly the most influential of the texts produced by that group: David S. Reynolds's *Beneath the American Renaissance: The Subversive Imagination in the Age of Emerson and Melville* (1989). Reynolds's book not only inspired our own book's title but influenced our contributors' vision for cultural biography, their use of popular literatures, and their rigorous contextual methodological practices. Moreover, in returning to his influential study, all of our contributors have consciously invoked another turn: one toward the above—that is, the spiritual or religious predilections of the authors we are studying. This spiritual turn is presently of surging interest in our profession; admittedly, at this late date, some of us may be a bit suspicious of yet another major critical redirection in American literary studies. In fact, given the commonplace view that our profession is dominated by a growing secularization, one might also be surprised to see this religious turn in our field. What accounts for a revival of interest in an approach that, only twenty years ago, was considered to be moribund?

During my doctoral studies at Indiana University, members of the graduate faculty urged me to let go of my interest in religion and focus on more important topics. They seemed to share an implicit sense, or prejudice, that attention to religion was incompatible with historicist scholarship. As Laura Levitt has written more recently, "Religion continues to carry the taint of abjection. It is primitive, outmoded, and dangerous."[3] Twenty-five years ago, the idea that literary scholars might wish to title a project *Above the American Renaissance*, referring as it does to those elements above and somehow separate from a culture, might have seemed oddly quaint. But nowadays the study of religion and literature (often abbreviated to "R & L") is a booming business and is no longer considered peripheral. In February 2015, an American Literature Association symposium astonishingly titled "God and the American Writer" (with a tip of the hat to Alfred Kazin's influential study) featured an exciting, mostly young cohort of scholars presenting their work. Likewise, as I sifted among the 177 job applications reviewed that year as chair of a departmental search for a nineteenth-century Americanist, I clearly saw that religious and spiritual approaches to the century's literature were constituting an emerging specialization in a field that remains very disjointed and impossible to pin down. These impressive research projects were being conceived, directed, and undertaken in many of the nation's top doctoral programs. The spiritual is now trending.[4]

The precise genealogy of this revival is hard to pin down, and a full historical analysis of the idea is certainly beyond the scope of this introduction. But many scholars often begin by pointing to the late Jenny Franchot's brief yet influential 1995 manifesto, "Invisible Domain," in which she lamented that religious approaches had gone to seed among Americanists.[5] Today critics commonly see her call to action as prescient, a reaction that gives her short article the feeling of a premature obituary. Scholars also commonly refer to the 9/11 attacks and the subsequent War on Terror as significant moments in the recovery of religion as a motivator of human action in American culture. In this regard, we may recollect the famous remarks of Stanley Fish in 2005, made soon after the death of the icon of theory, Jacques Derrida: "I was called by a reporter who wanted to know what would succeed high theory and the triumvirate of race, class and gender as the center of intellectual energy in the academy. I answered like a shot: 'religion.'"[6] Fish's off-the-cuff reaction, which has become a kind of disciplinary folk moment, has proven to be prophetic (though we might quibble about his prediction that religion would emerge as the center of the academy, especially in English departments). Finally, a rebirth of interest in the spiritual coincides with what some scholars of religion, such as Harvey Cox, are calling the "Age of the Spirit": "the threshold of a new chapter in the Christian story. Despite dire forecasts of its decline,

Christianity is growing faster than it ever has before, but mainly outside the West and in movements that accent spiritual experience, discipleship, and hope."[7] This explosive growth is commonly seen as most powerful in the global south and as Pentecostal or charismatic in nature, but its influence is significant in North America as well. Thus, the spiritual proclivities of the culture at large—and of individuals within it—may be provoking and shaping growth in the institutional study of religion and literature. The phenomenon is especially evident among a younger cohort of emerging scholars, many of whom count themselves as people of faith and are eager to find connections between their beliefs and literary texts.

Within the humanities, seminal works by Talal Asad, Charles Taylor, Leigh Schmidt, Robert Orsi, Tracy Fessenden, Charles Marsh, and Robert Wuthnow have gained traction among literary scholars. These writers are nurturing new ways of thinking about that mysterious phenomenon called *the secular,* a term that is rapidly being retrofitted for our times; and many focus on the lived religion of a subject under study as opposed to merely that person's beliefs. One of the most important of these works is Taylor's magnum opus *A Secular Age* (2007), which has radically recast the way in which many scholars think about the secular. In addition to redefining the term, Taylor brilliantly tracks what we label as secular as far back as the Protestant Reformation and notes how it has permeated western culture ever since. His argument complicates the secularization thesis that many have used to define the waning of faith and the disenchantment of the West. In the view of many academics, his account of a cross-pressured culture in which the religious and the irreligious dwell together in a vexed manner has come to seem much more plausible, especially alongside the resurgence of religious rhetoric and cultural power in American culture. By presenting new and exciting opportunities for practitioners in American literature to reexamine old and ingrained patterns of thought, Taylor and others have helped to trigger the turn to religion now being championed among Americanists.

It is notable, and perhaps not surprising, that none of the scholars I have just mentioned are members of English departments (though many of them, including Taylor, Schmidt, and Fessenden, frequently draw on literary examples). It seems that English professors are coming somewhat late to the party. Yet as one scholar of American literature, Michael Kauffman, notes, "histories of the profession of literary studies have long been underwritten by a narrative of secularization." Now, he believes, we must reexamine our assumptions about what we do, and why, in light of the abandonment of such narratives.[8] He is not the only literature scholar to take an interest in the religious turn. In *The Turn Around Religion in America,* a prominent collection of essays in honor of the career and achievement of Sacvan Bercovitch, the editor Nan Goodman writes that such a turn "provides a panoramic vision" and "invokes a metaphor common to recent studies."[9] Several other important and oft-cited volumes have appeared, including those by the critics John McClure, Amy Hungerford, John Modern, who have become touchstones in conversations about American literature.[10] Major journals such as *American Literature, American Literary History, Early American Literature,* and *Christianity and Literature* have hosted special issues that present new readings informed by a religious turn.[11] Moreover, certain works of influential critics who are themselves people of faith—perhaps most importantly the late Roger Lundin—have served as models for Christian scholars who are working to engage with American literature.[12]

During the past few years, several essayists have offered responses to influential monographs such as McClure's *Partial Faiths* in which they advance or question the theorization of this turn as a manifestation of what is now being described as the "postsecular." By positing yet another set of "turns"—the turn away from an outdated concept of the secular, and the turn to the terrain of a more progressive and enlightened view of how the secular has been previously misunderstood—these essays have confounded our understandings of what we might mean by such terms as "the religious." Among other things, the postsecular constitutes a powerful rejection of the so-called "secularization thesis" to which many had appealed as an organizing narrative of nineteenth- and twentieth-century American culture. That narrative focused on a steady diminishment of the authority of religion, a growing disenchantment among intellectuals, and the eventual but certain demise of the power of religion. Secularization, such works argued, was as sure as the rising of the sun—or perhaps as sure as its setting, if we see the sun as a representation of faith or enchantment. Lori Branch has recently asked if secularity still "functions in literary studies as something like Charles Taylor's 'immanent frame,' a combination of intellectual assumptions and political realities that make it hard to ascribe value to any intellectual position tainted by belief."[13] In response, one might offer the words of the influential religious studies scholar Robert Orsi: "Whether contemporary Americans working to understand particular religious phenomena know it or not, they bring to their inquiries local histories of talk about religion in the United States over time both within and outside the academy. Built into the very tools of analysis are hidden normativities, implicit distinctions between 'good' and 'bad' religions, and these need to be unpacked."[14]

The unpacking has begun in earnest. Suddenly, such sociological and cultural metanarratives and various local histories about religion have been called into question, if not abandoned outright, and scholars are beginning to take notice and to respond. Critics such as Fessenden are warning us of "the enduring hold of the secularization narrative" on our profession—"even on those who have supposedly rejected it."[15] Branch, who serves on the faculty of a major doctoral institution in literary studies, speaks forcefully of a desire to free her graduate students from the "stultifying misconceptions that plague our discipline . . . and so to enable them to unearth the strangeness and particularity of the acts of beliefs and disavowals of belief in the text."[16] Fessenden wryly notes that what Hungerford has written about contemporary novelists ("they want the fruits of religious power—or at least, they want to help us imagine compelling versions of religious power—without having to answer for the assumptions about the world, and about writing, upon which such visions are built") may ironically also be true for theorists of the postsecular.[17]

Riffing on some of Fessenden's concerns, I wonder about literary scholars' supposedly recent discovery of the weakened state of the notion of secularization, given the existence of pertinent religious scholarship—notably Philip Jenkins's *The Next Christendom* (2002). As we can clearly see in the wake of the 2016 presidential race and the morass of the administration of Donald Trump, religion, for better or worse, is alive and well in the American heartland. Why didn't the postmodern conceits of high theory, including the shibboleth of incredulity, provoke the literary crowd against the metanarratives of secularization? Given all of this evidence, what took so long? Despite some misgivings, at least the concept of the postsecular provides us with much additional grist for the mill as we reexamine how religion might open fruitful new approaches in the study of literature and culture. As Branch writes, the "presumed secularity of our field is being mitigated . . . by the emerging field of postsecular literature."[18] Though literature professors have arrived a bit late, the turn represented by postsecular studies is a welcome one.

All told, these are heady times for the study of religion and American literature. When Brian Yothers and I conceived of this book, we wanted to take advantage of this growth industry, exploit the theoretical and cultural shifts taking place, and recall the foundations set by the prolific cultural historian David S. Reynolds, whose work has been so crucial. His masterwork, *Beneath the American Renaissance*, is arguably the most significant volume in American literary studies to be published in the past three decades. It has influenced the methods and techniques of a generation of scholars and set the bar for the comprehensive attention required to speak authoritatively about various writers. Moreover, it greatly complicated the ways in which culture was informing biography; for as he pointed out, "far from being estranged from their context, [the major writers] were in large part created by it." Quoting Ralph Waldo Emerson, Reynolds showed how "the ideas of the time are in the air, and infect all who breathe it . . . almost through the pores of our skin."[19] He rigorously theorized and practiced the genre of cultural biography, a category that hardly existed prior to *Beneath the American Renaissance*. Several years later, in *Walt Whitman's America* (1995), he brought this methodology to its heights in the full treatment of a single individual.

In our book, we extend the cultural biographies of the writers under study by including their perceptions and experiences of what was "above" them—though, I hasten to note, such spiritual influences have always interested Reynolds. We also spill beyond the borders conventionally covered by the term *American Renaissance*, generally understood to be the first half of the 1850s. All of the writers discussed in our book published major works between 1840 and 1865, a period we might call the *long American Renaissance*. Each of our contributors attends to how the authors under study conceived of their works as deriving from or being inspired and informed by the spiritual realm. To some scholars, the category of the spiritual may seem hopelessly contemporary or even negative, perhaps connoting the New Age movement or various occult or mystical phenomena. However, the concept was very much part of the antebellum air—and not just among those who were involved in the spiritualist movement, with whom it is most commonly associated. Hebrews 12 assures us that we are "surrounded by a cloud of witnesses," and most intellectuals, writers, and artists found ways to employ the notion of the spiritual to their own ends, often in a positive light. They borrowed the terminology they found in their New Testaments, especially in the writings of Paul, who used the Greek word *pneumatikos* frequently in his description of the Christian life. In English translations of the Bible (for instance, in the King James Version), the term is most often rendered as "spiritual," thus connoting the way in which a disciple is driven by the spirit, like a sailboat is driven by the wind. Of the twenty-six appearances of *pneumatikos* in the New Testament, all but one are in the letters of Paul, with thirteen appearing in First Corinthians alone. In New Testament terms, a spiritual person is animated and led by a transcendent source called the Holy Spirit, one of three entities of the orthodox Godhead. Throughout his writings, Paul describes a spiritual person as one who walks by the spirit, listens attentively to the spirit, demonstrates the fruit of the spirit, and is filled with the spirit. It should be our goal, he says, to be spiritual as opposed to carnal or fleshly.

The writers discussed in our book all knew their King James Versions well, and they understood the centrality of the spiritual in the teachings of Paul. Thus, the term emerged frequently during the American Renaissance. For example, it appeared at least eleven times in Herman Melville's *Moby-Dick*, at least ten times in Harriet Beecher Stowe's *Uncle Tom's Cabin*, at least twenty-one times in Nathaniel Hawthorne's *The Blithedale Romance*, and at least seven times in Henry David Thoreau's *Walden*. Even Edgar Allan Poe used the word at least ten times in his tales. Certainly the New Testament warning that "the letter killeth, but the spirit giveth life" was an operative concept for these writers.[20]

A possible task for scholars who choose to study the spiritual lives of writers during this period is to consider how they sought guidance, counsel, and inspiration from the spirits of the air. For example, in *Harriet Beecher Stowe: A Spiritual Biography*, Nancy Koester takes seriously the task of identifying and clarifying the ways in which the spiritual influenced one of the century's most important and prolific novelists. Following that vein, several of the essays in our book also work to expand our understanding of Stowe's spiritual proclivities.

Specialists in the field will immediately recognize that the title of our collection complements Reynolds's gesture toward what was "beneath" an author: that is, the writer's cultural grounding. His account reveals that Emerson, Poe, Whitman, Dickinson, Hawthorne, and Melville were deeply embedded in their cultures and that their work depended on various subversive discourses underneath and within the mainstream. As Sean Wilentz has written, "after Reynolds' exploration of the unsounded depths of American culture, the nation itself, and not just its literary exemplars, looked very different than they had previously."[21] For instance, I recall being astonished by the sheer number of whale and other sea-monster stories that formed the foundation of *Moby-Dick* and by the number of popular preachers, beyond Edward Taylor, whose new religious style undergirded the famous sermon of Father Mapple in the opening section of that masterpiece.

In 2005, Reynolds followed up *Walt Whitman's America* with another impressive study, *John Brown, Abolitionist*. These titles, in tandem with his 2011 study, *Mightier Than the Sword: "Uncle Tom's Cabin" and the Battle for America*, mark him as not only a founder but also a master of the cultural biography. Moreover, as I have mentioned, he has long been a proponent of the field's spiritual turn, an interest he outlined in his first monograph, *Faith in Fiction* (1981). In *Mightier than the Sword*, he presents a detailed account of Stowe's adventures in the realm of the "ministering spirits" that she believed surrounded her on a daily basis. Although her affinity with spiritualism may seem eccentric or even heretical, her ideas follow a strong biblical theme: humankind's continuing bonds with the dead.[22]

As I was thinking about Reynolds's influence, I contacted numerous biographers who have themselves mastered the craft of cultural biography. One of them, Megan Marshall, told me, "It may be difficult now to judge whether Reynolds's *Beneath the American Renaissance* or the biographies themselves exert the greater influence. . . . His too, we can safely say, is a 'subversive imagination.'"[23] One of the strengths of Marshall's own cultural biography, *The Peabody Sisters*, is a similar ability to evoke subversive voices and communities. Her book draws her readers into the amazing community of intellectuals who gathered around Emerson in the 1830s and 1840s. Among all of these intriguing figures, she argues, the Peabodys have been largely ignored—especially the gifted Elizabeth, who is the heroine of her story. As Marshall has confirmed to me in personal correspondence, several aspects of *The Peabody Sisters* reflect Reynolds's work. In her preface, she comments on her theory of cultural biography, which, among other things, requires long and meticulous effort. "In the end, my work took most of two decades," she writes. "I became expert in deciphering the sisters' handwriting," and "I set out to read everything they ever wrote in letters and diaries and in print, along with most of the books they read and cared about."[24] These are daunting achievements, and they come back to all erstwhile cultural biographers with a certain alienated majesty, as Emerson might put it.

Reynolds has described his process in similar terms. While working on his epic biography of Whitman, he reports, "I dutifully read and reread all the letters, journals, conversations, and other private writings. I daresay I combed through them with an attentiveness never before attempted."[25] There is a kind of joyful boastfulness in that remark, and its implications have been ringing in my ears for many years now. In particular, his theory and method of paying scrupulous attention to the details of many fields simultaneously, along with his insistence on a comprehensive familiarity with primary and secondary materials, has marked the genre and become standard practice, setting the bar very high for those who follow him. Marshall's description of her own arduous process echoes precisely this concentration and joy.

Reynolds had help from forebears, of course—among them F. O. Matthiessen, whose 1941 *American Renaissance* remains surprisingly fresh in its cultural concerns. Marshall shared with me her thoughts about the genealogy of Reynolds's approach:

> In the mid-1980s, Phyllis Cole pioneered a style of literary analysis uniting close readings of biographical material (diaries and letters) and literary texts in her work on American Renaissance women, and Robert Richardson pursued a read-everything-he-read approach in his intellectual biographies of Thoreau and Emerson. [It is] possible to consider this triumvirate—Reynolds, Cole, and Richardson—as promoting a school of biographic literary criticism, emerging from the fertile ground of American Renaissance studies, running counter to, or at least alongside, the trend to "theorize," and infusing traditional literary humanism with a new rigor and expansiveness in use of materials and a much-needed diversity of subject matter.[26]

I spoke about Reynolds with John Matteson, a contributor to this book and author of the Pulitzer Prize–winning *Eden's Outcasts: The Story of Louisa May Alcott and Her Father* (2007). Matteson told me,

> Professor Reynolds's game-changing work had made that world more hospitable to the kind of work I was eager to do. Correcting the excesses of a field perhaps overly enamored with New Criticism and deconstruction, *Beneath the American Renaissance* bravely and persuasively affirmed that the authors of one of the great periods in American literature lived actual lives and that the cultural milieu from which they drew life had also enlivened and informed their work in myriad essential ways."[27]

Both Marshall and Matteson believe that Reynolds's work intervened in a field suffering from an excess of theoretical influence. But it is also important to notice how the form is a concrete instantiation of a theory of culture and the individual.

I also spoke with professional historians about Reynolds's influence, among them David Goldfield, author of the award-winning *America Aflame: How the Civil War Created a Nation* (2013). He told me,

David S. Reynolds's work was an important source for my book.... The thing about Reynolds [is this]: He not only writes well, but he evokes the time. This is especially true in his bio of Whitman. The first task of a biographer is to understand the time in which the subject lived, worked, and loved.... You need to know the times as well as possible.... Many historians working in this period know and admire Reynolds' work.[28]

Goldfield's remarks remind me of a quote that Reynolds is fond of—a comment that Melville made about Hawthorne: "geniuses are part of the times; they themselves are the times, and possess a corresponding coloring."[29] His words also invoke some favorite lines from Whitman: "Camerado, this is no book. / Who touches this touches a man."[30]

Many of the impulses behind Reynolds's work—such as democratizing literary and historical study, recuperating lesser-known works, listening closely to subversive voices, and taking seriously the relationship between popular or underground texts and canonical literature—have become fundamental to the various revisionist methodologies of the 2000s and beyond. But Judith Madera, author of *Black Atlas: Geography and Flow in Nineteenth-Century African American Literature* (2014), has another intriguing insight. In her view, "cultural biography's focus on both circuitry and material presence gives us more embodied writing."[31] I appreciate this idea of "embodied writing" and the notion of how we might truthfully represent full human experience. Madera's remark also reminds me of something Roger Lundin (himself the author of a fine cultural study of Emily Dickinson) wrote about the care with which biographers should approach their subjects: "the difficulty of writing a biography ha[s] to do with challenges unique to this craft. It is one thing to analyze a woman's poetry or ideas, quite another to cradle her life in your hands."[32] When we write about the lives of the past, a certain moral ethic requires us to recognize that we are indeed cradling vulnerable beings in our hands, and we should do so with seriousness, fairness, wonder, and a humility that takes into account a person's sincerest metaphysical preoccupations. Such an attitude is founded on painstaking effort and diligence and is modeled on the stringent methods of great cultural biographers like Reynolds and company.

Thus, there may be an important connection between Reynolds's rigorous methodology and the religious turn in literary studies—even in how a religious faith may enhance historical and literary research. The humble attitude of a religious believer, one who is steeped in a profound respect for truth seeking, who has a stake in the proper uses of evidence and a respectful approach to the past, could be an aid in historical writing rather than a hindrance. One controversial aspect of the postsecular has been that we no longer have clarity about why religion or belief should be separated out for special condemnation in the production of scholarship. Yet as some have noted, a religious sensibility may be a strength in this regard. As the historian David W. Bebbington writes in his convincing critique of the work of Hayden White (who famously described all history as mere "verbal fictions"):

> Christians will wish to affirm that evidence enables us to describe the past beyond reasonable doubt. Their faith is concerned with truth, and so there will be an enduring Christian insistence that truth about the past matters. The boundary between history and fiction does exist and ought to be respected. Christians may share the postmodernist suspicion about absolute rules for interpreting evidence, but they will urge that evidence needs to be deployed in order to discover the reality of the past.[33]

For Bebbington, a Christian commitment to an ethical use of evidence should provoke a greater care for historical accuracy. An intriguing implication of his argument is that those scholars who are devoted to historical religions are actually among those whom we should expect to be most invested in matters of historical truth and the sober uses of evidence, most committed to ethical uses of the past. Indeed, says Bebbington, perhaps it is the scholars of a Christian mindset who most aspire to represent a true history beyond a reasonable doubt. As we move deeper into this mode called the postsecular, we can free ourselves from the critical double-bind: on the one hand, invoking postmodern accounts of the constructed and fictive nature of history; on the other hand, warning that we must resist the temptations of prejudicial faith. There is a certain irony in seeing that a return to the religious, with its ethical demands for clarity and truthful witness, might help us revitalize how we do our scholarly work. The irony is due to some scholarly concerns that faith might color scholarship in negative ways rather than empower and enable it. This idea has grown more important today, I believe, in our era of post-truth, fake news, and other symptoms of media overload. Perhaps religious scholars can model a return to the real, given their ostensible commitment to historical truths.

Here, I note another irony, an unforeseen fruit of Reynolds's groundbreaking approach and achievements. As I've mentioned, the first word of his famous title, "Beneath," functions as an explanatory metaphor, indicating the direction from which literary texts emerge. Yet the concept of inspiration from above is quite old, dating back to Plato's *Ion* and to the Hebrew Bible's notion of prophetic inspiration—literally, the breath of God speaking through an artist or prophet. Despite this history, present-day American literary studies has long been dominated, even obsessed, by a focus on the great beneath—at least, until recently. Although such neglect was surely not Reynolds's intent, his deeply historicized methodology ultimately influenced the works that came in its wake in precisely that way.

I'm reminded of what Susan McClary identifies as an ongoing debate among musicologists regarding the sources of great music: as a confrontation between "non-social, implicitly metaphysical" approaches and those for whom music is essentially a "human, socially grounded, socially alterable construct." She argues that "most polemical battles in the history of music theory and criticism involve the irreconcilable confrontation of these two positions."[34] Likewise, American literary studies has been dominated by the approach from below, and some influential recent writings (including several labeled as postsecular) remain tone-deaf to the issues of spirituality at work in the lives of real authors. Why do scholars insist on seeing great authors as speaking merely through what comes from beneath? Is there still room for an appeal to what may come from above as well? Such a change of heart may be precisely what has animated the recent interest in the postsecular, but a turn, or return, to the spiritual includes much more than a mere rejection of secular framing devices. It also marks a moment of genuine longing, an insistence that whatever is beneath us is not enough. Even English professors pine for an elusive "something more."

Moving beyond a view of American literary culture as firmly secular may be good news for cultural biographers. By drawing on Paul Ricoeur's notion of a "second naivete," they may enjoy renewed vigor in discovering another sort of biography, a spiritual one that emerges from scholars who have survived a collective hermeneutic of suspicion and found themselves in some other site of interpretation—one that takes seriously the spiritual imaginations of our great writers.[35] Maybe it's time for younger critics to begin the task of writing such spiritual biographies. If so, I hope the essays in *Above the American Renaissance* can serve as models for them.

NOTES

1. See Harold K. Bush, *American Declarations: Rebellion and Repentance in American Cultural History* (Urbana: University of Illinois Press, 1999), 2–7.

2. Donald Pease, "New Americanists: Revisionist Interventions into the Canon," *boundary 2* 17 (Spring 1990): 1–37.

3. Laura Levitt, "What Is Religion, Anyway? Rereading the Postsecular from an American Jewish Perspective," *Religion and Literature* 41 (Autumn 2009): 110–11.

4. *Religious* and *spiritual* are loaded terms, of course, and the multiplicity of their distinctions is certainly part of the problem. For discussions of these thorny terms in present-day literary studies, see Tracy Fessenden, "The Problem of the Postsecular," *American Literary History* 26, no. 1 (2014): 154–67; Lori Branch, "The Rituals of Our Re-Secularization: Literature Between Faith and Knowledge," *Religion and Literature* 46 (Summer–Autumn 2014): 9–29; and Michael Kauffman, "The Religious, the Secular, and Literary Studies," *New Literary History* 38 (Autumn 2007): 607–28. On the meanings I use in this introduction, see Harold K. Bush, "Kissing the Bricks and Fly-Fishing for God: Teaching Literature as Spiritual Discipline," *Renascence* 62 (Spring 2010): 237–53.

5. Jenny Franchot, "Invisible Domain: Religion and American Literary Studies," *American Literature* 67, no. 4 (1995): 833–42.

6. Stanley Fish, "One University Under God?" *Chronicle of Higher Education*, January 7, 2005.

7. Harvey Cox, *The Future of Faith* (San Francisco: HarperOne, 2009), 8. Also see Phyllis Tickle, *The Great Emergence: How Christianity Is Changing and Why* (Grand Rapids, Mich.: Baker, 2012); Diana Butler Bass, *Christianity after Religion: The End of*

the Church and the Birth of a New Spiritual Awakening (San Francisco: HarperOne, 2012); and Philip Jenkins, The Next Christendom: The Coming of Global Christianity (New York: Oxford University Press, 2002).

8. Kauffman, "The Religious, the Secular, and Literary Studies," 607.

9. Nan Goodman and Michael P. Kramer, eds., The Turn Around Religion in America: Literature, Culture, and the Work of Sacvan Bercovitch (Burlington, Vt.: Ashgate, 2011), xix, xviii.

10. See John McClure, Partial Faiths: Postsecular Faith in the Age of Pynchon and Morrison (Athens: University of Georgia Press, 2007); Amy Hungerford, Postmodern Belief: American Literature and Religion Since 1960 (Princeton: Princeton University Press, 2010); and John Modern, Secularism in Antebellum Literature (Chicago: University of Chicago Press, 2011).

11. See the special issues of American Literature 86 (December 2014); American Literary History 26 (Spring 2014); Early American Literature 45 (2010); and Christianity and Literature 58 (2009). One exception is scholarship focusing on early American literature, in which studies of religion are common, due in large part to the fact that it would be very hard to avoid in that time period.

12. For an early engagement with high theory, see Roger Lundin, The Culture of Interpretation: Christian Faith and the Postmodern World (Grand Rapids, Mich.: Eerdmans, 1993). For examples of Lundin as an organizational leader, a mentor, and a visionary, see Roger Lundin, ed., There Before Us: Religion, Literature, and Culture from Emerson to Wendell Berry (Grand Rapids, Mich.: Eerdmans, 2007).

13. Branch, "The Rituals of Our Re-Secularization," 19.

14. Robert Orsi, Between Heaven and Earth: The Religious Worlds People Make and the Scholars Who Study Them (Princeton: Princeton University Press, 2005), 6.

15. Fessenden, "The Problem of the Postsecular," 154–55.

16. Branch, "The Rituals of Our Re-Secularization," 9.

17. Fessenden, "The Problem of the Postsecular," 157–58.

18. Branch, "The Rituals of Our Re-Secularization," 22.

19. David S. Reynolds, Beneath the American Renaissance: The Subversive Imagination in the Age of Emerson and Melville (New York: Oxford University Press, 1988), 3, 5.

20. II Corinthians 3:6.

21. Sean Wilentz, foreword to Beneath the American Renaissance, by David S. Reynolds, rev. ed. (New York: Oxford University Press, 2011), x.

22. See Harold K. Bush, Continuing Bonds with the Dead: Parental Grief and Nineteenth-Century American Authors (Tuscaloosa: University of Alabama Press, 2016), 36–69; and David S. Reynolds, Mightier Than the Sword: "Uncle Tom's Cabin" and the Battle for America (New York: Norton, 2011).

23. Megan Marshall, personal correspondence with the author.

24. Megan Marshall, The Peabody Sisters: Three Women Who Ignited American Romanticism (Boston: Houghton Mifflin, 2006), xix, xviii.

25. David S. Reynolds, "Writing Cultural Biography: In Pursuit of Walt Whitman," in *Biography and Source Studies*, ed. Frederick R. Karl, vol. 3 (New York: AMS Press, 1997), 76.

26. Marshall, personal correspondence with the author.

27. John Matteson, personal correspondence with the author.

28. David Goldfield, personal correspondence with the author.

29. Reynolds, *Beneath the American Renaissance*, 4.

30. Walt Whitman, "So Long!," *Walt Whitman Archive*, http://whitmanarchive.org.

31. Judith Madera, personal correspondence with the author.

32. Roger Lundin, *From Nature to Experience: The American Search for Cultural Authority* (Lanham, U.K.: Rowman and Littlefield, 2007), 128. Also see Harold K. Bush, "Cradling Lives in Our Hands: Towards a Theory of Cultural Biography," *Christianity and Literature* 57 (Fall 2007): 119–38.

33. David W. Bebbington, "The Discipline of History and the Perspective of Faith Since 1900," in Roger Lundin, ed., *Christ Across the Disciplines: Past, Present, Future* (Grand Rapids, Mich.: Eerdmans, 2013), 33.

34. Susan McClary, "The Blasphemy of Talking Politics during Bach Year," in Richard Leppert and Susan McClary, eds., *Music and Society: The Politics of Composition, Performance, and Reception* (New York: Cambridge University Press, 1987), 15.

35. Paul Ricoeur, *The Symbolism of Evil* (New York: Harper and Row, 1967), 347–57.

PART I
RECONSTRUCTING THE SPIRITUAL AND THE SECULAR

CHAPTER I

HAUNTED AMERICA

Reading the Spiritual Turn

Tracy Fessenden

ON MARCH 29, 1832, Ralph Waldo Emerson made a terse entry in his diary: "I visited Ellen's tomb & opened the coffin."[1] Emerson was twenty-eight, an obscure pastor who would some months later resign from his pulpit. Ellen, his bride of two years, had been dead for fourteen months, felled by tuberculosis before she reached the age of twenty. Emerson had visited her grave in Roxbury each day since her death, though after this entry his journal records no more visits that year.

The occasion for Emerson's subsequent resignation from Second Church in Boston was a disagreement with his congregation over the meaning of the body and blood of Christ. Emerson had wished to end his church's practice of the Lord's Supper. That Eucharistic rite remained central to Roman Catholics, he noted in a sermon preached in September 1832, but had "been very properly dropped by other Christians." To cling to it was to err on the side of Rome—that is, to mistake flesh and blood for the "redemption which they signified."[2] As his proof text, Emerson cited John 6:63: "It is the spirit that reviveth; the flesh profiteth nothing." Some months after his resignation he left off formal religious observance altogether, explaining in a December 1832 letter to his former congregation that he would be henceforth devoted to a "ministry of truth" and to "the liberty to seek, and the liberty to utter it."[3]

What lies beneath the American Renaissance? It's hard to imagine a more literal evocation of David S. Reynolds's masterwork than the scene of Emerson prying open his wife's casket just prior to his entrance onto the historical stage. This image of Emerson as the exhumer of decaying remains is a challenge to square with the Emerson who a decade later described himself as an "endless seeker" with "no Past at [his] back."[4] His turn away from canonical religious observance set a template for American spiritual seeking that endures to this day, as Leigh Eric Schmidt's magisterial *Restless Souls: The Making of American Spirituality* (2005) suggests. It also inaugurated a spiritual turn in American letters that is now in new flowering, with the present volume among its fruits.

Reynolds plumbed the subterranean literary currents that surfaced in the work of American Renaissance writers: pornography, dime novels, sensational journalism, and the mass-produced evangelical tracts that enlarged on their tales of dark adventure and their chilling dénouements. The graveyard scene in Emerson's journal points to more quotidian strata of underground knowledge in the literal fact of bodies returned to earth. This buried knowledge encompassed not only the ravages of war but also more mundane afflictions that made death an intimate visitor in nineteenth-century American families. In addition, death as subterranean presence extended to what might be called the structural fatality of American settlement, the predations to which whole populations were subject in service to American nationhood.

The term *American Renaissance* names a spiritual rebirth or reawakening in American letters, and *America* was a principle object of its writers' spiritual imagining. My effort to read the contemporary spiritual turn in American letters back through its grounding in the American Renaissance relies on the genealogical work undertaken in two authoritative histories of American spiritual striving: Schmidt's *Restless Souls* and Catherine Albanese's *Republic of Mind and Spirit* (2007). But I endeavor to read their overlapping histories of spiritual America somewhat against the grain—or, in the spirit of Reynolds, *from below*. "The only true America," declares Andrew Jackson Davis in Albanese's perfectly chosen epigraph, "is the coming spiritual Republic."⁵ The coming spiritual republic whose emergence Schmidt and Albanese track is an America at perpetual remove from the damage of history—in Sacvan Bercovitch's terms, an America forever being emptied of its "base historical content" to become, in the fleet and redemptive imaginings of ordinary and extraordinary Americans, a "trope of the spirit."⁶

What circuitry or turning conducts the mortal beneath of the American Renaissance to America imagined as a "trope of the spirit"? My project here is to consider a particular turn, in and around the American Renaissance, that begins in a literal seeing or other material witness to the dead and bends from there to imaginative contemplation of a spiritual entity identified with, or as, the nation itself.

Some who have grappled with the graveyard scene in Emerson's diary—"I visited Ellen's tomb & opened the coffin"—have decided it describes a deliberate leave-taking: a departure from mourning the dead, from the sepulcher of the past, and from the desiccated "stern old faiths," as Emerson would later write, that now send "a whole population of gentlemen and ladies out in search" of fresh sacralities.⁷ The need to cleave open Ellen's grave "was essential Emerson," writes Robert D. Richardson, whose biography of him begins with this story. "Some part of him was not able to believe she was dead. . . . Perhaps the very deadness of the body would help a belief in the life of the spirit."⁸ From that founding turn Emerson could cast formal religion "behind like an outgrown shell," as Laura Dassow Walls puts it, and enter into his expansive, enduringly influential ministry of spirit.⁹

Except that the leave-taking wasn't final. Emerson's journal entry for July 8, 1857, describes a visit to the tomb that now interred his son Waldo, who'd died at age five of scarlet fever and whose remains the father was moving to his own burial vault at Sleepy Hollow. "The sun shone brightly on the coffins, of which Waldo's was well-preserved—now fifteen years. I ventured to look inside the coffin." As in the 1832 account, he says nothing of what he saw. "I gave a few white-oak leaves to each coffin, after they were put into the new vault, and the vault was then covered with two slabs of granite."¹⁰

Sensory contact with the dead in the American Renaissance took many forms. Those who could do so laid out their dead at home, with all the intimate tending that such work entailed. Photography emerged as a popular medium in close conjunction with death. "Secure the shadow 'ere the substance fade," the tagline of American daguerreotypists, was specifically aimed at those who stood vigil over the dying. Itinerant photographers set up tents on the battlefields of the Civil War. "America swarms with the members of the mighty tribe of cameristas," the *London Photographic Journal* noted in December 1862, and "war has developed their business in the same way that it has given an impetus to the manufacturers of metallic air-tight coffins and embalmers of the dead."[11] Photographs of soldiers killed in battle might be sent home to grieving families in lieu of bodies, unrecoverable in the carnage, that were eventually plowed into the earth.

The perception of America as a literal field of death had earlier propelled the motions of Manifest Destiny. "Progress has never for a moment been arrested," Andrew Jackson noted in presenting his policy of Indian removal to Congress, "and one by one have many powerful tribes disappeared from the earth. To follow to the tomb the last of his race and to tread on the graves of extinct nations excites melancholy reflections."[12] Séance spiritualists would conjure the missing—Civil War dead, Indian guides—as material presences, winning the credulity or sympathetic interest of a vast demographic, including Harriet Beecher Stowe, Horace Greeley, Mary Todd Lincoln, and a young William James.

A richer account than mine might pay attentive care to any of the ways in which the nineteenth-century spiritual turn starts and pivots from the materiality of death. My interest is at once narrower and broader: I wish to focus on how this spiritual turn conjured, invoked, or sustained the *America* of the American Renaissance. As Benedict Anderson famously observed, the idea of nation comes into being in part by taking over a particular office of religion, which is to locate and compose our experience of death and loss within a spectral community of the blessed, conceived not as a heavenly kingdom but as the idea of the nation itself. "Strange, (is it not?)" Walt Whitman remarked of the death of Abraham Lincoln, "that battles, martyrs, agonies, blood, even assassinations should so condense—perhaps only really, lastingly condense—a Nationality."[13]

It's now a commonplace to situate the contemporary interest in spirituality, historical and otherwise, in relation to 9/11 and its aftermath. The events of September 11 showed us the power of religion in the world, we say, and led many to want more knowledge about religion generally. What is less often noted in these invocations of a post-9/11 spiritual turn is that the work of grieving had hardly begun when President George W. Bush, in a speech excerpted in the *New York Times* on September 28, 2001, urged us to move on, do our business, take the kids to Disney World.[14] Or that on October 7, 2001, the United States entered into what is now the longest military operation in our history. The number of U.S. military deaths in the wars in Afghanistan (underway since 2001) and Iraq (2003–11) now stands at well over twice the number of those lost in the September 11 terrorist attacks. As of this writing the number of direct kills in these wars, including civilian deaths, exceeds 300,000.[15] Both were launched under the penumbra of the War on Terror, whose hazy mission, non-state combatants, secret prisons, and stealth weaponry conspire to keep its operations at a ghostly remove from the day-to-day life of the United States.

In his introduction to this collection, Harold K. Bush notes that the term *spiritual* appears "at least eleven times in Herman Melville's *Moby-Dick*, at least ten times in Harriet Beecher Stowe's *Uncle Tom's Cabin*, at least twenty-one times in Nathaniel Hawthorne's *The Blithedale Romance*, and at least seven times in Henry David Thoreau's *Walden*. Even Edgar Allan Poe used the word at least ten times in his tales." Uses of the term clustered then as now in the overlapping precincts of "spirituality" and "spiritualism," the stout terrain of psychic wellness, on the one hand, and the rattling haunts of unresolved losses, on the other. Those who yearned for sensory communion with the Civil War dead conjured their spirits in parlors, on photographic plates, and in radiant, consoling dispatches from the world beyond. Such dispatches were a resilient franchise, one that has been renewed since 9/11 in books such as Alice Sebold's *The Lovely Bones* (2002), which sold 2 million copies in the year of its release. Like its post–Civil War precursor, Elizabeth Stuart Phelps's *The Gates Ajar* (1868), Sebold's novel of a murdered child's everyday life after death—peppermint ice cream on tap, the best kind of swings—reduces inassimilable grief to the scale of a bearable loss, one that finally isn't even reckoned as loss.

The American spiritual turn that has come into sharpened visibility after September 11 sustains a tacit, enduring tension between spirituality and spiritualism, between psychic quests for wholeness and self-sufficiency and the always-unfinished business of grief. For all its brave insistence on "epiphanic assurance," Leigh Schmidt suggests, the language of American spirituality is in fact shot through with "lacking and loss." He cites a twentieth-century spiritual seeker's prayer: "Oh God, if there be a God, make me a real person."[16] What would be a national equivalent of that search for realness or wholeness? Put another way, how does the Americanness of American spirituality, the national experience it invokes and composes, enter into as well as radiate from individual instances of grief or lack?

Consider Emerson's meditation on grief in "Experience" (1844):

> People grieve and bemoan themselves, but it is not half so bad with them as they say. There are moods in which we court suffering, in the hope that here at least we shall find reality, sharp peaks and edges of truth. But it turns out to be scene-painting and counterfeit. The only thing grief has taught me is to know how shallow it is. That, like all the rest, plays about the surface, and never introduces me into the reality, for contact with which we would even pay the costly price of sons and lovers. Was it Boscovich who found out that bodies never come in contact? Well, souls never touch their objects. . . . In the death of my son, now more than two years ago, I seem to have lost a beautiful estate,—no more. I cannot get it nearer to me. If tomorrow I should be informed of the bankruptcy of my principal debtors, the loss of my property would be a great inconvenience to me, perhaps, for many years; but it would leave me as it found me,—neither better nor worse. So is it with this calamity: it does not touch me; something which I fancied was a part of me, which could not be torn away without tearing me nor enlarged without enriching me, falls off from me and leaves no scar. It was caducous. I grieve that grief can teach me nothing, nor carry me one step into real nature.[17]

The chill of this passage is its testament to the dullness of mourning, a dullness amounting to denial of even the profoundest grief as brokenness, the most intimate loss as loss. The word *caducous* refers to vestigial parts of plants or animals, on the order of tender leaves or amphibious gills, that are shed without loss or damage to the organism in the proper course of its development. Emerson grieves that the grieving of loss will not itself forward his progress nor effect an opening into a reality for which, he wrenchingly avers, we would willingly barter the deaths of those we most love. He laments here not the death of his son but the fact that we are solitaries, intact, whom even the deaths of our sons do not pierce and break.

In "Experience," he then proceeds to observe that only in this unrent, ungrieving sufficiency do we experience "the Ideal journeying always with us." We bury our sons, we shed our grief, we find no lack or breakage in our inmost being even if we would seek it. Yet that unbroken vessel at the center of our being, "the heaven without rent or seam," is also the lamp that lights the spiritual path:

> Do but observe the mode of our illumination. When I converse with a profound mind, or if at any time being alone I have good thoughts, I do not at once arrive at satisfactions, as when, being thirsty, I drink water; or go to the fire, being cold; no! but I am at first apprised of my vicinity to a new and excellent region of life. By persisting to read or to think, this region gives further sign of itself, as it were in flashes of light, in sudden discoveries of its profound beauty and repose, as if the clouds that covered it parted at intervals and showed the approaching traveller the inland mountains, with the tranquil eternal meadows spread at their base, whereon flocks graze and shepherds pipe and dance. But every insight from this realm of thought is felt as initial, and promises a sequel.[18]

Emerson finds a name for this newness, these vistas of the spirit uncontaminated by grief and unsullied by loss: he calls it a "new yet unapproachable *America*" toward which the questing soul, refreshed, is ever drawing near.[19]

Benedict Anderson wondered how the idea of the nation-state managed over two centuries to "generate such colossal sacrifices," to compel so many millions not only to kill but "willingly to die for such limited imaginings" as that of the national community. He supposed the answer lay in the nation-state's capacity to absorb the charismatic authority of religion, to take up a self-evident plausibility at the point at which the no longer self-evident plausibility of religion leaves off. In the wake of religion's embattled sovereignty, the newly sovereign state and the ideals that animate it nurture such fatal attachments by offering "a secular transformation of fatality into continuity, contingency into meaning."[20] American spiritual belonging, Americanness, might be understood in this sense as the ongoing imaginative labor of transforming loss into freedom, fatality into national community; in Mitchell Breitwieser's resonant phrase, a practiced "calling it 'America' rather than 'the dead'"; a perpetual exhuming and hasty reburying of what Dana Luciano calls "the affective residue of the vanished past in the present tense, what we know as grief."[21]

Consider, for example, the oblique rhyme in the titles of Catherine Albanese's *A Republic of Mind and Spirit* (2007) and Drew Gilpin Faust's *This Republic of Suffering* (2008). Albanese's book is a sweeping reappraisal of American religion with an eye toward magical and metaphysical practices, including the long career of séance spiritualism in the middle decades of the nineteenth century. Faust's is a history of what she calls the "work of death" in Civil War America: that is, the work of killing and dying and of burying, naming, numbering, and mourning the dead. The *work* of death in *This Republic of Suffering* is both effort and outcome, labor and product. Death's labor is the labor of killing, dying, burying, naming, numbering, and mourning; death's product is the nation—this republic—that the labor of Civil War death brings into being. Every history is in some sense a history of the present, and Faust observes movingly near the end of her book that the Civil War "introduced a level of carnage that foreshadowed the wars of the centur[ies] to come. Even as individuals and their fates assumed new significance, so those individuals threaten to disappear into the bureaucracy and mass slaughter of modern warfare. We still struggle to understand how to preserve our humanity and ourselves within such a world."[22]

Albanese's very different book makes the case for a long New Age that reveals a home-grown metaphysics to be the nation's true spiritual currency. The cover of *A Republic of Mind and Spirit* shows an image from our monetary currency, the dollar's thirteen-step pyramid topped by the eye of Providence. The suggestion is one of steady ascent, transcendence of death's material plain as the ordained direction of progress. The work of death in *this* republic is to convert disquiet to psychic balm, haunting to wholeness. Albanese tells a story of Americans defined as such by their capacity to make of intimate and collective losses the materials of spiritual self-fashioning and national renewal.

Leigh Schmidt likewise contends that the liberal, free-floating, progressive spirituality he chronicles in *Restless Souls* is distinctively American, that it is "old and not other" within the deepest and defining currents of American life and thought, its influence formative, broad, and enduring. A representative voice in his narrative is that of an "early chronicler of Transcendentalism" who imagined the future religion of the United States to be a "liberal, universal one of the spirit" centered on the "soul's light, right, and freedom against ecclesiastical authority." Emersonian departures from "ecclesiastical authority," in Schmidt's account, would release the faithful "into a global field of spiritual appreciation, cosmopolitan rapport, and eclectic insight." Emerson is Schmidt's and his sources' touchstone throughout *Restless Souls*, a "prophet of spirituality" and a "lifelong believer in America" whose "sweeping effect on American religious life" and the spiritual aspirations of its citizenry extended well beyond the disaffections of a liberal Unitarian elite.[23]

Call it spiritual Manifest Destiny: *Restless Souls* describes American spirituality as a psychic terrain of open roads and democratic vistas, a lighting in rather than out for the territory, for fresh expanses of mind and spirit. Schmidt's first case study in illustration of this story belongs to an AWOL Danish lieutenant, Carl H. A. Bjerregaard, who abandoned his military post and his past for America, where he styled himself a philosopher and a mystic in the mode of Emerson. Bjerregaard entered the American lecture circuit in the 1890s to preach "the supreme freedom of aspirants to seek the truth of themselves within themselves" in whatever outward form the call might resound: "Bible passages, taoist sayings, pine trees and cones, Jewish Kabbalah, Zoroastrian fire imagery, yoga, Sufi poetry, American Transcendentalism, and the Christian mythology of the holy grail." That "cosmopolitan, sympathetic disposition," Schmidt contends, "fueled one innovation after another in American spirituality. It was a *sine qua non* of seeker culture."²⁴ Little wonder that this cosmopolitan spirituality's prophet should be Emerson, who made a national ethos of self-reliance, and imagined a future America in which the energy of the "Irish, Germans, Swedes, Poles, & Cossacks, & all the European tribes—of the Africans, & of the Polynesians, will construct a new race, a new religion, a new State, a new literature."²⁵

Emerson's was a cosmopolitanism poised over and against the constraints of home, an American quest for individual freedom pursued from an equally American foundation of slavery and dispossession. In a journal entry headed "Races," Emerson wrote, "Nature every little while drops a link. How long before the Indians will be extinct? then the negro? then shall we say, what a gracious interval of dignity between man and beast!" In a later entry, he contends, "The dark man, the black man declines. The black man is courageous, but the white men are the children of God, said Plato. It will happen by & by, that the black man will be destined for museums like the Dodo."²⁶ Barbara Packer suggests that Emerson's "desire to see black people disappear arose not from irrational prejudice but from [his] despair of seeing them successfully assimilated into a human race [he] needed to see as progressive."²⁷ His cosmic belief in America was a belief in progress to which laggards, as it were, could be sacrificed without loss. Progress compels a forgetting of loss, an obligatory leaving behind and moving forward in the ordained direction of national futurity. "It is very certain that the strong British race which have now overrun so much of this continent, must also overrun that tract [Texas], & Mexico & Oregon also, and it will in the course of ages be of small import by what particular occasions & methods it was done. It is a secular question."²⁸

The point I wish to make is that Emerson's America, imagined as both product and producer of a certain spiritual freedom, is an America whose past is not merely the past of outmoded and constraining "ecclesiastical authority." This America's darker, structural histories of conquest, subjugation, and violence are necessarily blurred or left in shadow in the dawning of a new age of spiritual emancipation. Religion makes a good alias or cover for the buried violence of progressive history insofar as religion, as opposed to spirituality, carries residual associations with forces to be left behind or disavowed: brute manipulations of the credulous, blind obedience to authority, irrational attributions of power to objects, idols, or bodies. (Emerson's career as a prophet of spirituality, recall, began in the desire to detach his ministry from the ritual re-membering of crucified flesh.) The American spiritual pilgrimage, says Schmidt, is the progress of "emancipated souls" who traversed a "disenchanted and divided terrain that they sought to reanimate and make whole through a universalized religion of the spirit." Spirituality, in Schmidt's historical mapping of it, is always on the go, "away from the old 'religions of authority' into the new 'religion of the spirit.'"[29]

But are Schmidt's restless souls, beginning with Emerson, really in flight from deadening *religion*? Or is that bleak terrain of disenchantment another terrain entirely: a continent wrested and riven by war, pitted with corpses, and rendered fertile and productive by slave labor? Alongside the better-known musings of Emerson and his circle, *Restless Souls* bears an epigraph from John Weiss's 1871 *American Religion*: "America is an opportunity to make a Religion out of the sacredness of the individual."[30] What is this spiritual disposition that claims identity with the nation itself? What palimpsestic shroud—*America, opportunity, sacredness, individual*—lies over the land, and what rattles and disturbs it from below?

In Emerson's "Experience," the questing soul whose motions track the dawning of a not-yet realized nation is an American whose identity with the nation, in sunlit future tense, is given as imperviousness to grief. Emerson finds solace from grief's muteness and inaccessibility in his "vicinity to a new and excellent region of life"—call it, with Emerson, *America*—less a confrontation with loss than a fantastic recompense for what is barely marked as missing. Consider Emerson's transcendentalist compatriot Margaret Fuller's record of a journey in *Summer on the Lakes in 1843*, which meditates upon the abandoned Indian settlements of the nation's receding frontier and concludes, in the manner of "Experience," in spiritual contemplation of America:

This aspect of this country was to me enchanting, beyond any I have ever seen, from its fullness of expression, its bold and impassioned sweetness. . . .

How happy the Indians must have been here! It is not long since they were driven away, and the ground, above and below, is full of their traces.

"The earth is full of men."

You have only to turn up the sod to find arrowheads and Indian pottery. On an island, belonging to our host, and nearly opposite his house, they loved to stay, and, no doubt, enjoyed its lavish beauty as much as the myriad wild pigeons that now haunt its flower-filled shades. Here are still the marks of their tomahawks, the troughs in which they prepared their corn, their caches.

A little way down the river is the site of an ancient Indian village, with its regularly arranged mounds. As usual, they had chosen with the finest taste. It was one of those soft shadowy afternoons when we went there, when nature seems ready to weep, not from grief, but from an overfull heart. . . . They may blacken Indian life as they will, talk of its dirt, its brutality, I will ever believe that the men who chose that dwelling-place were able to feel emotions of noble happiness as they returned to it. . . . The latter I visited one glorious morning; it was that, of the fourth of July, and certainly I think I had never felt so happy that I was born in America.[31]

Emerson's rhetorical figure of the transparent eyeball suggests a landscape from which difference has been more smoothly evacuated, leaving, as it were, no arrowheads or broken pottery in the sod—no fragments of alternative histories or their violent removal to obstruct the democratic vista, no particles of resistance to keep the mode of seeing from dissolving into what is seen. For Fuller, however, the shards of a vanished Indian world, violently felled, register inseparably as jagged lack and phantom wholeness, evidence of plunder and its enchanted recompense:

There was a peculiar charm in coming here, where the choice of location, and the unobtrusive good taste of all the arrangements, showed such intelligent appreciation of the spirit of the scene. . . . Seeing the traces of the Indians, who chose the most beautiful sites for their dwellings, and whose habits do not break in on that aspect of nature under which they were born, we feel as if they were the rightful lords of a beauty they forbore to deform.

"Even so," Fuller adds, "the white settler pursues the Indian, and is victor in the chase." And "this is inevitable, fatal; we must not complain, but look forward to a good result."[32]

A Republic of Mind and Spirit focuses on practices Emerson disdained; as he wrote, "Man is the Image of God. Why run after a ghost or a dream?"[33] Nor is Fuller, though a self-described "victim of spectral illusions," a player in Albanese's account.[34] Nevertheless, Fuller's rendering of the landscape in *Summer on the Lakes in 1843*—a world of the dead, broken and violently "driven away" to return, replete, in a mode of enchantment—might be taken, in broadest strokes, to describe the America that Albanese christens "A Republic of Mind and Spirit."

The spiritualist movement in America, Albanese argues, begins in the encounter of European Americans with native peoples and African slaves and in differently shared experiences of death and loss. Her portrait of American metaphysical religion, as she calls it, shows mostly Anglo-Protestant Americans turning to spiritualist practice to reach their own beloved dead while the collective, untold losses of enslaved Africans and displaced natives yield spiritual gifts born of the need, as W. E. B. Du Bois put it, to interpret the unknown, comfort the sorrowing, and express the "longing, disappointment, and resentment of a stolen and oppressed people."[35]

Albanese shows the world that made American metaphysical religion to be fractious, pain-filled, and above all in need of healing. "Along with celebrations of our basic connections to grandeur, a sense of sin and loss has haunted metaphysicians in Anglo-Protestant" America, who seek its solvents in the spirit world's tender of "a kind of cosmological forgiveness." For all their contributions to the larger story, Native Americans and the enslaved make mostly spectral appearances in this republic of mind and spirit. Thus, the familiar roster of spirit visitors to a polite séance includes "the dead who were known at an intimate level, the historically great and famous," and "hordes of Indians and other subalterns." However fraught the scenes of their deaths may have been with suffering, violence, or psychic irresolution, spirit visitors typically come unburdened from the world beyond to shed consoling benediction on the living. In a similar way, the violence of slavery and colonialism in the history Albanese recounts falls away, under the sign of spiritualism, from what are rendered instead as the "profusely rich and hybrid series of contacts" through which Native Americans, African Americans, and whites high and low collaborate in the creation of a "combinative American metaphysical religiosity."[36]

Here are two ways, then, of reading the contemporary spiritual turn—a turn that brings with it a new focus on the spiritual imagination of the nineteenth century. We might decide to read the post-9/11 spiritual turn as belonging to a structure of evasion, a national forgetting. What united Americans in the immediate aftermath of September 11, it appears, was a shared vulnerability both to the laying-to-ruins that is grief *and* to the proffered illusion of wholeness that comes in siding with the nation's violent and speedy assertion of its right to restored autonomy. How quickly, with what practiced attentions, the nation moved after September 11 to displace the ravages of grief onto a phantom of unalterable American sufficiency, Operation Enduring Freedom, to which so many thousands more would be sacrificed. To persist in mourning a brokenness at the nation's heart is what Americans must *not* do in order to sustain the fantasy of an America that protects us from having to mourn, an America that compensates us for the loss-but-not-loss it routinely exacts. If the landscape will be haunted by absence, let the haunting be felt as enchantment. If "the earth is full of men" whose brutal and untimely burial disquiets, let the restless souls who linger amid the shades be our own.

Another way of reading the spiritual turn: as acknowledgment, however hazy and halting or tidied and flattering, of the unknit bones that lie beneath the American Renaissance and the America it made. *Republic of Suffering, Republic of Mind and Spirit*: these are reciprocally haunting versions of nineteenth-century America as the history of our present. The photograph on the cover of Faust's book, a battlefield strewn knee-deep with corpses, recalls Walter Benjamin's angel of history, who sees "what we call progress" as a gathering storm that "pil[es] wreckage upon wreckage" at our feet.[37] The fact of slaughter in the work of national self-definition haunts any reading of American history as a progressive ascent under the watchful eye of Providence. Equally, the fact of slaughter in national self-definition offers every dreadful incentive to lift our eyes above the plain of carnage, to fasten our gaze instead on "the coming spiritual America." The ghostly prodding might be in either case how buried losses make themselves known, become what our spiritual strivings give breath or shape or answer to, however we choose to name them.

NOTES

I am grateful to Hal Bush for his generous engagement with this essay.

1. Ralph Waldo Emerson, *Journals and Miscellaneous Notebooks, 1832–1834* (Cambridge, Mass.: Belknap Press of Harvard University Press, 1964), 7.

2. Ralph Waldo Emerson, *Complete Works: Miscellanies*, ed. Edward Waldo Emerson (Boston: Houghton Mifflin, 1911), 11.

3. Ralph Waldo Emerson, *Selected Letters*, ed. Joel Myerson (New York: Columbia University Press, 1999), 116.

4. Ralph Waldo Emerson, *Essays and Lectures*, ed. Joel Porte (New York: Literary Classics of the United States, 1983), 412.

5. Catherine L. Albanese, *A Republic of Mind and Spirit: A Cultural History of American Metaphysical Religion* (New Haven: Yale University Press, 2007), vi.

6. Sacvan Bercovitch, *Rites of Assent: Transformations in the Symbolic Construction of America* (New York: Routledge, 1993), 19.

7. Emerson, *Essays and Lectures*, 1056.

8. Robert D. Richardson, *Emerson: The Mind on Fire* (Berkeley: University of California Press, 1995), 3.

9. Laura Dassow Walls, *Emerson's Life in Science: The Culture of Truth* (Ithaca: Cornell University Press, 2003), 83.

10. Ralph Waldo Emerson, *Journals and Miscellaneous Notebooks, 1854–1861* (Cambridge, Mass.: Belknap Press of Harvard University Press, 1978), 154.

11. "American Photographs," in the *Photographic Journal, Being the Journal of the Photographic Society of London,* December 15, 1862, 185.

12. Andrew Jackson, "Second Annual Message," December 6, 1830, *American Presidency Project,* http://www.presidency.ucsb.edu.

13. Walt Whitman, *Complete Prose Works: "Specimen Days" and "Collect," "November Boughs" and "Good bye My Fancy"* (New York: Appleton, 1910), 308–9.

14. George W. Bush, "Remarks to Airline Employees in Chicago, Illinois, September 27, 2001," in *Administration of George W. Bush, 2001* (Washington, D.C.: U.S. Government Publishing Office, 2001), 1170–73.

15. *Costs of War,* August 2016, Brown University, Watson Institute for International and Public Affairs, http://watson.brown.edu.

16. Leigh Eric Schmidt, *Restless Souls: The Making of American Spirituality* (San Francisco: HarperSanFrancisco, 2005), 58.

17. Emerson, *Essays and Lectures,* 472–73.

18. Ibid., 484–85.

19. Ibid., 485.

20. Benedict Anderson, *Imagined Communities: Reflections on the Origin and Spread of Nationalism* (London: Verso, 2006), 7, 19.

21. Mitchell Breitwieser, *National Melancholy: Mourning and Opportunity in Classic American Literature* (Stanford: Stanford University Press, 2007), 49; Dana Luciano, *Arranging Grief: Sacred Time and the Body in Nineteenth-Century America* (New York: New York University Press, 2007), 4.

22. Drew Gilpin Faust, *This Republic of Suffering: Death and the American Civil War* (New York: Knopf, 2008), 271.

23. Schmidt, *Restless Souls,* 286, 52, 108, 15, 21, 14.

24. Ibid., 26, 16.

25. Ralph Waldo Emerson, *Journals and Miscellaneous Notebooks, 1843–1847* (Cambridge, Mass.: Belknap Press of Harvard University Press, 1971), 299–300.

26. Ralph Waldo Emerson, *Journals and Miscellaneous Notebooks, 1852–1855* (Cambridge, Mass.: Belknap Press of Harvard University Press, 1977), 54, 286.

27. Barbara Packer, "Emerson and the Overgod," paper presented at the annual meeting of the American Historical Association, San Francisco, January 6–9, 1994.

28. Emerson, *Journals and Miscellaneous Notebooks, 1843–1847,* 74.

29. Schmidt, *Restless Souls,* 13, 7.

30. Ibid., vi.

31. Margaret Fuller, *Summer on the Lakes in 1843* (Boston: Little, Brown, 1944), 52–53.

32. Ibid., 46–47.

33. Ralph Waldo Emerson, *Early Lectures,* vol. 3, *1838–1842* (Cambridge, Mass.: Belknap Press of Harvard University Press), 170.

34. Margaret Fuller, *Memoirs of Margaret Fuller Ossoli* (Boston: Phillips, Samson, 1851), 15.

35. W. E. B. Du Bois, *The Souls of Black Folk* (New York: Oxford University Press, 2007), 93.

36. Albanese, *A Republic of Mind and Spirit,* 14, 187, 97.

37. Walter Benjamin, *Illuminations,* ed. Hannah Arendt (New York: Schocken, 1969), 257–58.

CHAPTER 2

"THE SPIRIT OF INSTRUCTIVE INVESTIGATION"

Bronson Alcott, Transcendental Childhood, and the Search for Divinity

John Matteson

Two DAYS after Christmas 1835, Bronson Alcott sat at his desk after sunset, writing. His life at this time was busy and, for him, unusually prosperous. His experimental Temple School in Boston was receiving lavish praise from the city's more progressive intellectuals, and the school's growing reputation had lately benefited from the publication of *Record of a School*, an account lovingly assembled by Alcott's classroom assistant, Elizabeth Palmer Peabody. Toiling by candlelight, he was writing with inspiration. He had lately undertaken a series of conversations with his young pupils about the true meaning of the Christian gospels. He was now planning further conversations that would unlock for them "the Facts of Genesis, as given by Moses." Alcott's new curriculum aimed to illuminate "the greatest problems that interest the mind of man—The Birth and Peopling of the Universe—the Origin and Consequences of Evil—the Destruction of the Vicious—the Preservation of the Righteous," and a good deal more. In exploring the life of Christ, he was sharing with his students "the genealogy of the Spiritual Universe." He now meant to balance that presentation by revealing "the Genesis of Material Nature."[1] The prospect excited him tremendously.

As thoughts of the new project filled his head, Alcott looked up at the shadows that his flickering candle was throwing onto the walls of the darkened room. Accustomed to regarding physical objects as the symbolic, outward clothing of a greater reality, he found much in the uncertain light to capture both his eye and his imagination. The flame's flicker fell upon his treasured bust of Socrates, an image of Saint John in the Wilderness, and a portrait of the Madonna. Alcott saw in each object a facet of his character: Socrates, the tireless teacher, risking all in the quest for truth; John, the self-exiled ascetic, forsaking material wants in the pursuit of purity; and Mary, the epitome of parental love. Even the flame itself seemed to emblematize Alcott's spirit: "a semblance of the evanescent, shapeless, yet ever-radiating life, that gleameth now, upon my mind, and anon, hath passed away, with dubious flutterings, yet not without promises and assurances of reappearance."[2]

Then his eyes fell upon what was, for him, a far fitter image of the all-pervading spirit. Near his chair, gazing up at him with a smile, sat his three-year-old daughter, Louisa May, the future children's author extraordinaire. Alcott paused and observed her shifting glance as Louisa looked first upon his face and then fastened her attention on his "quick-imaging pen," wondering, as it seemed to him, "at the meanings of the subtle characters"; and then, caught by same shadows that had piqued her father's fancy, followed their tracings across the wall.[3] Also within view was Louisa's older sister, Anna Bronson Alcott, who, imitating her father, had grasped a pen and was trailing it across a piece of paper, giving shape to her own private fancies.

Any father might have found the tableau charming. To Alcott, it was filled with ineffable significance. In his children, he saw the very image of divinity. As they contemplated the shadowy wall and the scribbled page, it seemed to him that their expressions became "more wise than the features of the Sage" and their apprehensions grew "more spiritual than those of the prophet or the seer."[4] He was certain that he sat in the presence of a miraculous phantom—a perfect embodiment of life and spirit. He was confronting a glorious mystery, a riddle that, if only he could solve it, might reveal the true essence of both God and man.

Before Ralph Waldo Emerson wrote *Nature*, while Henry David Thoreau was just another undergraduate at Harvard, while Margaret Fuller was mourning the death of her father and wondering what to do next with her life, Bronson Alcott was delving into questions that were to engross the American transcendental movement. What is the relation between perceived reality and ultimate truth? How does the soul of Creation make itself manifest on earth? Where, if not in scripture, can the real essence of divinity be discovered? Alcott did not invent these questions. Like his soon-to-be allies in transcendentalism, he had read Samuel Taylor Coleridge's *Aids to Reflection*, a book that, he observed, had formed "a new era in my mental and psychological life."[5] Among the questions that Coleridge explored was the relation of the world of the flesh to the realm of the spirit, which he analogized to the relation between the world and Christ. In each case, Coleridge observed, "these two opposites are connected by the middle term, birth, which is of course common to both."[6] Birth, be it the physical birth of an infant or the rebirth of a soul through baptism or spiritual awakening, was the critical nexus between the ideal and the real. For Coleridge, understanding this connection was vital, for, he observed, every object "becomes foreign to us as soon as it is altogether unconnected with our intellectual, moral, and spiritual life."[7] The physical needed to be understood in spiritual terms, and the spirit had to be traced to its discoverable origins. What made Alcott's reaction to Coleridge profoundly unusual was his confidence that he could prove the latter's spiritual theories by empirical research. To find the link between God and man, he turned to the beings who, he thought, bore the nearest relation to both: infants and children. His mission was mystical; more importantly, it was scientific.

This essay will attempt to correct a pair of common misconceptions about Alcott: first, that he was an aloof, almost indifferent father whose fondness for abstruse speculation blinded him to his family's emotional natures and needs; second, that, in his rampant idealism, he cared nothing about the practical applications of an idea. As his journals on childhood amply illustrate, his interest in his children bordered upon worship, and his understanding of them was thorough and precise. As for his supposed impracticality, we must understand it on terms quite different from those that are typically posited. Alcott's journals on childhood reveal that, more than any other major transcendentalist (except, possibly, Thoreau), he wanted to discover the empirical foundations and practical uses of transcendental philosophy.

Like the other contributors to this volume, I am working in this essay to offer an admiring counterweight to David S. Reynolds's great work, *Beneath the American Renaissance*. In it Reynolds boldly reveals the brash, earthy, vernacular culture that underlies the antebellum literary canon. Yet in doing so, Reynolds has made it almost too tempting to focus on the subterranean roots of the period's literature, to forget that it also aspired upward toward sunlight. Well into old age, Bronson Alcott handed out autographed sentiments to admirers that urged them to "Aim for the Highest."[8] He would never have written his journals on childhood had he not believed that the strongest forces in human existence came from a superior, ideal realm, a realm that was most visible in the uncorrupted spirits of children. Alcott sought, by the inadequate means at his disposal, to prove the existence of that realm by closely observing the behaviors of his daughters, who, he reasoned, were so recently arrived from heaven that they must surely carry with them the traces of their supernal origins. Emerson merely theorized about the Oversoul. Alcott hoped to track it to its lair. His impracticality lay in his willingness to seize hold of the highest ideas he could imagine and to take them seriously.

Alcott's quest to isolate and identify the great soul that he perceived within childhood is documented in the little-known half of a joint essay-writing project he undertook with Emerson. Emerson planned for his to deal with the physical world, while Alcott would focus on the world of the mind. Emerson's turned out well: every scholar of the American Renaissance has read and reread *Nature*. Almost no one, however, has examined Alcott's work on mysticism and infant psychology, *Psyche: The Breath of Childhood*. Equally obscure are his other manuscripts on the spiritual nature of childhood. From the day they were born, Alcott kept journals of the moral, physical, and spiritual growth of his two eldest daughters, Anna and Louisa. In these diaries he also strove to understand the mysteries of the spirit in scientific terms and to translate the soul into realistic terms. He was nothing if not ambitious: he intended not only to record his daughters' infancies but, when they were of a sufficient age, to instruct the girls to continue the journals themselves, to their own deathbeds if possible, thus creating the first complete cradle-to-grave records of a pair of human souls.[9]

Quixotic though Alcott's search may now appear, the philosopher himself was certain of both his eventual success and the supreme value of his research. He observed that, until the present moment, students of the human condition had focused their attention on either man's spiritual side or his material state; never had anyone made a sufficient attempt to bring the two inquiries together. In his introduction to his journals on Louisa, Alcott framed the problem as follows:

> Material-spiritual man, in connexion with the universe, should become united subjects of investigation. The study of life, however, as developed in humanity, has, heretofore been confined to but one of these forms, instead of being extended to them all in mutual connexion and dependence.
>
> While the materialist has confined his view to the consideration of man as an organic being, merging his spiritual movements into mere modifications of functions, and sinking the soul in subserviency to the material organs by which it is manifested, the spiritualist, on the other hand, disregarding its physiological connexions, has separated it from its constitutional basis, by formal abstractions, and thus thrown out of his view, a large class of influences which essentially modify all its phenomena.
>
> From the want of such an adequate foundation, on which to stand to apprehend all man's relations and trace them to their source in his constitution, the field of moral and spiritual relations has been, heretofore, imperfectly explored. No unified data are as yet established: a dark cloud rests on the operations of life, through which the light of the most piercing intellects has not penetrated.[10]

As befitted his desire to find a nexus between the worlds of spirit and matter, Alcott approached his work with an attitude that mingled holy reverence with an earnest desire to be as rigorously scientific as his abilities would allow. In passages like the one just quoted, he was trying desperately to write like a scientist. Yet as he beheld the spirit of uncorrupted childhood, a sense of awe overtook him, and he would sometimes wax rhapsodic, as in this passage from *Psyche: The Breath of Childhood*: "Mysterious essence! All-pervading, all-configuring, all-apprehending, all-meaning principle! Life! Spirit!—or, by what name soever, or under what form, thou art conceived, or presented—who shall apprehend thee, as thou art in thyself—or find thee, as thou art found in these *Little Ones* who have not left thee!"[11]

Alcott's oscillations between the vocabulary of scientific rigor and lexicon of quasi-religious ecstasy can feel symptomatic of a confusion of purpose. In his view, however, they were anything but. As he worked toward bringing together the realms of matter and spirit, it became clear to him that he would also need to merge the two languages: to speak to creation with idioms that were simultaneously rational and exultant—the better to show that the ultimate truth of existence, though grounded in observable fact, was also a pathway toward a glorious reunion with divine power.

Far from lacking interest in his children, Alcott argued that parents should assert strong and careful authority over their children's upbringing and that no degree of care in the execution of this duty could ever be thought excessive. Indeed, the world of the child "should be the creation of the parents' theory, the offspring of an enlightened mind and a feeling heart, and of this world the parent should be the sole director." Mothers and fathers, he asserted, should rule the home like benevolent gods, exerting "a special oversight over all the relations of the sphere in which [they move]." They should act as "the providence that fills, sustains, and protects, every member of [their] domestic relation."[12]

Alcott did everything in his power to make his children's home conducive to the growth of enlightened souls, and he strove to transform the Alcott nursery into a behavioral laboratory. Anna's and Louisa's infant eyes grew accustomed to seeing fresh flowers on the mantelpiece and prominently displayed busts of Isaac Newton, John Locke, and their father's other intellectual heroes. Alcott took upon himself as much of his daughters' care as he could manage and sought to guard the girls against sudden movements, loud voices, and "incessant prattle."[13] He conducted experiments to determine when they began to recognize colors and acquire object permanency. The following list of observations regarding Anna is typical:

> Identifying her own image, as reflected in the mirror, with her own person. . . . Habits assume the form of personal character. . . . An active desire to exercise her vocal organs, with improved power of enunciation, approaching faintly to forms of speech. . . . Appreciates relations. Perceives the relation of cause and effect; observes the intimations of experience; and acts upon it, both in the form of faith, and submission. . . . Obvious physical improvement from her taking of vegetable and animal food.[14]

These physical observations underlay the question that defined the center of Alcott's research on his children: By what means does a child acquire a personality and a sense of self that is distinct from the surrounding world? Part of his answer had to do with the child's innate power to comprehend symbolism. He took as given a doctrine that Emerson was soon to elaborate in *Nature:* that all material objects are symbolic manifestations of unseen qualities and truths and that this relation can be found continually in language—a cunning person is a fox; a firm person is a rock. Emerson quoted French Swedenborgian Guillaume Oegger concerning the principle that "material objects . . . are necessarily kinds of *scoriæ* of the substantial thoughts of the Creator, which must always preserve an exact relation to their first origin; in other words, visible nature must have a spiritual . . . side." Thus, he continued, "every object rightly seen unlocks a new faculty of the soul."[15] Assuming these conclusions to be true, Alcott maintained that, when a child becomes aware of the difference between herself and the things beyond herself, the recognition is not only a sensory awakening but also a moral one. He wrote:

> The analogy of the symbols of the outward world to the spiritual sense, is apparent during the early experiences of existence. The child obviously finds in the visual, vocal, minute symbols of the outward objects, Conscious expressions, and representations of the spirit's

instincts and ideas. He experiences his connexions with things and persons, he dimly appreciates the harmonies and relations of his being to surrounding phenomena and agents. He sees himself pictured forth in objectivity. He feels his own soul radiated through the constancy of others. He enjoys communion . . . by sympathetic affinities, with the manifestations of the infinite through finite forms.[16]

In the earliest development of an infant's mind, Alcott believed that he saw the confluence and the inseparability of sense and spirit. He framed the argument this way:

The question has often been asked, "At what period of its existence does the child become a moral being?" . . . May we not say that susceptibility begins with the [perception] of relations; that the child feels a sense of this [awareness] as soon as experience has shed upon his mind a sensation of his being, and suggested to him his power of volition, by which he may control his actions in reference to it? He learns by . . . his relations to physical, surrounding objects: he perceives by the careful observation of these objects their power of imparting happiness or misery; he learns that he may avoid the one [and achieve] the other; and gains a knowledge of will; he feels the consciousness of volition, he discovers the [operation] of cause and effect; he detects a general law . . . and . . . he is thus put in possession of himself.[17]

Viewing the matter theistically, Alcott attributed the shock of the child's first awareness to her having left her celestial home and being thrust into a sinful, inharmonious world. But one need not accept the religious gloss to embrace at least a portion of his reasoning. A child develops in vitro unaware that her environment is separate from herself. Only at birth does she begin to experience the world as something foreign and as a source of challenge. The life that ensues is one of struggle to achieve a manageable relation between self and other. But whereas we may tend to see the conflict as unending, Alcott saw the possibility of reconciliation and restored harmony. He sought to explain that, with careful guidance, the child might progress from her original innocence, through the experience of conflict, to a state of wise submission to the forces of God and nature. His thinking on this point merits quotation at length:

> Is not nature, is not the spirit of man, *quick* with divinity? How else doth the one undergo its manifold changes, and the other put on so many varying phases? Do not these come from the ever-shifting, evanescent life, that acteth within? . . . The spiritual senses drink in the life of the spiritual, as the material sense doth the material influence. . . . God floweth in; God floweth out; God encompasseth around, and in this eddy of affinitive forces, man holdeth his being. . . . In the confluence of these agencies, he attaineth a force that he calleth his own free-will, and acteth with the laws that he cannot master, and by which he becometh a separate will—an individual. Upborne, as on these flowing waters, he becometh, as it were, a part of the tide, and ebbeth and floweth, with it, as he willeth to follow its celestial courses on the ocean of the Infinite![18]

The biblical verb endings are, I confess, a bit of a bother. Yet they succeed in conveying Alcott's sense of the grand transformation he is attempting to describe: a mystical conjoining of the spirit of the individual person with the all-encompassing spirit of the universe. And, as he goes on to explain, this union results when the person, having acquired a sense of separateness and self, renounces it in favor of the greater, uplifting spirit:

> Man's force, his individual will, his free-agency, cometh by submission to the superior force that ever presseth against him [and] penetrateth into his very nature. . . . He findeth his own strength, as he yieldeth up, and is upborne by these superior forces. . . . By this docility, this suffering of the Divinity, doth he lade his spirit with Divinity; and all his powers are renewed. His *Senses* are quickened; his *sentiments* vivified . . . and he flourishes as a tree planted by the waterside, and putteth forth leaves, blossoms, fruit, in his person.
>
> Accepting the conditions of his being, he [protesteth] against nothing. He obeys the Divine Laws, and obedience bringeth life and light to his spirit. He is filled with the inspiration of the Divinity. God

floweth into him; he floweth and commingleth with God, and is laden with the fullness that he thirsteth after. . . . Thus, by descending into nature, spurning its frail instruments, suffering its conditions, with meek, yet patient endeavors, doth the spirit rise again from its mission of self-sacrifice, as did Jesus, to the glorious liberty of a Son of God.[19]

Alcott's narrative of the birth of the soul found its type in the Christian mythos. The child's birth was analogous to the Fall; the infant's gradual acceptance of the laws of nature served the same function as repentance and atonement. Yet even though his writings on child development are rife with invocations of divinity, he perceived a pathway to salvation that was not stained with the sacrificial blood of Christ. As the last sentence of the quotation reveals, he believed that one could be saved through the *imitation* of Christ—through a merging of one's independent will with the will of God and a surrender of oneself to the flow of celestial energies.

Alcott presumed the forces of nature and divinity to be wholly beneficent. Resisting them, therefore, was irrational. One had only to open oneself to these forces—to see them not as opposition but as allies—and one's spirit would be upraised and absorbed into the sweet truth of divine being. A newborn child, he argued, has set forth "out of the pure realm of spirit . . . on an expedition against matter." By the very process of feeling "the infirmities and weaknesses" of the world of flesh, the child learns to subordinate the self "to the higher life which he bringeth with him. He liveth in nature. He dwelleth in the flesh. The Incarnate One is he; and he . . . entereth upon the mission of his own redemption from the tempting body. . . . He laboreth in every little function of his body to regain the seeming good . . . and to throw off the encumbrance that checketh his ascension."[20] Alcott imagined that this process was underway in the spirits of both Anna and Louisa, even when the two girls were only four and three years old. As the year 1835 drew to a close, he observed:

> The . . . two little ones are finding that deep stream of quietude, which, at times, they have left, and sailed forth, on the purturbid waters of the fleshly lusts. . . . Anna is becoming daily more conscious

of the loves that calm and soften; Louisa of the impolicy of reaction. Both are in the way of recovery; both shall return to the fold that they have left, in quest of the liberty that they love, but the means of which they had misconceived. Through the school of disobedience they are learning . . . lessons. . . . If they have put forth their hands and taken of the fruit of the tree of knowledge—the sense-growth of the nature of the [flesh], they have also partaken of the tree that groweth in the midst of the Garden, even the tree of Life, the Holiness that cometh through the spirit of conscience, and they are not only sensible of their nakedness, but ready to put on the [garments?] of The Lord.[21]

Alcott conceded that even spiritually minded people went through periods when "a sense of loneliness comes over the spirit and the idea of isolation from the universal . . . overpowers . . . the associations of the mind."[22] These moods, however, were likely to be short lived if the person possessed a truly firm foundation in both understanding and community. For this, he offered an illustration. His infant daughter Elizabeth, while sleeping, had been carried into a strange room by the family's housekeeper. As she opened her eyes and failed to recognize her surroundings, "her first expression was that of surprise; then came fear at the strangeness . . . and then, the loss of wonted hold on the familiar things and faces that had ever been around her. Then came the vague & dark sense of loneliness—being unsupported by aught that her heart loved; and tears came quick into her eyes."[23]

Promptly, his wife, Abba Alcott, began to caress the child. Anna and Louisa gathered close, and Bronson soothed Elizabeth with his words. In short order, the little girl "found her position again in the universe; and [a] smile of joy, as expressive as the preceding one of grief, came to her relief. . . . The saddening thought had passed away forever."[24] One may smile at Alcott's tendency to find mighty signs and portents in the seemingly trivial griefs and disappointments of childhood. His tales of a baby recovering her place in the universe and of two preschoolers navigating "the purturbid waters of the fleshly lusts" can seem laughably hyperbolic. Yet they reveal his conviction that, where a child's development is concerned, the stakes are always tremendously high. He understood that, to a child too young to have developed a sense of perspective, the commonplace can seem cataclysmic. He also had seen enough of life to know that even a seemingly small event can have powerful, unforeseeable consequences in the life of a child. In his writings about the task and art of child rearing, he consistently conveys urgency; a soul is always too precious to be trifled with.

One evening, after Alcott had read her the biblical story of Lazarus, Louisa, then three years old, asked whether she would one day die. He assured her "that if she *loved* her friends as she ought, as Jesus wanted to have her, she would never die—so Jesus told Martha. Love makes us live. Love keeps us from dying. Naughtiness makes us die but love kept us alive."[25] Reflecting on their conversation, he set down in his journal some precepts on discussing death with children:

> It is safer to make statements to children that hold true in a spiritual sense, and which their opening consciousness will reveal the more and more fully as they advance in understanding, than to state merely appearances of the senses. . . . Details concerning the process of decay, mislead their simple sense, and fill the imagination with disturbing images. . . . Life is but a transit of the spirit across time, in the drapery of the body, and this a child apprehends. He has as distinct sense of something *not* his body, as he has of the body itself. Yea, this sense is more distinct and vivid—for a child lives in this spiritual self, more than the adult.[26]

These thoughts led Alcott to consider as well the duty of parents to "present [the] primal facts of the spirit, in fit manner to the awestruck minds of childhood."[27] It was paramount for a mother or a father to encourage and develop the child's sense of ethical mission and to foster in her a confidence in immortality. He pressed what he deemed the ultimately crucial question:

> Parent, dost thou hope? Hast thou a faith in the immortality of the Soul? Canst thou apprehend the full meaning, and receive, with a glad assurance, without a shadow of doubt, the life-giving, life perpetuating [words] "I am the resurrection and the life, he that believeth in me, though dead, shall live; and he that believeth shall never die." If thou

leave me to feel my bereavement, and to cherish, with fond recollection, the words that thou didst faintly whisper in mine ears, while thou wert in my presence—Childhood is thus *meaning* to me, because it reminds me of thee. In it I behold the memories of a lost life: I feel the relics of an age of innocence—of holiness, of [purity?] that neither time, nor revolution have defiled, nor destroyed. Thou comest unto me, in the forms of these little ones, as an inhabitant of a country, all mine own—and thy familiar tones, and gentle ways, seem the manners of my native home—the language of my mother-tongue; and I seem beside thee, but a stranger and sojourner here below.[30]

Alcott devoted countless days and well upwards of 1,500 pages to his researches on childhood. In the end, he felt that he had come nowhere near to discovering the essence of infant consciousness or tracing the connection between the ideal and the actual. He had dreamed of chronicling his children's entire spiritual lives; he abandoned the task when his eldest was only five. Although he vowed to take up the project again, the following words, written in 1836, were among the last that he would give to the effort:

I now leave these little ones, for a time. Other labours claim my attention, for which I am better armed. Long have I assayed to seize, for this record, some sketch of the inner life that goeth on in the . . . heart of childhood. But faint has been my sketch—imperfect my copy. Still I do not despair. Again I will resume the work, when, after years of insight, I shall be permitted to apprehend the phenomena that I now but notice. Life shall not be barren; for I shall linger around *the refreshing fount of Infancy and Childhood* if, perchance, I may be purified . . . therein.[31]

Alcott's last metaphor on the subject of Psyche was one of metamorphosis. He depicted the childish mind "as the creeping worm, just winding itself in the . . . shroud, [but which] shall, in due time, escape from her confinement [to] be the joyous being of the air and the light."[32] Now, 180 years since Alcott put them aside, his manuscript volumes on the spirit of childhood sleep in their cocoon at Houghton Library, disturbed only by a few scholars, who occasionally comb the pages for a glimpse or two into the lives of the Alcott family. That these journals, or even extended excerpts of them, have never been published is a misfortune. If they offered no more than a fascinating glimpse of a little girl who happened to grow up to become a world-famous author, they would deserve a broader circulation. But they are more than this. They are, in addition, one of the first concerted attempts by an American to create a science of child psychology. And they are a vibrant testament to the spirit of an era, a time when the prospect of uniting the mundane with the eternal seemed possible and when divine truth seemed to be waiting just on the other side of an infant's smile.

NOTES

1. A. Bronson Alcott, "Journal for 1835," Houghton Library, Harvard University, MS Am 1130.12 (8), 533–35.
2. A. Bronson Alcott, "Psyche, or, The Breath of Childhood," Houghton Library, Harvard University, MS Am 1130.10 (8), 261.
3. Ibid., 263.
4. Ibid., 263–64.
5. A. Bronson Alcott, "Journals for 1832–1833," Houghton Library, Harvard University, MS Am 1130.12 (6), 1:41.
6. Samuel Taylor Coleridge, *Aids to Reflection* (Burlington, Vt.: Chauncey Goodrich, 1840), 299.
7. Ibid., 68.
8. A. Bronson Alcott, unpublished manuscript, collection of the author.
9. Alcott's prose style, though not nearly so disastrous as some readers have claimed, was certainly not Emersonian. Emerson adored the aphorism, and he was blessed with an almost journalistic capacity for stating an idea in a terse, quotable form. Alcott tended to write around his ideas, giving the reader a full sense of his thinking process but seldom bothering to reduce his core contention to a pithy, accessible bottom line. Thus, his work is fiendishly difficult to excerpt. Moreover, the manuscripts on which I principally draw are available only to those who are able to spend days at Harvard's Houghton Library. For these reasons, I feel compelled to quote more extensively in this essay than I would typically recommend.
10. A. Bronson Alcott, "Observation[s] on the Life of My Second Child [Louisa May Alcott] During the First Year. 1832–1833," Houghton Library, Harvard University, MS Am 1130.10 (3), ii–iii.
11. Alcott, "Psyche, or, The Breath of Childhood," 265.

12. A. Bronson Alcott, "Observations on the Spiritual Nurture of My Children," Houghton Library, Harvard University, MS Am 1130.10 (6), 69.

13. John Matteson, *Eden's Outcasts: The Story of Louisa May Alcott and Her Father* (New York: Norton, 2007), 45.

14. A. Bronson Alcott, "Observation[s] on the Life of My First Child During Her First Year, 1831[–1832]," Houghton Library, Harvard University, MS Am 1130.10 (1), 260.

15. Ralph Waldo Emerson, *Nature*, in *Essays and Lectures* (New York: Library of America, 1983), 25.

16. Alcott, "Observation[s] on the Life of My Second Child," 161.

17. Alcott, "Observation[s] on the Life of My First Child," 262. The difficulty of Alcott's handwriting has left me unable to decipher a handful of the words in some of the quotations presented in this essay. The words in brackets are not the ones Alcott used, but I insert them to give the best rendering I can of what I take to be his intended meaning.

18. Alcott, "Psyche, or, The Breath of Childhood," 251–53.

19. Ibid., 253–55.

20. Ibid., 387.

21. Ibid., 259–60.

22. Ibid., 161.

23. Ibid., 163–64.

24. Ibid., 165.

25. Ibid., 343.

26. Ibid., 343–44.

27. Ibid., 345.

28. Ibid., 346.

29. Alcott, "Observation[s] on the Life of My First Child," 79–80.

30. Alcott, "Psyche, or, The Breath of Childhood," 265–66.

31. Ibid., 502.

32. Ibid.

CHAPTER 3

SECULAR MELANCHOLY

Religious Skepticism and the "Literature of Misery"

Dawn Coleman

IN "THE American Women's Renaissance and Emily Dickinson," chapter 14 of *Beneath the American Renaissance*, David S. Reynolds argues that mid-nineteenth-century American women's writing contains a distinctly melancholy strand that constitutes a veritable "literature of misery." He distinguishes this dark thread from two other dominant, and more easily mapped, literary styles that define U.S. women's writing of the 1850s. The literature of misery is not "conventional literature," epitomized by Susan Warner's *The Lamplighter* (1852) and Harriet Beecher Stowe's *Uncle Tom's Cabin* (1852) and featuring pious female exemplars who exercise moral and religious influence over their loved ones while conforming to sanctioned gender roles. Nor is it "women's rights fiction," such as Hannah Gardner Creamer's *Delia's Doctors* (1852) and Laura Curtis Bullard's *Christine* (1856), which argues for an expansion of women's opportunities through heroines who claim social and political power. Less invested in moral didacticism or political change, the literature of misery limns the psyches of unconventional women and reveals the performativity of gender. Fiction in this mode uses narrative fragmentation, an emotionally detached style, mordant wit, and strange silences to challenge gender scripts while granting art status as a realm for self-expression and representational control. It is "an ironic, stylized genre" that "set the stage for Dickinson's elliptical poems." The best fiction of this type, Reynolds holds, adumbrates the sophisticated realism of Henry James and Edith Wharton: for example, Alice Cary's *Hagar* (1852) and *Married, Not Mated* (1859), Lillie Devereux Blake's *Southwold* (1859), Fanny Fern's *Ruth Hall* (1855), Louisa May Alcott's *Behind a Mask* (1866), and Elizabeth Stoddard's *The Morgesons* (1862).[1]

Reynolds's chapter does invaluable work in rescuing from oblivion a trove of culturally significant novels and illuminating the variously conventional, activist, and artistic approaches that midcentury women took to representing womanhood. Doubtless, his taxonomy needs revamping in light of both the massive digital archives of nineteenth-century fiction now available and the surge in scholarship on women writers since 1988, much of which troubles assumptions about the artistic and political conservatism of so-called conventional literature. Here, however, I attempt the more modest task of rethinking a single branch of midcentury fiction: the literature of misery. We might choose to revisit this category if only to rid ourselves of its unfortunate name, which, by foregrounding emotion rather than circumstances, effect rather than cause, implies that women of the 1850s were overreacting to their many legitimate sources of unhappiness, including political disenfranchisement, economic disempowerment, and social subordination. To be fair, the term is not Reynolds's own. He borrows it from the editorial "When Should We Write," published in an 1860 issue of the *Springfield Republican*, which lamented a then-current strain of writing that appeals to sympathy but not judgment, "clouds, withers, distorts" its subject, is written by "poor, lonely, and unhappy women," and obscures reality "through a mist of tears."[2] Tacitly recognizing the callousness of this appraisal, Reynolds counterbalances it with more sympathetic perspectives, such Caroline Dall's, who noted the undercurrent of dissatisfaction in women's writing but found just cause in their oppression.

Yet gender inequalities, significant as they were, do not fully explain the downcast mood of some midcentury women's writing. As I will discuss, that malaise arose at times from a non-gender-specific cause common in the United States and Europe: the pain of confronting the existential uncertainties of religious skepticism and the possibility of a godless universe or one in which a deity is absent, unknowable, or unconcerned with human affairs. A surprising number of midcentury novels by women navigate the treacherous transition from the once-safe harbors of faith to the open seas of secular modernity; from a stable, inherited, religiously grounded sense of identity to a destabilizing, open-ended, secular selfhood. Like Ishmael in Herman Melville's *Moby-Dick*, the protagonists of these fictions are "quick to perceive a horror" and unafraid to inhabit religious doubt, however unhappy it might make them.[3]

Aside from Dickinson and Margaret Fuller, the century's religiously skeptical women writers have made barely a ripple in U.S. literary history. In contrast, we are well aware of skeptical male contemporaries such as Melville, Edgar Allan Poe, and Nathaniel Hawthorne and British luminaries such as George Eliot, whose deconversion story and humanist novels loom large in the canon. Yet America had its own Eliots, who, if less magisterial in scope and masterly in execution, also wrote accomplished, thought-provoking fictions that critiqued conventional religion and explored secular ways of being. Sympathetic narratives of religiously skeptical women became a recognizable subgenre in the United States only after 1850. Before that, few such women appear in novels, and those who do serve as negative examples.[4] The shift may have been due in part to the March 1850 publication of Hawthorne's *The Scarlet Letter*, which centers on heroic, defiant Hester Prynne, who was modeled in part on Fuller. Transfigurations of Hester appear in fiction throughout the 1850s and beyond, and a heightened interest in women's religious iconoclasm owed a great deal, I suspect, to Fuller's tragic, spectacular death in July 1850. After that tragedy she became a martyr figure and an icon of free thought in ways that were often difficult to reconcile with her documented spiritual views. Numerous novels with heterodox heroines were published in the decade following her death. Two pointedly took her for a template: Caroline Chesebro's *Isa: A Pilgrimage* (1852) and, a few months later, Hawthorne's *The Blithedale Romance* (1852). Subsequent fictions reflected her legacy while incorporating elements from the authors' own histories: not only Blake's *Southwold* and Stoddard's *The Morgesons* but also Mary Gove Nichols's

Mary Lyndon (1855), Eliza Farnham's *My Early Days* (1859), and Augusta Jane Evans's *Beulah* (1859).

While *The Scarlet Letter* and the empowering memory of Fuller were important catalysts for the midcentury emergence of skeptical women in American fiction, an even more significant one came via a transatlantic zeitgeist that was circulating new theories about deep time, deep space, biblical hermeneutics, materialism, pantheism, and other faith-disrupting ideas. As Charles Taylor writes in *A Secular Age,* in about 1850 Europe and North America experienced a "nova effect" in religion: an explosion of new possibilities for religious belief and unbelief. He explains that this proliferation hastened processes of modernity that had begun in about 1500, when North Atlantic peoples went from being "porous" selves—connected to spiritual realities, vulnerable to ghosts and devils, yet capable of transcendent "fullness"—to being modern, "buffered" selves, forced to pick and choose religious beliefs and thus condemned to regard their own faith or lack thereof with a certain alienation.[5] John Modern substantiates the relevance of Taylor's observations about the "nova effect" for the mid-nineteenth-century United States while usefully challenging the neat distinction between buffered and porous selves. He describes "the secular imaginary" that emerged midcentury as a matter of embodied affect that "occurred at the levels of emotion and mood, underneath the skin," and thus was not wholly subject to rational control.[6] In this way, Modern troubles an insistence on choice (the idea that in the secular age we navigate religious options) and argues that Taylor assumes an unduly ratiocinative, agentive, modern selfhood. His revision of Taylor, with its messier, less autonomy-affirming description of selfhood, resonates with the models of subjectivity in nineteenth-century novels, which often represent contingency and embodied affect as crucial to identity formation.

Reading fiction about religiously skeptical women in light of Modern's insights can create new respect for the affective dimension of novels long disparaged for their perceived emotionalism. Such books offer lush representations of the lived experience of secularization. Despite the occasional intrusion of pious narrators and didactic coverplots, they depict skepticism as a wellspring of power and freedom, an ally of unconventionality and heroic individualism. Yet many are also infused with a gloom that, while recognizable as misery, can be understood more precisely as the distinctive form of unhappiness that the British romanticist Colin Jager has called "the melancholy of the secular."[7] Like Modern, Jager takes issue with Taylor's understanding of the modern self as inherently buffered and holds that the secular is a "pretheoretical way of life that bequeathed to modernity a particular phenomenology," one that individuals register more than they control.[8] Again, contingencies matter. As Jager details, a dominant aspect of this secular phenomenology is melancholy, an ennui and dissatisfaction rooted in the sense that religious belief and belonging are not viable now and perhaps never were, that religious doctrines and teachers provide no trustworthy guidance, that solitary paths to spiritual enlightenment are illusory, and that secular pursuits cannot produce lasting happiness. He sees such secular melancholy as the opposite of Taylor's "fullness." It is the perception of "possibilities only as impossible, untried experiences encountered as irrecoverable, losses ungrievable because fullness was never there to begin with."[9] Bracingly authentic, secular melancholy confronts present realities without illusion or residual faith, in contrast to its starry-eyed twin, nostalgia, which tends to idealize the past, however unjust or unsatisfying. This affective orientation is less abject "misery" than the grim endurance of a world in which, if God exists, he offers neither comfort nor direction.

To explore the significance of this form of melancholy for American women at midcentury—the moment when religion went nova—I begin with *The Scarlet Letter*, which established a template for later representations of discontented, freethinking women. I then turn to two geographically antipodal novels that feature religiously skeptical, melancholic protagonists: Evans's *Beulah*, set in a fictive Montgomery, Alabama, and Stoddard's *The Morgesons*, set largely in the coastal villages of Massachusetts. All three novels urge the idea that midcentury women experienced rather than chose secularity and its melancholy and that this negative affect, though perceived as a problem to be solved, could also confer formidable psychic and social advantages.

In U.S. literature, Hester Prynne inaugurates the tradition of the skeptical woman as a sympathetic character type. She does not, of course, begin life as a skeptic. Having traveled to the New World as a Puritan, she feels the internal tug of Puritan morality even after the community ostracizes her for violating the regnant sexual ethic. She tells herself, in what the narrator calls "half a truth, and half a self-delusion," that she stays in the colony because here "had been the scene of her guilt, and here should be the scene of her earthly punishment." Conscientiously, if unsuccessfully, she strives to repress her unquenched passion for Dimmesdale and to accept Puritan justice. But once she is made an outcast, she gradually and inadvertently strays from the ways of righteousness. She "[forbears] to pray for her enemies," lest, supposedly, she curse them by accident; and when the narrator says that, if she enters a church, she might hear a sermon taking her and the "A" she wears as a text, the subtext of that "if" is that she often avoids church altogether. During the long years of virtual exile, she glides through the town like a mournful spirit, neither idealizing the past nor hoping for the future. She seems to find no solace in the church, the Bible, prayer, pastoral counsel, or other means of grace. With time she becomes an antinomian, perhaps even a transcendentalist *avant la lettre:* she seldom "measure[s] her ideas of right and wrong by any standard external to herself."[10] Crucially, she does not choose this renegade life; communal scapegoating and social isolation have changed her. Her lonely cottage by the sea, set on barren soil and half-hidden by a scrubby brake, is the emblem of secular melancholy, a New World analogue to the dismal shores of Matthew Arnold's "Dover Beach."

After seven years of living in, but not of, the Puritan community, Hester's faith has evaporated. Now she is not merely an antinomian but a freethinker: "She assumed a freedom of speculation, then common enough on the other side of the Atlantic, but which our forefathers, had they known it, would have held to be a deadlier crime than that stigmatized by the scarlet letter." This "freedom of speculation" touches both politics and religion. The narrator explains that the new thought of that age had political repercussions—"Men of the sword had overthrown nobles and kings"—yet that even deeper transformations of history were afoot: "Men bolder than these had overthrown and rearranged—not actually, but in theory, which was their most real abode—the whole system of ancient prejudice, wherewith was linked much of ancient principle." The suggestion is that Hester, too, balks at musty pieties and feels the humanizing, secularizing impulses of early modernity. Her powder-keg musings are less political than social and religious; she might have been a "prophetess" or "the foundress of a religious sect." Her meditations chiefly concern the status of women: "Was existence worth accepting, even to the happiest among them?" For herself, she says no—a heretical drive to self-erasure—and despairs of any change in women's social position. Her discouragement eventuates in melancholy, with the narrator explaining that here she fulfills a general truth: "A tendency to speculation, though it may keep woman quiet, as it does man, yet makes her sad."[11] Patronizing as this axiom may seem, as if sadness were a sign of feminine weakness, it underscores how religious skepticism could unsettle a woman's equanimity when experienced in a social context that anathematized women who rejected the community's religious beliefs.

Yet Hester's separation from Puritanism affords her unwonted power, suggesting how secular melancholy might contain the seeds of nonreligious sources of redemption. She is the "rightful inmate" of houses "darkened by trouble," nursing the sick and holding vigils at deathbeds with a sense of belonging and purpose she enjoys nowhere else. Social and religious estrangement fires the creativity evinced in her lavish, original needlework. Most strikingly, her "A" displays a "delicate and imaginative skill" that betokens "human ingenuity." Its contrast with her dress, "of the coarsest material and the most somber hue," emblematizes how irreligious human vitality can flourish against a backdrop of melancholy. This vitality eventually erupts into plot when Hester meets Dimmesdale in the forest and, with her hair down and the glow of womanhood again upon her, revolts against the religious interpretation of her life—"What we did had a consecration of its own"—and audaciously proposes flight. The narrator famously censures her errancy: "Shame, Despair, Solitude! These had been her teachers—stern and wild ones—and they had made her strong, but taught her much amiss." But the portrait of brave, beautiful, sexy freethinking remains.[12]

Years later, after the dream of a fairy-tale ending has vanished and Dimmesdale and Chillingworth have crumbled to dust, Hester's melancholy again takes center stage, now with newly redemptive power.

Following a tradition stretching back to Aristotle, Hawthorne in the novel's conclusion links melancholy to prophecy.[13] Hester's perpetual sorrow generates her far-seeing intimations of that "brighter period" when "a new truth would be revealed, in order to establish the whole relation between man and woman on a surer ground of mutual happiness." Though unable to imagine herself as the "destined prophetess," she in fact serves this function through her comfort and counsel to other suffering women and in her predictions of a future that does not claim to find authority or guidance in scripture or theology but in happiness, that most secular of human goods.[14] Thus, the novel argues that the sadness associated with a woman's disaffection from religion can inspire visions of a better, more humane world, one that does not take its bearings from ministers or magistrates, churches or scriptures, but from a commitment to improved gender relations.

A woman's generative secular melancholy is also the main event in *Beulah*, which offers nineteenth-century America's most penetrating fictive exploration of the intellectual challenges facing Christian faith in the secular age. The story is deceptively formulaic in its outline, following the script that Nina Baym traces for nineteenth-century "woman's fiction": an intelligent orphan girl ventures alone into the world, works hard and overcomes obstacles to achieve success, and then creates in adulthood the magic family circle she herself lacked in childhood.[15] Like many such fictions, *Beulah* borrows liberally from Charlotte Brontë's *Jane Eyre* (1847). In Evans's book, the wealthy, Rochester-esque Dr. Guy Hartwell takes Beulah into his care when she is thirteen years old and educates her, offering her an adoption she wisely, as it turns out, refuses. Inevitably, an attraction between the two develops, with her pride and his petulance thwarting its immediate fulfillment in marriage. Many years must pass, in which Guy wanders the "East" (a vast expanse that includes palm trees and pagodas, deserts and the Himalayas, as well as Morocco, Tartary, India, and China) while Beulah slowly recognizes the strength of her feeling for him. When he finally returns from his travels, weary and graying, they fall into each other's arms.

This predictable romantic plot encircles the far more gripping and original story of Beulah's disillusionment with religious faith and her radical, individualistic quest to discover the nature of reality and the meaning of human life by reading her way through romanticism's leading writers. Beulah gets her first taste of skepticism from Hartwell's library; but when she defiantly leaves his care in late adolescence, she seeks to make her spiritual journey her own. Financially and intellectually independent, she teaches school and by night writes for publication and seeks answers to the mysteries of the universe in books. In the course of her philosophical inquiries, she reads works by Poe, Samuel Taylor Coleridge, Thomas De Quincey, William Wordsworth, Jean Paul Richter, Lord Byron, Charles Kingsley, William Cowper, Alfred Tennyson, Ralph Waldo Emerson, Thomas Carlyle, Johann von Goethe, Victor Cousin, Theodore Parker, John Ruskin, and various unnamed scientists and German philosophers. That some permutation of Beulah's startlingly erudite reading list appears in nearly all criticism on the novel suggests the rarity of encountering a nineteenth-century fictional American heroine—or hero, for that matter—with such voracious reading habits and intense philosophical proclivities. Perhaps no other U.S. novel so thoroughly registers midcentury transatlantic currents of secular thought. *Beulah* is, as the historian Michael O'Brien writes, "*Middlemarch* before its time, a meditation on the intellectual problem of modern knowledge."[16]

Evans modeled *Beulah*'s storyline on her own experience of religious skepticism in early adulthood, which involved a multiyear, study-intensive pursuit of answers to the philosophical conundrums of the age.[17] Having closed this episode by returning to the Methodism of her youth, she claimed that she wrote *Beulah* to warn vulnerable young people of the perils of skeptical thought. However, despite her own reconversion to Christian faith, much in the novel seeks to defend Beulah's explorations among the metaphysicians and to recover the complexity of thought and feeling that accompanied Evans's sojourn in the land of faithlessness. Even more so than *The Scarlet Letter*, *Beulah* presents a thoughtful, sustained imagining of a religiously skeptical woman.[18] As in Hawthorne's novel, freethinking is thrust upon the heroine. Beulah loses faith due to an overwhelming confluence of reasons: her sister's death, her hatred of her sister's adoptive mother, her grief at having lost her entire family, her intellectualism, her reading in Hartwell's library, her lack of a pious mother, her stubbornness, her pride, and arguably

God himself, who tries her soul without compensatory comfort. The sheer plenitude of reasons for her lack of faith upends the evangelical teaching, echoed in the novel, that unbelievers living in Christian lands "willingly walk in darkness." Of the multitudinous contingencies that push Beulah toward skepticism, the most important, it seems, is her avid curiosity: "From her earliest childhood she had been possessed by an active spirit of inquiry, which constantly impelled her to investigate, and as far as possible explain the mysteries which surrounded her on every side." Yet Evans also stresses that Beulah's struggles are representative. At one point, for instance, the kindly Dr. Asbury, himself an agnostic, tells his wife, "This spirit of skepticism is scattered far and wide over the land.... It broods like a hideous nightmare over this age, and Beulah must pass through the same ordeal which is testing the intellectual portion of every community."[19] Repeatedly, the novel seeks to exonerate Beulah for her skepticism, to reframe it as not a sin but a bleak psychological and historical necessity.

The emotional corollary of Beulah's unbidden skepticism is a persistent melancholy.[20] If her sadness is linked to her lingering grief for her dead mother, father, and sister, it arises as well from the loss of her heavenly Father, a keen awareness of the silence of the universe, and the growing plausibility that no divine Parent ever existed. Others see her as "dismal and graveyardish," and at one point she spends a dreary winter day brooding on the idea that all life returns to the "charnelhouse" and wondering whether the human spirit, like the flowers and trees, might also be reborn, despite the lack of concrete evidence for that eventuality. In taking a walk near her old orphanage, she ruminates on bitter thoughts and "speculative doubts" and feels upon returning home that "'If a man die shall he live again?' seemed [to be] echoing on the autumn wind."[21] She turns to the Bible but finds no satisfactory answers. Such episodes strike the keynote of *Beulah*: for adults, childhood faith is not a pleasant home inviting return but a rent scrim that no longer veils material realities.

Yet as in *The Scarlet Letter*, secular melancholy, a stern and wild teacher, makes Beulah strong. Like Hester, she demonstrates striking autonomy and individualism. During her extended period of pronounced religious skepticism, she leaves Hartwell's home, earns her own living, establishes her own home, and achieves a moderate sense of peace and contentment. She rejects not only her guardian's offers of adoption and then marriage but also the repeated suits of the respectable and pious Reginald Lindsay. As with Hester, secular melancholy intensifies her sympathy with suffering and grants her a special place at sickbeds and deathbeds. Even more so than in *The Scarlet Letter,* exemplary nursing acquits the skeptical heroine, decoupling lack of faith from lack of charity and lack of womanliness. Beulah's sickbed talents save a baby in her care, numerous cholera victims, and Eugene Graham, her brother-like friend from the orphanage. Somewhat less conventionally, secular melancholy serves as a font of artistic and intellectual creativity for Beulah, as it also does for Hester. Over time she comes to play the piano rapturously, to sing opera airs with virtuosic grace, to express herself through drawing and sculpture, and to write learned essays for publication. These talents assert the sensitivity of her soul, errant though it is. Flourishing as her faith dies, her creative endeavors represent the siren song of a beguiling, aesthetically rich paganism that allows her to take unapologetic joy in art.

But unlike *The Scarlet Letter,* which in the end represents Hester's dissatisfaction with Puritanism as the kindling fire of the social energies that will create a new secular social order, *Beulah* closes by renouncing secularity altogether. One night, after years of lonely intellectual questing and in keen emotional need, when depression ratchets up to despair, Beulah returns to God. Why? Because relentless doubt has made her unhappy. Moreover, although she considers the Christian creation story implausible, she finds the materialist theory that mind emerged from matter even more unlikely. Buoyed by that particular incredulity and all too aware that her metaphysical studies will never provide the certainty she craves, she submits to God: "My God, save me! Give me light: of myself I can know nothing!"[22] She does not so much choose faith at this moment as stumble back into it, seeing dimly through her tears. Nor does the novel here affirm the saving grace of a loving God. He does not speak or send his spirit, and neither scripture nor preachers nor believing friends act with providential power to effect her conversion. Her faith is the flag of surrender, a choice she feels compelled to make not out of conviction but out of desperation.

Frustrated with the ricketiness of the novel's bridge between metaphysical uncertainty and Methodist piety, Evans's fellow southerner Henry Timrod wrote to a friend, "Beulah's transition from scepticism [sic] to Faith is left almost wholly unaccounted for. How much I should like to have my own doubts settled in the same satisfactory, yet most inexplicable manner!"[23] Dwelling on this same problem, a latter-day critic explains that, despite occasional affirmations of divine agency and the reliability of religious teachings, the novel effectively endorses psychological relativism: Evans at times "seems to argue, not that religion is true, just that it works, and for her."[24] Indeed, one of Beulah's mentors makes much this point: "I have never yet known a happy man or woman, who did not reverence God and religion."[25] Enlisting happiness—not blessedness, not peace, not truth—to champion Christian faith, the novel's didacticism sounds an unexpectedly secular note.

The Morgesons presents the melancholy of unbelief without even the semblance of Christian remedy. Stoddard, who was openly secular while living in New York City in the latter half of the nineteenth century, centered her semi-autobiographical novel on Cassandra Morgeson, a young woman reared in a coastal Massachusetts village. Though she is descended from the Puritans, Cassandra is constitutionally irreligious. As a child, she puts her hands over her ears when her aunt sings a hymn and cannot believe in the sanctity of communion after she sees the leftover bread made into pudding. She is miserable during the year she lives with her Grandfather Warren, who enforces a near-comatose Sabbath and countenances no pleasures for himself or others. She sits torpidly through revivals and amuses her family by burlesquing ministers. When she falls in love with Charles Morgeson, a distant cousin and a married man, and their simmering, unconsummated affair ends in catastrophe, she feels no compunction. She tells her father that examining love, like theology, "makes one skeptical" but if she ever examines theology, it must be off-stage.[26]

The novel traces no path from childhood faith to adult skepticism; Cassandra's inability to believe is a given, a fact of temperament. As retrospective narrator, she claims that as a child she never looked on nature "with the curiosity of thought, or spiritual aspiration" but "was moved and governed by my sensations, which continually changed, and passed away." Her incurious, irreverent skepticism stirs no inner turmoil, and no censorious narrator frowns on her heterodoxy. Rather, she describes the religious practices of New England with anthropological distance, as local tribal customs. The town of Surrey, based on Stoddard's native Mattapoisett, is "lonely, evangelical, primitive." In the factory town of Rosville, "the rich and fashionable [are] Unitarians" who endure tired sermons on "Human Nature." Yet these, dull as they are, prompt in Cassandra something like a moral awakening: "When I felt an emotion without seeing the shadow of its edge turning toward me, I discovered my conscience, which hitherto had only been described to me." But that is the last one hears of Cassandra's conscience or of the Unitarians until she is in Belem (that is, Salem), where, as she helps sort old books and papers in the Somers's third story, she finds, in a seeming homage to Hawthorne's "The Old Manse," "piles of Unitarian sermons."[27] In this novel all things ecclesiastical feel quaint and superannuated.

Despite an unblinking acceptance of secularity, Cassandra is no happier than Hester or Beulah is. Without one of the local faiths to guide her or any inclination to seek a new one, she drifts rudderless through adolescence and early womanhood, a creature of moods who lacks a reliable hermeneutic for interpreting herself and her relationships. Even the surges of sexual desire that constitute the most stirring incidents of life—her infatuations with Charles Morgeson and Desmond Somers—are only temporary respites from listlessness. When, for instance, she returns from Rosville to Surrey, she finds in the sea an echo of her soul sickness: "it seemed to express my melancholy." In Belem, contemplating her return to Surrey, she sees before her "joyless, vacant, barren hours," yet the specter of boredom inspires no action. At one point she announces that she has "no plans" and that if she has "a Purpose, it is formless yet."[28] Putatively a comment on the uncertainty of her relationship to Desmond, her words reflect her existential aimlessness. She cannot escape what Reynolds calls the "benign boredom of [her] bourgeois background."[29]

What can redeem this melancholy? Not a return to the religion of yore. Though of Puritan stock, Cassandra regards the ancestral faith without nostalgia or even interest. The stories and artifacts of her father's family have disappeared: *"Morgeson—Born—Lived—Died*—were all their archives." Their imagined epitaph bears, like Young Goodman Brown's, no hopeful verse, no pious sentiment; the Morgesons have endured without perpetuating their faith in any meaningful way. Nor does Cassandra find a spiritual resource in the religious heritage of her mother's family, embodied in Grandfather Warren's rigidity and her mother's ambivalent piety. Religious traditions are part of the problem, not the solution. As the worldly wife of Charles Morgeson tells Cassandra, "the Puritans have much to answer for in your mother." Stoddard also remains skeptical of that quintessentially Victorian response to waning faith: hard work. Whereas Beulah, the southerner, leaves Hartwell's home with Carlylean ambitions to confront the mystery of existence with diligent toil, Cassandra, Yankee born and bred, regards labor with a jaundiced eye. A Bartleby among women, she prefers not to teach, serve, write, nurse, or fill any of the male professions. Of her father and his business associates, she observes, "They appeared to me . . . as if pursuing something beyond Gain, which should narcotize or stimulate them to forget that man's life was a vain going to and fro."[30] Industry cannot still the tooth that nibbles at the soul.

The silver lining of Cassandra's melancholy is an ability to perceive and describe the world in vibrant, non-moralistic terms. Just as Hester and Beulah transform their misery into art, Cassandra in narrating *The Morgesons* tells a story rich in secular details: the shifting, enigmatic character of the Atlantic seacoast, the fitful household routines of her idiosyncratic family, the annoyances of travel, and the egotistical impulses animating the social world. She dwells perceptively on her physical sensations: for instance, in Rosville, "I was conscious of the ebb and flow of blood through my heart, felt it when it eddied up into my face, and touched my brain with its flame-colored wave"; in Belem when Desmond speaks to her, "The accent with which he spoke my name set my pulses striking like a clock."[31] *The Morgesons* excels, as Reynolds writes, in "quietly potent, often wryly subversive images that attest to woman's artistic power."[32] Cassandra can have this compelling, disruptive perspective on the world only by ignoring the usual religious modes of interpreting a woman's life as a character-building, soul-trying pilgrimage toward the afterlife.

Following Ben's death, Desmond declares in the novel's final line, "God is the ruler. Otherwise, let this mad world crush us now," but we need not assume that Stoddard endorses this backhanded affirmation of providential order. In the novel's closing paragraphs, Cassandra offers an alternative cosmic vision: the sea "wears a relentless aspect to me now; its eternal monotone expresses no pity, no compassion." Such a sea symbolizes the only deity she can acknowledge after her mother's death: "the One above human emotion." In the face of existential uncertainty and the dispiriting probability of divine absence, *The Morgesons* counsels a sporadic zest for embodied existence—"'Have then at life!' my senses cried"—and the steady endurance of misfortune.[33] Alternately epicurean and stoic, Cassandra's materialist response to God's seeming indifference may be the nineteenth century's most defiantly secular affirmation of a woman's heterodoxy.

American women of the mid-nineteenth century faced strong social pressures to conform to and perpetuate religious traditions, with disbelief often bringing with it emotional travail and social isolation. Some of the most engaging novels of the "literature of misery" tradition reflect these struggles. Based on women's personal stories while reflecting a dawning secularity widely felt across the United States and Europe, the novels of women's skepticism are among the most revelatory documents in American letters for understanding the phenomenology of secularization. Complex meditations on difficult experiences, they vividly convey the affective texture of an emergent secularity. They suggest that skeptics might not choose faith or doubt, opt in or out of religion, but find themselves, regardless of will or desire, unable to believe or to be comfortable in their unbelief, to borrow from Hawthorne's well-known gloss on Melville. Yet these novels also intimate that the discomfort, or melancholy, of unbelief might blossom in partial redemptions: resilient individualism, sympathy for suffering, artistic creativity, and visions of social transformation. Unhappiness has its rewards.

NOTES

1. David S. Reynolds, *Beneath the American Renaissance: The Subversive Imagination in the Age of Emerson and Melville* (Cambridge, Mass.: Harvard University Press, 1988), 387, 388–410.

2. Ibid., 395. Reynolds attributes the editorial to Samuel Bowles, but Alfred Habegger has since shown that the author was most likely Fidelia Hayward Cooke, the *Republican*'s new literary editor (*My Wars Are Laid Away in Books: The Life of Emily Dickinson* [New York: Random House, 2001], 383–84).

3. Herman Melville, *Moby-Dick, or the Whale*, vol. 6 of *The Writings of Herman Melville*, ed. Harrison Hayford, Hershel Parker, and G. Thomas Tanselle (Evanston: Northwestern University Press and Newberry Library, 1988), 7.

4. U.S. novels published before 1850 that feature unsympathetic portraits of skeptical women include Susanna Rowson's *Sarah, or the Exemplary Wife* (1813), Catharine Sedgwick's *Redwood: A Tale* (1824), Lydia Maria Child's *The Rebels, or Boston Before the Revolution* (1825), Eliza Lee Cabot Follen's *The Skeptic* (1835), and J. H. Ingraham's *The Gipsy of the Highlands* (1843).

5. Charles Taylor, *A Secular Age* (Cambridge: Belknap Press of Harvard University Press, 2007), 5–10, 35–42, 299–300.

6. John Modern, *Secularism in Antebellum America* (Chicago: University of Chicago Press, 2011), 6. On the rise of religious skepticism in the United States in this period, see James Turner, *Without God, Without Creed: The Origins of Unbelief in America* (Baltimore: Johns Hopkins University Press, 1985).

7. Colin Jager, *Unquiet Things: Secularism in the Romantic Age* (Philadelphia: University of Pennsylvania Press, 2015), 56–75.

8. Ibid., 10.

9. Ibid., 56. In contrast, Sigmund Freud offers a far more pathological definition of melancholia as a state of "profoundly painful dejection, abrogation of interest in the outside world, loss of the capacity to love, inhibition of all activity, and a lowering of the self-regarding feelings to a degree that finds utterance in self-reproaches and self-revilings, and culminates in a delusional expectation of punishment" ("Mourning and Melancholy," in Jennifer Radden, ed., *The Nature of Melancholy: From Aristotle to Kristeva* [New York: Oxford University Press, 2000], 283).

10. Nathaniel Hawthorne, *The Scarlet Letter and Other Writings: Authoritative Texts, Contexts, Criticism*, ed. Leland S. Person (New York: Norton, 2005), 56, 59, 104.

11. Ibid., 107, 108.

12. Ibid., 105, 57, 58, 126, 128.

13. See Aristotle [or a follower of Aristotle], "Problems Connected with Thought, Intelligence, and Wisdom" (ca. 2nd century BCE), in Radden, *The Nature of Melancholy*, 57–60. Melancholy is here connected to "diseases of madness or frenzy, which accounts for the Sibyls, soothsayers, and all inspired persons" (58).

14. Hawthorne, *The Scarlet Letter*, 166.

15. See Nina Baym, *Woman's Fiction: A Guide to Novels by and about Women in America, 1820–70*, 2nd ed. (Urbana: University of Illinois Press, 1993).

16. Michael O'Brien, *Conjectures of Order: Intellectual Life and the American South, 1810–1860* (Chapel Hill: University of North Carolina Press, 2004), 1163.

17. William Perry Fidler, *Augusta Evans Wilson, 1835–1909: A Biography* (Birmingham: University of Alabama Press, 1951), 47–55; and Sara S. Frear, "'You My Brother Will Be Glad with Me': The Letters of Augusta Jane Evans to Walter Clopton Harriss, January 29, 1856, to October 29, 185[8?]," *Alabama Review* 60, no. 2 (2007): 111–41.

18. *Beulah* has a precursor of sorts in Orestes Brownson's semi-autobiographical novel *Charles Elwood; or the Infidel Converted* (1840), which also gives skepticism a full and fair hearing. Evans may have taken inspiration from Brownson, though she does not mention him in her surviving letters.

19. Augusta Jane Evans, *Beulah*, ed. Elizabeth Fox-Genovese (Baton Rouge: Louisiana State University Press), 385, 208, 248.

20. Elizabeth Fox-Genovese regards the character's sadness more pessimistically than I do; for her, the novel "figures as a protracted account of melancholia, of pathological and self-destructive mourning" (introduction to Evans, *Beulah*, xxxiiii). In what seems to me a strained reading, she links Beulah's melancholy not to her skepticism but to the long-ago loss of her mother.

21. Ibid., 63, 131, 180.

22. Ibid., 371.

23. Henry Timrod, letter to Rachel Evans, July 7, 1861, in William Perry Fidler, ed., "Unpublished Letters of Henry Timrod," *Southern Literary Messenger*, n.s. 2 (1940): 605.

24. O'Brien, *Conjectures of Order*, 1170.

25. Evans, *Beulah*, 315.

26. Elizabeth Stoddard, *The Morgesons*, ed. Lawrence Buell and Sandra A. Zagarell (New York: Penguin, 1984), 137.

27. Ibid., 14, 96, 73–74, 171.

28. Ibid., 127, 188, 194.

29. Reynolds, *Beneath the American Renaissance*, 410.

30. Stoddard, *The Morgesons*, 9, 153, 142.

31. Ibid., 77, 184.

32. Reynolds, *Beneath the American Renaissance*, 410.

33. Stoddard, *The Morgesons*, 253, 252, 212, 214.

CHAPTER 4

WHITTIER AND THE MORMONS

From Folk Magic to Freedom and Back Again

Zachary McLeod Hutchins

BEFORE JOHN Greenleaf Whittier won wealth and popularity with prematurely nostalgic celebrations of normative white American culture, he worked with the supernatural myths and folk traditions that David S. Reynolds has described as popular irrationalisms.[1] Whittier's first book, *Legends of New England* (1831), was a volume of prose and poetry documenting the colonial superstitions, folkways, and spiritual traditions of the Northeast. Recounting tales of rattlesnake fascination and Indian religion, *Legends* aimed for the commercial success that Washington Irving had already won with his sketches of Dutch folklore.[2] Whittier would return to these themes sixteen years later in *The Supernaturalism of New England* (1847); but as he earned a national reputation as an abolitionist and a poet, he eventually came to view his early writings with embarrassment and hoped to distance himself from the style and content of *Legends*. According to his biographer Samuel T. Pickard, "Whenever, in later life, Mr. Whittier obtained possession of a copy, he destroyed it. On one occasion he paid five dollars for a copy, and burned it."[3] In his earliest work Whittier attempted to establish the "native idiom" that Reynolds discerns beneath the subversive fiction that F. O. Matthiessen discusses in *American Renaissance*. In that book, Matthiessen suggests dismissively that Whittier's "bare prose and honest doggerel verse" were more concerned with recounting "the sources of our rural life" than with "the problem of language itself." As his reputation grew, Whittier strove to distance himself from the naïve perspective of *Legends* and its unabashed embrace of "the popular traditions and legends of New-England."[4] Instead, he increasingly turned his attention to unpopular battles for social reform and human rights.

As Whittier's writing shifted from folk magic to freedom, a group with roots in New England supernaturalism came briefly and sharply into focus: Mormons. Whittier had taken passing notice of Joseph Smith and the Church of Jesus Christ of Latter-day Saints (LDS) during his time as a folklorist but preferred documenting colonial wonders to publicizing the sensational claims of Smith and his contemporaries. Notwithstanding his respect for historical accounts of spectacular heavenly signs, the Quaker poet was skeptical of new religious movements and pseudosciences such as phrenology or animal magnetism, regarding nineteenth-century religious innovators with suspicion. He accordingly dismissed the LDS church as a bastion of superstition and fanaticism until, in the late 1840s and 1850s, the Saints were driven from Nauvoo and their Illinois homes across the Great Plains to Utah. These setbacks reframed the cultural significance of the Mormon movement, as news reports emphasized the unwarranted suffering of LDS church members rather than their credulity. "The history of the Mormons is one of persecution," editorials declared in 1848, and Whittier took up the cause of Mormon suffering as part of his broader campaign for the rights of enslaved African Americans and other oppressed peoples.[5] But when, in 1852, word of Mormon polygamy surfaced in the newspapers, Whittier—and other members of the New England intelligentsia—dropped their support for the LDS church immediately. The Mormons became again personae non gratae, irrational enthusiasts associated with the Yankee supernaturalism of Whittier's youth rather than an oppressed sect deserving his sympathy.

The shifting moral valence of Mormonism in Whittier's writing, from fanatical folk magicians to an unjustly persecuted minority and back again, suggests that the antebellum divide between the form and content of lowbrow (regional legends or superstitious ballads) and high culture (essays on liberalism) was permeable. Groups and belief systems moved along that spectrum fluidly over a fairly short period of time. Political casuistry shaped the contours of the ground beneath and the sky above the American Renaissance, as writers opportunistically elevated or rejected ideas and institutions depending on their significance to extant, ongoing cultural debates. The moral valence of Mormonism fluctuated according to its utility for politicians and social activists. As reflected in the changing tastes of Whittier and the public for which he wrote, midcentury Mormonism rode the rollercoaster of popular opinion from the skeptical fringes of supernatural religion to the thick of debates about who is entitled to the protection of American laws and back again. That journey charts the fickle contours of a cultural map whose topography shifted in response to the fluctuating popularity and ideological utility of someone like Smith and of the church he founded.

IN JUNE 1838, at the close of the New England Antislavery Convention, Whittier drafted an editorial for the *Pennsylvania Freeman* considering the events of the convention's closing days. Disappointed that discussion had strayed from the cause of immediate emancipation, he regarded the final day's debate as a waste and suggested that "a discussion of the merits of animal magnetism, or of the Mormon Bible would have been quite as appropriate" as the conversation which actually took place.[6] In identifying the Book of Mormon, Smith's volume of ancient American scripture, with the principles of animal magnetism, Whittier signaled his dismissal of both. Smith made claims of angelic visitations and Franz Anton Mesmer promoted the study of scientific fluids connecting all matter, but both men asked their followers to acknowledge supernatural phenomena of which Whittier was deeply skeptical. Of course, David Meredith Reese and others of Whittier's contemporaries characterized the principles of abolitionist thought as a form of fanaticism just as absurd as Smith's revelations or Mesmer's science. Anticipating objections to his use of the word *humbug* to describe religious sects, scientific theories, and philosophies,

Reese wrote: "Believers in the 'celestial science of Animal Magnetism,' for example, will be shocked at the high handed wickedness of placing them on a level with the deluded victims of Ultra-Abolitionism;—while the disciples of the latter delusion will be so outraged in their pious feelings, at being classed with the former, that they will anathematize the author."[7] Whittier dismissed Mormonism and mesmerism as supernatural distractions from the most important issues of the age, belief systems diverting attention and energy away from ending the evils of slavery—but he also knew that others saw the fight for abolition as an equally misguided pursuit.

Appropriately, Whittier's next mention of Mormons differentiated between the serious cultural work of abolitionists and the entertainment provided by gulls who believed in the supernatural. In 1842, while inviting his friend Elizabeth Neall to visit him in Boston, Whittier wrote, "I think thou would be pleased to make a visit to the 'city of notions'—we have transcendentalism, Swedenborgianism, Mormonism, Elder Knapp—Abby Folsom, and many other isms—to say nothing of good and true friends of Freedom and humanity."[8] To speak of Mormons and Swedenborgians was to say nothing of truth, goodness, or the friends of freedom because Whittier saw the misguided followers of Smith and Emanuel Swedenborg as notional: impulsive adherents of a passing fancy, not committed defenders of essential truths.

Mormonism was distanced, in Whittier's early writing, from the realm of serious ideas and also from meaningful aesthetic accomplishment. Reflecting on the ways in which an early 1830 poem in praise of Henry Clay had been appropriated to support Thomas H. Benton and other political candidates, Whittier lamented that "as General Joseph Smith from the latest accounts is about to run as the Presidential candidate of the Latter Day Saints I confess I should not be surprised to see this unlucky bit of rhyme appear in the Nauvoo Times and Seasons, addressed to the Great Mormon Prophet himself!"[9] Whittier's fears were apparently realized; he reported some decades later that "the Saints of Nauvoo" had embraced the "partisan enthusiasm of that boyish production" as part of their campaign for "the apotheosis of the Prophet Joseph Smith."[10] Whittier's poem on Clay, like *Legends*, came to be a source of embarrassment for the poet, and he links the

Mormons' misplaced zeal for Smith's supernaturalism to their immature grasp of aesthetics. An unsophisticated regard for poetic form—as though a bit of boyish rhyme was what distinguished good verse!—was to be expected of Mormon enthusiasts with a questionable grasp of religion and politics. Whittier characterized them as both irrational and literarily unsophisticated, firmly in the cultural underbelly of what would become the American Renaissance.

The Saints built two temples that were praised for their architectural sophistication—the first in Kirtland, Ohio, during the 1830s; the second in Nauvoo during the 1840s. Yet Whittier insists, in an early essay on Smith's followers, that notwithstanding their success in building a highly regarded Greek Revival–style temple on the banks of the Mississippi River, Mormons were cultural outsiders and aesthetic rubes (figure 1).[11] He praised the temple envisioned and commissioned by Smith as "the most splendid and imposing architectural monument in the New World" but refused to accept this work of art as evidence of a refined or genteel culture. Establishing his own aesthetic bona fides with quotations from Ralph Waldo Emerson's poem "The Priest" and Lord Byron's *Manfred*, he ridiculed the Book of Mormon as an apocryphal delusion and rejected "the coarse and vulgar character of the Mormon Prophet." Smith may have demonstrated, in the Nauvoo Temple, an LDS awareness of "dignity and beauty," but Whittier found the building and its virtues aberrant, atypical of Mormon culture. Smith was not an urbane artist like Byron or a respected philosopher like Emerson but a rustic, regional folk hero: "Once in the world's history we were to have a Yankee prophet, and we have had him in Joe Smith. For good or for evil, he has left his track on the great pathway of life—or, to use the words of [the British poet Richard Henry] Horne, 'knocked out for himself a window in the wall of the nineteenth century,' whence his rude, bold, good-humored face will peer out upon the generations to come."[12] Smith's theology and art were transgressive, his character uncouth. In Whittier's view, Mormonism arrived through a hole knocked in the wall of American culture, a hole that was retrospectively dignified with the word *window*. Whittier framed Smith's character and his contributions to literature, theology, and art in terms of his capacity to subvert or reject nineteenth-century norms.

FIGURE 1: This 1890 lithograph depicts the original Nauvoo temple, which was burned to the ground shortly after the Saints were forced to abandon the city. Courtesy of the Library of Congress.

In the fall of 1844, when Whittier met with two LDS evangelists and their congregants in a rented room in Lowell, Massachusetts, he found his prejudices confirmed. Feeling uncharacteristically flighty, "in the mood to welcome any thing of a novel character," he stepped inside Classic Hall and took his seat among the sect's "honest and sincere fanatics." The preacher was "a young man, with dark, enthusiast complexion" (Whittier does not explain what an enthusiast complexion looks like) "gesticulating with the vehemence of Hamlet's player, 'tearing his passion to rags.'"[13] Citing Hamlet's well-known speech to the company of actors who visit Elsinore, Whittier used William Shakespeare's words to condemn the Mormon preacher and his eager auditors for their collective lack of artistic judgment. In the play, Hamlet instructs the players,

> Do not saw the air too much with your hand, thus, but use all gently; for in the very torrent, tempest, and, as I may say, whirlwind of your passion, you must acquire and beget a temperance that may give it smoothness. Oh, it offends me to the soul to hear a robustious periwig-pated fellow tear a passion to tatters, to very rags, to split the ears of the groundlings, who for the most part are capable of nothing but inexplicable dumb shows and noise.[14]

In Whittier's terms, Mormons are capable of appreciating nothing but Smith's noise and dumb shows; they are groundlings who are literally beneath the literary and cultural stage on which the American Renaissance is being performed, as yet unable to follow the leads of Whittier, Emerson, and others in appreciating the beauties and internalizing the lessons of Shakespeare's plays.

Although Whittier was aware, in 1844, that the Saints had endured "severe and protracted persecution for their faith," he came to think more kindly of the LDS church after the Mormon sympathizer Thomas Kane began an extended public relations campaign in 1847.[15] In a March 1850 lecture to the Pennsylvania Historical Society, published by the Mormon leader John Bernhisel and excerpted or reprinted in newspapers across the country, Kane painted the pioneer church in moving terms that spoke to Whittier's core interests. In his lecture, he noted that Mormons had been harassed by mobs in Missouri, Illinois, and Iowa, and he chose sentimental tropes to emphasize the injustice of this abuse: "Mothers and babes, daughters and grandparents, all of them alike, were bivouacked in tatters, wanting even covering to comfort those whom the sick shiver of fever was searching to the marrow."[16] According to Kane's biographer, Matthew J. Grow, here and in similar passages he "portrayed the saints as noble victims, morally and socially superior to their persecutors, much like abolitionists portrayed the 'suffering slaves' as a civilized contrast to their brutish masters."[17] The *North Star*, an antislavery newspaper published by Frederick Douglass, referred to Kane's pamphlet as "one of the most entertaining, eloquent and exciting publications with which it has recently been our privilege to meet from the American press." Douglass's review, which appeared just below news of "The First Victim under the New Fugitive Slave Bill," invited his readers to compare the suffering of Mormons with that of slaves and described crimes against Mormons as "outrages the most cruel and monstrous against humanity."[18] As a result of Kane's published lecture, the LDS church became a symbol of the fight for human rights that abolitionists and other activists were waging; and Whittier accordingly reexamined his original assessment of the Saints.

Even before Douglass identified the Mormons as fellow sufferers, Whittier had taken their cause as his own. Writing in the *National Era* in August 1850, he paraphrased Kane's sentimental account of the Mormon exodus:

> Bearing with them their aged and infirm, their sick and dying, they passed in mournful processions through the streets of Nauvoo, and through their corn fields and orchards, the fruit of which they could no longer gather. Pausing on the swell of the last wave of prairie from whence the gilded spire of the great Temple was visible, they bade farewell forever to their homes, hearths, and altars, and then set their faces resolutely towards the setting sun.[19]

The gilded temple that Whittier admired in 1844, despite his reservations about Smith's rough edges, had now become an appropriately majestic monument to Mormon refinement and mistreatment.

A scathing 1844 newspaper editorial by "J. T. M." compared Nauvoo to John Milton's depiction of Sin in *Paradise Lost*, but Whittier came to identify the Mormons with other, more admirable characters from the epic. J. T. M. wrote that Nauvoo was full of "boys untutored and wild, and girls bare-footed and bare-legged with hair so matted and tangled, that vermin could not thread the labyrinth. The city was like Milton's personification of Sin, 'Woman to the waist and fair, / But ending foul in many a scaly fold.'" Whittier, by contrast, compared the Saints to Milton's Adam and Eve as they are driven out of the Garden of Eden:

> Some natural tears they dropp'd, but wip'd them soon;
> The World was all before them, where to choose
> Their place of rest, and Providence thir [sic] guide.[20]

Here, as in his account of meeting Mormon missionaries in Massachusetts, Whittier illustrated the scene with a quotation from a masterpiece of the British Renaissance. However, the difference between those accounts is stark: the Mormons were no longer bit players being lectured by Hamlet but sympathetic and heroic protagonists of their own religious epic. Quoting Kane, Whittier described the "well-cultivated mezzo-soprano voice" of a Mormon singer whose rendition of Psalm 137 nearly drew tears from her audience during the trek west.[21] The LDS church had risen, in six years, from beneath the American Renaissance to a height of cultural respectability, filled with people whose lives and art belonged at center stage in the national drama of expansion and self-governance.

And in 1850, Utah was, as Whittier knew, at the center of national politics. Abolitionists and slaveholders were fighting for political influence over territory newly acquired in the Mexican-American War. Each side strove to persuade territorial governments to prohibit or establish slavery; and when rumors "that slaves are now held in Utah" made their way east, Whittier penned his editorial. He pleaded with "Utah [to] take her stand by the side of California and New Mexico as a free State, and, like them, present herself at the door of the Union with the Declaration of Independence embodied in her Constitution." His newfound respect for the Mormon people was conceived during—and, in all likelihood, as part of—a campaign to win the support of a group at the pivot point of racial politics, and he warned that an LDS embrace of slavery would come with negative consequences for the church: "It becomes the people of Utah to consider that, in their peculiar circumstances, the religious faith for the quiet enjoyment of which they have made so many sacrifices will be justly held responsible for their action in this matter. Toleration of slavery will not be likely to facilitate the popular recognition of their claim as Saints of the Latter Day."[22] Whittier extended an olive branch and a hand up to his Mormon readers, but his offer was clearly conditional; a failure to reject slavery would bring renewed condemnation and rejection.

At this crossroads, Whittier acknowledged a superstitious LDS past and pointed toward a socially inclusive future in which Mormons might come to be recognized as valued civic partners in the American project. Historically, he wrote, the Mormon faith resembled "the enthusiasm of the old Crusaders and the fanaticism of Musselmen propagandists"; Mormons were often demonized as violent and crazed zealots or New World Muslims.[23] But this repugnant reputation for spiritual excess and whispered rumors of immoral behaviors had been quelled, for Whittier, by Kane's lecture and other eyewitness reports:

> They have shrewd, intelligent men at the head of affairs, and are evidently losing a great deal of the fanaticism of their early time. They have a regularly organized Government, and all accounts agree in representing them as an orderly and peaceful people. The author of the "Discourse" before us, denies emphatically the charges which have been preferred against their habitual purity of life, integrity of dealing, their toleration of religious differences, their regard for law, and their devotion to constitutional government.

The opportunity and invitation were clear: join the cause of abolition, and the supernaturalism that had characterized the Mormon religion would be forgotten in exchange for a future devotion to liberal values, political cohesion, and economic prosperity. Salt Lake "must be the grand central station of the future railroad which is to unite the two oceans and to open to us the golden stream of oriental traffic by the way of California."[24] Whittier reminded the LDS church of its painful history and proposed a new path forward, offering public respect and the gold of California in exchange for abandoning its fanatic devotion to the martyred Smith and his golden plates.

Briefly, the LDS church stood atop a pinnacle of public opinion, forgiven for its early enthusiasm by Whittier and embraced by prominent public figures from Douglass and Emerson to Charles Sumner and Wendell Phillips.[25] In the fall of 1850, Grow reports, it was briefly "fashionable to sympathize with the downtrodden Mormons."[26] Over the next year Whigs and Democrats courted the Saints and sought to win their support. It might have seemed, in Utah, that a corner had been turned and that the country would soon accept the sect as a colorful but welcome thread in the national fabric.

Then, in 1852, amid proliferating rumors of sexual malfeasance, the LDS church publicly embraced the doctrine of plural marriage, a practice that had been shrouded in secrecy for two decades.[27] After the Mormon apostle Orson Pratt avouched and publicly defended the theology of polygamy in an August address, the nation erupted into condemnations and invective.[28] Predictably, this disclosure damaged the public image of the church and its support among the intelligentsia, who understood Mormon polygamy to be an expansion of the patriarchal authority propping up the institution of slavery. Noting that the church was arguing "that to condemn men for polygamy, is to condemn the patriarchs and saints whom God is represented in the Bible as honoring and blessing," Joseph Barker, writing for William Lloyd Garrison's abolitionist newspaper the *Liberator*, pointed out that "slaveholding, which is the sum of all villanies," was similarly "cherished by the churches, and justified on Scripture grounds." He asked, "Would God hold up for our imitation men who were liars, adulterers, slaveholders and murderers?"[29] Abolitionists such as Whittier undoubtedly abandoned their support of Mormonism even more precipitously than the general public did. Scholars have recovered, from the archive, a series of editorials and novels warning that white women were being enslaved by lascivious Mormon men; and at the first Republican National Convention, slavery and polygamy were dubbed the twin relics of barbarism.[30] Whatever goodwill and public support the church had won during its passage across the prairies evaporated in the aftermath of Pratt's announcement.

Popular American writers quickly incorporated sensational stories of Mormon polygamy into the erotic literature they wrote for the masses.

Tales of Mormon debauchery contributed to what Reynolds has called a literary "miasma in which morality, sex, self-righteous indignation, and exploitative sensationalism on all sides became mingled in a swirling maelstrom of values."[31] George Thompson, for example, drew on the popular belief in Mormon sexual excesses to criticize the immorality of New York Protestants, "lecherous lepers of civilized society [who hold] their orgies as openly as the half crazed fanatics of barren Utah."[32] Thanks to Thompson's erotica and similarly sensational portrayals of Mormonism, the Saints again became—as in Whittier's earlier invocation of *Hamlet*—aesthetic incompetents incapable of understanding the lofty sentiments and artistic achievements of an American Renaissance. In the 1858 theatrical farce *Deseret Deserted; or, the Last Days of Brigham Young*, an actor portraying Young reclines in the heavenly paradise of the deceased prophet Mohammed, lustily watching the dancing of half-clad houris. When, after the dance, Young asks for an opportunity to "mingle with the ladies," Mohammed contrives an excuse to introduce him to the dancers:

> Mah. [*A la Hamlet taking the instrument.*] Will you play upon this pipe?
> Brig. My lord I cannot.
> Mah. I pray you.
> Brig. Believe me, I cannot.
> Mah. I do beseech you. [*This is imitated from Shakspeare.*]
> Brig. Well, since you insist upon it I don't mind if I do have a shy at it.
>
> [*Takes the ophicleide and plays a few notes of recitative (piccolo flute at wing) then relapses into "The Arkansaw Traveller," dancing to the air. After a few bars the ballet join in. Then Brigham, at the close, falls exhausted into the arms of the women. Tableau. Drop.*][33]

By characterizing Young as both a hopelessly outwitted Polonius and a lascivious boor who prefers a popular jig to the plaintive tones of serious music, this scene reinscribes the prejudices apparent in Whittier's earlier encounter with Mormon preachers. The suggestion is that Mormons can't recognize Shakespeare even when they are reciting his lines, much less understand the implications of his art. Even the stage directions, which misspell Shakespeare's name and twice—twice!—remind the reader/actor that this scene is adapted from *Hamlet*, emphasize the cultural illiteracy of the Saints and those who desire to be entertained by a glimpse of their sexual excesses.

When Whittier eventually found occasion to reconsider the cultural status of the LDS church, he returned to his earlier opinion: that the Mormons were a superstitious sect believing in folk magic and presumably lacking aesthetic judgment. Whittier's 1864 volume of poems, *In War Time*, included the ballad "Cobbler Keezar's Vision," a narrative description of a colonial artisan in possession of a magical lapstone through which he sees a vision of the future. Keezar is a "cunning man" with power over nature:

> Well he knew the tricks of magic,
> And the lapstone on his knee
> Had the gift of the Mormon's goggles
> Or the stone of Doctor Dee.[34]

Joseph Smith used multiple interpretive aids in his translation of the Book of Mormon, including a seer stone such as that in Keezar's lap and a pair of translucent stone spectacles mounted on a breastplate and identified as the biblical Urim and Thummim—the "goggles" of Whittier's poem.[35] The poet here reduces Smith's declarations of divine inspiration to claims no more credible than those advanced by John Dee, a Renaissance alchemist.

Keezar's vision is inspiring but false. He writes at the turn of the eighteenth century and looks, through his lapstone, 150 years into the future.[36] He foresees idyllic times for his rural Massachusetts town, in which the enmity between priests and Quakers, cats and dogs will cease. The stocks and the gallows will become unnecessary and be dismantled. But 1860, the year when Whittier first published this poem in the *Atlantic*, was hardly a tranquil fulfillment of millennial prophecies, as the poet—writing at the brink of the violence and discord of the Civil War—well knew.[37] At vision's end the lapstone rolls from Keezar's lap "like a wheel bewitched" and plunges to the bottom of a millpond, recalling the biblical injunction in the Gospel of Matthew warning Keezar and all men against sin: "it were better for him that a millstone were hanged about his neck, and that he were drowned."[38] The scholar John B. Pickard argues against attempts to find a "moral purpose" in Whittier's ballads, but the poem seems to demand such a reading; the utopia Keezar anticipates is a sham.[39] His vision is no more accurate or truthful than the revelations of Smith or the predictions of Dee, and Whittier hints that anyone who gives credence to such supernatural claims will soon be disenchanted.

WHITTIER'S RAPIDLY shifting views of the LDS church and its founder suggest the imprecise and constantly fluctuating boundaries of cultural standards. Mormons were uneducated backwoods fanatics until their expulsion from Illinois, at which point they came to represent liberal values and good taste; months later, the revelation that the church endorsed polygamy reversed whatever progress it had made in the court of public opinion, and Mormons were again thought of as superstitious fanatics with a questionable grasp of literature, culture, and the arts. The rapidity and the undulating trajectory of that shift only underscore the subjective and casuistic nature of artistic judgments promoting individual authors and texts as models of cultural excellence. Our own conception of Whittier's achievement and his place in the American Renaissance, for instance, has changed dramatically over the past fifty years; the Quaker poet who was celebrated and analyzed by so many scholars of the mid-twentieth century has since been relegated to long-term storage in most libraries.

That Whittier condemned the aesthetic judgment of Mormons is ironic because the LDS church seems to be one of the few groups in the country who still think Whittier's poetry is worth reading. Over the past forty years, he has been quoted eleven times in sermons delivered during the church's biannual General Conference, more often than Henry David Thoreau (nine) and far more frequently than fixtures of the American Renaissance such as Emily Dickinson (three), Nathaniel Hawthorne (two), and Walt Whitman (none). Among nineteenth-century American authors, only Emerson (twenty-one) is more popular than Whittier.[40] Whittier's most devoted twenty-first-century readers include the religious fanatics whose taste he once questioned, and the Saints are, apparently, one of the few groups that still see him as an important contributor to the literature of his era.

NOTES

1. For an excellent account of Whittier's portrayal of a white, mainstream American sensibility, see Angela Sorby, *Schoolroom Poets: Childhood, Performance, and the Place of American Poetry, 1865–1917* (Durham: University of New Hampshire Press, 2005), 35–67.

2. As John A. Pollard notes, Irving's "influence was painfully obvious in the book," but "the melodramatic flourishes that marred the *Legends* were not the best things an imitator could have learned from Irving" (*John Greenleaf Whittier: Friend of Man* [Boston: Houghton Mifflin, 1949], 92).

3. Samuel T. Pickard, *Life and Letters of John Greenleaf Whittier*, 2 vols. (Boston: 1888), 1:92.

4. David S. Reynolds, *Beneath the American Renaissance: The Subversive Imagination in the Age of Emerson and Melville* (Cambridge, Mass.: Harvard University Press, 1988), 5; F. O. Matthiessen, *American Renaissance: Art and Expression in the Age of Emerson and Whitman* (New York: Oxford University Press, 1941), 204, 34; John Greenleaf Whittier, *Legends of New England*, ed. John B. Pickard (Delmar, N.Y.: Scholars' Facsimiles and Reprints, 1965), 3.

5. John Greenleaf Whittier, "Charities for the Mormons," *American and Commercial Daily Advertiser*, September 28, 1848.

6. John Greenleaf Whittier, *The Letters of John Greenleaf Whittier*, 3 vols. (Cambridge, Mass.: Harvard University Press, 1975), 1:301. Edward Wagenknecht describes Whittier's polite skepticism with regard to spiritualism, animal magnetism, phrenology, and physiognomy in his biography *John Greenleaf Whittier: A Portrait in Paradox* (New York: Oxford University Press, 1967), 182–85.

7. David Meredith Reese, *Humbugs of New-York: Being a Remonstrance against Popular Delusion; whether in Science, Philosophy, or Religion* (New York, 1838), v. Reese also castigated Mormons, lumping Smith's adherents with "Multitudes who believe in 'Animal Magnetism,' subscribe to 'Phrenology,' are the willing victims of every form of 'Quackery,' and have adopted the creed and practice of 'ultraism;'— multitudes of such, have gathered around this *Mormon oracle*, and drank in wisdom from his 'golden bible!'" (265). Whittier and Reese saw Mormons and the adherents of Mesmer's science as equally deluded individuals drawn from a single, gullible crowd. For a history of animal magnetism, see Bruce Mills, *Poe, Fuller, and the Mesmeric Arts: Transition States in the American Renaissance* (Columbia: University of Missouri Press, 2006).

8. Whittier, *The Letters of John Greenleaf Whittier*, 1:555.

9. Ibid., 1:639. The poem, "Henry Clay," not included in any of the collections of Whittier's poetry that I surveyed, appeared in the *American Advocate*, May 29, 1830, and was reprinted in several other newspapers of the period.

10. As quoted by C., "Henry Clay, John G. Whittier and Horace Greeley," *Sacramento Daily Union*, June 7, 1873.

11. On the architecture of these and subsequent early Mormon temples, see Laurel B. Andrew, *The Early Temples of the Mormons: The Architecture of the Millennial Kingdom in the American West* (Albany: State University of New York Press, 1978).

12. John Greenleaf Whittier, *The Stranger in Lowell* (Massachusetts, 1845), 29–32. See R. H. Horne, *A New Spirit of the Age*, 2 vols. (London, 1844), 2:263; Whittier paraphrases Horne's description of Thomas Carlyle.

13. Whittier, *The Stranger in Lowell*, 26, 29. Connell O'Donovan speculates that this unnamed preacher may have been Enoch Lovejoy Lewis, a son of one of the few African American men ordained as an elder in the LDS church during the nineteenth century. However, the unnamed apostle who spoke at the meeting was likely Wilford Woodruff, who visited Lowell in October and November of 1944, not Orson Hyde, as O'Donovan suggests ("The Mormon Priesthood Ban and Elder Q. Walker Lewis: 'An Example for his More Whiter Brethren to Follow,'" *John Whitmer Historical Association Journal* 26 (2006): 75–77.

14. William Shakespeare, *Hamlet*, in *The Complete Works of Shakespeare*, ed. David Bevington, 6th ed. (New York: Pearson, 2008), 1121.

15. Whittier, *The Stranger in Lowell*, 29.

16. Thomas L. Kane, *The Mormons: A Discourse Delivered before the Historical Society of Pennsylvania* (Philadelphia, 1850), 10.

17. Matthew J. Grow, *"Liberty to the Downtrodden": Thomas L. Kane, Romantic Reformer* (New Haven: Yale University Press, 2009), 83.

18. Frederick Douglass, "A Discourse, Delivered Before the Historical Society of Pennsylvania by Thomas S. Kane," *North Star*, October 3, 1850.

19. John Greenleaf Whittier, "The Mormons and Their City of Refuge," *National Era*, August 15, 1850.

20. J. T. M., "Nauvoo in 1844," *Wisconsin Herald*, January 1, 1848; John Milton, *Paradise Lost*, in *Complete Poems and Major Prose*, ed. Merritt Y. Hughes (Indianapolis: Prentice Hall, 1957), 469.

21. Whittier, "The Mormons and Their City of Refuge."

22. Ibid. John B. Pickard writes that this casuistic change of views was characteristic of Whittier: "In public and political action Whittier took men as they were, neither 'saints [n]or angels,' and was willing to lobby, compromise, and shift to obtain necessary votes" (*John Greenleaf Whittier: An Introduction and Interpretation* [New York: Holt, Rinehart, and Winston, 1961], 24). Whittier's essay on the LDS settlement of Utah was one of several related pieces; as Pollard notes, opposing slavery's "extension was the steady and informing principle of all his Abolitionist articles in the *Era*" (*John Greenleaf Whittier*, 227).

23. Whittier, "The Mormons and Their City of Refuge." See also Timothy Marr, *The Cultural Roots of American Islamicism* (New York: Cambridge University Press, 2006), 185–218.

24. Whittier, "The Mormons and Their City of Refuge."

25. See the correspondence between Kane and Charles Sumner, Wendell Phillips, and Walter H. Channing held in the Special Collections of Brigham Young University and at the American Philosophical Society.

26. Grow, *"Liberty to the Downtrodden,"* 84.

27. Todd Compton offers persuasive evidence that Joseph Smith inaugurated the practice in 1833, when he married Fanny Alger (*In Sacred Loneliness: The Plural Wives of Joseph Smith* [Salt Lake City: Signature, 1997]). For excellent overviews of polygamy's spread and eventual curtailment, see Kathryn M. Daynes, *More Wives Than One: Transformation of the Mormon Marriage System, 1840–1910* (Urbana: University of Illinois Press, 2001); and Sarah Barringer Gordon, *The Mormon Question: Polygamy and Constitutional Conflict in Nineteenth-Century America* (Chapel Hill: University of North Carolina Press, 2002).

28. See David J. Whitaker, "The Bone in the Throat: Orson Pratt and the Public Announcement of Plural Marriage," *Western Historical Quarterly* 18, no. 3 (1987): 293–314.

29. Joseph Barker, "The Bible Question," *Liberator*, April 22, 1853.

30. On patriarchy and the racialization of Mormon sex, see Peter Coviello, *Tomorrow's Parties: Sex and the Untimely in Nineteenth-Century America* (New York: New York University, 2013), 104–28; Nancy Bentley, "Marriage as Treason: Polygamy, Nation, and the Novel," in *The Futures of American Studies*, ed. Donald E. Pease and Robyn Wiegman (Durham, N.C.: Duke University Press, 2002), 341–70; and Bruce Burgett, "On the Mormon Question: Race, Sex, and Polygamy in the 1850s and the 1990s," *American Quarterly* 57.1 (2005): 75–102.

31. Reynolds, *Beneath the American Renaissance*, 214.

32. George Thompson, *The Mysteries of Bond Street, or The Seraglios of Upper Tendom* (New York, 1857), 46.

33. Anonymous, *Deseret Deserted; or, The Last Days of Brigham Young* (New York: French, 1858), 17.

34. John Greenleaf Whittier, *The Complete Poetical Works of John Greenleaf Whittier* (Boston: Houghton Mifflin, 1894), 78.

35. See John W. Welch, "The Miraculous Translation of the Book of Mormon," in *Opening the Heavens: Accounts of Divines Manifestations, 1820–1844*, ed. John W. Welch and Erick B. Carlson (Provo, Utah: Brigham Young University Press, 2005), 118–213; D. Michael Quinn, *Early Mormonism and the Magic World View*, 2nd ed. (Salt Lake City: Signature, 1998), 42–44, 242–47; and Richard S. Van Wagoner and Steven Walker, "Joseph Smith: 'The Gift of Seeing,'" *Dialogue* 15, no. 2 (1982): 48–68.

36. Keezar, a colonist in the Merrimack Valley, was a contemporary of the Massachusetts Puritans who were "Hunting of witches and warlocks, / Smiting the heathen horde" (Whittier, *The Complete Poetical Works*, 78). He acquired some small

fame for his role in warning the colonists of Indian attack during the Haverhill massacre in 1708.

37. Whittier reportedly submitted the poem with a note: "I send thee an absurd ballad which I like *for* its absurdity" (Pickard, *Life and Letters of John Greenleaf Whittier*, 2:430).

38. Whittier, *The Complete Poetical Works*, 79; Matthew 18:6.

39. John B. Pickard, "Whittier's Ballads: The Maturing of an Artist," in *Critical Essays on John Greenleaf Whittier*, ed. Jayne K. Kribbs (Boston: Hall, 1980), 155.

40. These statistics were accurate as of September 2015. General Conference is held in April and October of each year; Whittier was quoted in April 1972, October 1975, October 1980, April 1997, October 1997, April 2002, October 2009, April 2010, April 2012, April 2013, and April 2014 (http://www.lds.org).

CHAPTER 5

"WILL HE PERISH?"

Moby-Dick *and Nineteenth-Century Extinction Discourse*

Timothy Sweet

WHEN HERMAN Melville's character Ishmael asserts that "the whale [is] immortal in his species, however perishable in his individuality," he does so against mounting concerns that the whaling industry is threatening the extinction of whales.[1] Over the centuries, such concerns, though motivated primarily by economic interest, have raised the general issue of human impact on the nonhuman world.[2] In *Notes on the State of Virginia,* Thomas Jefferson, for example, denied the extinction of the American mammoth (though he later reversed his position) because he felt that any such gap in "the oeconomy of nature" would reveal a flaw that allowed for the ultimate extinction of humankind.[3] Repairing such a flaw would require a supernatural "restoring power" to prevent nature from being "reduced to a shapeless chaos."[4] Although sciences such as geology and biology increasingly removed the theological underpinnings of models such as Jefferson's, they persisted nevertheless—as is evident, for example, in Darwin's explicit insertion of divine agency, via the phrase "by the Creator," into the concluding sentence of the second (1860) edition of *Origin of Species.*[5] Throughout the mid-nineteenth century, then, scientific and theological discourses frequently intersected in conversations about extinction, and reconstructive criticism regarding them can show how Melville's engagement with extinction was part of his larger project of religious investigation in *Moby-Dick*.[6]

One of Darwin's most important influences, Charles Lyell's *Principles of Geology* (1830–33), attempted to avoid theological discourse and its attendant moral implications by claiming purely naturalist grounds.[7] In his account of the various causes of extinctions, Lyell argued, in contrast to Jefferson, that even anthropogenic extinctions give no cause for lament. That is, he refused the emerging modern elegiac narrative of extinction as loss: "If we wield the sword of extermination as we advance, we have no reason to repine at the havoc committed. . . . We have only to reflect, that in this obtaining possession of the earth by conquest, . . . we exercise no exclusive prerogative. Every species which has spread itself from a small point over a wide area, must, in like manner, have marked its progress by the diminution, or the entire extirpation, of some other." As part of the ordinary course of nature, consistent with Lyell's uniformitarian thesis, the extirpation of other species was thus a feature of humankind's own species being. This feature had become more rapidly evident in the early nineteenth century, Lyell asserted, because humankind had taken on a larger geohistorical role as "highly-civilized nations spread themselves over unoccupied lands."[8]

Even so, the fact that Lyell paused to moralize in his account of extinction suggests that he was working against a powerful impulse to repine. Casting his account as an ontological claim about species being rather than a moral claim, he both conflated and marked animality and humanity. By identifying a state of life that is neither human nor animal and merely embodies the potential for extirpation, he collapsed the distinction between *zoe* (bare life) and *bios* (political life) that was later clarified by Giorgio Agamben: all life, according to Lyell, is merely life.[9] Yet in claiming exception for the more "highly-civilized nations" of humans as the greater exterminators who are at the same time capable of reflecting on the fact of extermination in their self-recognition of humankind *as* a species, he reinstated the distinction between bare life and political life as the difference between animal and human. This account of species being encodes the "sacrificial structure" according to which the animal is separated from the human through its designation as the potential object of "a noncriminal putting to death."[10] Thus, Lyell's ontological claim rests on a moral-juridical assumption that cuts against his denial of a theological foundation—for bare life, as theorized by Agamben, originally "belonged to God as creaturely life," in relation to which the "highly-civilized nations" that were the nineteenth century's primary agents of extirpation have, by virtue of their political sophistication, taken on a godlike role.[11] Ishmael, more ontologically attuned than Lyell, remains skeptical of this godlike usurpation.

Melville specified the conditions for answering the question of the whale's extinction in the memorable quarter-deck scene in which Ahab first addresses the crew of the *Pequod*. Sometimes read as political allegory, the scene stages an investigation into the nature of species being.[12] Ahab seeks vengeance on the great whale Moby Dick as either "agent" or "principal" of the "unknown but still reasoning thing" that has wounded him, psychically as much as physically. Ahab—and, for a time, Ishmael and the rest of the *Pequod*'s crew—understands the whale not as a natural resource, a "dumb brute," much to the pragmatist Starbuck's dismay, but as a deliberating, intending being. This understanding, which is emphasized during the concluding three-day chase, blurs the conventional boundary between human and nonhuman. Moreover, in construing the whale as either agent or principal, Ahab leaves room for, though does not absolutely insist on, the possibility of supernatural agency. As the narrator Ishmael reframes the difference between Ahab and Starbuck to draw out its ontological and moral significance, he imagines "admonitions and warnings" not only in Starbuck's sense of "foreboding" but even in the natural environment, as potentially signified by the "presaging vibrations of the winds in the cordage." For Ishmael, these "vibrations" register our common existential condition: "not so much predictions from without, as verifications of the foregoing things within. For with little external to constrain us, the innermost necessities in our being, these still drive us on."[13] Over the course of his narrative, Ishmael comes to recognize that what Ahab regards as the whale's intelligence (natural or supernatural) and Starbuck regards as the whale's animality is merely behavior—that is, a configuration of species being unknowable by humans either in terms of a common understanding, which Ahab posits and resents, or in terms of mastery, which Starbuck assumes to legitimate the whale's sacrificial commodification. Knowable neither in terms of mutuality nor property, the whale's species being thus poses to us the question: In humankind's historical relation to whales (or mammoths, dodos, bison, and so on), are other terms of response possible than those proposed by Lyell's assumption of sovereignty, with its implications of either lament or justification for anthropogenic extinctions?

Melville's novel does not deny the logic of Lyell's narrative of competitive extermination. Yet his narrator Ishmael argues that whales will not be exterminated through human agency, despite the concerns of some contemporary observers. Rather, in a narrative that begins as displaced suicide and is preoccupied throughout with human mortality, the whale offers hope for the infinite extension of conscious life. Ishmael reserves supernatural narrative for human fate, leaving whales to persist according to their own natural agency. Against mounting concerns regarding anthropogenic extinction, he marshals his cetological investigations in support of the proposition that "the unspeakable terrors of the whale, which, having been before all time, must needs exist after all humane ages are over."[14] The effect is twofold. First, Ishmael's argument, like Lyell's, positions species as responsible for their own preservation or extinction. Second, the narrative structure and imagery through which he frames this argument links Ahab rather than Moby Dick with extinction, thus displacing the predatory violence of the whaling industry away from whales and onto humankind's fate. With this displacement, Ishmael fantasizes the eternal persistence of consciousness—that is, a version of eternal life but configured as life on earth.

WHEN ISHMAEL calls the whale the "salt-sea mastodon," evoking the question of extinction early on in the novel, he alludes to the attributes of ancientness and power that made the mastodon an aspirational symbol for the young and vulnerable nation during the early federal period.[15] The symbol did not gain long-term traction, likely because, on reflection, the mammoth's extinction augured ill for the continuance of a nation-state. Nevertheless, these attributes of ancientness and power remained compelling, and Ishmael draws on them to argue against the possibility of the whale's extinction. As he surveys the fossil record of various kinds of "annihilated antechronical Leviathans," Ishmael is, "by a flood, borne back to that wondrous period, ere time itself can be said to have begun, for time began with man. Here Saturn's grey chaos rolls over me." In an oscillation that recurs throughout the novel between deep geological time and shallow human time (the latter often measured by the traditional biblical chronology of 6,000 years), Ishmael reserves deep time as the whale's domain, which antecedes and succeeds human time.[16] Thus, he "account[s] the whale immortal in his species, however perishable in his individuality." Ishmael takes this position against the concerns of certain "recondite Nantucketers" who worry that, as a result of overhunting, the whale "cannot now escape speedy extinction."[17]

Such "recondite Nantucketers" were not alone discerning a pattern of population decline that threatened extinction. In retrospect, the pattern is all too clear in the history of industrial whaling's expansion from the New England coast outward to the Pacific. Each new whaling ground yielded the bulk of its harvest in the first few years. Increased exploitation led to the failure of the ground and the search for new grounds.[18] In the late eighteenth century, J. Hector St. John de Crèvecoeur reported, in his history of the Nantucket fishery, that "when the whales quitted their coasts . . . by degrees they went whaling to Newfoundland, to the Gulph of St. Laurence, . . . the coasts of Labrador. . . . In time they visited the western islands, the latitude of 34°, famous for that fish, the Brazils, the coast of Guinea. Would you believe that they have already gone to the Falklands, and that I have heard several of them talk of going to the South Sea!"[19] As Crèvecoeur indicated with his verb *quitted*, commentators understood that this pattern indicated the retreat of whales from areas of hunting pressure to those in which they were not hunted rather than seeing it as a sign of the extirpation of local populations.

Yet the potential endpoint of the narrative of retreat was extinction, as even some optimistic commentators came to recognize. In an 1834 review of four books on the whale fishery—including two of Melville's source texts, William Scoresby's *An Account of the Arctic Regions* and Scoresby's *Journal of a Voyage to the Northern Whale Fishery*—the North American

Review observed that, with the industry's global expansion, whales "have been driven to the deepest recesses of Baffin's Bay" or to "the very confines of the Pacific." As a result, "whether their mammoth bones in some distant century shall indicate to the untaught natives of the shores they now frequent that such an animal *was*, or whether, lurking in the inaccessible and undisturbed waters north of Asia and America, the race shall be preserved, is almost a problem." *Almost*, because in the view of this writer, the whale would not suffer the mammoth's fate at the hands of humankind: "the exhaustless resources of nature" would "never fail."[20] Others were less optimistic regarding nature's "exhaustless" potential, especially after the industry expanded into the Pacific. One such was M. E. Bowles, an officer on a New England whaling ship and a frequent contributor to shipping newspapers published in Hawaii, the cultural center of the Pacific fleet during the mid-nineteenth century. Reviewing the past "ten or fifteen years" of the Pacific whale fishery in 1845, Bowles concluded "that the poor whale is doomed to utter extermination, or at least, so near it as that too few will remain to tempt the cupidity of man, I have not a doubt."[21]

Melville might not have been aware of Bowles's writings, but one of his source texts had taken up the topic. Borrowing silently from Bowles and from the 1834 *North American Review*, the Reverend Henry T. Cheever's *The Whale and His Captors* did predict the extinction of whales. In this account of a Pacific whaling voyage, Cheever concluded his discussion of the industry's unsustainability by assigning whales' extinction to divine ordination, using quotations spliced together from an undersea vision in canto 2 of James Montgomery's poem "The Pelican Island" (1828):

> They roamed, they fed, they slept, they died, and left
> Race after race to roam, feed, sleep, then die,
> And leave their like through endless generations:
> So HE ordained, whose way is in the sea,
> His path amid great waters, and His steps
> Unknown![22]

Cheever significantly altered the original poem. After the first three lines of the six just quoted, Montgomery's account of oceanic life reads:

>   —Incessant change of actors, none of scene,
>   Through all that boundless theatre of strife!
>   Shrinking into myself again, I cried,
>   In bitter disappointment,—"Is this all?"[23]

But Cheever substituted his passage to emphasize God's power rather than humankind's existential despair. Through his revision of Montgomery, then, he maintained Bowles's description of human agency in cutting off the generations but departed from Bowles's moral assessment by absolving humankind of responsibility for what God had "ordained." Thus, he supplied a theological warrant for Lyell's refusal to mourn the natural act of one species exterminating another. Assessments such as Cheever's, whether or not they appeal to a theological warrant, treat whales as animal resources. Their primary concern is not so much for the preservation of whales in their species being—the question that animated Melville's inquiry—but for the continuance of an extractive industry.

A different sort of assessment appeared in 1850 in the seaman's newspaper the *Friend*. Signed "Polar Whale" and dated "Anadir Sea, North Pacific, The Second Year of the Trouble," "A Polar Whale's Appeal" presents the voice of an "Old Greenland" whale pleading for mercy on his kind.[24] Using a disorienting alternative chronology to plunge the reader into whales' subjective being, Polar Whale refers to a potentially apocalyptic event in whale history. The year 1848 marked the first penetration of a whaling ship north of the Bering Strait—where, to anticipate one of Melville's arguments against the likelihood of extinction, one might have expected whales to find safe haven from the predation of the Pacific whaling fleet.[25] Thus, in the article, the spokes-whale pinpoints 1850 as the "Second Year of the Trouble." Having established this whale-oriented chronology, he begins an appeal to the "friends of the whale":

> A few of the knowing old inhabitants of this sea have recently held a meeting to consult respecting our safety, and in some way or other, if possible, to avert the doom that seems to await all of the whale *Genus* throughout the world, including the Sperm, Right, and Polar Whales. Although our situation, and that of our neighbors in the Arctic, is remote from our enemy's country, yet we have been knowing [sic] to

the progress of affairs in the Japan and Otchosk seas, the Atlantic and Indian oceans, and all the other "whaling grounds." We have imagined that we were safe in these cold regions; but no; within these last two years a furious attack has been made upon us, an attack more deadly and bloody, than any of our race ever experienced in any part of the world.[26]

Polar Whale measures local suffering as more intense than distant suffering in a very human way, yet he links that suffering to a universal cause, reporting on a meeting of whales who form a genus-based collective encompassing several species united by a common threat from another species, humankind. This collective has somehow found voice—as Bruno Latour claims nonhuman nature can do through human-scientific "speech prostheses"—and now claims representation.[27] The spokes-whale thus enlists human communicative media, "the power of the 'Press,'" and begs readers to "pray give these few lines a place in your columns, and let them go forth to the world." Mixing pathos with grim humor that shows cross-species awareness of the human bodily perspective—"Multitudes of our species (the Polar) have been murdered in 'cold' blood"—he elaborates a petition whose generic form is familiar from antebellum American reform rhetoric— for example, activism against slavery or Indian removal, which counts on powerful "friends" to take up the cause of the powerless oppressed: "We polar whales are a quiet, inoffensive race, desirous of life and peace, but, alas, we fear our doom is sealed. . . . Is there no redress? I write in behalf of my butchered and dying species. I appeal to the friends of the whole race of whales. Must we all be murdered in cold blood? Must our race become extinct? Will no friends and allies arise to revenge our wrongs? Will our foes be allowed to prey upon us another year?"[28] Extinction's melancholic nostalgia begins to shadow activist exhortation as Polar Whale imagines the demise of his kind. Like Thomas Jefferson's Mingo warrior Logan or James Fenimore Cooper's Mohican chief Chingachgook, they may be the last of their lines.[29]

How many "friends and allies" did Polar Whale hope to find among the readership of a seaman's newspaper? One historian of the industry imagines whalemen "doubled over with laughter" as they read the article.[30] It is possible that the author intended the text to be an elaborate satire on the idea that whales deserved something like *The Rights of Man*, as many argued that Africans and Native Americans did. Such claims depended on drawing a distinction between those who did and did not deserve such rights, a distinction that asserted some configuration of the human-animal boundary.[31] Melville's Ishmael, however, is one whaleman who would not have read the text as satire (though he would have appreciated its punning humor). For, like Polar Whale, he realizes that the context of extinction invites considerations of agency that may trouble the distinction between humans and animals.[32]

Just as Polar Whale asserts the quasi-humanity of whales, Ishmael argues that whales will escape extinction, despite the increasing pressure of human predation, through the apparently humanlike means of developing new behaviors. These developments vary within natural constraints according to the species' jaw shapes. Krill-straining baleen whales such as Greenlands and humpbacks possess little capacity for attack: "driven from promontory to cape" by whalers, they will retreat "at last resort to their Polar citadels, and diving under the ultimate glassy barriers and walls there, come up among icy fields and floes, and in a charmed circle of everlasting December, bid defiance to all pursuit from man." In the mid-nineteenth century, Melville's assumptions about the climate stability of polar ice were reasonable—though, as Polar Whale's appeal indicates, whether or not it would provide enough of a refuge was another question. Ishmael reports that sperm whales, who find the polar seas less congenial, have developed other strategies. Possessing predatory jaws, they have become more aggressive. They have also taken to congregating for mutual protection in response to increasing attacks by whalers. Thus, "as of late, the Sperm Whale Fishery ha[s] been marked by various and not infrequent instances of great ferocity, cunning, and malice in the monster attacked." He continues, "In more than one instance, [a sperm whale] has been known, not only to chase the assailing boats back to their ships, but to pursue the ship itself"—as reported, for example, in Owen Chase's narrative of the destruction of the whale ship *Essex*, a key source text for *Moby-Dick*.[33] Moreover, in response to "unwearied" pursuit, "Sperm Whales, instead of almost invariably sailing in small detached companies, as in former times, are now frequently met with in extensive herds, . . . as if numerous nations of them had sworn solemn league and covenant for mutual assistance and protection." They travel in "widely separated, unfrequent armies" such as the "Grand Armada" that the *Pequod* encounters in chapter 87. Moby Dick himself combines both of these behavioral developments—increased aggression and mutual assistance—when he frees a fellow whale by "snapping furiously at [the] fast-line" that secures it to a boat commanded by Captain Boomer of the *Samuel Enderby*.[34] Melville posited these developments contrary to the arguments of one of his most important scientific sources, Thomas Beale's *Natural History of the Sperm Whale* (1839). Beale had described the sperm whale as "a most timid and inoffensive animal" that "shew[s] extreme activity in avoiding [its] foes" and causes harm to humans only inadvertently as the result of its great bulk.[35]

Ishmael's emphasis on the development of evasive, aggressive, defensive, or mutually protective behaviors suggests that he understands species evolutionarily—or, to use mid-nineteenth-century language, developmentally. Here, he resembles some of Melville's pre-Darwinian contemporaries such as Johann von Goethe and Jean-Baptiste Lamarck. Perhaps the most famous, at the time, was Robert Chambers, whose *Vestiges of the Natural History of Creation* (1844), with its hypothesis of divine "creation by law," convinced Ralph Waldo Emerson of the truth of evolution.[36] "May there not be," Henry David Thoreau asked, "a civilization [process] going on among brutes as well as men?"[37] Yet whereas romantic developmentalists held a teleological view of evolution as progress, especially regarding human life, *Moby-Dick* withholds the possibility of *human* progress.[38] By contrast, whales seem, in the novel, to have developed both behaviorally and morphologically (that is, by becoming larger over geological time), changes that will enable them to survive well beyond the point when "the last man" will "smoke his last pipe."[39] The allusion here to Mary Shelley's novel *The Last Man* (1826), about a plague that decimates humankind, exemplifies a thematic contrast evident throughout *Moby-Dick* between whales' immortality and human vulnerability.[40]

Ishmael's developmental account of the whale contrasts with Ahab's fateful refusal to change his course—a refusal that renders him vulnerable even as it binds the *Pequod*'s crew to his purpose. Melville's characterization of Ahab's refusal and the *Pequod*'s fate may have resonated, for nineteenth-century American readers, with predictions of the supposed extinction of Native Americans who refused to change their savage ways.⁴¹ Ahab, who "lived in the world like the last of Grisly Bears lived in settled Missouri," is comparable to Jefferson's "wild Logan of the woods." The Native American harpooner Tashtego goes down, as D. H. Lawrence observed nearly a century ago, with the "Red Indian bird" hammered to the *Pequod*'s main topmast.⁴² The *Pequod* itself, "a noble craft but somehow a most melancholy [one]," is said to be named after "a celebrated tribe of Massachusetts Indians, now extinct."⁴³

Such allusions to human extinction encourage the projection of individual mortality onto species mortality. Heightening this effect is the depiction of the whaling industry itself as death-bound, especially in chapter 96, which concludes the account of the industry prior to the final chase narrative. Earlier associated with Starbuck's prudent rationality, here the industrial ship, "laden with fire, burning a corpse, and plunging into that blackness of darkness, seem[s] the material counterpart of her monomaniac commander's soul." Affected by this underworldly experience, Ishmael feels that the *Pequod* is "bound not so much to any haven ahead as rushing from all havens astern. A stark, bewildering feeling of death came over me."⁴⁴

In the subsequent chapter, as the narrative approaches its conclusion, the novel addresses human mortality from another direction, that of reproductive futurity. This engagement is interwoven with accounts of the ships *Rachel* and *Delight*, which have lost men to Moby Dick. The captain of the *Rachel* begs Ahab to help him search for a lost whaleboat whose crew includes his twelve-year-old son. Ahab refuses, and *Rachel* is left "weeping for her children, because they were not."⁴⁵ The *Delight* is a floating hearse, fulfilling the first part of Ahab's harpooner Fedallah's prophesy regarding his captain's death.

Finally, the chapter just before the beginning of the *Pequod*'s chase after Moby Dick opens on a revealing ontological-environmental meditation. While such meditations are characteristic of the novel's texture, this one particularly evokes possibilities of reproductive sexuality, pairing the "gentle thoughts of the feminine air" with the "murderous thinkings of the masculine sea" in a dialectic in which the apparent "contrast was only without." Within, "those two seemed one; it was only the sex, as it were, that distinguished them." In this moment, in which "the step-mother world, so long cruel—forbidding—now threw affectionate arms round [Ahab's] stubborn neck," the captain recalls his wife in Nantucket, whom he has hardly seen: "I widowed that poor girl when I married her." In this mood, Ahab begs Starbuck not to lower his boat in the hunt for Moby Dick: "I see my wife and child in thine eye." Yet as the captain articulates his sense of fate, in which he is compelled in the chase "by some invisible power," reproductive futurity ceases to matter: "toil how we may, we all sleep at last on the field. . . . Aye, and rust amid greenness; as last year's scythes flung down, and left in the half-cut swaths." Listening to Ahab's meditation on death, Starbuck "blanche[s] to a corpse's hue with despair," recognizing his own removal from the reproductive narrative.[46] He will go down with the rest of the *Pequod*'s crew. The only survivor will be Ishmael, whose role in the reproductive future remains in question.

THE SINKING of the *Pequod* confirms the human vulnerability that is the source of Ahab's rage. Describing the event's aftermath, Ishmael reports that "the great shroud of the sea rolled on as it rolled five thousand years ago." Thus, the narrative ends on an apocalyptic image, the biblical flood, echoing Ishmael's earlier reflections on extinction in chapter 105: "In Noah's flood [the whale] despised Noah's Ark; and if ever the world is to be again flooded, . . . then the eternal whale will survive, and rearing upon the topmost crest of the equatorial flood, spout his frothed defiance to the skies."[47] The whale survives to spout defiance where Ahab does not. The whale therefore displaces him as the figure who names and rages against our human pain, our vulnerability, our mortality, translating these into the fantasy of our "eternal" persistence. This translation depends on Melville's oscillation between two chronological scales. Having posited deep geological time in his natural history of the whale to index its invulnerability—from the epoch of the fossil zeuglodon to the endless future beyond "all humane ages"—Melville reverts in his concluding measure of "five thousand years" to the shallow time that had traditionally measured human history, thus contrasting whales' immortality with human finitude.[48]

No rainbow appears to signal God's covenant as the *Pequod* sinks beneath the flood; but if it had appeared, it would have suggested to readers the fire of final judgment. Such a conflagration would destroy whales as well as humankind: "the elements shall melt with fervent heat, the earth also and the works that are therein shall be burned up."[49] Yet as Polar Whale informs us, whales use their own chronology, marked by crises such as the first penetration of human predators into the Bering Sea. In writing the novel, Melville found that the whale exceeded the scope of the biblical chronology that served as a common reference point for human history. The undecidability of biblical versus geological chronotopes in *Moby-Dick* thus differentiates humankind's fate from whalekind's fate, rendering extinctive agency either natural or supernatural—but, in either case, other than human.

Lyell had resolved the implicit moral question regarding extinctive agency by appealing to an earthly morality not grounded in theology. For him, the extirpation of one species by another was a natural phenomenon for which his uniformitarian thesis could supply no ultimate origin. This line of reasoning did not satisfy Melville, as is evident not only in Ahab's and Ishmael's ontological inquiries but also in the narrative's oscillation between biblical and geological time scales to measure and predict species' fates. In Polar Whale's presentation of the moral question, whales deserve rights ordinarily accorded to human beings, but they are helpless to protect those rights. In other words, he attempts to bring whales into the human domain of politics, though as dependent subjects. In exploring and blurring the human-animal boundary throughout *Moby-Dick*, Ishmael in effect entertains Polar Whale's appeal, though he denies its accession to dependency.

Yet as Ishmael comes to recognize during the three-day chase after Moby Dick—even as he repeatedly characterizes the whale using quasi-human qualities such as volition, deliberation, calculation, retribution, and malicious intent—the inscrutable whale is another form of life. This other form of life is not finally reducible to the terms of the human distinction between *zoe* and *bios*—that is, between bare life premised on mere existence and political life premised on communicability. Questions of the whale's deliberation, retribution, mutual protection, and other such qualities remain indeterminate, however much these qualities, whether evolutionarily developed or originally inherent, seem to invite human recognition. The category of *bios*, or political life, constituted through instruments such as declarations of rights and responsibilities, is a key feature of both Polar Whale's appeal for sovereign recognition and Ahab's mastery of the *Pequod*'s crew. Yet Ishmael's account of the whale, however much it alludes to political criteria such as mutual protection or deliberation, remains grounded in the onto-theological concerns of bare or creaturely life, which, as Agamben reminds us, originally "belonged to God."[50] If, as Lyell's account of extinction suggests, there is no onto-theological ground either for an interspecies ethic of protection, as Polar Whale would wish, or for Ahab's vengeful metaphysical quest—"Sometimes I think there's naught beyond," he admits—then, as Ishmael interprets Ahab's quarter-deck speech, "with little external to constrain us, the innermost necessities in our being, these still drive us on."[51] Locating the problem of extinction in the nature of species being, Ishmael finds species responsible for their own fates—and thus imagines the self-replicating perpetuation of cognizant life—while marking humankind as an indeterminate exception. Yet by displacing the violence emblemized by the whaling industry away from whales and onto humankind's fate while transcoding Ahab's ontological defiance as the whale's ontological defiance, Ishmael projects human consciousness into the deep whalekind chronology that, he says, will outlast humankind's biblically specified time.

NOTES

1. Herman Melville, *Moby-Dick, or, The Whale* (New York: Penguin, 2003), 503–4.

2. The first comprehensive account was George Perkins Marsh's *Man and Nature: Or, Physical Geography as Modified by Human Action* (1864; reprint, Cambridge, Mass.: Harvard University Press, 1965); on whales, see 99–102. For a history of local cases through the mid-nineteenth century, see Mark Barrow, *Nature's Ghosts: Confronting Extinction from the Age of Jefferson to the Age of Ecology* (Chicago: University of Chicago Press, 2009), 15–77.

3. Thomas Jefferson, *Notes on the State of Virginia*, ed. Frank Shuffelton (New York: Penguin, 1999), 55. On Jefferson's concerns, see Timothy Sweet, "The Eighteenth-Century *Archives du Monde*: The Question of Agency in Extinction Stories," in *The Year's Work in the Oddball Archive*, ed. Jonathan Eburne and Judith Roof (Bloomington: Indiana University Press, 2016), 219–45.

4. Thomas Jefferson, letter to John Adams, April 11, 1823, in *The Writings of Thomas*

Jefferson, ed. Andrew A. Lipscomb and Albert Ellery Bergh, 20 vols. (Washington, D.C.: Jefferson Memorial Association, 1903), 15:427.

5. See the Darwin Variorum, http://darwin-online.org.uk.

6. On Melville's religious investigations, see, for example, David S. Reynolds, *Beneath the American Renaissance: The Subversive Imagination in the Age of Emerson and Melville* (Cambridge, Mass.: Harvard University Press, 1999), 27–30; and Brian Yothers, *Sacred Uncertainty: Religious Difference and the Shape of Melville's Career* (Evanston, Ill.: Northwestern University Press, 2015), 73–98. As Reynolds observes, these investigations were so complex that they were largely ignored by mainstream religious writers (*Faith in Fiction: The Emergence of Religious Literature in America* [Cambridge, Mass.: Harvard University Press, 1981], 214).

7. In the first chapter of *Principles of Geology* (3 vols. [London: Murray, 1830–33]), Charles Lyell warns against confusing geology with cosmogony and identifies Charles Hutton as the first to draw a clear distinction (1:4).

8. Ibid., 2:156.

9. See Giorgio Agamben, *Homo Sacer: Sovereign Power and Bare Life*, trans. Daniel Heller-Roazen (Stanford: Stanford University Press, 1998); and Giorgio Agamben, *The Open: Man and Animal*, trans. Kevin Attell (Stanford: Stanford University Press, 2004).

10. Jacques Derrida, "'Eating Well,' or the Calculation of the Subject: An Interview with Jacques Derrida," in *Who Comes After the Subject?*, ed. Eduardo Cadava, Peter Connor, and Jean-Luc Nancy (New York: Routledge, 1991), 112.

11. Agamben, *Homo Sacer*, 127.

12. On the quarter-deck scene as political allegory, see, for example, Donald Pease, "Melville and Cultural Persuasion," in *Ideology and Classic American Literature*, ed. Sacvan Bercovitch and Myra Jehlen (New York: Cambridge University Press, 1986), 384–417.

13. Melville, *Moby-Dick*, 178, 179.

14. Ibid., 498.

15. Ibid., 70. See Paul Semonin, *American Monster: How the Nation's First Prehistoric Creature Became a Symbol of National Identity* (New York: New York University Press, 2000).

16. That Melville was familiar with current geological thought by the time he wrote *Moby-Dick* is evident from his parodic rehearsal of both catastrophist and uniformitarian theories in chapter 132 of *Mardi*.

17. Melville, *Moby-Dick*, 498, 503–4, 501, 502.

18. See, for example, Robert Lloyd Webb, *On the Northwest: Commercial Whaling in the Pacific Northwest, 1790–1967* (Vancouver: University of British Columbia Press, 1988).

19. J. Hector St. John de Crèvecoeur, *Letters from an American Farmer* (Oxford: Oxford University Press, 1997), 110–11.

20. "The Whale Fishery," *North American Review* 82 (January 1834): 115.

21. M. E. Bowles, "Some Account of the Whale-Fishery of the N. West Coast and Kamschatka," *Polynesian* [Honolulu], October 4, 1845, 83. Bowles signed himself

as an officer of the Rhode Island whale ship *Jane* in "She Would Have Him: A Temperance Tale," *Friend* [Honolulu], November 1, 1845, 161.

22. Henry T. Cheever, *The Whale and His Captors; Or, the Whaleman's Adventures and the Whale's Biography* (New York: Harper, 1850), 108–9. On Melville's use of Cheever, see Howard Vincent, *The Trying Out of "Moby-Dick"* (Boston: Houghton Mifflin, 1949), 131, 212–13, 256, 260, 266–67, 292, 323–24.

23. James Montgomery, "The Pelican Island," in *The Poetical Works of James Montgomery*, 2 vols. (Boston: Houghton Mifflin, 1880), 2:19–20.

24. "A Polar Whale's Appeal," *Friend* [Honolulu], October 15, 1850, 82–83.

25. On this first polar whaling expedition, see Eric Jay Dolin, *The History of Whaling in America* (New York: Norton, 2007), 226–31. The Anadir Sea was a nineteenth-century name for the Bering Sea.

26. "A Polar Whale's Appeal," 82.

27. Bruno Latour, *The Politics of Nature: How to Bring the Sciences into Democracy*, trans. Catherine Porter (Cambridge, Mass.: Harvard University Press, 2004), 66–68.

28. "A Polar Whale's Appeal," 83.

29. On the supposed lastness of Jefferson's Logan and Cooper's Chingachgook, see Jonathan Elmer, *On Lingering and Being Last: Race and Sovereignty in the New World* (New York: Fordham University Press, 2008), 118–46, 195–96.

30. Dolin, *The History of Whaling*, 84.

31. See, for example, Cary Wolfe's critique of the sacrificial logic of humanism in *Animal Rites: American Culture, the Discourse of Species, and Posthumanist Theory* (Chicago: University of Chicago Press, 2003).

32. As several critics have remarked, Melville questions the human-animal distinction throughout *Moby-Dick*. See, for example, Elizabeth Schultz, "Melville's Environmental Vision in *Moby-Dick*," *Interdisciplinary Studies in Literature and Environment* 7, no. 1 (2000): 97–113; Eric Wilson, "Melville, Darwin, and the Great Chain of Being," *Studies in American Fiction* 28, no. 2 (2000): 131–50; Lawrence Buell, *Writing for an Endangered World* (Cambridge, Mass.: Harvard University Press, 2001), 205–14; and Philip Armstrong, "*Moby-Dick* and Compassion," *Society and Animals* 12, no. 1 (2004): 19–37.

33. Melville, *Moby-Dick*, 502, 503, 195, 228. On the destruction of the *Essex*, see Nathaniel Philbrick, *In the Heart of the Sea: The Tragedy of the Whaleship* Essex (New York: Viking, 2000). As Ishmael reports in chapter 45, Melville had spoken with Chase's son in the Pacific in 1841 and later acquired a copy of the narrative (Vincent, *Trying Out*, 47–48).

34. Melville, *Moby-Dick*, 417, 502, 415, 478.

35. Thomas Beale, *The Natural History of the Sperm Whale; To which is Added, a Sketch of a South-Sea Whaling Voyage* (London: Van Voorst, 1839), 6, 5. On Melville's use of Beale, see Vincent, *Trying Out*, 164–66.

36. Robert Chambers, *Vestiges of the Natural History of Creation* (London: Churchill, 1844), 156. On pre-Darwinian developmentalism, see Ernst Mayr, *The*

Growth of Biological Thought: Diversity, Evolution, and Inheritance (Cambridge, Mass.: Harvard University Press, 1982), 343–62, 381–85; and Robert J. Richards, *The Romantic Conception of Life: Science and Philosophy in the Age of Goethe* (Chicago: University of Chicago Press, 2002), 407–508. For an analysis of Melville's interest in romantic protobiology, see Jennifer Jordan Baker, "Dead Bones and Honest Wonders: The Aesthetics of Natural Science in *Moby-Dick*," in *Melville and Aesthetics*, ed. Samuel Otter and Geoffrey Sanborn (New York: Palgrave Macmillan, 2011), 85–101.

37. Henry David Thoreau, *Walden* (Princeton: Princeton University Press, 1989), 273.

38. Chambers, for example, located the European "race" at the pinnacle of human development (*Vestiges*, 217).

39. Melville, *Moby-Dick*, 500, 501.

40. In 1849, Melville bought an edition of *Frankenstein* that was advertised as "By the Author of 'The Last Man.'" He would also have been familiar with other examples of romantic apocalypticism such as Lord Byron's poem "Darkness." See Merton M. Sealts, Jr., *Melville's Reading: A Check-List of Books Owned and Borrowed* (Madison: University of Wisconsin Press, 1966), 46, 94.

41. On the resonance of Ahab and the vanishing Indian motif, see Wai Chee Dimock, "Ahab's Manifest Destiny," in *Macropolitics of Nineteenth-Century Literature: Nationalism, Exoticism, Imperialism*, ed. Jonathan Arac and Harriet Ritvo (Philadelphia: University of Pennsylvania Press, 1991), 184–212.

42. Melville, *Moby-Dick*, 166. D. H. Lawrence, *Studies in Classic American Literature* (New York: Viking, 1964), 159.

43. Melville, *Moby-Dick*, 77.

44. Ibid., 463, 464.

45. Ibid., 579. Melville quotes from Jeremiah 31:15 (King James Version). The allusion suggests that it is doubtful that the *Rachel* ever finds the missing whaleboat; she does, however, later rescue the *Pequod*'s lone survivor, Ishmael.

46. Ibid., 589, 590, 591–93.

47. Ibid., 624, 504. On traditional biblical time scales such as the 6,000-year chronology popularized by James Ussher's *Annals of the World* (1650), 5,000 years ago is a reasonable date for the flood. Genesis 7:6 reports Noah's age at the time as six hundred years.

48. Melville, *Moby-Dick*, 498.

49. 2 Peter 3:10, King James Version.

50. Agamben, *Homo Sacer*, 127.

51. Melville, *Moby-Dick*, 178, 179.

PART II
RECONSTRUCTING THE SCRIPTURES

CHAPTER 6

HIGHER READING

Uncle Tom's Cabin *and Biblical Higher Criticism*

Gail K. Smith

DAVID S. REYNOLDS broke new ground in *Beneath the American Renaissance* by demonstrating how the so-called major antebellum American authors drew from the popular and the lowbrow (even the downright seamy) in their cultural milieu to produce high art. For instance, in his brief treatment of Harriet Beecher Stowe's *Uncle Tom's Cabin*, he argued that its popular appeal in the 1850s had much to do with the ways in which it pulls together subversive popular elements, including religious skepticism and sensational slave horror stories, and tethers those elements to reassuring conventional pieties and narrative structures.[1] Yet a major gap remains in Stowe studies: there has not been sufficient attention to the *highbrow* cultural context that shaped her work throughout her career, from the 1830s to the 1870s.

To date, two primary intellectual influences have been studied in connection with Stowe's work: her reworking of Edwardsean theology and her uses of sympathy, which many critics attribute to her exposure to the Scottish common sense philosophy taught in antebellum American schoolrooms.[2] Missing from our understanding, however, has been a recognition of her involvement in the revolutionary critical biblical studies that made their way to the United States from Europe, especially from Germany, when she was in her teens and that particularly influenced her via the biblical scholar and seminary professor she married in 1836: the Reverend Calvin Stowe, one of America's early and important adopters of the German higher criticism. Although its influence has been noted in a handful of nineteenth-century American writers, few scholars have recognized the higher criticism's significance in Stowe's work.[3] In *Uncle Tom's Cabin*, on which I will focus here, understanding how Stowe synthesized and responded to the new biblical scholarship of her day casts new light on some of the novel's most hotly contested scenes and issues: its use of the idea of sympathy, its idealization of childlike readers, and its frequent juxtapositions of scholarly questions with an unlearned faith.

The higher criticism—a term coined by the German theologian and orientalist J. G. Eichhorn (1752–1827)—shook the foundations of biblical understanding in the transatlantic world, reaching the United States from Europe in the 1820s. In addition to Eichhorn, its pioneers included the Anglican bishop and Oxford University professor Robert Lowth (1710–87) and, in Germany, the biblical scholar J. D. Michaelis (1717–91); the poet, philosopher, and theologian Johann Gottfried von Herder (1744–1803); and the theologian and biblical scholar W. M. L. de Wette (1780–1849). The higher critics read the Bible as a collection of miscellaneous pieces of ancient "Oriental" literature written by ordinary human authors in recognizable literary genres. Using the same historical and literary tools one would apply to Homer's or Shakespeare's works, they studied the ancient manuscripts to show that Genesis and a number of other biblical books were cobbled together from multiple sources written at different times, that hundreds of variants existed among manuscripts of the same biblical book, that the gospels date from decades after the life of Christ, that the stories of the Old Testament are best understood as formative cultural myths of the ancient Hebrew people rather than as literal history, and so on—insights that continue to undergird much academic study of the Bible today. The most radical higher-critical wing, including Eichhorn, de Wette, and the theologian and writer David F. Strauss (1808–74), turned the same demythologizing impulse to the New Testament accounts of the miracles, resurrection, and ascension of Jesus.[4]

Moses Stuart of Andover Theological Seminary in Andover, Massachusetts, was one of the first Americans to study the new criticism. His student Calvin Stowe carried Stuart's legacy forward when he became professor of biblical literature at Cincinnati's Lane Theological Seminary, the new school Presbyterian seminary where Harriet's father, Lyman Beecher, served as president from 1832 to 1850.[5] Following Lowth and Herder, Calvin Stowe valued the Old Testament for its poetry and as the record of the gradual refinement of an ancient culture under divine tutelage. Like Stuart, he taught the Bible as sacred literature, analyzing each biblical book within the conventions of its literary genre and taking care to interpret figurative language as a literary device. And he railed against the popular academic practice of hunting up decontextualized biblical prooftexts to support an argument. As Harriet Beecher Stowe explained in a biographical sketch of her brother, Henry Ward Beecher, who studied under Calvin Stowe at Lane,

> The old and the new school [of Presbyterianism] were both too much agreed in using the Bible as a carpenter does his nail-box, going to it only to find screws and nails to hold together the framework of a theological system. Professor Stowe inspired [Henry] with the idea of surveying the books of the Bible as divinely inspired compositions, yet truly and warmly human, and to be rendered and interpreted by the same rules of reason and common sense which pertain to all human documents.[6]

Harriet, too, picked up a great deal from her scholarly husband, including alternatives to what she had already felt were the inadequacies of Scottish common sense philosophy. Looking back in an 1874 letter to George Eliot, she explained,

> From my childhood I have been brought up upon a priori metaphysical discussion. My father a disciple of the Scotch school of metaphysicians applied their methods to theology and discussed the doctrines of human responsibility of repentance, conversion, and holy living in ways that all along it appeared to me the *facts* of daily observation and universal human consciousness did not justify—

> When I married, I found a man of unusual reading and great love of facts whose first work was to upset all of *technical* orthodoxy my own reflections had left—and replace it by a wide insight in *facts* of which his reading in many languages gave him the command.[7]

A few scholars have acknowledged Calvin Stowe's deep impact on his wife's thought and work.[8] As Marie Caskey observes, "not only his biblical studies but also his pulpit views were, as Harriet herself indicated time and again, the single most important influence on her theological development."[9] Under Calvin's direction she studied the Bible, biblical commentaries, the church fathers, even Talmudic material. She shared his admiration for de Wette and Herder: on her European trip of 1853 she visited de Wette's widow in Geneva and found Herder's signature on the roof of the Strasbourg cathedral, and she included a hymn of de Wette's in her 1877 *Footsteps of the Master*.[10] She also adopted a number of higher-critical approaches in her private and public religious life. She explained the gospels in the same terms that Calvin used, as collections of remembered anecdotes rather than chronological biographies.[11] She discussed the Old Testament as Herder did—as a treasury of ecstatic poetry and as the record of God's gradual education and refinement of the people of Israel.[12] Late in life she echoed Eichhorn by discussing the Genesis story of the Fall as "symbolic" and a "parable."[13]

Above all it was Herder to whom Calvin Stowe owed much of what he emphasized throughout his life in the classroom and the pulpit. He bought volumes of Herder on his 1836 European book-buying trip for Lane's library, taught Herder's books in his classes, recommended Herder texts to his readers, and even used "Herder" as his own pseudonym in some of his published work.[14] Key for Calvin Stowe was Herder's concept of *Einfühlung*, then typically translated as "sympathy." (The word *empathy* was later created specifically as a translation for the term.)[15] For Herder, *Einfühlung*—"in-feeling" or "feeling [one's way] into"—was specifically readerly, an imaginative entry into the times and spirit of an ancient biblical writer. Applying "this *living reading*, this divination into the author's soul" enabled one to read "in the spirit of the author" rather than simply "in the book."[16] As he wrote in an often-quoted exhortation, "If you would enjoy these writings in their original air, you must become a shepherd with shepherds, a peasant with an agricultural people, an oriental with the primitive inhabitants of the East."[17] Or, as Calvin Stowe expressed it, "the interpreter must be able to put himself in the exact place where the Hebrew stood when God spake to him, if he would hear God's voice as the Hebrew heard it."[18] This readerly form of sympathy—a "strong, living sympathy with the writers whom you undertake to interpret"—appears over and over again in Calvin Stowe's writing, and it is prominent in Harriet Beecher Stowe's work as well, particularly in *Uncle Tom's Cabin*.[19] And it owes far more to German biblical criticism than it does to Dugald Stewart or Adam Smith.

The other Herderian touch that appears often in both Calvin's and Harriet's writings is the description of the ancient Hebrew writers as "simple" and "childlike." Herder always identified "Oriental" culture with the childhood of humanity, "the infancy of our race."[20] The Bible "was hardly written for us of the eighteenth century," he explained. "We must take the pains to go back to its connexion, to the childhood of our race."[21] The best readers of the Bible, then—the ones with the best *Einfühlung*—are childlike as well. "In this feeling of natural beauty and sublimity" found in the Hebrew poetry, says Herder, "the child often has the advantage of the man of gray hairs."[22] To enter into the spirit of the ancient biblical writer, the western adult reader must recapture a childlike spirit: "We must learn to dwell long upon plain and simple imagery, to revolve them over in our contemplations, to excite the sense of wonder, and picture them in gigantick forms. Such are the views, the language, and the feelings of children."[23] Following Herder, Calvin Stowe explained that the biblical writers in the "patriarchal period of childlike simplicity" were writing not for the educated but for a simple readership.[24] Harriet wrote that "the promises of the Bible are everywhere made to the simple—the confiding—the childlike" and noted that Jesus routinely addresses his disciples as "My little children."[25]

This context gives new insight into *Uncle Tom's Cabin*'s many scenes of Bible reading. In particular, it has puzzled many critics that Stowe presents Tom and Eva, two "childlike" characters with imperfect literacy, as her model Bible readers. Tom reads slowly because, she tells us, he learned to read "late in life"; Eva, with her child's vocabulary, does not always fully understand the words she reads.[26] But Stowe reminds her readers that the Bible was written by "ignorant and unlearned men," an allusion to the Book of Acts: "Now when [the Jewish leaders] saw the boldness of Peter and John, and perceived that they were unlearned and ignorant men, they marvelled."[27] Eva and Tom, as readers without sophisticated literacy skills, are closest to the condition of the biblical authors. Like the biblical writers, too, they are both "childlike." Stowe refers to them as "the old child and the young one"—Eva obviously because of her youth, Tom because of what Stowe often calls his "childlike" and "simple" trusting faith as well as "the soft, impressible nature of his kindly race, ever yearning toward the simple and childlike."[28] Both characters therefore have a built-in *Einfühlung* with the scriptures.

And according to Stowe, reading the Bible does not depend on an intellectual understanding of all the words: "All that [Tom and Eva] knew was, that they spoke of a glory to be revealed,—a wondrous something yet to come, wherein their soul rejoiced, yet knew not why; and though it be not so in the physical, yet in moral science that which cannot be understood is not always profitless."[29] As Calvin Stowe explained, "with the poetic element strongly developed and under the guidance of a pure and powerful religious sentiment, the general teachings of the Bible will be clearly apprehended, however erroneous may be the understanding of some particular words and phrases."[30] Eva, despite her limited vocabulary, brings the necessary qualities to the text: "a quick poetic fancy, and an instinctive sympathy with what is grand and noble."[31] Moreover, her favorite biblical books, "the Revelation and the Prophecies," are the books most lauded by the "spirit of Hebrew poetry" school of Lowth and Herder.[32] Her response to her reading is precisely the childlike wonder Herder hoped for: the "dim and wondrous imagery, and fervent language" "woke in her strange yearnings, and strong, dim emotions."[33] Her ecstatic reverie upon reading a line from Revelation, "And I saw as it were a sea of glass mingled with fire," matches what Calvin Stowe had hoped readers of Revelation would do: "Read it simply for the sake of enjoying it; read it as a glowing description of a series of magnificent pictures which were passing before the eye of the writer; read it for the sake of throwing your soul into its sublime acts of adoration of the Great Supreme."[34]

Tom, too, may not grasp the Bible's textual subtleties, but, like Eva, he has what matters more—a childlike faith that comprehends the spirit of scripture. When he and St. Clare discuss the Bible, St. Clare muses, "It seems to be given to children, and poor, honest fellows, like you, to see what we can't. . . . How comes it?" Tom responds by quoting from Jesus' prayer, recorded in Matthew and Luke: "Thou hast 'hid from the wise and prudent, and revealed unto babes.'"[35] St. Clare points out that he himself has "a great deal more knowledge" than Tom does, and Tom replies that he knows what the Bible means because he "feels it in [his] soul. Oh, Mas'r! The love of Christ, that passeth knowledge.'"[36] His faith is a different kind of knowledge, like that of the poverty-stricken mother who faithfully reads her Bible in Stowe's 1855 sketch "How Do We Know?":

> Could she give the arguments from miracles and prophecy? Could she account for all the changes which might have taken place in it through translators and copyists, and prove that we have a genuine and uncorrupted version? Not she! But how, then, does she know that it is true? How, say you? How does she know that she has warm life blood in her heart? How does she know that there is such a thing as air and sunshine? She does not *believe* these things—she *knows* them; and in like manner, with a deep heart consciousness, she is certain that the words of her Bible are truth and life. Is it by reasoning that the frightened child, bewildered in the dark, knows its mother's voice? No! Nor is it only by reasoning that the forlorn and distressed human heart knows the voice of its Savior, and is still.[37]

Similarly, Tom has no knowledge of the hot topics of biblical criticism in Stowe's day, but simply reads the Bible and knows that its "words . . . are truth and life."

Tom's Bible reading, however, has repeatedly served as the basis for arguments that Stowe is uninterested in or even hostile to scholarship, especially biblical scholarship. It has also undergirded related and, I think, equally mistaken interpretations of Tom as a passive reader and assumptions about Stowe's designs to make her readers similarly unquestioning and passive. The key passage from which these arguments stem is the scene when Tom, on board the riverboat from Kentucky to New Orleans, turns to his Bible. At this moment, after he has been sold away from the Shelby plantation and is mourning for his lost family, he opens his Bible and, "with patient finger, threading his slow way from word to word, traces out its promises":

> Having learned late in life, Tom was but a slow reader, and passed on laboriously from verse to verse. Fortunate for him was it that the book he was intent on was one which slow reading cannot injure,—nay, one whose words, like ingots of gold, seem often to need to be weighed separately, that the mind may take in their priceless value. Let us follow him a moment, as, pointing to each word, and pronouncing each half aloud, he reads,—
>
> "Let—not—your—heart—be—troubled. In—my—Father's—house—are—many—mansions. I—go—to—prepare—a—place—for—you."
>
> Cicero, when he buried his darling and only daughter, had a heart as full of honest grief as poor Tom's,—perhaps no fuller, for both were only men;—but Cicero could pause over no such sublime words of hope, and look to no such future reunion; and if he *had* seen them, ten to one he would not have believed,—he must fill his head first with a thousand questions of authenticity of manuscript, and correctness of translation. But, to poor Tom, there it lay, just what he needed, so evidently true and divine that the possibility of a question never entered his simple head. It must be true; for, if not true, how could he live?[38]

Using this and other passages as evidence, critics have described Tom's degree of literacy as everything from "dyslexic" to "barely literate" to "marginally literate" to "semiliterate" to "literate."[39] He is a "big, simple child," "infantile" in his "autodidactic antics"; or a model self-teacher in the Franklinian mode; or a learner "gradually acquiring and sharing a very complex range of literary practices."[40] Depending in part on the degree of literacy they attribute to Tom, critics have concluded from this passage that Stowe is expressing deep ambivalence or even hostility toward intellectual analysis, particularly toward biblical exegesis, while idealizing the idea of a "passive" and "unquestioning" reader.[41]

This passage, however, is neither an attack on intellectual analysis, nor one on biblical exegesis, nor a call for a passive reader uninvolved in the interpretive process. Rather, Stowe is presenting specific conditions under which scholarly approaches can hinder the best use of the Bible—namely, in times of personal anguish and loss of the sort that Cicero and Tom experience. No spiritual comfort is going to come to such a person through the study of variants in biblical manuscripts. The passage is not a denigration of scholarship but an appeal for a faith-based *Einfühlung* with the text as more important than scholarship—precisely what Herder and Calvin Stowe argued throughout their lives.

Stowe's choice of Cicero is significant as well. He is not simply an intellectual but a learned, pre-Christian-era pagan in dire need of spiritual comfort after the death of a child. According to Stowe, if given the scriptures, he would have only been able to turn (because of his lack of Christian faith and his scholarly bent) to academic questions about the text's material production. As a result, his pain could not be assuaged; intellectual inquiry in this situation would have never led him to the heartfelt engagement with scripture that a faithful believer such as Tom experiences. As Calvin Stowe put it, "For the full understanding of the Scriptures there must be faith. . . . This faith is the only inlet by which spiritual truth, deep and full, can pass into the soul."[42] No skeptic is going to be led to faith by poring over "questions of authenticity of manuscript, and correctness of translation." In Harriet's imagined scenario, Cicero would be going about the task backward: he would be doing scholarship first rather than approaching the text in the context of faith.[43]

Moreover, Stowe's assertion that Cicero could not look forward to "any . . . future reunion" with his dead daughter was part of a long-standing conversation among educated western Christians on whether Cicero believed in an afterlife. There "has been," said one writer in 1851, the year *Uncle Tom's Cabin* appeared in the *National Era*, "considerable dispute [over] . . . Cicero's belief in a future state."[44] Article after article on this issue appeared in the antebellum popular press.[45] Most of them based their claims on the first book of Cicero's *Tusculan Questions*, which consists of an extended Socratic dialogue on whether the soul is immortal. The dialogue ends with two possibilities unresolved: death as merely a restful oblivion or as a pathway to a future state. Some nineteenth-century readers—including Calvin Stowe's mentor, Moses Stuart—argued that Cicero's true views were represented by the character in the dialogue who supports the idea of an afterlife.[46] Others maintained that the dialogue was inconclusive either because Cicero was philosophically opposed to dogmatic statement or because he could not bring himself to believe in an eternal existence.[47]

Why did this seemingly esoteric question about an ancient Roman author claim so much attention in antebellum America? Because if a wise pagan could reason his way to a belief in the soul's immortality, then the church's claims for the uniqueness and necessity of the Christian revelation would receive a severe blow. As Cicero's English translator explained in his introduction to the first book of the *Tusculan Questions*, printed in two installments in the *Christian Examiner* in 1842,

> [Before the birth of Christ] the human mind had tried every expedient to solve the great mystery of being. . . . The argument of Cicero must be read, as a cry to heaven for light and guidance; as a confession of human weakness and want. Only in this way can it be understood. The argument is not conclusive. It could not be so. Had it been, what necessity for a revelation? It is a proof of that necessity from its very incompleteness; and herein lies its great value.[48]

In the spring of 1851 Harvard University's bookstore brought out an edition of *Cicero on the Immortality of the Soul* that gave new energy to the conversation in the periodical press.[49] With the debate ongoing, Stowe could assume that many in her audience would be aware of it as the first installments of *Uncle Tom's Cabin* began appearing in the *National Era* in June of that year. For Stowe, Cicero demonstrates that human reason is an insufficient tool in our search for consolation during a "dread soul-crisis" such as the death of a child.[50] As Harold K. Bush has noted, Stowe had herself lost a child to cholera in 1849; like many of her readers, she knew firsthand the need for the consoling power of a faith in the "continuing bonds" between the dead and the living.[51]

Stowe's description of Cicero's doubt also echoes Jesus' admonishment of his doubting disciple Thomas in the gospel of John. Had the Bible's promises of an eternal home been available to Cicero, she says, even "if he *had* seen them, ten to one he would not have believed." The phrasing recalls Jesus' words to Thomas: "Because thou hast seen me, thou hast believed: blessed are they that have not seen, and yet have believed."[52] Stowe could count on the biblically literate readers of the *National Era* to recognize her allusion, reinforcing her central contrast between a Ciceronian doubt that intellectualizes and a Tom-like faith that lives without proof.

It is surely no coincidence that in the very next paragraph after Stowe's Cicero-Tom comparison we are introduced to Augustine St. Clare, whose doubt and cynicism quickly unfold as he converses with Haley about Tom's religion. As a writer in the *Southern Literary Messenger* noted in 1850, Cicero's "brilliant intellect understood everything, his faint heart believed nothing. He doubted forever, and in each crisis of his life, he hesitated, deliberated and when he at last made up his mind, invariably preferred half measures, spoke of expediency and left the door open for the morrow"—a perfect description of St. Clare.[53] Further, St. Clare will soon face the same grief Cicero experienced when he loses his beloved only daughter, Eva.

With a fuller understanding of the allusive richness of this scene in *Uncle Tom's Cabin*, we can turn to the argument that Stowe uses Tom in this passage to privilege a "passive" or "unquestioning" reader. A passive reader, however, would not have a Bible "marked through, from one end to the other," with his marginalia.[54] On the contrary, with his repeated and concentrated study of one book, Tom is what book historians call an intensive reader.[55] Instead of "annotations and helps in margin from learned commentators,"

> Tom's Bible . . . had been embellished with certain way-marks and guide-boards of Tom's own invention, and which helped him more than the most learned expositions could have done. It had been his custom to get the Bible read to him by his master's children, in particular by young Master George; and, as they read, he would designate, by bold, strong marks and dashes, with pen and ink, the passages which more particularly gratified his ear or affected his heart. His Bible was thus marked through, from one end to the other, with a variety of styles and designations; so he could in a moment seize upon

his favorite passages, without the labor of spelling out what lay between them.[56]

As Martin Luther had encouraged his students to do, Tom reads for himself and creates his own marginal glosses, following the Reformation-era Protestant watchword *sola scriptura* ("scripture alone").[57] Rather than relying on the opinions and interpretations of church authorities, such reading requires an active interpreter.

Tom's interpretive abilities are evident throughout the novel, and both St. Clare and Eva acknowledge his skill at explaining biblical passages. His deep familiarity with scripture and his system of markings enable him on numerous occasions to "seize upon" the perfect verses in order to minister to others and to himself—whether to admonish St. Clare for his drinking, to prepare himself and Ophelia St. Clare for Eva's death, to touch a grieving father's numbed heart with the account of the raising of Lazarus, to comfort the exhausted slaves at Legree's plantation, or to encourage Cassy and himself not to despair of God's presence in the midst of suffering.[58] Nor is Tom "unquestioning" in his reading. On the contrary, at Legree's plantation, he undergoes "weeks and months" of anguished religious questioning while he struggles to gain consolation from the Bible.[59] For a time, the scriptures even cease to speak to him as he confronts "the gloomiest problem of this mysterious life . . . souls crushed and ruined, evil triumphant, and God silent." "There were all the marked passages, which had thrilled his soul so often. . . . Had the word lost its power, or could the failing eye and weary sense no longer answer to the touch of that mighty inspiration? Heavily sighing, he put [the Bible] in his pocket."[60] P. Gabrielle Foreman argues that, when Tom ultimately regains his faith as he faces a Christlike death, "he becomes the living word, rather than a reader of the written word."[61] But it is his intensive reading of the scriptures that enables him to quote a verse from Romans as his dying words—"Who shall separate us from the love of Christ?"—again selecting the passage that is precisely appropriate to the situation.[62]

Both in *Uncle Tom's Cabin* and in her own life, then, Stowe was an active biblical student, questioner, and interpreter at a time of unprecedented upheaval in both lay and clerical understandings of the Bible.

In this novel and in other works throughout her career, she popularized some of the higher criticism's emphases and applied them in new ways to her contemporary context, demonstrating what Jacqueline R. deVries calls "the less obvious role of women in reshaping widely held Christian beliefs in the nineteenth century."[63] Tracing the ways in which Stowe synthesized and responded to the new biblical scholarship of her day illustrates her intimate relationship with intellectual developments above the popular and lowbrow influences on which Reynolds has concentrated and her deep commitment to the faith that, for her, was above all else.

NOTES

I wish to thank Kent Andersen, Clare Emily Clifford, and Ted Farrell for their insightful comments on earlier versions of this essay and thank Anne-Marie Bogdan for bibliographic assistance.

1. David S. Reynolds, *Beneath the American Renaissance: The Subversive Imagination in the Age of Emerson and Melville* (New York: Knopf, 1988), 74–79. A fuller treatment of *Uncle Tom's Cabin* appears in David S. Reynolds, *Mightier Than the Sword: "Uncle Tom's Cabin" and the Battle for America* (New York: Norton, 2012).

2. On Stowe's reworking of Edwardsean theology, see Kimberly Van Esveld Adams, "Family Influences on *The Minister's Wooing* and *Oldtown Folks*: Henry Ward Beecher and Calvin Stowe," *Religion and Literature* 38 (Winter 2006): 27–61; Marie Caskey, *Chariot of Fire: Religion and the Beecher Family* (New Haven: Yale University Press, 1978), 169–207; Charles Foster, *The Rungless Ladder: Harriet Beecher Stowe and New England Puritanism* (Durham: Duke University Press, 1954); Joan D. Hedrick, *Harriet Beecher Stowe: A Life* (New York: Oxford University Press, 1994), 280–81. On Stowe's uses of sympathy, see Maurice Lee, *Slavery, Philosophy, and American Literature, 1830–1860* (New York: Cambridge University Press, 2005), 52–92; Naomi Z. Sofer, *Making the "America of Art": Cultural Nationalism and Nineteenth-Century Women Writers* (Columbus: Ohio State University Press, 2005), 25–30; Patricia Hill, "*Uncle Tom's Cabin* as a Religious Text," 2007, *Uncle Tom's Cabin and American Culture*, http://utc.iath.virginia.edu; Elizabeth Barnes, *States of Sympathy: Seduction and Democracy in the American Novel* (New York: Columbia University Press, 1997), 4–5; Gregg Camfield, *Sentimental Twain: Samuel Clemens in the Maze of Moral Philosophy* (Philadelphia: University of Pennsylvania Press, 1994), 22–59; and Gregg Crane, *The Cambridge Introduction to the Nineteenth-Century American Novel* (New York: Cambridge University Press, 2007), 105.

3. For the higher criticism's influence on Emerson, see Barbara Packer, "Origin and Authority: Emerson and the Higher Criticism," in *Reconstructing American*

Literary History, ed. Sacvan Bercovitch (Cambridge, Mass.: Harvard University Press, 1986), 67–92. On Emerson and Melville, see Lawrence Buell, *New England Literary Culture from Revolution through Renaissance* (New York: Cambridge University Press, 1986), 166–85. On Elizabeth Stuart Phelps, see Gail K. Smith, "From the Seminary to the Parlor: The Popularization of Hermeneutics in *The Gates Ajar*," *Arizona Quarterly* 54 (Summer 1998): 99–133. On Mark Twain, see Harold K. Bush, *Mark Twain and the Spiritual Crisis of His Age* (Tuscaloosa: University of Alabama Press, 2007), 207. For scholarship that addresses the influence of the higher criticism on Stowe, see Gail K. Smith, "Reading with the Other: Hermeneutics and the Politics of Difference in Stowe's *Dred*," *American Literature* 69, no. 2 (1997): 289–313; Sofer, *Making the "America of Art*,*"* 40–41; and Hill, "*Uncle Tom's Cabin* as a Religious Text."

4. For useful accounts of biblical higher criticism, including its influence on European and American literature, see Jerry Wayne Brown, *The Rise of Biblical Criticism in America, 1800–1870: The New England Scholars* (Middletown, Conn.: Wesleyan University Press, 1969); Hans W. Frei, *The Eclipse of Biblical Narrative: A Study in Eighteenth and Nineteenth Century Hermeneutics* (New Haven: Yale University Press, 1974); Robert Grant, with David Tracy, *A Short History of the Interpretation of the Bible* (Philadelphia: Fortress, 1984); E. S. Shaffer, "*Kubla Khan*" and "*The Fall of Jerusalem*": *The Mythological School in Biblical Criticism and Secular Literature, 1770–1880* (Cambridge: Cambridge University Press, 1975); Gerald L. Bruns, *Hermeneutics Ancient and Modern* (New Haven: Yale University Press, 1992); and Jonathan Sheehan, *The Enlightenment Bible: Translation, Scholarship, Culture* (Princeton: Princeton University Press, 2005).

5. For an account of the new school–old school split in the Presbyterian church in 1837, see Randall Balmer and John R. Fitzmier, *The Presbyterians* (Westport, Conn.: Greenwood, 1993).

6. Harriet Beecher Stowe, *Men of Our Times; or, Leading Patriots of the Day. Being Narratives of the Lives and Deeds of Statesmen, Generals, and Orators* (Hartford, 1868), 537–38.

7. Harriet Beecher Stowe, letter to George Eliot, August 20, 1874, Henry W. and Albert A. Berg Collection of English and American Literature, New York Public Library. (Emphasis, spelling, and punctuation in the text match the original.) The letter continues with descriptions of Calvin Stowe's sermons on the "facts" of the spiritual experiences of believers and unbelievers, including those of Goethe, Paulus, and other rationalists—a contrast between lived experience and the theoretical approach of Harriet's father and Scottish common sense philosophy. See also Harriet Beecher Stowe, *Uncle Tom's Cabin* (1852; reprint, New York: Signet, 1981): "Moore, Byron, Goethe, often speak words more wisely descriptive of the true religious sentiment, than another man, whose whole life is governed by it" (327–28).

8. Adams, "Family Influences," 27–28;. Caskey, *Chariot of Fire*, 180–83; Hedrick, *Harriet Beecher Stowe*, 122–32; Hill, "*Uncle Tom's Cabin* as a Religious Text"; Edward Wagenknecht, *Harriet Beecher Stowe: The Known and the Unknown* (New York: Oxford University Press, 1965), 203.

9. Caskey, *Chariot of Fire*, 181.

10. Harriet Beecher Stowe, *Sunny Memories of Foreign Lands*, 2 vols. (Boston, 1854), 2:277–79, 307; Harriet Beecher Stowe, *Footsteps of the Master* (London, 1877).

11. Harriet Beecher Stowe, letter to Hatty Stowe, n.d., Beecher-Stowe Collection, Arthur and Elizabeth Schlesinger Library on the History of Women in America, Radcliffe College, Cambridge, Mass.; Calvin Stowe, letter to Harriet Beecher Stowe, February 9, 1857, Harriet Beecher Stowe Center, Hartford, Ct.

12. See Harriet Beecher Stowe, *Woman in Sacred History: A Series of Sketches Drawn from Scriptural, Historical, and Legendary Sources* (New York, 1874).

13. Harriet Beecher Stowe, letter to Charles E. Stowe, [early February 1881], Beecher-Stowe Collection; Harriet Beecher Stowe, letter to Charles E. Stowe, fragment, n.d., Beecher-Stowe Collection.

14. Calvin Stowe, description of Lane Seminary Library, in "Miscellany," *Western Christian Advocate*, October 6, 1837, 96; Lane Theological Seminary, "Appendix," in *Fifth Annual Report of the Trustees of the Cincinnati Lane Seminary: Together with the Laws of the Institution, and a Catalogue of the Officers and Students* (Cincinnati, 1834), 17–19; Calvin E. Stowe, preface to *Lectures on the Sacred Poetry of the Hebrews*, by Robert Lowth, trans. G. Gregory (Andover, 1829), xi; Herder [Calvin Stowe], "Ecclesiastes," *Western Monthly Magazine* 2 (September 1834): 458–63. Calvin Stowe often recycled material; the first half of "A Lecture on the First Chapter of Ecclesiastes" (*Biblical Repository and Classical Review*, April 1, 1850, 274–83), published under his name, is the "Ecclesiastes" article almost verbatim, indicating that the "Herder" pseudonym is his. See also T. J. S.'s "Stilling, Tholuck and the Universalists" (*Trumpet and Universalist Magazine*, January 28, 1843, 125), which refers to "Prof Stowe, the 'Herder' of the Cincinnati, Ohio, 'Watchman of the Valley.'"

15. Mark H. Davis, *Empathy: A Social Psychological Approach* (Madison, Wisc.: Brown and Benchmark, 1994), 5, 8–11; Michael L. Frazer, "John Rawls: Between Two Enlightenments," *Political Theory* 35 (December 2007): 779; Gustav Jahoda, "Theodor Lipps and the Shift from 'Sympathy' to 'Empathy,'" *Journal of the History of the Behavioral Sciences* 41 (Spring 2005): 154; Robert C. Solomon, *In Defense of Sentimentality* (New York: Oxford University Press, 2004), 72–73.

16. Johann Gottfried von Herder, "On the Cognition and Sensation of the Human Soul," in *Johann Gottfried von Herder: Philosophical Writings*, ed. and trans. Michael N. Forster (Cambridge: Cambridge University Press, 2002), 218.

17. Johann Gottfried von Herder, "Herder's Letters Relating to the Study of Divinity. Letter II," trans. Henry Ware, *Christian Disciple and Theological Review*, November 1, 1820, 418.

18. Calvin E. Stowe, *The Right Interpretation of the Sacred Scriptures: The Helps and the Hindrances. An Inaugural Discourse Delivered at Andover, Sept. 1, 1852* (Andover, 1853), 15.

19. Ibid., 19. See, for instance, Harriet Beecher Stowe, "Old Testament Pictures.—No. 1," *New-York Evangelist* 15, no. 46 (Nov. 14, 1844): 1.

20. Johann Gottfried von Herder, "Herder's Letters Relating to the Study of

Divinity. Letter III," trans. Henry Ware, *Christian Disciple and Theological Review*, January 1, 1821, 7.

21. Herder, "Letter II," 425.

22. Herder, "Letter II," 425; Johann Gottfried von Herder, *The Spirit of Hebrew Poetry*, 2 vols., trans. James Marsh (Burlington, Vt., 1833), 2:8.

23. Ibid., 2:9.

24. Calvin Stowe, *Right Interpretation*, 10. Also see Calvin Stowe, introduction to *Philosophy of the Plan of Salvation: A Book for the Times*, [by James Barr Walker] (Salem, Ohio, 1845), 7; Calvin Stowe, *Introduction to the Criticism and Interpretation of the Bible, Designed for the Use of Theological Students, Bible Classes, and High Schools*, 2 vols. (Cincinnati, 1835), 1:19; and Calvin Stowe, "On Expository Preaching and the Principles Which Should Guide Us in the Exposition of Scripture," *Biblical Repository and Quarterly Observer* 5 (April 1835): 394.

25. Harriet Beecher Stowe, "Heinrich Stilling," *New-York Evangelist*, February 6, 1851, 1. See also Harriet Beecher Stowe, letter to Mary Claflin, March 2, 1872, in which she refers to the Old Testament as "those childlike old days of simple faith"; and Harriet Beecher Stowe, letter to Charles E. Stowe, June 24 1879, both at the Harriet Beecher Stowe Center.

26. Stowe, *Uncle Tom's Cabin*, 132.

27. Ibid.; Acts 4:13, King James Version.

28. Stowe, *Uncle Tom's Cabin*, 280, 162. I acknowledge the arguments regarding the negative uses of the romantic racialist thought behind descriptions of African Americans as "simple" and "childlike." However, the evangelical context of the childlike character in Stowe—especially the childlike reader—has largely been missed. As Miriam Elizabeth Burstein notes, "the figure of the godly child, inspired by Matthew 18:2–5, whose innocence enables him or her to read and even expound on the Bible in a way that educated adults cannot," had become "a staple of evangelical fiction" by the time of Sir Walter Scott (*Victorian Reformations: Historical Fiction and Religious Controversy, 1820–1900* [Notre Dame, Ind.: University of Notre Dame Press, 2014], 42). In various works, Stowe attributes positive childlike qualities to men, women, adults, children, whites, African Americans, intellectuals, and those with little formal education. For critiques of romantic racialist childlike traits that are applied to African Americans, see Elizabeth Ammons, "Freeing the Slaves and Banishing the Blacks: Racism, Empire, and Africa in *Uncle Tom's Cabin*," in *Harriet Beecher Stowe's "Uncle Tom's Cabin": A Casebook*, ed. Elizabeth Ammons (New York: Oxford University Press, 2007), 241; and Robin Bernstein, *Racial Innocence: Performing American Childhood from Slavery to Civil Rights* (New York: New York University Press, 2011), 25. On childlike men as devalued in British Victorian literature, see Claudia Nelson, *Precocious Children and Childish Adults: Age Inversion in Victorian Literature* (Baltimore: Johns Hopkins University Press, 2012), 8–9.

29. Stowe, *Uncle Tom's Cabin*, 280–81.

30. Stowe, *Right Interpretation*, 11.

31. Stowe, *Uncle Tom's Cabin*, 280.

32. Herder, *Spirit*, 2:312.

33. Stowe, *Uncle Tom's Cabin*, 280.

34. Ibid., 281; Revelation 15:2, King James Version; H., "Professor Stowe's Lectures. Lecture IX. Subject.—Genuineness of the Apocalypse or Revelation of St. John," *Cincinnati Journal*, January 9, 1835, 7; Stowe, *Introduction to the Criticism and Interpretation of the Bible*, 1:151.

35. Stowe, *Uncle Tom's Cabin*, 324. The prayer is recorded in Matthew 11:25 and Luke 10:21, King James Version.

36. Ibid., 325–26.

37. Harriet Beecher Stowe, "How Do We Know?," in *The May Flower, and Miscellaneous Writings* (Boston, 1869), 245–46.

38. Stowe, *Uncle Tom's Cabin*, 160.

39. Hortense Spillers, "Changing the Letter: The Yokes, the Jokes of Discourse, or, Mrs. Stowe, Mr. Reed," in *Slavery and the Literary Imagination: Selected Papers from the English Institute 1987*, ed. Deborah McDowell and Arnold Rampersad (Baltimore: Johns Hopkins University Press, 1989), 56; Colleen Glenney Boggs, *Transnationalism and American Literature: Literary Translation, 1773–1892* (New York: Routledge, 2007), 136; Spillers, "Changing the Letter," 45; Roger Thompson, "Stowe, Slavery, and the Culture of Literacy Reform" (paper presented at the annual conference of the American Literature Association, San Francisco, May 2004); Mason I. Lowance, Jr., "Biblical Typology and the Allegorical Mode: The Prophetic Strain," in *The Stowe Debate: Rhetorical Strategies in "Uncle Tom's Cabin,"* ed. Mason I. Lowance, Jr., Ellen E. Westbrook, and R. C. De Prospo (Amherst: University of Massachusetts Press, 1994), 174.

40. Marcus Wood, *Slavery, Empathy, and Pornography* (Oxford: Oxford University Press, 2002), 186–87; Gregg Crane, *The Cambridge Introduction to the Nineteenth-Century American Novel* (New York: Cambridge University Press, 2007), 112; Sarah Robbins, *Managing Literacy, Mothering America: Women's Narratives on Reading and Writing in the Nineteenth Century* (Pittsburgh: University of Pittsburgh Press, 2004), 273, 129–134.

41. Jan Pilditch, "Rhetoric and Satire," in Lowance et al., *Stowe Debate*, 62–63; Josephine Donovan, *Uncle Tom's Cabin: Evil, Affliction, and Redemptive Love* (Boston: Twayne, 1991), 46; Christina Zwarg, "Fathering and Blackface in Uncle Tom's Cabin," *NOVEL* 22 (Spring 1989): 283; Gregg Camfield, *Sentimental Twain: Samuel Clemens in the Maze of Moral Philosophy* (Philadelphia: University of Pennsylvania Press, 1994), 53–54; Wood, *Slavery*, 188; Les Harrison, *The Temple and the Forum: The American Museum and Cultural Authority in Hawthorne, Melville, Stowe, and Whitman* (Tuscaloosa: University of Alabama Press, 2007), 126, 136; Boggs, *Transnationalism*, 137.

42. Stowe, *Right Interpretation*, 21.

43. On the relationship of academic theology to the faith of "the lowly" in Stowe, see Nancy Koester, *Harriet Beecher Stowe: A Spiritual Life* (Grand Rapids,

Mich.: Eerdmans, 2014), 187; and Clíona Ó Gallchoir, "*Uncle Tom's Cabin* and the Irish National Tale," in *Transatlantic Stowe: Harriet Beecher Stowe and European Culture*, ed. Denise Kohn, Sarah Meer, and Emily B. Todd (Iowa City: University of Iowa Press, 2006), 39, 43.

44. E. D., "Cicero on Immortality," *Literary World*, July 12, 1851, 29.

45. For an overview of Cicero's continuing influence in nineteenth-century Anglo-American culture, see Mary Rosner, "Cicero in Nineteenth-Century England and America," *Rhetorica* 4 (Spring 1986): 153–82. For a representative antebellum account of Cicero's grief over his daughter's death, see "The Ancients. Cicero" [excerpted from *Universal Biography*], *Family Lyceum*, January 5, 1833, 81.

46. Marcus Tullius Cicero, *Cicero on the Immortality of the Soul or Quaestionum Tusculanarum*, ed. M[oses] Stuart (Andover, 1833); E. D., "Cicero on Immortality," 29.

47. J. N. B., "Cicero on the Immortality of the Soul. [From the Tusculan Questions.]" *Christian Examiner and General Review* 33 (November 1842): 129–30; "Cicero on the Immortality of the Soul," *Literary World*, May 10, 1851, 378; "Cicero on the Immortality of the Soul," *Southern and Western Monthly Magazine and Review* 2 (December 1845): 416.

48. J. N. B., "Cicero on the Immortality of the Soul," 129–30.

49. "Publishers' Circular," *Literary World*, May 3, 1851, 361; "Cicero on the Immortality of the Soul," *Literary World*, 378; E. D., "Cicero on Immortality," 29.

50. Stowe, *Uncle Tom's Cabin*, 417.

51. Harold K. Bush, *Continuing Bonds with the Dead: Parental Grief and Nineteenth-Century American Authors* (Tuscaloosa: University of Alabama Press, 2016), 36–64.

52. John 20:25–29, King James Version.

53. "A Few Thoughts on Cicero," *Southern Literary Messenger* 16 (August 1850): 499.

54. Stowe, *Uncle Tom's Cabin*, 161.

55. Matthew P. Brown, "Book History, Sexy Knowledge, and the Challenge of the New Boredom," *American Literary History* 16, no. 4 (2004): 698.

56. Stowe, *Uncle Tom's Cabin*, 160–61.

57. Bruns, *Hermeneutics Ancient and Modern*, 139.

58. Stowe, *Uncle Tom's Cabin*, 203, 223, 316, 326, 374, 386–87.

59. Stowe, *Uncle Tom's Cabin*, 416, 374–417; Wood, *Slavery*, 188; Boggs, *Transnationalism*, 136–37; Harrison, *The Temple and the Forum*, 126, 136.

60. Stowe, *Uncle Tom's Cabin*, 416.

61. P. Gabrielle Foreman, "'This Promiscuous Housekeeping': Death, Transgression, and Homoeroticism in *Uncle Tom's Cabin*," in Ammons, *Harriet Beecher Stowe's "Uncle Tom's Cabin*," 190.

62. Stowe, *Uncle Tom's Cabin*, 446; Romans 8:35, King James Version.

63. Jacqueline R. deVries, abstract of "Rediscovering Christianity after the Postmodern Turn," *Feminist Studies* 31 (Spring 2005): 135.

CHAPTER 7

THE "ART OF ATTAINING TRUTH" IN *MOBY-DICK*

Print Technologies, Hermeneutics, and Castaway Readers

Jeffrey Bilbro

AFTER SURVIVING his first night of sharing a bed with a cannibal, Ishmael finds that bedfellow attempting to read a book. Queequeg's manner of interacting with this foreign technology is rather odd: he simply counts the pages, pausing at times to look "vacantly around him, and giving utterance to a long-drawn gurgling whistle of astonishment."[1] While some of my students also do this when they first pick up *Moby-Dick*, they generally discover more effective ways of reading. Yet although Queequeg's method doesn't lead to a determinate meaning, he models a humble approach to an uninterpretable text.

As we discover later, Queequeg's own body is tattooed with another text. These "hieroglyphic marks" inscribe "a complete theory of the heavens and the earth, and a mystical treatise on the art of attaining truth; so that Queequeg in his own proper person [is] a riddle to unfold; a wondrous work in one volume; but whose mysteries not even himself [can] read." This unreadable text infuriates Ahab, who exclaims, "Oh, devilish tantalization of the gods!"[2] Yet Queequeg's response to his unreadable body parallels his attitude toward the wondrous printed book; he is content to be a living witness to truths he cannot read or understand. Through such contrasting attitudes toward textually mediated truth, *Moby-Dick* suggests that, even when aided by print technology, texts cannot contain and master meaning. In fact, the hermeneutic posture that can lead us into greatest intimacy with truth is not a panoptic position of control and mastery but a humble, castaway perspective, one willing to be swallowed by truth.[3]

Many critics have discussed *Moby-Dick*'s concern with questions of epistemology and interpretation. As David S. Reynolds has demonstrated, situating the novel within its cultural, religious, and even technological context brings Melville's literary masterpiece into greater focus. A consideration of nineteenth-century claims to textual authority and perspicuity reveals the significance of the hermeneutic postures and methods that Melville depicts in his narrative. Readers in the early republican print culture were conditioned to presume that printed texts could clearly communicate meaning: Protestants emphasized *sola scriptura* and the plain sense of the Bible, and citizens of the new republic relied on the Constitution as the textual authority that would knit together a diverse nation. These traditions asserted that if readers just read in the right way, they could agree on the essential meaning of a given text. From its beginnings, however, the republic witnessed vigorous disputes about these authoritative texts, leading, in the antebellum period, to a proliferation of Protestant denominations and the constitutional crises that culminated in the Civil War. In light of these interpretive disagreements, Melville had little faith in textual perspicuity; instead, he considered what readerly attitudes and virtues might be required for a community based on opaque, polysemous texts. *Moby-Dick* thus imagines different textual forms and different reading practices to explore which ones foster the kinds of virtuous reading necessary to form and sustain community. From the nautical charts Ahab uses to track Moby Dick, to the print forms Ishmael experiments with to contain the meaning of the whale, to the doubloon that the *Pequod*'s crew members strive to interpret, Melville's book encourages its readers to consider how they make meaning from texts. When perspicuity is the ultimate goal of textual forms and interpretive practices, readers become prone to vices such as arrogance and coercion. The novel, then, aims at fostering hermeneutic virtues—particularly humility and a willingness to listen to marginalized readers—rather than pursuing clarity. *Moby-Dick* suggests that even if interpretive consensus remains elusive, *how* Americans go about seeking such agreement determines the difference between civil war and union, chaos and harmony, death and life. Cultivating such humility and contentment with mystery may lead a community of readers closer to the truth than does an obsessive pursuit of certainty.

In *The New Organon* Francis Bacon marvels at the "force, power and consequences" of three technologies: "the art of printing, gunpowder and the nautical compass."[4] While printing may not appear powerful to us, its strength was readily apparent to those such as Bacon who lived in the wake of its invention. Particularly in America, it became a means of controlling and unifying a sprawling, chaotic culture. Any powerful technology brings temptations to abuse it, and in *Moby-Dick* Melville probes the ways in which print's ability to arrange and control ideas can tempt readers to use that power for selfish ends.

The development of print and the complex influences of this technology on western culture have been the subject of much scholarly debate, and the precise contours of this influence remain contested.[5] Nevertheless, most scholars agree that print facilitated the rise of the Protestant Reformation, republican government, and the scientific revolution. None of these developments originated in America, but for a variety of reasons their combination proved particularly powerful there.[6] By making texts accessible, perspicuous, and thus controllable, print makes the world itself appear to be similarly manageable. American print culture fostered the belief that print could represent truth, rendering it democratically perspicuous so that everyone could control and master truth.

Walter Ong traces the way in which Ramist logic and the development of print combined to make knowledge more spatial and visual, which renders ideas more discrete and manipulable.[7] Following these developments, "an epistemology based on the notion of truth as 'content' begins to appear. Out of the twin notions of content and analysis is bred the vast idea-, system-, and method-literature of the seventeenth and eighteenth centuries . . . [which] conceived of . . . box-like units laid hold of by the mind in such a way that they are fully and adequately treated by being 'opened' in an analysis."[8] As Chad Wellmon aptly summarizes, "the technology of print made knowledge manageable, accessible, and available."[9] As we will see, however, Ishmael and Ahab discover that Moby Dick embodies a kind of truth that cannot be reduced to the confines of print.

In part, appeals to textual authorities played such a large role in America's early republican culture because of the lack of institutional authorities—king, aristocracy, centralized church structure—that could unify the culturally and geographically diverse population. The absence of these other forces of social cohesion put an immense burden on texts.[10] This burden became particularly heavy because it was reinforced by the domains of both religion and politics. In each of these domains, texts were elevated to authoritative roles under a twin set of philosophical justifications: Scottish common sense held that everyone had the basic capacity to reason and interpret, and Baconian induction provided the method that each person could follow to reach the truth about a given phenomenon or text. Antebellum America comprised diverse and wildly disparate communities, and in the midst of this rather chaotic situation, a national unified culture was formed by reference to the Bible and the founding documents.[11] These appeals shaped an understanding of print as definitive, authoritative, and unifying, when, as the facts on the ground stubbornly indicated, print does not always have these effects.

American Protestants, particularly after the Revolutionary period, took the Reformation credo of *sola scriptura* more seriously than its European adherents ever did. As the historian Mark Noll explains in describing the shift from the religion of the revolutionary period to that of the antebellum era, "divine revelation was equated more simply with the Bible alone than with Scripture embedded in a self-conscious ecclesiastical tradition. . . . Theological method came to rely less on instinctive deference to inherited confessions and more on self-evident propositions organized by scientific method."[12] Whereas the original European Reformers such as Martin Luther and John Calvin maintained the need for ecclesially sanctioned biblical interpretation, by the mid-eighteenth century many Americans embraced a more democratic view of interpretation, claiming that any individual could examine the scriptures and determine their clear meaning.[13]

As the works of Charles Hodge demonstrate, many American theologians had confidence in the ability of individuals to read the Bible and inductively determine its clear meaning. Hodge, who became the principal of Princeton Theological Seminary in 1851, famously declares in the introduction to his *Systematic Theology*, "The Bible is to the theologian what nature is to the man of science. It is his store-house of facts; and his method of ascertaining what the Bible teaches, is the same as that which the natural philosopher adopts to ascertain what nature teaches."[14] This view of the Bible as a "store-house" parallels Ong's observation that print encourages readers to imagine knowledge in spatial metaphors and then to access and manipulate it via proper analysis. Later in his book, Hodge asserts under the heading "Perspicuity of the Scriptures. The Right of Private Judgment" that the "Bible is a plain book. It is intelligible by the people. And they have the right, and are bound to read and interpret it for themselves; so that their faith may rest on the testimony of the Scriptures, and not on that of the Church."[15] He recognizes the dangers of such a position: "if every man is at liberty to exalt his own intuitions, as men are accustomed to call their strong convictions, we should have as many theologies in the world as there are thinkers." Yet he quickly asserts this won't be a problem because the Bible is so obviously perspicuous: "What is self-evidently true, must be proved to be so, and is always recognized in the Bible as true."[16] The passive construction of the sentence indicates the flaw in Hodge's logic; his sentence leaves out the subject, the interpreter who must do this "recogniz[ing]," a flaw that Melville also points out in "The Doubloon" chapter in *Moby-Dick*. It was exactly this issue—the ability of different interpreting subjects to recognize vastly different truths in the Bible—that led to the proliferation of Protestant sects in the first half of the nineteenth century.

Similar interpretive problems marked the political debates of the early republic. It is hard today to recognize the audacious innovation the nation's founders made when they based the legitimacy of the new nation on a printed document. One of the purposes of that document was to "form a more perfect Union," yet the Constitution arose out of fierce debate. As Cathy Davidson observes, "popular history—and especially our legal system's continual reference back to Constitutional precedence—has made the Constitution a monument, not the result of a process, representing only a fraction of those living in what would become the United States, that was sometimes divisive, contentious, and even cynical."[17] The wide dissemination that print made possible helped enshrine the Constitution as a monument held in common by all; yet as each person made reference to this monument, fierce interpretive disputes arose.

By the time Melville wrote *Moby-Dick*, these religious and political divisions could not be ignored and, by threatening the confidence that readers had in printed texts, caused many authors in the antebellum period to question the authority and perspicuity of print. As Brian Yothers observes, "an often-overlooked source of the epistemological uncertainties that pervade the gothic works of Poe, Hawthorne, and Melville is the frequently chaotic religious pluralism of nineteenth-century America. Nineteenth-century Americans faced a bewildering variety of religious options that offered widely disparate ontological, ethical, and epistemological bases for understanding their world."[18] Michael Warner makes a similar argument in the context of the political sphere, noting that as the "republican ideology of print eroded, . . . an official hermeneutics emerged."[19] He points out that this shift had important consequences for antebellum literature: "It was of no small importance that the years in which literary culture was established in this country were also the years of protracted constitutional crisis. . . . [I]t became possible to locate in language the conflicted and mediated character of truth, nonetheless maintaining the authoritative character of that truth."[20] Language continued to be the means of ascertaining and understanding truth, but authors were increasingly aware that, even when allied to print technology, language was not perspicuous and could not easily unify disparate readers.

In fact, the print technology that once seemed to promise the diffusion of language and promote unity across the sprawling American culture became increasingly divisive in the 1830s and 1840s with the development of new paper-making and printing technologies—for instance, the cylinder press—that made newspapers and pamphlets much cheaper.[21] While Reynolds rightly observes that "it is impossible to measure precisely the effects of a journalistic revolution that had a lasting impact upon all aspects of America's cultural life, including its major literature," what does seem clear is that the increasingly varied and sensational perspectives appearing in print counteracted the unifying influence of authoritative texts such as the Bible and the Constitution.[22] As Nathan Hatch argues about the expansion of cheap religious print, "a profound irony, in fact, surrounds the success of religious printing. Instead of the press serving as truth's herald, it often amplified a welter of competing voices, proving, if anything, that no truth had inherent power."[23] Whether or not it proves that truth had no inherent power, the proliferation of cheap print at least cast doubt on print's ability to render truth accessible and perspicuous.

Thus, the irony that Hatch describes was the great paradox of print in the antebellum period. Earlier, there had been a sense that the diffusion of print was itself a guarantee of the diffusion of republican, Christian virtue.[24] But the rise of new religious movements, constitutional crises, and the penny press undermined this naïve confidence. In the face of a chaotic proliferation of viewpoints, readers were tempted to interpret selectively and selfishly, choosing meanings that suited their private interests. In response, authors such as Melville attempted to reimagine print technologies and reading practices in ways that would enable readers to navigate this sea of print and approach truth. *Moby-Dick* dramatizes the perils of selfish interpretation, of using print technologies in an attempt to control and limit complex meaning, but it also offers glimpses of more virtuous reading practices: reading marked by humility and intimacy may not lead to perspicuous truth, but it leaves the reader open to truth's self-revelation.

Print enables readers to imagine that they can stand outside and above the play of meaning to control and manipulate words on a spatial plane. This panoptic, divine perspective offers readers the illusion that they will be able to manage and grasp the truth. Ong links this spatial orientation with the rise of modern cartography: "Only after print and the extensive experience with maps that print implemented would human beings, when they thought about the cosmos or universe or 'world,' think primarily of something laid out before their eyes, as in a modern printed atlas, a vast surface or assemblage of surfaces (vision presents surfaces) ready to be 'explored.'"[25] Other scholars have considered the ways in which print and the ability to reproduce accurate copies of charts and images led to a reimagination of space and cartography, facilitating the development of modern maps that furthered exploration and navigation and, in the American context, national identity.[26] This is the process that Peter Candler, drawing on the work of Michel de Certeau, describes in terms of a contrast between medieval itinerary maps, which represent humans on a journey toward God, and modern spatial maps, which place humans in the position of God.[27]

In "The Chart" chapter, Ahab enacts this print-derived orientation toward space, relying on his nautical charts to track down and capture the elusive Moby Dick. "Almost every night" he retires to "the solitude of his cabin [and] ponder[s] over his charts." He does this in a quest for certitude: "with the charts of all four oceans before him, Ahab was threading a maze of currents and eddies, with a view to the more certain accomplishment of that monomaniac thought of his soul." The narrator acknowledges that it may seem to be "an absurdly hopeless task thus to seek out one solitary creature in the unhooped oceans of this planet"; but armed with his charts and his knowledge of ocean currents, Ahab has confidence that he can master these chaotic "unhooped oceans." This mastery serves his quest to find the "particular set time or place . . . when all possibilities would become probabilities, and, as Ahab fondly thought, every possibility the next thing to a certainty." The captain strives to turn the possibilities of Moby Dick's location into probabilities and then certainties, and he relies on his charts to achieve this mastery of space. He even figures his technical ability in textual images: "And have I not tallied the whale, Ahab would mutter to himself, as after poring over his charts till long after midnight he would throw himself back in reveries—tallied him, and shall he escape?"[28] *Tallied* is a textual mark made over a word to cross it off and thus control it. Ahab tries to control Moby Dick via his charts and tallies, yet the whale escapes textual boundaries.

The chapter ends with a reference to Prometheus and his eternal punishment, foreshadowing the price Ahab will pay for his technical mastery. While the captain's charts enable him to stand in the place of the gods, looking out over the globe and plotting his movements, they cannot make his hunt successful. Like Prometheus' fire, the charts bring only a pyrrhic victory. Ahab realizes this later in the narrative when the *Pequod* finally reaches the fateful Season-on-the-Line. As he uses his quadrant to calculate the ship's latitude, he complains to the sun that, while he can use his charts and quadrant to make the sun tell him where he is, he cannot extract information about where he or others will be: "thou high and mighty Pilot! thou tellest me truly where I *am*—but canst thou cast the least hint where I *shall* be? Or canst thou tell where some other thing besides me is this moment living? Where is Moby Dick?"[29] Medieval itinerary maps provided the opposite kind of information; rather than representing space as passive and "laid out before [the viewer's] eyes," they oriented all space around the holy city of Jerusalem where the creator of the world was born and died.[30] In this way, medieval maps told pilgrims where they should go, even if they weren't much help in the mundane matters of travel. In the absence of such prescriptive, hierarchical guidance, Ahab becomes frustrated with his quadrant, throws it to the deck, and stomps on it, determining to be guided only by horizontal instruments such as "the level ship's compass, and the level dead-reckoning."[31] Ahab desperately desires to occupy the panoptic, divine position to which charts promise to elevate the viewer; and when he realizes this status is an illusion and that his charts won't tell him where his prey is, where he will be, or where he should go—in other words, that they won't make him godlike—he prefers to travel without vertical guidance rather than cede this place of authority to the sun or to God.

Ishmael never displays the blind arrogance that characterizes Ahab's use of print technology; his efforts to use print to render a chaotic world perspicuous and controllable are marked by irony and an awareness that, for all its power, print cannot adequately represent, much less contain and manage, authoritative truth. His textual methods and reading practices, then, point toward a more humble way of relating to meaning: "Surely all this is not without meaning. And still deeper the meaning of that story of Narcissus, who because he could not grasp the tormenting, mild image he saw in the fountain, plunged into it and was drowned. But that same image, we ourselves see in all rivers and oceans. It is the image of the ungraspable phantom of life; and this is the key to it all."[32]

All of these facts aren't without meaning, but they nonetheless remain unclear. The lesson Ishmael manages to draw from the myth of Narcissus bears an all too clear relevance to Ahab's fate, and Ishmael's word *grasp* identifies the captain's primary disposition, which we have already seen modeled in his use of his charts. Yet Ishmael's grammar here remains ambiguous and his meaning ungraspable. What is the "it" that is the image of the ungraspable phantom of life? What is the "this" that is the "key to it all"? Is "it" the meaning of water's pull upon humans, which remains unstated, the still deeper meaning of Narcissus, which also remains unstated, or the image that we see—perhaps our own image reflected—in bodies of water? Ishmael's grammar, like the list of facts he piles up, remains ambiguous and open to conflicting interpretations.

Perhaps most obviously, these conflicting voices and the different interpretations they offer are dramatized in "The Doubloon" chapter. Early in the voyage, Ahab nails a gold doubloon to the mast and declares that the first crew member who hails Moby Dick will receive the coin as his reward. This doubloon, stamped with "strange figures and inscriptions," is certainly an accessible text, but it defies all attempts at interpretation. On one particular morning, Ahab pauses in front of the coin "to interpret for himself in some monomaniac way whatever significance might lurk in [it]." As a train of interpreters troops in front of the coin—Ahab, Starbuck, Stub, Flask, the Manxman, Queequeg, Fedallah, and finally Pip—it, as Ahab remarks, "to each and every man in turn but mirrors back his own mysterious self." To paraphrase Hodge, we appear to have as many interpretations of the coin as there are readers. Stubb, attempting to use a printed text to clarify the ambiguous coin, brings out the almanac, but when that doesn't solve his perplexity, he becomes frustrated and exclaims, "Book! you lie there; the fact is, you books must know your places. You'll do to give us the bare words and facts, but we come in to supply the thoughts." Unable to make heads or tails of the coin itself, Stubb proceeds to supply thoughts as he pleases, inventing a story out of the zodiac symbols. At one point, while watching this ongoing drama, he observes, "There's another rendering now; but still one text." His insight is seconded by Pip, the African American boy who earlier in the novel went mad after

Stubb abandoned him in the ocean while their boat was tied to a fleeing whale. Watching this series of interpreters, Pip comes up to the coin and begins conjugating: "I look, you look, he looks; we look, ye look, they look." He repeats this conjugation three times, flustering Stubb, who feels guilty for causing the boy's apparent imbecility. Yet as Ishmael notes elsewhere in reference to Pip, "man's insanity is heaven's sense."[33]

Stubb flees Pip's prophetic diagnosis of the interpretive chaos wrought by individual, narcissistic modes of looking. When he is frustrated by the obduracy of the world, he either retreats behind his "invulnerable jollity of indifference and recklessness" or resorts to might-makes-right violence.[34] Reynolds links Stubb's attitude to the "comic violence of frontier humor," and this anarchic setting coincides with Ishmael's earlier description of the fast-fish, loose-fish legal code, a code whose "commentaries" on hard-to-interpret texts consist of "hard words and harder knocks."[35] If a community can't reach interpretive consensus, those individuals who have authority get to force their interpretation on those beneath them.[36]

Stubb's sharkish propensities are highlighted when, after killing a whale, he eats a blubber steak while, in the water below, the sharks feast on the same whale, "mingling their mumblings with his own mastications." While eating his whale, he mercilessly berates Fleece, the African American cook, for supposedly overcooking his steak and, as a sort of punishment, commands him to preach to the sharks below. After enduring Stubb's abuse as best he can, the cook finally gets away, commenting to the reader, "Wish, by gor! whale eat him, 'stead of him eat whale. I'm bressed if he ain't more of shark dan Massa Shark hisself."[37] Like Pip, Fleece voices the final and most perceptive interpretation of the preceding scene; both these characters are on the bottom of the *Pequod*'s social hierarchy, yet this position provides more interpretive insight than being on top does. Readers who have power are more tempted to see their own desires reflected in texts and to use those texts as means of control. But Melville figures outcasts and castaways as more receptive and thus more perceptive readers.

Fleece's wish that the whale would eat Stubb recalls the other sermon in *Moby-Dick* when Father Mapple preaches about the story of

Jonah. In that biblical story, a man is eaten by a whale. Rather than trying to contain the whale inside the covers of a book, which Ishmael's efforts show is a futile hope, Jonah is himself contained inside the whale's covers, and from this uncomfortable, humbling position he finally listens to God's call. Being eaten, being at the bottom of the sharkish heap—whether as the swallowed prophet, the castaway Pip, or the outcast Ishmael—seems to be the place where one learns to obey and love God. God rescues those who are lost, but those who think they are found may end up resisting his redemptive aims. At the end of the book, Ishmael is saved not by mastering some perspicuous print text but by clinging to an indecipherable pagan "mystical treatise on the art of attaining truth," a treatise originally tattooed on Queequeg's body and then carved on a wooden coffin.[38] A divine text may be a life buoy, but its salvific revelation does not depend on Ishmael being able to grasp its meaning.

The biblical yarns from which Ishmael weaves the conclusion of his narrative likewise suggest the necessity of humbly bearing witness to a truth that can save those who accept their inability to comprehend it. The "Epilogue" begins with an epigraph from Job that links Ishmael to one of Job's servants delivering news of the disasters that wipe out his wealth and family. Ishmael—whose name recalls the son whom Abraham orphaned and cast out—thus becomes one who bears witness to us, his readers, about an overwhelming tragedy. He can only testify to us because when he became a castaway adrift on the open ocean, he was picked up by *Rachel*, a ship searching for "her missing children."[39] The captain of this ship has lost a son, along with a boat's crew, to Moby Dick, and his ship's name alludes to the mothers who mourned when Herod killed all the boys around Bethlehem who were under two years of age.[40] Herod's reaction to a strangely significant star and an incarnate Word whose meaning he couldn't master was to lash out in violence. His response to an opaque sign prefigures those of both Ahab and Stubb. The *Pequod* begins her voyage on Christmas Day, and her tragic end stands as an example of what happens when readers in power are unable to gain mastery over a word of divine revelation. The castaway, the orphaned Ishmael, unlike these more powerful readers, bears witness to a redemption that he cannot explain or understand.

In Melville's world, what you don't know can still hurt you. But it may also save you. Ahab and Stubb both respond to indeterminacy with print technologies—charts and almanacs—and then, when these fail, with indifference or violence. Stubb avoids the prophetic words of his subordinates, and Ahab tries to wreak his rage on the whale. Ishmael and Queequeg model a more healthy alternative to opaque texts; their inability to read each other's texts—and, in Queequeg's case, even his own text—does not prevent them from being friends. And, of course, when the *Pequod* goes down and Ishmael is left a castaway on the wide ocean, Queequeg's coffin-turned-life buoy, inscribed with "a mystical treatise on the art of attaining truth," bobs up from the sinking ship to save Ishmael's life. It turns out that the unreadable text, like the Word born on Christmas Day, can save even those who do not understand it. This realization can lead to humble piety or, as it seems to do in Ishmael's case, may engender an "easy sort of genial, desperado philosophy."[41] In either case, Melville critiques the understanding, derived from American print culture, that truth is perspicuous and can be easily grasped. Rather than basing unity, whether political or religious, on the ability of individual readers to reach the same interpretation of printed texts, Melville suggests that recognizing our shared befuddlement before the mysteries of the world may lead us to humbly bear witness to one another about the words that have saved us.

NOTES

1. Herman Melville, *Moby-Dick: Or, The Whale*, ed. Harrison Hayford, Hershel Parker, and G. Thomas Tanselle (1851; reprint, Chicago: Newberry Library and Northwestern University Press, 1988), 49.

2. Ibid., 480–81.

3. On this use of panoptic, see Michel Foucault, *Discipline and Punish: The Birth of the Prison*, trans. Alan Sheridan (New York: Pantheon, 1977).

4. Lisa Jardine and Michael Silverthorne, eds., *The New Organon* (Cambridge: Cambridge University Press, 2000), 100.

5. See, for example, Marshall McLuhan, *The Gutenberg Galaxy: The Making of Typographic Man* (Toronto: University of Toronto Press, 2011); Walter J. Ong, *Ramus, Method, and the Decay of Dialogue: From the Art of Discourse to the Art of Reason* (Chicago: University of Chicago Press, 2004); Walter J. Ong, *Orality and Literacy: The*

Technologizing of the Word (London: Routledge, 1991); and Elizabeth L. Eisenstein, *The Printing Press as an Agent of Change: Communications and Cultural Transformations in Early Modern Europe* (Cambridge: Cambridge University Press, 1980).

6. For an analysis of print culture and politics in early America, see Michael Warner, *The Letters of the Republic: Publication and the Public Sphere in Eighteenth-Century America* (Cambridge, Mass.: Harvard University Press, 1990); and Larzer Ziff, *Writing in the New Nation: Prose, Print, and Politics in the Early United States* (New Haven: Yale University Press, 1991).

7. Ong, *Ramus, Method, and the Decay of Dialogue*, 309–11. See also Ong, *Orality and Literacy*, 116–132.

8. Ong, *Ramus, Method, and the Decay of Dialogue*, 315.

9. Chad Wellmon, *Organizing Enlightenment: Information Overload and the Invention of the Modern Research University* (Baltimore: Johns Hopkins University Press, 2015), 43.

10. Mark Noll, for instance, notes the emergence of increasingly authoritative written confessions among American Protestants; in the absence of a central church hierarchy, these texts came to delimit the faith (*America's God: From Jonathan Edwards to Abraham Lincoln* [Oxford: Oxford University Press, 2002], 20–21).

11. On the religious shift toward textual authority in antebellum America, see Ibid., 4ff; and Nathan O. Hatch, *The Democratization of American Christianity* (New Haven: Yale University Press, 1989), 179–83.

12. Noll, *America's God*, 4.

13. Hatch, *The Democratization of American Christianity*, 179–83.

14. Charles Hodge, *Systematic Theology* (Grand Rapids, Mich.: Eerdmans, 1979), 10.

15. Ibid., 183. Noll claims that Hodge nuances this statement elsewhere, but he also points to Hodge as an exemplar of the common sense, inductive mode of reading the Bible (*America's God*, 316–19).

16. Hodge, *Systematic Theology*, 15.

17. Cathy Davidson, *Revolution and the Word: The Rise of the Novel in America*, rev. ed. (New York: Oxford University Press, 2004), 5.

18. Brian Yothers, "Terrors of the Soul: Religious Pluralism, Epistemological Dread, and Cosmic Exaltation in Poe, Hawthorne, and Melville," *Poe Studies/Dark Romanticism* 39–40, nos. 1–2 (2006): 136. George Marsden makes a similar observation: "Everything in the Common Sense Baconian system assumed the stability of truth which could be known objectively by careful observers in any age or culture. Almost all the other trends in nineteenth-century thought, however, pointed toward an opposite conclusion" ("Everyone One's Own Interpreter? The Bible, Science, and Authority in Mid-Nineteenth-Century America," in *The Bible in America: Essays in Cultural History*, ed. Nathan O. Hatch and Mark Noll [New York: Oxford University Press, 1982], 92). Drawing on one of these other trends, Thomas Werge situates *Moby-Dick* in the Calvinist epistemic tradition of human depravity, one opposed to

the optimistic common sense philosophy ("*Moby-Dick* and the Calvinist Tradition," *Studies in the Novel* 1, no. 4 [1969]: 484–506).

19. Warner, *The Letters of the Republic*, 114.
20. Ibid., 115.
21. David Hall traces the shift in reading practices brought about by the increased quantity and cheapness of print ("The Uses of Literacy in New England, 1600–1850," in *Printing and Society in Early America*, ed. William Leonard Joyce, David D. Hall, Richard D. Brown, and John B. Hench [Worcester, Mass.: American Antiquarian Society, 1983], 1–47).
22. David S. Reynolds, *Beneath the American Renaissance: The Subversive Imagination in the Age of Emerson and Melville* (New York: Oxford University Press, 2011), 171.
23. Nathan O. Hatch, "Elias Smith and the Rise of Religious Journalism in the Early Republic," in Joyce et al., *Printing and Society in Early America*, 277.
24. Warner, *The Letters of the Republic*, 118–50.
25. Ong, *Orality and Literacy*, 72.
26. For an analysis of printed maps and national identity in early America, see Martin Brückner, *The Geographic Revolution in Early America: Maps, Literacy, and National Identity* (Chapel Hill: University of North Carolina Press, 2006).
27. Peter M. Candler, Jr., *Theology, Rhetoric, Manuduction, or Reading Scripture Together on the Path to God* (Grand Rapids, Mich.: Eerdmans, 2006), 21–51. See also Michel de Certeau, *The Practice of Everyday Life* (Berkeley: University of California Press, 1988).
28. Melville, *Moby-Dick*, 198, 199, 200, 201.
29. Ibid., 501.
30. Ong, *Orality and Literacy*, 72.
31. Melville, *Moby-Dick*, 501.
32. Ibid., 5.
33. Ibid., 430, 431, 433, 434, 414.
34. Ibid., 186–87.
35. Reynolds, *Beneath the American Renaissance*, 546; Melville, *Moby-Dick*, 396.
36. Foucault also links a desire for a panoptic interpretive perspective that provides clarity with a willingness to resort to violence; see *Discipline and Punish*.
37. Melville, *Moby-Dick*, 293, 297.
38. Ibid., 480.
39. Ibid., 573.
40. Matthew 2:18.
41. Ibid., 480, 226.

CHAPTER 8

"NEW-BORN BARD[S] OF THE HOLY GHOST"

The American Bibles of Walt Whitman and Joseph Smith

Michael Robertson

DURING THE summer of 1857, Walt Whitman was afire with possibilities for a third, enlarged edition of *Leaves of Grass*. Confiding his ambitions to his notebook, he wrote hurriedly, "*The Great Construction* of the *New Bible*. Not to be diverted from the principal object—the main life work." In another note he grandiosely labeled *Leaves of Grass* the "Bible of the New Religion."[1] Viewed in isolation, Whitman's scriptural ambitions seem stunning, but David S. Reynolds has pointed out that antebellum America was "a remarkably fertile breeding ground of new religions." He explains, "The Shakers, the Mormons, the Oneidan perfectionists, Phoebe Palmer's perfectionist Methodists, the Seventh-Day Adventists, the spiritualists, and the Harmonialists all sprang up between the Revolution and the Civil War. . . . Several of the new movements were based on freshly inspired sacred writings meant to supplant or complement the Bible."[2]

The most famous—and, as time was to reveal, the most widely successful—of these new movements was Mormonism, which was founded following Joseph Smith's publication of the Book of Mormon in 1830. Reynolds mentions Smith only briefly in *Walt Whitman's America* in the course of placing Whitman in the context of antebellum Americans who sought to inaugurate a new religion. Other critics—I among them—have also noted the parallel ambitions of Walt Whitman and Joseph Smith but have then quickly moved on to seemingly firmer and certainly more comfortable historical and theological ground.[3] In this essay, however, I want to build on the project that Reynolds began in *Beneath the American Renaissance* of illuminating canonical works of American literature by placing them in dialogue with "submerged" writing of the nineteenth century.[4] Reading *Leaves of Grass* and the Book of Mormon side by side can not only shed light on Whitman's scriptural ambitions and the religious dimensions of *Leaves of Grass* but also contribute to recent efforts to bring the Book of Mormon into American literary studies, giving this complex text the sort of attentive reading that *Leaves of Grass* has long received.[5]

No one has previously compared *Leaves of Grass* and the Book of Mormon, although some critics have addressed the similarities between Whitman's poems and Smith's later revelations and prophecies.[6] Like those critics, I do not think that Whitman was directly influenced by Smith: the multitudes the poet contained did not include Mormon doctrine. While Whitman certainly knew of the Book of Mormon and may have authored an 1858 squib in the *Brooklyn Daily Times* about its new edition, there is no evidence that he ever opened its covers.[7] Rather, I want to locate both *Leaves of Grass* and the Book of Mormon in what Richard Brodhead has called "the history of prophetism in their time," a moment when "the category of the prophetic was unusually accessible in America."[8] Prophetic ambitions inspired figures as diverse as Ralph Waldo Emerson, who attacked the notion that prophetic revelation had ceased with the death of Jesus and urged readers to become themselves "new-born bard[s] of the Holy Ghost," and the enslaved Nat Turner, who in his *Confessions* detailed the divine revelations that had led to his revolt.[9] Smith and Whitman—along with Emerson, Turner, and a host of now lesser-known contemporaries—eagerly assumed the role of prophet. Yet at the same time both wore the prophetic mantle uneasily, for their claims to a unique gift were at odds with their democratic impulses. Thus, the Book of Mormon and *Leaves of Grass* are deeply conflicted texts that valorize the divinely inspired prophet even as they suggest that the prophetic gift is broadly accessible.

Visionary Origins of the New Scriptures

Here is a story about the origins of an American masterwork. In antebellum New York, a lightly educated man from a family barely clinging to the edges of respectability is vocationally and intellectually adrift. Dissatisfied with all existing churches, he becomes a religious seeker committed to forging his own spiritual path.[10] Although possessed of a fertile imagination, he has shown no evidence of special literary gifts. Then, abruptly, he brings forth a visionary prophetic work that offers itself as a new bible uniquely appropriate to the American nation. The work initially attracts relatively few readers, a substantial proportion of whom dismiss it as worthless. However, it wins some fervent adherents and, over a period of years, is issued in successive editions that, with increasing clarity, call attention to its scriptural dimensions.

I am speaking of Walt Whitman and *Leaves of Grass*. And I am speaking of Joseph Smith, Jr., and the Book of Mormon. Smith never had the opportunity to remark upon the striking parallels between his career and Whitman's; he was killed by a mob in 1844, eleven years before the first edition of *Leaves of Grass* appeared. However, Whitman made several comments on Mormonism, all of which were surprisingly favorable, given how widely reviled the religion, its founder, and its central text were in nineteenth-century America. "I have even heard him speak kindly of the Mormons," Whitman's friend Horace Traubel marveled in an article about the poet.[11] Whitman's favorable—or at least indulgent—attitude to Mormonism may well have come about because he recognized his commonalities with Joseph Smith and perceived that the abuse heaped on Smith for writing a supposedly inspired religious text was not unlike the attacks on the spiritually fervid *Leaves of Grass*. Joseph Smith and Walt Whitman were brothers under the skin.

The full story of the Book of Mormon's visionary origins is not widely known outside the field of American religious studies.[12] Smith was born in 1805 into a family of religious seekers who, when he was ten years old, moved from Vermont to western New York State, an area that during the early nineteenth century was swept by so many fiery religious revivals that the evangelist Charles Grandison Finney dubbed it the "burned-over district." "Millennial revivalism flourished more strongly here than in any other part of the country," according to Whitney R. Cross, the region's foremost historian.[13] Methodist and Baptist evangelical revivalism, with its emphasis on an intensely emotional conversion experience, was the best-known and most widespread expression of the era's religious fervor, but New York State proved hospitable to a wide array of lesser-known religious movements, including the communal kingdom of Robert Matthews, who reinvented himself as the prophet Matthias; the Oneida Perfectionists led by John Humphrey Noyes; and the Adventists inspired by William Miller, who prophesied that Christ's second coming would occur in 1844. The area was a "paradise of heterodoxy," according to one observer.[14] These new religious movements shared a distrust of existing churches and traditional religious authority, along with a corresponding conviction that individual experience and belief are the bedrock of religion. Other common features followed from these central premises: an emphasis on ecstatic personal experience; confidence that an unschooled layperson might well become a religious leader; a belief in continuing revelation, or illuminism (the idea that new light was being shed on God's nature and purpose); and an understanding that new sects and churches might spring from individual experience of the divine.[15]

Given the example of his spiritually questing parents and the intense religious atmosphere of the burned-over district, it is no surprise that Smith had his first religious vision at age fourteen. Retiring into the woods to pray, he saw a pillar of light descend and two personages, whom he identified as God and Christ, emerge from it. The boy earnestly asked them which sect he should join. They replied that he should "join none of them, for they were all wrong; and . . . all their creeds were an abomination." When he shared his vision with a Methodist preacher, the clergyman swatted away the young man's experience, saying that "it was all of the devil, that there were no such things as visions or revelations in these days; that all such things had ceased with the apostles, and that there would never be any more of them."[16] Richard Bushman argues convincingly that the preacher rejected Smith's vision not because of its strangeness but because of its familiarity. Ecstatic religious visions were common among people in the burned-over district, and these powerful personal experiences had the potential to disrupt church doctrine and a minister's pastoral authority over his congregation.[17]

Despite the disapproval of religious authorities, Smith's visions continued throughout his adolescence, culminating in September 1827, when the angel Moroni delivered to him the golden plates containing the text of the Book of Mormon. Because the plates were written in a previously unseen language, Smith required divine assistance to translate them. Fortunately, two "interpreters," or seer stones, which Moroni identified as the "Urim and Thummim" mentioned elliptically in the Hebrew Bible, accompanied the gold plates.[18] By looking through the stones, Smith was able to translate the text, which he dictated to a scribe.

Smith and his contemporaries provided extensive commentary about the process that resulted in the Book of Mormon.[19] We know much less about Whitman's composition of the first edition of *Leaves of Grass* (1855). However, analysis of his notebooks over the past twenty years has revealed that its composition took place within a much shorter time frame than scholars had previously believed.[20] Before the 1850s, Whitman never tried out the long unrhymed lines and ecstatic content that distinguish *Leaves of Grass*. Instead, throughout the 1840s he produced a limited number of conventional poems indistinguishable from the verse of other antebellum rhymesters. *Leaves of Grass* seemed to come out of nowhere. Yet unlike Smith, who put on record the angelic visitations that lay behind the Book of Mormon, Whitman made few comments about the composition of *Leaves*. His silence left acolytes such as Richard Maurice Bucke, a physician and amateur theorist of religion, free to speculate. How, Bucke wondered, could "writings of absolutely no value" be "*immediately* followed . . . by pages across each of which in letters of ethereal fire are written the words ETERNAL LIFE"?[21]

Bucke found his answer in "Song of Myself," Whitman's longest, most celebrated poem and the first poem in the first edition of *Leaves of Grass.* Bucke reprinted what he believed to be the key passage from "Song" in *Cosmic Consciousness* (1901), his study of religious visionaries.

> I believe in you my soul . . . . the other I am must not abase itself to you,
> And you must not be abased to the other.
>
> Loafe with me on the grass . . . loose the stop from your throat,
> Not words, not music or rhyme I want . . . not custom or lecture, not even the best,
> Only the lull I like, the hum of your valved voice.
>
> I mind how we lay in June, such a transparent summer morning;
> You settled your head athwart my hips and gently turned over upon me,
> And parted the shirt from my bosom-bone, and plunged your tongue to my barestript heart,
> And reached till you felt my beard, and reached till you held my feet.
>
> Swiftly arose and spread around me the peace and joy and knowledge that pass all the art and argument of the earth;
> And I know that the hand of God is the elderhand of my own,
> And I know that the spirit of God is the eldest brother of my own,
> And that all the men ever born are also my brothers . . . and the women my sisters and lovers,
> And that a kelson of the creation is love.[22]

Bucke was certain that this passage revealed that Whitman had experienced a mystical union with the divine, most likely in June 1853 or 1854. Given the absence of any confirmation of that hypothesis, subsequent biographers and critics have been more circumspect. However, the passage clearly falls into the tradition of mystical literature, which includes numerous instances of illumination depicted, as it is here, as an erotic encounter between the narrator and a divine personage. Critics have seen this passage as both homoerotic mysticism and an originary account of his poetic project, in which the poet's soul functions simultaneously as sexual partner and muse. It is, after all, the soul's tongue, an organ of speech as well as of sexual pleasure, that plunges to the poet's heart.[23]

A mystical homoerotic encounter was also central to Joseph Smith's life work. In an autobiographical account he described the first appearance of the angel Moroni:

> He had on a loose robe of most exquisite whiteness. . . . His hands were naked, and his arms also, a little above the wrist; so, also, were his feet naked, as were his legs, a little above the ankles. His head and neck were also bare. I could discover that he had no other clothing on but this robe, as it was open, so that I could see into his bosom.
>
> Not only was his robe exceedingly white, but his whole person was glorious beyond description, and his countenance truly like lightning. . . . He called me by name, and said unto me that he was a messenger sent from the presence of God to me, and that his name was Moroni; that God had a work for me to do.[24]

Both "Song of Myself" and the Book of Mormon arise from a visionary encounter with the personified divine, encounters that are simultaneously spiritual and sexual, that mix bared bosoms with a call to poetic-religious vocation.

Miriam Levering has noted that religion scholars tend to define scripture in three nonexclusive ways: as texts of supernatural origins, as texts that define our relationship to the sacred, or simply as texts that readers treat as sacred.[25] However, these categories miss a fourth way in which to define scripture: as material manifestation. Over successive editions, both the Book of Mormon and *Leaves of Grass* highlighted their scripturism through changes in physical format. The first edition of *Leaves* (1855) had no table of contents and the poems were untitled so that to the casual reader the entire volume appeared to be one long continuous poem. By the third edition (1860), not only were the poems titled but the stanzas numbered so that they had the appearance of verses in biblical books. That edition began with a new poem, "Proto-Leaf," which functions as a preview of the volume as a whole. "Proto-Leaf" trumpets Whitman's ambition to be the poet of the New World, glides over images that will appear later in the book, and with a crescendo of capital letters announces his two great themes, love and democracy, plus one more, which is "inclusive" of the other two and even "more resplendent": religion. "I . . .

announce that the real and permanent grandeur of These States must be their Religion," he proclaims. Whitman does not systematically describe the new American religion he is proposing, but he repeatedly emphasizes the sacredness of the individual ("I say no man . . . has begun to think how divine he himself is") and the divinity immanent within the material world ("Was somebody asking to see the Soul? / See! your own shape and countenance—persons, substances, beasts, the trees, the running rivers, the rocks and sands.")[26]

Remarkably, it took much longer for the Book of Mormon to assume its current format, which closely mimics conventional editions of the Bible. The first edition (1830) had a binding similar to that of mass-circulation Bibles distributed by the American Bible Society, but in all other ways the book's physical format resembled that of conventional texts.[27] Smith was listed on the title page as "Author and Proprietor," and the text itself was formatted in lengthy unnumbered paragraphs. Starting with the 1837 edition, Smith became identified as translator rather than author, but the chapters of the work's sixteen sections, or books, were not divided into short numbered verses until 1879, and the work was first issued in the double-column format traditional to Bible printings in 1920.[28]

As the Book of Mormon became more scriptural in its physical format, *Leaves of Grass* became less so. Whitman abandoned the numbered stanzas in the fourth (1867) and all succeeding editions of *Leaves of Grass*, and he replaced "Proto-Leaf" as the book's first poem with "One's-Self I Sing," a poem that highlights his work's political rather than religious dimensions. Nevertheless, visionary experience remained at the heart of every edition of *Leaves of Grass* and, of course, the Book of Mormon.

Re-enchantment, Democracy, Prophecy, and Narrative Frailty

The first six of the Book of Mormon's sixteen divisions, or books, are ascribed to Nephi, an Israelite living in Jerusalem early in the sixth century BCE. At the text's opening, Nephi's father, Lehi, hears with alarm multiple prophets' declarations that Jerusalem is damned. As he prays to the Lord, a pillar of fire descends, after which he throws himself onto his bed and is "carried away in a vision, even that he saw the Heavens open; and he thought he saw God sitting upon his throne."[29]

God tells Lehi that Jerusalem shall be destroyed and the Jews taken captive into Babylon.

Lehi's initial vision sets into motion the events that dominate almost all of the six hundred pages that follow. The Lord instructs Nephi to build a boat and sail with his family to the Promised Land—that is, the Americas. While this vision initiates the book's plot, it is not the last—or even the most consequential—of the prophecies revealed to Lehi, Nephi, and their descendants, the Nephites. Visions and revelations are at the heart of the Book of Mormon and its central claims: that the advent of Christ was revealed to the Nephites some six hundred years before the birth of Jesus, that God repeatedly spoke to the Nephites to remind them that their salvation depended on their Christian belief, and that the resurrected Christ appeared among the Nephites in America following his crucifixion in Jerusalem.

The Book of Mormon is centered around the idea of continuing revelation. God speaks directly to virtually every major character in the book, and the Nephites inhabit a world in which religious revelations are as common as dreams—where, in fact, the distinction between human dream and divine vision is obliterated, as Lehi emphasizes to his sons: "Behold, I have dreamed a dream; or, in other words, I have seen a vision." In the book's divinely suffused milieu, miracles become commonplace. On the voyage to the Promised Land, for example, Nephi's evil older brothers rebel against his leadership, tie him up, and take over the ship. Immediately, the ship's compass, "which had been prepared of the Lord, did cease to work," and a great storm arises that nearly destroys the ship.[30] However, as soon as the terrified brothers release Nephi, the compass returns to truth north, and the storm ceases.

"Why, who makes much of a miracle?"[31] The speaker is Walt Whitman, but it could be any of the Book of Mormon's multiple narrators, who inhabit an ancient world in which miracles are one of the ways in which God reveals himself. Whitman similarly regards miracles as evidence of the divine, but in his immanentist theology miracles are redefined:

Whether I walk the streets of Manhattan,
Or dart my sight over the roofs of houses toward the sky,

Or wade with naked feet along the beach just in the edge of the water,
Or stand under trees in the woods,
Or talk by day with any one I love, or sleep in the bed at night with any one I love,
. . . .
Or watch honey-bees busy around the hive of a summer forenoon,
. . . .
Or the exquisite delicate thin curve of the new moon in spring;
These with the rest, one and all, are to me miracles.[32]

The thriving city, the nearness of friends, the processes of nature—all are everyday miracles. *Leaves of Grass* sacralizes human beings, nature, and the created world, paralleling the Book of Mormon's insistence on continuing revelation and ongoing miracles.

Leaves of Grass and the Book of Mormon are both responses to what Max Weber called "the disenchantment of the world." Weber argued that the history of western culture since ancient times constituted a process of disenchantment in which "mysterious incalculable forces" such as gods and demons had been superseded by a rational, impersonal, and scientific orientation.[33] The adolescent Joseph Smith ran up against this disenchanted worldview when he detailed his first visionary experience to the Methodist preacher who assured him that "there were no such things as visions or revelations in these days." Walt Whitman entered a largely disenchanted world from birth, thanks to his father, a freethinker who revered Thomas Paine and passed on to his son a fondness for freethinkers' classics such as *The Age of Reason*. Yet *Leaves of Grass*, as fully as the Book of Mormon, can be seen as an instrument of what historians of modernity call *re-enchantment*—a restoration of the awed sense of mystery and wonder common in earlier eras and non-western cultures.[34]

Whitman's path to re-enchantment led through the corridors of nineteenth-century scientific empiricism. "Hurrah for positive science! long live exact demonstration!" cheers the speaker of "Song of Myself," who studs his poem with references to recent scientific discoveries: mastodons and nebulae, sauroids and gneiss. Yet the same poem includes the poet's mystical encounter with his soul and his paeans to the miracles of everyday life. "Gentlemen, to you the first honors always!" he says in salute to scientists, but he continues, "Your facts are useful, and yet they are not my dwelling, / I but enter by them to an area of my dwelling."[35] The poet's dwelling is, ultimately, the domain of the miraculous and soulful.[36]

The Book of Mormon's means of re-enchantment are both textual and extratextual. The textual narrative is filled with God's miraculous interventions on behalf of his previously unknown chosen people, the Nephites, who emigrated from Israel to America in the sixth century BCE. Yet the extratextual origin story is as powerfully miraculous as anything within its pages. In Richard Bushman's words, Joseph Smith's discovery of the golden plates of Moroni buried in a hillside in upper New York State presented "the tantalizing possibility of another world having invaded this one."[37]

The Book of Mormon and *Leaves of Grass* offer themselves not only as instruments of re-enchantment but as foundational texts for a revivified American nation. The Book of Mormon imagines a nation equally committed to the Christian religion and political liberty, commitments spelled out in a passage in which Moroni—a Nephite military commander in the first century BCE and father of one of the book's narrators—goes into battle carrying a banner that he calls the "title of liberty" and prays "for the blessings of liberty to rest upon his brethren so long as there should a band of Christians remain to possess the land."[38] The story of Moroni makes explicit the Book of Mormon's yoking of nationalism and Christianity, and those dual commitments are at the heart of the book's narrative of a tribe of Israel venturing to America. The book rewrites American history, locating America's origins not among seventeenth-century Protestants or pagan natives but among highly civilized Jews to whom, thanks to a miraculous extension of God's grace, the salvific truths of Christianity are revealed six hundred years before the birth of Jesus. The Book of Mormon takes American exceptionalism to stirringly unparalleled levels, suggesting to readers in the nineteenth century, when the nation's manifest destiny was being formulated in geographic terms, that the country's true destiny was to recover the militant devotion to liberty and powerful Christian faith that characterized its ancient foundations.

Walt Whitman's American nationalism is scarcely visible in the poems of the first edition of *Leaves of Grass*. The brashly patriotic note that readers associate with his poetry did not appear until later editions, with poems such as "I Hear America Singing." However, the preface to the first edition, which Whitman later dropped, can be seen as a massive prose poem that, like the Book of Mormon, redefines the American nation. Percy Bysshe Shelley, in "The Defence of Poetry," argues that poets are "the unacknowledged legislators of the World"; Whitman's visionary preface prophesies that in America poets shall become the *acknowledged* legislators.[39] Whitman bases his prophecy on the ideas that "the United States themselves are essentially the greatest poem" and that "the Americans of all nations at any time upon the earth have probably the fullest poetical nature." The opening paragraphs of the preface defend these assertions, detailing the physical grandeur of the American continent, the success of America's democratic institutions, and the nobility of the American people. "Of all nations," he concludes, "the United States with veins full of poetical stuff most need poets and will doubtless have the greatest and use them the greatest. Their Presidents shall not be their common referee so much as their poets shall."[40] In Whitman's vision, the central cultural role that Shelley claimed for the poet will be recognized by all Americans.

The democratic celebration of the common person that suffuses *Leaves of Grass* is a powerful theme in the Book of Mormon as well. The latter work values the unlearned over the learned, the humble over the "stiffnecked," the poor over the wealthy.[41] Borrowing a phrase from twentieth-century Catholicism, Nathan O. Hatch argues that the Book of Mormon exhibits a "preferential option for the poor."[42] Repeatedly, Nephite prophets warn against piling up riches and emphasize the need to share one's wealth with the poor. Discussing the book's reception among nineteenth-century Americans, at a time when the Jacksonian market revolution offered some people a quick path to wealth but thrust many into poverty, Terryl Givens writes that it offered a "utopian alternative to class conflict."[43] The Book of Mormon as a whole is filled with tribal battles; yet as Givens suggests, it also contains utopian interludes that must have been deeply appealing to the book's first readers. Notably, shortly after the resurrected Christ appears to the Nephites following his crucifixion in Jerusalem, they are reconciled with their centuries-old adversaries, the Lamanities, "and there was no contentions and disputations among them, and every man did deal justly one with another; and they had all things common among them, therefore there were not rich and poor, bond and free, but they were all made free, and partakers of the Heavenly gift."[44] *Leaves of Grass* also offers a vision of reconciliation between classes, although Whitman's utopia is enacted in the present moment. He writes in his visionary poem "I Sing the Body Electric":

> The man's body is sacred and the woman's body is sacred,
> No matter who it is, it is sacred—is it the meanest one in the
>   laborers' gang?
> Is it one of the dull-faced immigrants just landed on the wharf?
> Each belongs here or anywhere just as much as the well-off, just
>   as much as you,
> Each has his or her place in the procession.[45]

This utopian procession is part democratic political ceremony, part spiritual pilgrimage in which the holiness of each of the participants has already been achieved.

Celebration of the common person is central to both *Leaves of Grass* and the Book of Mormon, but the books' democratic commitments sit uneasily with their prophetic projects. That tension is easily discernible in the Book of Mormon. On the one hand, the book depicts dozens of characters who share the prophetic gifts of major figures such as Lehi, Nephi, Mormon, and Moroni; on the other, it suggests that the prophetic gift is limited to men. Its six hundred closely printed pages contain almost 250 named characters, only six of whom are women. Prophets in the Book of Mormon are invariably male, and they are part of a hierarchical system in which the prophet's gift is inferior to that of the most favored of God's agents, the seer. The seer—and there can be only one in any generation—is the man who has possession of the "interpreters," which are "two stones . . . fastened into the two rims of a bow . . . and . . . handed down from generation to generation, for the purpose of interpreting languages; . . . and whosoever has these things is called seer." The two "interpreters" are not named in the Book of Mormon, but they correspond exactly to the Urim and Thummim that Smith received along with the golden plates. In a famous passage, Nephi's brother Joseph prophesies that a seer shall arise in the latter days to come, "and his name shall be called after me; and it shall be after the name of his father."[46] In other words, this seer Joseph will have a father of the same name—a prophecy that Latter-day Saints take to be realized in Joseph Smith, Jr. The Book of Mormon veers between an inclusive conception of prophetic power as potentially available to any (male) believer and celebration of the unique, world-changing seer.

Leaves of Grass proclaims the democratic inclusiveness of its prophetic vision more obviously and insistently than the Book of Mormon does. "I am the poet of the woman the same as the man, / And I say it is as great to be a woman as to be a man," exclaims the speaker of "Song of Myself." The grass grows "among black folks as well as white," he says earlier in the same poem. Throughout "Song of Myself," the poet-seer insists that prophetic power is available to all, without exception. The speaker's insistence on his readers' equality with him verges on the strident: "I speak the pass-word primeval, I give the sign of democracy, / By God! I will accept nothing which all cannot have their counterpart of on the same terms."[47] The syntactical ejaculation in the second line cannot entirely draw our attention away from the difficulties inherent in simultaneously making "democracy" the keyword of this poetic project while also insisting on the poet's "primeval" powers.

Leaves of Grass is a new bible that testifies to the always already achieved salvation of every person; at the same time it is a celebration of the unique powers of the poet-seer. "Song of Myself," Whitman's greatest poem, is the most powerful demonstration of this contradiction. The poem's lengthy catalogues can be understood as democratic litanies that sacralize their subjects, whether hunter or farmer, mill girl or matron, prostitute or president. Moreover, the speaker tells his readers from the poem's beginning that he is no different from them, that every atom belonging to him as good belongs to us. Yet he also repeatedly emphasizes his superhuman abilities to assume others' identities:

> I am the man, I suffer'd, I was there
> ... I am the hounded slave, I wince at the bite of the dogs,
> ... Agonies are one of my changes of garments,
> I do not ask the wounded person how he feels, I myself become
>   the wounded person.[48]

These flamboyant displays of empathy, this insistence that he understands others' experiences so perfectly that he can assume them as his own, can strike readers as arrogant. They can seem like forms of appropriation—even of theft.

The tensions between democratic sympathies and prophetic authority, between celebration of the common person and trumpeting of the seer's unique power, are never resolved in either the Book of Mormon or *Leaves of Grass*. Instead, the clash of irreconcilable ideals results in a powerful rhetorical trope that I call *narrative frailty*. In the Book of Mormon, this narrative frailty is manifested in the extraordinary amount of attention given to the identity and subjectivity of the text's multiple authors and the material conditions of its production. Nephi, the text's first narrator, begins by drawing attention to his authorship, even at the cost of considerable syntactical awkwardness: "This is according to the account of Nephi; or, in other words, I Nephi wrote this record."[49] "I, Nephi" is a recurring textual formula, an irregular drumbeat reminding us of the text's authorship.

The two other principal narrators of the Book of Mormon—Mormon and his son Moroni—are as eager as Nephi to emphasize their role as authors and their process of composition. For example, in the Book of Helaman, Mormon begins telling about Gadianton, the leader of a band of robbers, but then cuts off his narrative: "And more of this Gadianton shall be spoken hereafter. . . . And behold, in the end of this book, ye shall see that this Gadianton did prove the overthrow, yea, almost the entire destruction of the people of Nephi. Behold I do not mean the end of the Book of Helaman, but I mean the end of the Book of Nephi, from which I have taken all the account which I have written."[50] Mormon leads readers into his workshop, reminding us that his narrative is actually an abridgment of a narrative composed much earlier by Nephi, founder of the Nephite tribe to which Mormon belongs.

The narrators of the Book of Mormon—and there are several in addition to the three principals—repeatedly draw attention to their work of composition, in part because of what they claim is the physical difficulty of the process. All of them engrave their words on metal plates in a language not their own. They write in "Reformed Egyptian" because, as Moroni explains, this script takes up less room on the plates than their native Hebrew does. The process is so painstaking that one narrator, Jacob, breaks off his narrative in frustration: "Now behold, it came to pass, that I, Jacob, having ministered much unto my people in word (and I cannot write but a little of my words, because of the difficulty of engraving our words upon plates)." No other narrator expresses Jacob's frustration with the task, but each reminds readers that he is writing on metal plates. The effect is twofold. The narrators' attention to their process of composition and the incompleteness of their record—they can "write but a little" of their story—suggests that no scripture can be considered definitive and final. The very existence of the Book of Mormon as a supplement to the Christian Bible depends on the possibility of continuing revelation and the emergence of multiple scriptures. Recording the word of God, Nephi writes, "Many of the Gentiles shall say, 'A Bible, a Bible, we have got a Bible, and there cannot be any more Bible. Thou fool, . . . wherefore murmur ye, because that ye shall receive more of my word? . . . Because that I have spoken one word, ye need not suppose that I cannot speak another: for my work is not yet finished."[51] Acknowledging that the Book of Mormon will not be the last scripture to be revealed, the text relinquishes sole authority; however, it does claim authority from the divine. God himself speaks to Nephi and the other narrators, and the book's attention to its own composition and materiality can serve as a means of authentication, an insistence that it is to be read not as one more production in a crowded literary marketplace but as a unique event. The Book of Mormon, as Terryl Givens argues, cannot be understood apart from its manner of origin—Joseph Smith's discovery of the golden plates of Moroni buried in the hill Cumorah in upstate New

York. As Givens writes, Smith's prophetic writings are "grounded in artifactual reality."[52]

Leaves of Grass is as attentive as the Book of Mormon is to narrative voice and the material conditions of its own production, but its narrative frailty is used to very different effect. The speaker of Whitman's poems continually reaches out to his readers, seemingly desperate to connect with them and fill the well of loneliness that exists deep within him, as in this passage from "So Long!":

> Camerado, this is no book,
> Who touches this touches a man,
> (Is it night? are we here together alone?)
> It is I you hold and who holds you,
> I spring from the pages into your arms—decease calls me forth.
>
> O how your fingers drowse me,
> Your breath falls around me like dew, your pulse lulls the
>   tympans of my ears,
> I feel immerged from head to foot,
> Delicious, enough.[53]

This remarkable passage is both naïve and crafty, earnest and witty. The speaker wants to break the bounds of writing, spring from his pages, and erotically "immerge" himself in the reader's lap. Yet at the same time the passage reminds us of the materiality of the book, the way in which one's fingers touch the page while the cover presses against the pulse point of one's wrist.

Without "you," the "I" of *Leaves of Grass* is nothing. Throughout the book the poet yearningly invokes the reader. "I stop some where waiting for you," reads the last line of "Song of Myself"; the poem is incomplete without its readers. Like the Book of Mormon, *Leaves* claims to offer salvific good news, yet Whitman's greatest, most spiritually charged poems are suggestive, not explicit. He defines his poetic project as being "a few diffused faint clews and indirections," and he delights in challenging his readers to construct his poems' meanings for themselves.[54] For instance, in the climax to the spiritually charged "Crossing Brooklyn Ferry":

We understand then do we not?
What I promis'd without mentioning it, have you not accepted?
What the study could not teach—what the preaching could not accomplish is accomplish'd, is it not?[55]

With its succession of paradoxes—promises made without mentioning them, lessons learned without studying—the passage demands readers' active engagement with the text. Whitman's prophetic speech is designed to generate our own prophetic responses. He believed that the act of reading should be "a gymnast's struggle; . . . the reader is to do something for himself, must be on the alert, must himself or herself construct indeed the poem."[56] If the Book of Mormon invites belief, Walt Whitman's new American bible demands action. Go, it tells us, and do thou likewise.

NOTES

I am grateful for the generous assistance of several friends and colleagues: Andrew Kimball and Peter Robertson assisted with research; Richard Bushman and Ed Whitley guided my research on the Book of Mormon and responded to an early draft; and David Blake, Hal Bush, and Ryan Harper commented on drafts.

1. Walt Whitman, *Notebooks and Unpublished Prose Manuscripts,* vol. 1, ed. Edward F. Grier (New York: New York University Press, 1984), 353; Richard Maurice Bucke, ed., *Notes and Fragments Left by Walt Whitman* (London, Ont.: Talbot, 1899), 55.

2. David S. Reynolds, *Walt Whitman's America: A Cultural Biography* (New York: Random House, 1995), 256–57.

3. See Lawrence Buell, *New England Literary Culture: From Revolution through Renaissance* (Cambridge: Cambridge University Press, 1986), 183; W. C. Harris, *E Pluribus Unum: Nineteenth-Century Literature and the Constitutional Paradox* (Iowa City: University of Iowa Press, 2005), 78; M. Jimmie Killingsworth, *Whitman's Poetry of the Body* (Chapel Hill: University of North Carolina Press, 1989), 44; David Kuebrich, *Minor Prophecy: Walt Whitman's New American Religion* (Bloomington: Indiana University Press, 1989), 25–26; and Michael Robertson, *Worshipping Walt: The Whitman Disciples* (Princeton: Princeton University Press, 2008), 16.

4. David S. Reynolds, *Beneath the American Renaissance: The Subversive Imagination in the Age of Emerson and Melville* (Cambridge, Mass.: Harvard University Press, 1989), 10.

5. For recent literary readings of the Book of Mormon, see Elizabeth Fenton, "Open Canons: Sacred History and American History in *The Book of Mormon,*"

J19 1, no. 2 (2013): 339–61; Terryl L. Givens, *By the Hand of Mormon: The American Scripture That Launched a New World Religion* (New York: Oxford University Press, 2002); Grant Hardy, *Understanding the Book of Mormon* (New York: Oxford University Press, 2010); and Jared Hickman, "The Book of Mormon as Amerindian Apocalypse," *American Literature* 86, no. 3 (2014): 429–61. Laura Thiemann Scales offers an overview of these and other critical essays in "A New 'Mormon Moment'? The Book of Mormon in Literary Studies," *Literature Compass* 13, no. 11 (2016): 735–43.

6. See Peter Coviello, *Tomorrow's Parties: Sex and the Untimely in Nineteenth-Century America* (New York: New York University Press, 2013), 104–28; and Harold Bloom, *The American Religion* (New York: Simon and Schuster, 1992). I have also benefited from Edward Whitley's comparison of Whitman and the Mormon poet Eliza R. Snow in *American Bards: Walt Whitman and Other Unlikely Candidates for National Poet* (Chapel Hill: University of North Carolina Press, 2010), 67–112.

7. The squib reads, "It is quite a curiosity in its way and should find a place in the library of every diligent book-collector" (*Brooklyn Daily Times*, November 19, 1858). Mormonism was mentioned respectfully in the *Brooklyn Daily Times* on four other occasions during the period when Whitman was associated with it: July 9, 1857; July 10, 1857; March 19, 1858; and June 14, 1858.

8. Richard Brodhead, "Prophets in America circa 1830: Ralph Waldo Emerson, Nat Turner, Joseph Smith," in *Joseph Smith Jr.: Reappraisals after Two Centuries*, ed. Reid L. Neilson and Terryl L. Givens (New York: Oxford University Press, 2009), 18, 20. See also Laura Thiemann Scales's analysis of the prophetic in Nat Turner and Joseph Smith in "Narrative Revolutions in Nat Turner and Joseph Smith," *American Literary History* 24, no. 2 (2012): 205–33.

9. Ralph Waldo Emerson, "Divinity School Address," *Emerson's Poetry and Prose*, ed. Joel Porte and Saundra Morris (New York: Norton, 2001), 79; Kenneth S. Greenberg, ed., *The Confessions of Nat Turner* (Boston: Bedford, 1996).

10. I employ the anachronistic term *religious seeker* to describe Smith and Whitman, inspired in part by Dan Vogel, *Religious Seekers and the Advent of Mormonism* (Salt Lake City: Signature, 1988). Robert V. Remini describes Smith as part of a "generation of seekers" in *Joseph Smith* (New York: Viking Penguin, 2002), 6.

11. Horace Traubel, "Walt Whitman as Both Radical and Conservative," *New York Times*, July 12, 1902. Whitman speaks kindly of the Mormons in Horace Traubel's *With Walt Whitman in Camden*, vol. 4 (Philadelphia: University of Pennsylvania Press, 1953), 32–33.

12. I have taken my account of Joseph Smith and the origins of the Book of Mormon principally from Richard Lyman Bushman, *Joseph Smith: Rough Stone Rolling* (New York: Knopf, 2006); Givens, *By the Hand of Mormon*; and the primary documents reprinted in John W. Welch, "The Miraculous Translation of the Book of Mormon," in *Opening the Heavens: Accounts of Divine Manifestations, 1820–1844*, ed. John W. Welch with Erick B. Carlson (Provo, Utah: Brigham Young University Press and Deseret Books, 2005), 76–213. Also see Fawn Brodie, *No Man Knows My*

History: The Life of Joseph Smith, the Mormon Prophet (New York: Knopf, 1946); Paul C. Gutjahr, *The Book of Mormon: A Biography* (Princeton: Princeton University Press, 2012); and Remini, *Joseph Smith*. In discussing Smith and the Book of Mormon's creation, I have avoided scare quotes and the use of terms such as *alleged* and *purported*. I agree with Fenton that one can analyze the Book of Mormon "without either falling back on or merely resisting its truth claims" ("Open Canons," 342).

13. Whitney R. Cross, *The Burned-over District* (Ithaca: Cornell University Press, 1950), 79.

14. Terryl L. Givens, *The Book of Mormon: A Very Short Introduction* (New York: Oxford University Press, 2009), 105.

15. I take the term *illuminism* from Sydney Ahlstrom, *A Religious History of the American People*, 2nd ed. (New Haven: Yale University Press, 2004), 476.

16. Joseph Smith, Jr., "History of Joseph Smith, the Prophet," in *The Pearl of Great Price* (Salt Lake City: Church of Jesus Christ of Latter-day Saints, 1973), 48, 49.

17. Bushman, *Joseph Smith*, 40–41.

18. See, for example, Exodus 28:30.

19. See the excerpts from 202 contemporary documents collected in Welch, "The Miraculous Translation of the Book of Mormon."

20. See Andrew C. Higgins, "Wage Slavery and the Composition of *Leaves of Grass*: The 'Talbot Wilson' Notebook," *Walt Whitman Quarterly Review* 20 (Fall 2002): 53–77.

21. Richard Maurice Bucke, *Cosmic Consciousness* (1901; reprint, New York: Penguin Arkana, 1991), 226.

22. Bucke chose to use the first (1855) edition of *Leaves of Grass* for this passage. I have followed the text of that edition as printed in Walt Whitman, *Complete Poetry and Collected Prose*, ed. Justin Kaplan (New York: Library of America, 1982), 30–31. Unless otherwise indicated, all subsequent quotations from *Leaves of Grass* are from the 1891–92 "deathbed" edition, which is included in *Complete Poetry and Collected Prose*.

23. For critical responses to this passage, see Edwin Haviland Miller, *Walt Whitman's "Song of Myself": A Mosaic of Interpretations* (Iowa City: University of Iowa Press, 1989), 59–67.

24. Smith, "History of Joseph Smith, the Prophet," 50–51.

25. Miriam Levering, "Scripture and Its Reception: A Buddhist Case," in *Rethinking Scripture*, ed. Miriam Levering (Albany: State University of New York Press, 1989), 58. Givens applies Levering's categories to the Book of Mormon in *By the Hand of Mormon*, 4.

26. Whitman, "Proto-Leaf, " in *Leaves of Grass* (Boston: Thayer and Eldridge, 1860), 13, 12, 16. "Proto-Leaf" became "Starting from Paumanok" in the 1867 and later editions. All of these editions are available at http://www.whitmanarchive.org.

27. Paul C. Gutjahr, *An American Bible: A History of the Good Book in the United States, 1777–1880* (Stanford: Stanford University Press, 1999), 152–53.

28. Gutjahr, *The Book of Mormon: A Biography*, 97–98.

29. *The Book of Mormon* (Palmyra, N.Y.: Grandin, 1830), 6. All quotations from the Book of Mormon are from this first edition and cited by page number. For readers' convenience, I also cite chapter and verse from the widely available *The Book of Mormon* (Salt Lake City: Church of Jesus Christ of Latter-day Saints, 1981), 1 Nephi 1:8. Grant Hardy's "Reader's Edition" (*The Book of Mormon* [Urbana: University of Illinois Press, 2003]) is an invaluable resource.

30. *The Book of Mormon*, 18 (1 Nephi 8:2), 48 (1 Nephi 18:12).

31. Whitman, *Complete Poetry and Collected Prose*, 513.

32. Ibid., 513–14.

33. Max Weber, "Science as a Vocation," in *From Max Weber: Essays in Sociology*, ed. and trans. H. H. Gerth and C. Wright Mills (Oxford: Oxford University Press, 1946), 155, 139.

34. See Joshua Landy and Michael Saler, eds., *The Re-Enchantment of the World: Secular Magic in a Rational Age* (Stanford: Stanford University Press, 2009).

35. Whitman, *Complete Poetry and Collected Prose*, 210.

36. See Reynolds's discussion of science and religion in *Leaves of Grass* in *Walt Whitman's America*, 235–78.

37. Richard Bushman, personal communication with the author, August 9, 2015.

38. *The Book of Mormon*, 351 (Alma 46:13).

39. Percy Bysshe Shelley, "A Defence of Poetry," in *Shelley's Poetry and Prose*, ed. Donald H. Reiman and Sharon B. Powers (New York: Norton, 1977), 508.

40. Whitman, *Complete Poetry and Collected Prose*, 8.

41. The adjective *stiffnecked* is used twenty times in the Book of Mormon, the noun *stiffneckedness* four times.

42. Nathan O. Hatch, *The Democratization of American Christianity* (New Haven: Yale University Press, 1989), 120.

43. Givens, *Very Short Introduction*, 115.

44. *The Book of Mormon*, 514 (4 Nephi 1:2–3).

45. Whitman, *Complete Poetry and Collected Prose*, 254–55.

46. *The Book of Mormon*, 173, 216 (Mosiah 8:13, 28:13–16); 67 (2 Nephi 3:15).

47. Whitman, *Complete Poetry and Collected Prose*, 207, 193, 211.

48. Ibid., 225.

49. *The Book of Mormon*, 5 (1 Nephi headnote).

50. Ibid., 411 (Helaman 2:12–14).

51. Ibid., 536 (Mormon 9:32–33), 129 (Jacob 4:1), 115–16 (2 Nephi 29:3–9).

52. Givens, *By the Hand of Mormon*, 80.

53. Whitman, *Complete Poetry and Collected Prose*, 611.

54. Ibid., 247, 171.

55. Ibid., 312.

56. Ibid., 992.

CHAPTER 9

THE OTHER *TRADITIONS* OF PALESTINE

An 1863 Novel by Ebenezer Wheelwright

Richard Kopley

I suppose it was a fan letter of sorts. On May 1, 1988, I wrote to David S. Reynolds, "I have read only the Introduction and the Poe sections of *Beneath the American Renaissance*, but I can already tell that this book is the book we needed. It is a landmark work which will, I hope and expect, inaugurate a renaissance in the study of the American Renaissance."[1] For a young scholar who had been writing, in part, about the cultural connections of Edgar Allan Poe's *The Narrative of Arthur Gordon Pym* and "The Murders in the Rue Morgue" and of Herman Melville's "Bartleby the Scrivener," Reynolds's call for reconstructive scholarship was truly welcome. His book was heartening and emboldening—confirmation to me that I was on the right track.

In the years since its publication, *Beneath the American Renaissance* has, of course, come to be recognized as a scholarly classic. The book's openness to—indeed, its seeking out of—noncanonical texts was exciting and anticipated decades of scholarly recovery in American literary study. Reynolds was prescient when he wrote, "It should be expected that the reconstructive enterprise will lead to the discovery of lost literary texts."[2] In my own case, the study of Nathaniel Hawthorne, by way of James Russell Lowell's 1843 magazine the *Pioneer,* led to the discovery of a lost literary text, an important source for *The Scarlet Letter:* the 1842 novel *The Salem Belle: A Tale of 1692.* Hawthorne transformed three passages in the final third of *The Salem Belle* (a forest scene, a harbor scene, and a scaffold scene) for three passages in the final third of his masterpiece. He drew on *The Salem Belle,* I argue, to intimate the identity of its unnamed author, Ebenezer Wheelwright, a direct descendant of John Wheelwright, who was Anne Hutchinson's partner in the Antinomian controversy. Through his three transformations of Wheelwright's novel, Hawthorne linked not only Hester Prynne with Anne Hutchinson but also Arthur Dimmesdale to John Wheelwright. And the Antinomian controversy, concerning a man and a woman who disobeyed authority and were expelled, suggested allegorically the story of the Fall and its consequences, Hawthorne's lifelong theme.[3]

The Salem Belle might have seemed to be beneath the American Renaissance in its focus on the sensational witchcraft delusion, but it was actually above the American Renaissance in its piety and in its facilitation of Hawthorne's delineation of the Genesis story. Reynolds had already suggested the importance of works above the American Renaissance in his 1981 book *Faith in Fiction.* Of particular interest to me is the chapter "Biblical Fiction," which adumbrates the development in American literature of works that creatively render scriptural narratives.[4] Particularly relevant to that category is Wheelwright's 1863 novel *Traditions of Palestine; or, Scenes in the Holy Land in the Days of Christ.* Harriet Martineau's *Traditions of Palestine* (1830) is known to scholarship, but Wheelwright's *Traditions of Palestine* is not.[5] The "reconstructive enterprise" here yields yet another lost literary text.

Harriet Martineau (1802–76) was an eminent and successful writer of fiction and nonfiction. She had been brought up in Norwich, England, as a Unitarian, and she decided, as a young woman, that, "of all delightful tasks, the most delightful would be to describe, with all possible fidelity, the aspect of life and land of the Hebrews at the critical period of the full expectation of the Messiah."[6] Her story "The Hope of the Hebrew—A Tale" appeared in William J. Fox's *Monthly Repository* in February 1830, and her novel *Traditions of Palestine,* of which this story was the first chapter, was published in London the same year. It was, she wrote, her "first decisive success."[7] The book was later published in Boston in 1831 and 1832 as *The Times of the Saviour* and then in 1839 as *Traditions of Palestine*.[8]

Martineau's narrative features seven chapters and relates "the approach" but not the "presence" of Jesus.[9] The work conveys the growing Christian faith of a young Jewish man, the fictional Sadoc, from the time of Jesus' ministry to the destruction of Jerusalem. Martineau focuses on miracles, including the healing of the blind, Jesus' walking on water, the cleansing of the lepers, and Jesus' returning from the tomb. Much is related indirectly through the dialogue of the characters. Jesus himself is never described; however, the landscapes are richly elaborated. Jefferson J. A. Gatrall calls the use of landscapes "Martineau's most important formal innovation" in the novel.[10] The book is short and simple, accessible to adults and children alike.

Ebenezer Wheelwright (1800–77) was brought up in Newburyport, Massachusetts, as a Congregationalist, and he worked as a bookseller in Newburyport; a flour merchant in Portsmouth, New Hampshire; and a West Indies trader in Boston. He was a very poor businessman, declaring bankruptcy in 1842.[11] However, he was an interesting, though largely anonymous, writer. We can attribute *The Salem Belle* to him based on a range of evidence, from a contemporary attribution to his inscription.[12] And we can attribute *Traditions of Palestine* to him (the "Wayfarer" of the title page) in part because a Portsmouth reviewer observed, "Although the name of the author does not appear, yet we have reasons for believing that it is from the pen of one who thirty years ago was the Superintendent of a Sabbath School in this city. Those who there frequently listened with interest to the addresses of Mr. E. Wheelwright, will find in this book something worth treasuring up in his remembrance."[13] As I will discuss, elements of *Traditions of Palestine* (theme, plot, and language) notably resemble elements of *The Salem Belle*.[14] Moreover, in a copy owned by Reverend Andrew Preston Peabody, the handwriting of the author's inscription is recognizably Wheelwright's.[15] Finally and definitively, Wheelwright wrote to John A. Vinton on October 10, 1867, that he had written "several works—one of which, 'Traditions of Palestine' has seen 3 editions."[16]

The novel, registered for copyright on October 2, 1863, by M. H. Sargent (identified as the publisher in the third edition [1864]), appeared serially in the *Newburyport Herald* from June to October 1863 as well as in the *Herald of Gospel Liberty,* beginning in July 1863.[17] However, it was written significantly earlier. Wheelwright notes in the preface, "As one or two works, in some respects similar to this, have been published within a few years, it is proper to state that this narrative was written more than twenty years ago."[18] He thereby disavows indebtedness to works such as Maria T. Richards's 1854 novel *Life in Judea: or, Glimpses of the First Christian Age* and J. H. Ingraham's 1855 novel *The Prince of the House of David.* "More than twenty years ago" puts the composition of *Traditions of Palestine* before October 1843. Whether this novel's composition preceded that of *The Salem Belle* is not clear, but I should note a matter of geography: in 1842 the publisher of *The Salem Belle,* Tappan and Dennet, was located at 114 Washington Street in Boston, and the publisher of the 1839 edition of Martineau's *Traditions of Palestine,* William Crosby, was located a few buildings down at 118 Washington Street.[19] Because he had been living in Boston since 1834, Wheelwright would probably have seen the Martineau volume. The coincidence of the shared title—*Traditions of Palestine*—suggests this as well. It is possible that Wheelwright read a review of the 1839 edition of Martineau's book that stated, "We think several [books] similar to Miss Martineau's, might be written with excellent effect."[20] Perhaps her famous speech against slavery at an 1835 abolitionist meeting in Boston would have increased his interest in the book.[21] Furthermore, we may infer from the Portsmouth reviewer that there was a resonance between Wheelwright's *Traditions of Palestine* and his "Sabbath school" "addresses" "thirty years ago." The novel was probably long in its development.

Wheelwright's *Traditions of Palestine* is more ambitious than Martineau's earlier volume. His novel includes fifteen chapters and braids multiple narrative strands, sometimes out of chronological sequence. We follow Rabbi Nathan, his daughter Mary, and the Jewish officer Carmi, but we also learn the back story of the young Roman woman whom they befriend, Corinna, and that of the robber chief, Hakem, who nearly kills Selma Nicodemus and later guides Corinna to her lost love, Lucius. The novel provides romance and adventure, and it dramatizes the power of Jesus on a variety of people—the Jewish and the pagan, the law-abiding and the criminal. Hakem, it turns out, is one of the two thieves crucified with Jesus, the one who says, "This man hath done nothing amiss."[22] Wheelwright ably blends the imagined and the scriptural, acknowledging that "some of the characters presented exist only in fancy; others are but faintly seen in tradition; while others still are invested with all the solemn verities of the most impressive history the world ever saw." And he states the overall object of his work: "If they [the characters] do but illustrate the beauty of the gospel, so that any may be led thereby to embrace it, the great purpose of these pages will be answered." He considers his audience to be both the adult and the young; indeed, early on he refers to "our youthful readers."[23] He was clearly a devout writer, unlike Martineau, who described herself as moving "from the dreamland or fairyland of the Bible to the perception that the Holy Land had a geographical place in our world."[24] Indeed, she eventually moved from Unitarianism to agnosticism.

Wheelwright was a pious Christian, and his themes in *Traditions of Palestine* are familiar teachings of the New Testament: love, mercy, repentance, forgiveness. These teachings are, unfortunately, accompanied toward the book's close by the also familiar blood libel against the Jews. He evidently accepted what he had been taught, what he had read. We are reminded, then, that to recover a lost literary text is not necessarily to recover an entirely unobjectionable one.

Although Wheelwright does occasionally describe a disciple physically (for instance, John has "hair, flowing over his neck in graceful ringlets") he does not describe the physical appearance of Jesus, focusing instead on his qualities of calm and compassion.[25] Perhaps Wheelwright avoids a physical characterization as a possible perceived affront. Accordingly, the reader is able to imagine the specific appearance of Jesus as he or she wishes.[26] Like Martineau, Wheelwright does provide rich, detailed descriptions of the landscapes.

Wheelwright relies primarily on the New Testament, but he draws also from the Old Testament as well as the apocryphal Acts of Nicodemus or Acts of Pilate and the writings of the British Calvinist minister William Huntington, the British Congregationalist minister William Jay, and the British bishop Thomas Dawson.[27] Gatrall notes, "What distinguishes the Jesus novel from its literary antecedents as well as from most other varieties of nineteenth-century Jesus fiction is its reliance on extrabiblical intertexts."[28] Interestingly, Hawthorne wrote of the library that he had found in his home, the Old Manse, in Concord, Massachusetts: "I tossed aside all the sacred part [the old folios and recent tracts], and felt myself none the less a Christian for eschewing it." Perhaps Wheelwright would have found more sustenance in the "frigid" books.[29]

There are parallels between *Traditions of Palestine* and *The Salem Belle*, novels written by Wheelwright in proximate years.[30] Certainly, both advocate a Christian orthodoxy, but the former critiques non-Christian views and the latter superstition. Remarkably, they offer similar plots. Lucius' rescue and then wedding of Flavia Marcella (renamed Corinna) echoes Walter Strale's rescue and then wedding of Mary Lyford (renamed Mary Graham). In both cases, the woman is innocent: Flavia Marcella sees the forbidden rite at the Temple of Apollo inadvertently, and Mary is no witch. Hakem and Pilate are, in different ways, persecutors of the innocent and are then wracked by guilt, just as Trellison is the persecutor of the innocent and is later wracked by guilt. And balancing the sinful and tormented are a pair of happy marriages—not just Lucius and Flavia Marcella but also Carmi and Mary in *Traditions of Palestine*; not just Walter and Mary but also her brother James and Margaret Elliott in *The Salem Belle*. Finally, both novels offer similar language, as the following two instances show. In *Traditions of Palestine*, "the winds ... sighed mournfully along, as if they bore on their wings the dying cadences of the Nazarene's voice."[31] In *The Salem Belle*, "the wind sighed mournfully along, as if in sympathy with the sadness which had fastened deeply on the minds of brother and sister."[32] Likewise, in the former novel, Carmi says, "Time will reveal his [Jesus'] character and mission. Meanwhile, he seems to me a Messenger from God."[33] In the latter, James advises Mary, "Time will soon disclose all; meanwhile have courage, my dear sister."[34] It therefore seems critical to study each work with reference to the other, and as we think about Hawthorne's debt to *The Salem Belle* in *The Scarlet Letter*, we should also consider Wheelwright's later novel, *Traditions of Palestine*. All three concern persecution, guilt, and atonement.

Traditions of Palestine was advertised as early as December 14, 1863, with great enthusiasm: "This is an intensely interesting book, abounding in beautiful description and full of impressive scenery and startling interest. It is written in a style which adds a charm to its every feature. It is eminently fitted to afford pleasure and profit to all. Its pictures of History and Tradition are all limited to the days of Christ, a period of the world more interesting than any or all others. As a Christmas gift none can be more appropriate."[35] A later advertisement offered an extensive plot summary and concluded with the assurance that "there is no poison in this hive; no serpent lurks under its flowers."[36] A plot summary in another advertisement ends with these words: "This book challenges the attention of the reader. The scenes are lifelike and deeply impressive. The same testimony of commanding and absorbing interest comes from all who have perused it. The wonder is that it has been withheld from the public so long."[37]

Response to the book was largely positive. The author of the notice for the *Boston Journal* wrote, "Early traditions, incidents from the old apocryphal works, and imaginary scenes are blended in this pleasing work, forming a graphic picture of the days of Christ."[38] The Portsmouth reviewer stated, "We have read this book with no little interest; in its plan and execution, throwing light on sacred history, with all the attractions of a novel. The leading personages presented are prominent in holy writ, and are brought vividly before us. We seem to live for a time with them in the first century." The reviewer observes that "fancy has wrought a network of circumstances which presents the imagined history of Nathan, of Joseph of Arimathea, of the thieves on the cross, and of others whose names are associated with the history of the holy Nazarene."[39] In a letter to the editor, the Episcopalian bishop of Rhode Island, Thomas M. Clark, asserted, "I have read the 'Traditions of Palestine' with very deep interest, and predict for the work a wide circulation. It should be placed in every Sunday School library."[40] Another letter to the editor, signed "F," noted, "This little work is attracting much notice. Even though it be carelessly taken up, it rivets the attention of the reader."[41]

There are several extant gift copies of the book that suggest that readers were responding positively to it. One features the inscription "Mother A Christmas gift from Susan."[42] Another includes the inscription "Nellie M. Warren / From Cousin Albert / Jan. 1st, 1865."[43] An object that expressed affection for the story of Christ had evidently become an object that expressed affection for family.

Yet the reviewer for the *Vermont Chronicle* had reservations about the book's moral effectiveness: "Such commingling of fact and fancy, the authentic with the visionary, has, we think, far less moral power than the simple gospel history. It is something like attempting to catch birds with chaff."[44] Different readers might have faulted the book for other reasons. In 1838, Ralph Waldo Emerson had attacked "Historical Christianity" in "The Divinity School Address," contending, "It has dwelt, it dwells, with noxious exaggeration about the *person* of Jesus."[45] Though "the *person* of Jesus" is handled discreetly in *Traditions of Palestine*, it is still vital to the book, and if Emerson had read the novel, he might have felt some ambivalence or even resistance. Emerson and Wheelwright were clearly at opposite poles religiously—the former liberal, the latter conservative.

Nonetheless, Wheelwright was concerned with not only Christian faith but also what he considered Christian good works. He was, like Martineau before him, an abolitionist; he "espoused early the antislavery cause and wrote frequently on its behalf."[46] As a merchant trading with the West Indies, he was especially focused on Haiti. Emerson, too, a renowned abolitionist, was devoted to justice in the West Indies (consider "Emancipation in the British West Indies"). So despite their great religious differences, the two shared social views. Wheelwright's dedication of *Traditions of Palestine* to Benjamin C. Clark indicates the common ground: "THE CAUSE OF HUMANITY."[47] Hawthorne, who had found *The Salem Belle* so conducive to his literary art, may not have found the reformist touch in the dedication of *Traditions of Palestine* especially consonant with his own social views. But here Emerson and Wheelwright were in agreement: both were social progressives.

The full dedication to *Traditions of Palestine* is as follows:

To

HON. BENJAMIN C. CLARK,
IN
MEMORY OF
REPEATED ACTS OF FRIEND-
SHIP, AND OF THE MANY PUBLIC AND
PRIVATE VIRTUES WHICH ADORN YOUR CHAR-
ACTER, AND ESPECIALLY OF THE SIGNAL ABILITY WITH
WHICH YOU HAVE VINDICATED THE CAUSE OF HUMANITY,
BUT MOST OF ALL AS YOU ARE A FOLLOWER OF THE
CRUCIFIED NAZARENE, WHOSE WORKS
OF LOVE YOU HAVE SO
EARNESTLY SOUGHT
TO IMITATE,
THIS LITTLE VOLUME IS GRATEFULLY INSCRIBED.[48]

According to an obituary in *Zion's Herald and Wesleyan Journal,* Clark (1800–63) was "one of the merchant princes" of Boston.[49] According to another obituary, this one in the *Boston Post,* he had "a large circle of relatives, intimate personal friends and business and social acquaintances." Wheelwright was probably a business acquaintance who became a personal friend. And perhaps there was a literary component to their friendship—after all, the obituary states that Clark "had much taste for literature, and was familiar with the works of the best writers of the day."[50]

Clark's *Post* obituary observes,

> As a true friend of Hayti he is entitled to the lasting gratitude of that nation. He did more to infuse a correct knowledge of their government, their actual condition, embarrassments and capabilities, than any other writer or speaker within our recollection, and the final acknowledgment of Haytien nationality by our Government was more owing to his exertions than to the efforts of any other individual.[51]

An obituary in the *Boston Daily Advertiser* expands on that history:

> His commercial relations made him intimately acquainted with the character of the black man, and he labored with untiring zeal in his cause. The recognition of the Haytian government and independence, was a subject near to his heart, and from the days of President Jackson until the successful result under the present administration, he labored, he wrote, he spoke and he travelled, as if it were the only object of his regard.[52]

According to an obituary in the *Boston Traveller*, "as a mark of appreciation of his services, he was appointed Acting Haytien Consul at this port, a position he occupied at the time of his death."[53] Clark had written three books about Haiti—*Biographical Sketch of St. Domingo, Cuba, Nicaragua* (1850), *A Plea for Hayti* (1853), and *Remarks upon United States Intervention in Hayti* (1853)—and he had been the advisor on Haiti to Massachusetts senator Charles Sumner, whose legislation had led to the formal U.S. recognition of Haiti in 1862.[54]

On November 26, 1863, shortly after Clark's death on November 13 and before the publication of *Traditions of Palestine* on about December 14, Wheelwright wrote a letter to Senator Sumner extolling the late consul's devotion to "the improvement of the colored race, especially in Hayti," and to "the Christian elevation, the material prosperity & the social improvement of the Haytien Republic." In that letter, Wheelwright also recommended that Clark's son, also named Benjamin, become the new consul.[55] At the same time, "many of our [Boston's] prominent merchants" presented "a memorial" to the president of Haiti, Fabre Geffrard, who did appoint Clark's son to replace his father as consul.[56]

So *Traditions of Palestine* is a work of Christian piety that, in its dedication, pays tribute to social reform. Wheelwright was both conventional and unconventional—a latter-day Puritan with an abiding concern for the oppressed. The writer of a Wheelwright obituary captured the combination well:

> Trained from infancy to a rigid Calvinism, his inner life was somewhat clouded with its gloomy dogmas, and his large and liberal soul contracted by its stern demands but it could not subdue the kindliness of

his nature; and he will long be remembered for his genial disposition, for the unstinted hospitality of a home made beautiful by a saintly companion, whose very presence dropped continued blessings, even as the clouds distil the dew, and for his fearless advocacy of every good work for his suffering fellow men.[57]

Wheelwright's novel *Traditions of Palestine* is a significant minor work in nineteenth-century American literature, one that offers elements of the traditional biblical story of the ministry of Jesus with engaging accounts of fictional characters from the time. It is a notable contribution to the subgenre of the Jesus novel (which culminates with Lew Wallace's 1880 bestseller *Ben-Hur*), a representative work in the larger category of biblical fiction, and a reflection of the reading culture of the time (including the time of its composition and that of its publication). While scholars are right to pay careful attention to Boston's remarkable transcendentalists, we should note as well those who adhered to more established thinking, especially the ones who did so imaginatively.

For readers who wish to explore Wheelwright further, I suggest archival research to help us to recover and interpret his publications—especially additional periodical publications, possibly even book publications. For instance, scholars might examine the newspaper that Wheelwright edited, the *Panoplist* (1867–68), which sheds light on sectarian religious differences of the time. His contributions to the *Congregationalist* (1875–76) should also help us clarify his thinking and lead us to additional information about his life. The pleasure of reconstructive criticism endures: discovery opens up literary history and allows the past to be more fully understood.

It seems fitting to return, finally, to the work of Reynolds, who ably recommended reconstructive criticism so many years ago. I therefore quote again from the fan letter with which I began: "Let me close by offering my congratulations on your fine book. I look forward to reading it in its entirety. I can readily see that it is a cause for celebration."[58] Inasmuch as reconstructive criticism continues to thrive, the celebration continues.

NOTES

1. Richard Kopley, letter to David S. Reynolds, May 1, 1988, in the author's personal archive.

2. David S. Reynolds, *Beneath the American Renaissance: The Subversive Imagination in the Age of Emerson and Melville* (New York: Knopf, 1988), 564.

3. Richard Kopley, *The Threads of "The Scarlet Letter": A Study of Hawthorne's Transformative Art* (Newark: University of Delaware Press, 2003); Richard Kopley, "The Missing Man of *The Scarlet Letter*," in *Nathaniel Hawthorne in the College Classroom*, ed. Christopher Diller and Samuel Coale (Norwalk, Conn.: AMS Press, 2016), 13–23; Richard Kopley, introduction to *The Salem Belle: A Tale of 1692*, by Ebenezer Wheelwright, ed. Richard Kopley (State College: Pennsylvania State University Press, 2016), 1–21.

4. David S. Reynolds, *Faith in Fiction: The Emergence of Religious Literature in America* (Cambridge, Mass.: Harvard University Press, 1981), 123–44.

5. Shelagh Hunter, *Harriet Martineau: The Poetics of Moralism* (Hants, U.K.: Scolar, 1995), 125–31; Jefferson J. A. Gatrall, *The Real and the Sacred: Picturing Jesus in Nineteenth-Century Fiction* (Ann Arbor: University of Michigan Press, 2014), 31–36.

6. Harriet Martineau, *Traditions of Palestine: Times of the Saviour* (London: Routledge, 1870), vii.

7. Ibid., viii.

8. Joseph B. Rivlin, *Harriet Martineau: A Bibliography of Her Separately Printed Books* (New York: New York Public Library, 1947), 140–43.

9. Martineau, *Traditions of Palestine*, vii.

10. Gatrall, *The Real and the Sacred* 31.

11. Kopley, *The Threads of "The Scarlet Letter,"* 69.

12. Kopley, introduction to *The Salem Belle*, 2–3; Kopley, *The Threads of "The Scarlet Letter,"* 68–69.

13. Review of [Ebenezer Wheelwright's] *Traditions of Palestine; or, Scenes in the Holy Land in the Days of Christ*, *Portsmouth Journal of Literature and Politics*, February 20, 1864, 2. The reviewer was probably referring to Portsmouth's North Parish Sabbath School (James Smith, personal communication with the author, August 27, 2015).

14. Kopley, *The Threads of "The Scarlet Letter,"* 71–72.

15. Ibid., 70, 148.

16. Ibid., 70.

17. Ibid., 70–71.

18. [Ebenezer Wheelwright], *Traditions of Palestine; or, Scenes in the Holy Land in the Days of Christ* (Boston: Graves and Young, 1863), v.

19. *Stimpson's Boston Directory* (Boston: Stimpson, 1842), 455, 154.

20. Review of Harriet Martineau's *Traditions of Palestine*, *Christian Register and Boston Observer*, August 31, 1839, 138.

21. Harriet Martineau, *Harriet Martineau's Autobiography*, 2 vols. (1877; reprint, London: Virago, 1983), 2:23–40.

22. [Wheelwright], *Traditions of Palestine*, 208. Here Wheelwright is quoting Luke 23:41, King James Version.

23. Ibid., v–vi, 15.

24. Martineau, *Traditions of Palestine*, vi. Mark Twain reverses Martineau's direction in *The Innocents Abroad* (1869). Finding the place "a hopeless, dreary, heartbroken land," "desolate and unlovely," he wrote, "Palestine is no more of this work-day world. It is sacred to poetry and tradition—it is dream-land" (in *The Oxford Mark Twain*, ed. Shelley Fisher Fishkin [New York: Oxford University Press, 1996], 606, 608).

25. [Wheelwright], *Traditions of Palestine*, 121.

26. On the varied depictions of Jesus in nineteenth-century novels, see Jefferson J. A. Gatrall, "The Color of His Hair: Nineteenth-Century Literary Portraits of the Historical Jesus," *Novel* 42, no. 1 (2009): 109–30.

27. [Wheelwright], *Traditions of Palestine*, 194, 202, 235–38.

28. Gatrall, *The Real and the Sacred*, 29.

29. Nathaniel Hawthorne, *Centenary Edition of the Works of Nathaniel Hawthorne*, ed. William Charvat, Roy Harvey Pearce, Claude M. Simpson, and Thomas Woodson, 23 vols. (Columbus: Ohio State University Press, 1962–97), 10:20.

30. Kopley, *The Threads of "The Scarlet Letter,"* 71–72.

31. [Wheelwright], *Traditions of Palestine*, 39.

32. Wheelwright, *The Salem Belle*, 139.

33. [Wheelwright], *Traditions of Palestine*, 124–25.

34. Wheelwright, *The Salem Belle*, 140.

35. Advertisement for [Ebenezer Wheelwright's] *Traditions of Palestine*, *Boston Daily Advertiser*, December 14, 1863, [2].

36. Advertisement for [Ebenezer Wheelwright's] *Traditions of Palestine*, *New York Observer*, January 14, 1864, 11.

37. Advertisement for [Ebenezer Wheelwright's] *Traditions of Palestine*, *Independent*, January 14, 1864, 6.

38. Notice for [Ebenezer Wheelwright's] *Traditions of Palestine*, *Supplement to the Boston Journal*, December 23, 1863, [1].

39. Review of [Wheelwright's] *Traditions of Palestine*, *Portsmouth Journal of Literature and Politics*.

40. Thomas M. Clark, letter to the editor, *Boston Recorder*, March 18, 1864, 47. An extant copy of Wheelwright's *Traditions of Palestine* bears the "Rules" of the East Dedham [Massachusetts] Baptist Sabbath School Library (collection of the author). According to the *Nation*, *Traditions of Palestine* was published in 1864 by the Massachusetts Sabbath School Society, whose "business agent" was Moses H. Sargent, a man "most admirably . . . fitted for his responsible post" (January 30, 1864, 3).

41. F., letter to the editor, *Boston Daily Advertiser*, April 2, 1864, 79.

42. [Inscription from Susan], in [Wheelwright], *Traditions of Palestine*, Pitts Theology Library, Candler School of Theology, Emory University.

43. [Inscription from Albert], in [Wheelwright], *Traditions of Palestine*, Kendrick Library, Evangel University.

44. Review of [Ebenezer Wheelwright's] *Traditions of Palestine; or, Scenes in the Holy Land in the Days of Christ*, *Vermont Chronicle*, January 16, 1864, 8.

45. Ralph Waldo Emerson, *The Collected Works of Ralph Waldo Emerson*, ed. Alfred R. Ferguson, Robert Ernest Spiller, Joseph Slater, and Jean Ferguson Carr, 10 vols. (Cambridge, Mass.: Harvard University Press, 1971–2013), 1:82.

46. Genealogical notes, Wheelwright family papers, box 4, Massachusetts Historical Society, Boston.

47. [Wheelwright], *Traditions of Palestine*, [iii].

48. Ibid.

49. "Hon. Benjamin C. Clark," *Zion's Herald and Wesleyan Journal*, November 25, 1863, 186.

50. "The death of the Hon. B. C. Clark," *Boston Post*, November 16, 1863, [1].

51. Ibid.

52. R. G. P., "Hon. Benjamin Cutler Clark," *Boston Daily Advertiser*, November 18, 1863, n.p.

53. "Death of Hon. B. C. Clark," *Boston Traveller*, November 14, 1863; reprinted in *Boston Daily Advertiser*, November 16, 1863, [1].

54. On Clark's service as advisor to Sumner, see Edward L. Pierce, *Memoir and Letters of Charles Sumner*, vol. 4 (London: Sampson Low, Marston, and Company, 1893), 69. For Sumner's speech on behalf of his legislation and the consequences of that speech, see Charles Sumner, *Charles Sumner: His Complete Works.*, 19 vols. (Boston: Lee and Shepard, 1900), 8:307–35. For the law itself, signed by President Abraham Lincoln, see Fritz Daguillard, *A Jewel in the Crown: Charles Sumner and the Struggle for Haiti's Recognition* (Washington, D.C.: Haitian Embassy, 1999), 35. The Sumner Collection at Harvard University's Houghton Library holds forty-three letters from Clark to Sumner, written between 1853 and 1862. Most are about Haiti.

55. Ebenezer Wheelwright, letter to Charles Sumner, November 26, 1863, in Sumner Papers, MS Am 1, Houghton Library, Harvard University.

56. "Haytien Consul in Boston," *Boston Advertiser*; reprinted in *Boston Daily Evening Transcript*, January 27, 1864, 4.

57. "Mr. Ebenezer Wheelwright, Aged 77," *Newburyport Daily Herald*, June 13, 1877, [3].

58. Kopley, letter to Reynolds.

CHAPTER 10

THE MILLENNIAL IMPULSE ABOVE THE AMERICAN RENAISSANCE

From Jonathan Edwards to Charles Grandison Finney and the Second Great Awakening

Mason I. Lowance, Jr.

IN 1988, when David S. Reynolds produced his award-winning study *Beneath the American Renaissance*, he announced, "This study compares the major literature with a broad range of lesser-known works, combines literary analysis with social history, and discusses writings of various geographical regions and of both sexes." In that pioneering work, he demonstrated how the "major writers" canonized by F. O. Matthiessen in 1940, "owed a profound debt to lesser (contemporary) writers."[1] Since 1988, Reynolds has developed a sound methodology that he calls *contextual studies*, persisting in this quest at a time when literary analysis has focused on theory and textual philosophy rather than texts and contexts. He has expanded this methodology in subsequent works such as *Waking Giant: America in the Age of Jackson* (2008), *Mightier Than the Sword: "Uncle Tom's Cabin" and the Battle for America* (2011), and especially *Walt Whitman's America: A Cultural Biography* (1995).

Reynolds commenced his contextual studies with *Faith in Fiction: The Emergence of Religious Literature in America* (1981), and much of his subsequent scholarship has focused on lesser-known literary and religious texts that form the context of the American Renaissance, which he has embraced throughout his distinguished career. Thus, it is appropriate that the editors of this volume have chosen to focus on spiritual contexts above the American Renaissance, for Reynolds's own scholarship cites many examples of sermons, pamphlets, and religious tracts that greatly influenced midcentury American literary writers. As recent studies clearly illustrate, Ralph Waldo Emerson's "Nature" (1836), Henry David Thoreau's *Walden* (1854), Nathaniel Hawthorne's *The Scarlet Letter* (1850) and *The Blithedale Romance* (1852), Herman Melville's *Moby-Dick* (1851), and Harriet Beecher Stowe's *Uncle Tom's Cabin* (1851–52) all owe a tremendous debt to the now neglected sermon writers and ministers of the nineteenth-century's Second Great Awakening.

Harold K. Bush's *American Declarations* (1999) and *Continuing Bonds with the Dead* (2016) both reflect the Reynolds methodology, and Nancy Koester's *Stowe: A Spiritual Life* (2014) amplifies his concerns about a theological cultural context and links Stowe's progressive thinking to contemporary feminist assertions:

> The first phase of feminism was closely tied to the anti-slavery movement. Many reformers hoped that women would get the vote along with freedmen after the war. In 1866 the American Equal Rights Association was formed to push for the enfranchising of blacks and women. Hopes for women's suffrage were dashed when the Fifteenth Amendment granted voting rights to black males but not to women. Moderate reformers supported the Fifteenth Amendment, preferring gradual progress to none at all. But radical reformers felt betrayed. Rejecting the idea that black males deserved the vote more than any women, black or white, these feminists were dubbed "irreconcilables." Led by Susan B. Anthony and Elizabeth Cady Stanton, they formed the Boston-based National Woman's Suffrage Association (NWSA) in 1869. Then a moderate group, led by Lucy Stone and others, formed the American Woman Suffrage Association (AWSA), headquartered in New York, with Henry Ward Beecher as president.[2]

Claudia Stokes also argues that Stowe's writings significantly link to contemporary social and political movements:

> Throughout the nineteenth century, it was a widely held belief that the millennium was imminent. Established denominations and new religious movements alike shared the belief that the divine kingdom would soon be established on Earth, and religious leaders as diverse as Lyman Abbott, Henry Ward Beecher, Horace Bushnell, Alexander Campbell, Lorenzo Dow, Dwight L. Moody, John Humphrey Noyes, and Joseph Smith all maintained that the religious fulfillment of human history was impending. . . .
>
> The closing chapter [of *Uncle Tom's Cabin*] offered the most famous literary avowal of millennialist belief in the entire century, let alone among nineteenth-century women's writing. Insisting that the impending millennium necessitates the abolition of slavery, Stowe enlists the thundering oratory of the pulpit to urge readers to "read the signs of the times." The imminence of the millennium, she proclaims, is evident in the revolutionary upheaval sweeping Europe and encroaching on the United States.[3]

Stowe's powerful work reflects the context of contemporary spiritual values and religious beliefs. Reynolds opened the floodgates for a new direction in literary and cultural studies by analyzing "the bearing that exterior circumstances and the social world have upon the literary text." He argues that *Uncle Tom's Cabin* "suggests that during the American Renaissance literariness resulted not from a rejection of socioliterary context, but rather from a full assimilation and transformation of key images and devices from this context."[4] According to Bush, the most prominent theme in nineteenth-century America was regeneration and fulfillment emphatically expressed in evangelical sermons of the Second Great Awakening and echoed in the writings of Emerson, Stowe, Abraham Lincoln, and Walt Whitman: "The most important sources of the regenerative theme central to antebellum America's regnant myths were the Bible and the Christian religion. As the young nation's preeminent and pervasive religious tradition, the Christian mythos constitutes the logical starting point for an analysis of the American myth."[5]

In this chapter, I examine the spiritual context of Stowe's novel *Uncle Tom's Cabin* (1852) following Reynolds's and Bush's contextual methodology. I focus particularly on the long tradition of millennial sermon writing in the United States after the Great Awakening of the eighteenth century and extending through the Second Great Awakening of the nineteenth century. This tradition inspired Stowe, who was one of the most influential writers of the period; in fact, *Uncle Tom's Cabin* concludes with an apocalyptic warning taken from the Book of Revelation and the Old Testament prophets: "Are not these dread words for a nation bearing in her bosom so mighty an injustice? Christians!! Every time that you pray that the kingdom of Christ may come, can you forget that prophecy associates, in dread fellowship, the day of vengeance with the year of his redeemed?"[6] Here, Stowe controls both language and imagery appropriated from the Bible and the Puritan jeremiad tradition to caution the United States against continued hypocrisy and degradation in the un-Christian practice of slavery. Yet immediately she follows this prophetic threat with an evangelical exhortation to return to biblical morality, using the language of adumbration and fulfillment, in a millennial vision of America's future. "A day of grace is yet held out to us. Both North and South have been guilty before God, and the Christian Church has a heavy account to answer."[7] For both Emerson's antislavery writings and Stowe's theology, transformation of the individual heart, repentance for the national sin of slavery, and the rebirth of the nation would necessarily precede the millennium and Christ's return to earth.

Stowe's conclusion to *Uncle Tom's Cabin* is often cited as one of the strongest antebellum warnings against slavery. In it she deliberately links the Old and New Testament doctrines of justice and mercy, noting that the salvation of humankind depends on how human beings respond to the teachings of Christ and thus treat their fellow men. While this stand is hardly a return to the notion of salvation by works, which the Protestant tradition rejected along with medieval iconography and stained glass, it does emphasize the importance of individual piety and morality in the process of salvation and redemption, a central principle of Emerson, Charles Grandison Finney, and the evangelical ministers of the nineteenth century. Both Stowe and Finney, for instance, focus on a restoration of covenant theology through which individuals may enter into a divine partnership to assist in effecting their own salvation.[8] In their view, humanity will ultimately be saved by grace, yet human behavior and moral principles will determine whether this predetermined grace will be made available to individuals, communities, or nations. For Stowe, as for Emerson and Finney, repentance and transformation must precede regeneration, which does not come like a bolt out of the blue but is the result of a lengthy process of individual reform and change.

As Sacvan Bercovitch has shown in *The Puritan Origins of the American Self* (1975) and *The American Jeremiad* (1979), as Harold Bush argues in *American Declarations* (1999), and as the evangelical ministers of the Second Great Awakening demonstrated, millennial expectations and the jeremiad were both grounded in the personal and national covenant. In the jeremiad, calamities that threatened society became God's calls to reformation and proved his covenantal relation with his elect nation. Through the millennium and its attendant judgment and eternal glory, God was expected to fulfill the national covenant and save New England and the so-called New English Israel from destruction. This union of jeremiad and the millennial prospects of repentance preceding regeneration was powerfully evoked in the sermons of ministers such as Finney and in the exhortations of Stowe's antislavery brothers during the Second Great Awakening.

In the antebellum era, ideas about millennialism and the attendant jeremiad were not peculiar to minor sects such William Miller's Millerites and other utopian socialists, and the onset of the Civil War did not destroy evangelical ministers' fervent belief that the judgment of sinners was imminent and that God would reward his elect saints during the thousand years of peace, prosperity, and plenty. The abundant natural resources of the United States supported expansion westward, and belief in manifest destiny suggested that the end of human time anticipated in the Book of Revelation could be viewed as a positive experience for God's elect saints while becoming a moment of dread, apprehension, and fear for those sinful Americans who had not repented and been transformed. As in Emerson's philosophy, reform of each individual sinner was a necessary prerequisite for the salvation and redemption of the entire nation. And the Bible was clear concerning Jesus' requirements for salvation. For instance, consider these words from the books of Luke ("I tell you, unless you repent, you will all perish just as they did"), Matthew ("Repent ye, for the Kingdom of Heaven is at hand"), and Mark ("The time is fulfilled, and the Kingdom of God is at hand: repent ye, and believe the gospel").[9] Evangelical ministers did not have to look far to find scriptural authority for their warnings about the judgment and the millennium. Finney may have been the most prolific preacher in antebellum America, but Harriet Beecher Stowe was the most influential antislavery "minister" of the era.[10] Their theological positions were very similar.

Like Finney, Stowe was a postmillennialist, a much-abused term label that refers simply to the belief that Christ would most likely appear at the end of the thousand years millennium rather than as a wrathful judge at the beginning of the millennium. (In contrast, premillennialists argued that the believers' harmony and prosperity sought by believers would only come only as a result of the last judgment and the cleansing of the earth, when everyone except God's elect and predetermined saints would be swept away.) Stowe's condemnation of slavery in the United States and her graphic depiction of moral degradation of America's promise through chattel slavery inspired readers all over the world. (*Uncle Tom's Cabin* sold 10,000 copies in America by the end the first week and by the end of 1852, some 350,000 copies in English. By 1860, it had sold 4.6 million copies in English and had been translated into sixteen languages, including Welch and Bengali). Her "Concluding Remarks" in *Uncle Tom's Cabin* suggest that she was willing to accept a transformed America, one that rejected slavery and embraced Republican ideals, those dual cornerstones on which her Christian faith rested. The rhetorical power of the Puritan jeremiad that she appropriated places such a resolution in jeopardy so that her reader is held between alternative modes of spiritual fulfillment. Thus, by concluding her novel with a great moral dilemma, she was positing alternatives that were very familiar to Second Great Awakening congregations, including Finney's. That is, continued immersion in individual sin or collective sin (such as slavery) would lead only to death and destruction, whereas repentance, transformation, and regeneration might lead to progressive improvement and the gradual development of a restored social order, a "new birth of freedom," as Lincoln later said in the Gettysburg Address.

As a young person, Stowe was steeped in antislavery rhetoric, the Bible, and Christian theology. Her father, Lyman Beecher, was the president of Lane Seminary in Cincinnati; and all six of her brothers were ministers, including the famous Brooklyn preacher Henry Ward Beecher and the abolitionist preachers Charles Beecher and Edward Beecher. Moreover, she was married to Calvin Stowe, who was both a minister and a professor of religion at Bowdoin College in Brunswick, Maine. Stowe's exceptionally influential novel was clearly the most powerful antislavery sermon "preached" before the Civil War. It is appropriate to connect her rhetorical strategies to those she absorbed from these many influences. For the evangelists and for her, the postlapsarian human condition, manifested in contemporary ills such as chattel slavery, required repentance and salvation through Christ. Only by atoning for the sins of mankind could believers realize their individual and communal millennial expectations through Christ's kingdom on earth.

Stowe was not the only writer of the early antebellum period who was caught up in evangelical and millennial enthusiasm. Poems such as David Humphreys's "The Glory of America" (1773), Joel Barlow's "The Columbiad" (1806), and Timothy Dwight's "The Conquest of Canaan" (1772) embrace millennial doctrines inherited from the Bible. One of the most eloquent verse expressions of these doctrines appears in Philip Freneau's "The Rising Glory of America" (1774), which argues that the peaceable kingdom so anticipated in millennial writing (and represented visually in Edward Hicks's contemporaneous paintings) is imminent in America:

> And when a train of rolling years are past,
> (So sung the exiled seer in Patmos isle)
> A new Jerusalem, sent down from heaven,
> Shall grace our happy earth—perhaps this land,
> Whose ample bosom shall receive, though late,
> Myriads of saints, with their immortal king,
> To live and reign on earth a thousand years,
> Thence called Millennium.[11]

This postmillennial optimistic view contrasts sharply with Dwight's premillennial conviction in "The Conquest of Canaan" that Christ will return to earth to judge, purify, and then usher in the thousand years. Yet however the details vary, in sermons and in verse the use of biblical images to explore the future promise of the new nation in its new land was pervasive from the Revolution until the Civil War. At that juncture most perceptions of biblical prophecies for the United States were altered, and Union sympathizers came to view victory as a long-awaited judgment (the jeremiad) on slavery and the purging of sin from the national landscape.

The Negro spirituals of antebellum America also reflect the evangelical emphasis on millennial eschatology—for instance, in this famous first line: "Swing low, sweet chariot, coming for to carry me home." Chattel slavery in plantation America was so hopeless and brutal an experience that most spirituals focused on salvation and eternal life, when human earthly travail would be replaced by a spiritual existence overseen by a benevolent God. Spirituals such as "We Are Climbing Jacob's Ladder" and "The Gospel Train," which recapitulate metaphors from John Bunyan's *Pilgrim's Progress* (1678), prophesied eschatological events vividly described in the Bible, particularly in the Book of Revelation. There is no question that the pervasive theme of freedom in spirituals was linked to a desire to escape from earthly bondage into earthly freedom; yet for the evangelists, who had considerable influence among the enslaved population of antebellum America, *bondage* also referred to the shackles of sin and the need for redemption. Evangelical Christianity had become deeply ingrained in African slave culture, and the hope for a better life in this world was coupled with a longing for the forgiveness of sin and more rewards in the next life. Spirituals, then, reinforced the evangelical emphasis on both the need for forgiveness (the jeremiad tradition) and the rewards that await God's faithful followers (the millennial tradition). Both had been transformed by the evangelical Puritan preacher Jonathan Edwards, reaching fruition in Stowe's literary masterpiece and in the sermons of the Second Great Awakening. Evangelical sermons such as Finney's provided a spiritual and cultural context for the "moral suasion" of William Lloyd Garrison's *Liberator* editorials (Boston, 1831–65) and Stowe's rhetorical strategies in *Uncle Tom's Cabin*, such as the sermonic warnings in her "Concluding Remarks."

Theologically speaking, the term *millennium* denotes the thousand years of the kingdom of Christ on earth, which is detailed in the Book of Revelation.[12] *Millenarianism* (or the corresponding word of Greek derivation, *chiliasm*) is the belief in the millennium. More specifically, it is the belief that Christ will reign personally on earth with his saints for one thousand years (or for an indefinitely long period) at the end of the world. As writers explored the metaphorical possibilities of this eschatological figure, the emphasis would shift from one biblical prophecy to another, but the rich figural language that expressed future judgment and restoration remained constant. The biblical prophecies of the millennium are varied, but preachers of the two Great Awakenings repeated a few central passages from the books of Isaiah, Daniel, and Revelation.[13] Particularly important was this verse from Psalm 90: "For a thousand years in thy sight are but as yesterday when it is past, and as a watch in the night."[14] Some evangelical ministers used the psalm as their basis for constructing a historical scheme that began more than 4,000 years before Christ and culminated in the nineteenth century—for example, in the Millerite adventist prophecies of the coming of the kingdom in the 1840s and 1850s. As I have discussed, many evangelists shared a literal chiliasm that looked forward to a judgment that was would precede the millennium of Christ's personal glory. Opposed to this position is the spiritual or allegorical view, which held that the millennium would consist of a spiritual transformation of the world, during which Christ would reign in spirit but not in person. Like the literalists, the spiritualists viewed the happy paradise as being a future state, but they argued that man's estate would become so blessed that a perfect society of gathered saints would constitute the visible church of Christ on earth, even before the second coming and judgment. Put simply, the premillennial interpretation held that Christ's second coming would occur before the millennium could begin, whereas the postmillennial view held that Christ would come in person at the end of the thousand years of peace and prosperity, but in spirit before the advent through personal regeneration and progressive reforms in society. Obviously, there is a close relationship between the literal and premillennial, the spiritual and postmillennial, but the association is not as clear as it might seem. The tensions between attempts to maintain a literal veracity in prophetic interpretation and the tendency to endow biblical and contemporary events figures with allegorical and metaphorical value were present in the jeremiads *and* in millennial discourse throughout the eighteenth and nineteenth centuries. The postmillennial "New Light" followers simultaneously argued from a strong scriptural foundation taken from the harsh prophetic language of the jeremiad, but they succeeded in renewing the eschatology of hope and regeneration available to the saints also found in biblical prophecy. The postmillennial "new lights" argued that through Christian agency the Gospel would gradually permeate the entire world and become more effective than at present, without the personal arrival of Christ, and that eventually, after a thousand year period of peace and prosperity, there would simultaneously occur the advent of Christ, the general resurrection, the judgment, the destruction of the old world by fire, and the revelation of the new heavens and the new earth foretold by Isaiah and Revelation. Obviously, this view was influential in thinking of progressive idealists of New England including Emerson, the reformers, and Stowe's contemporary evangelical writers.

The two American dreams—the spiritual "errand into the wilderness" associated with the Puritan impulse to establish a "city upon a hill" and the more contemporary economic democracy that has attracted waves of immigrants to American shores since the writing of the Constitution—have more in common than one might think. The rationalist eighteenth century witnessed a secularizing of the original errand impulse, a transformation reflected in the contrast between Joel Barlow's two long poems, "Prospect of Peace" (1778) and "The Columbiad" (1806), but the language of America's mission and its millennial promise remained spiritual and biblical, even following the loss of pietistic force that accompanied the rise of secular progress in the nineteenth century. The millennial idea passed into the hands of minor sects, but traditional arguments for its imminent arrival were advanced by nineteenth-century evangelists such as Finney and Miller. Miller's failed prophetic announcements and predictions of specific years for Christ's arrival may have doomed his movement (he kept postponing the day of Christ's return as each year passed into history), but they advanced the emphasis on Biblical chiliasm and the necessity for reforming and purifying American society.[15]

The foundation for the Second Great Awakening prophecies was laid in the eighteenth century in Jonathan Edwards's "Miscellaneous

Notebooks" and *A History of the Work of Redemption*. In the latter work, which contains a vivid description of the arrival of millennial peace and the coming of the kingdom, Edwards envisioned the setting up of Christ's kingdom as a succession of great events, each revealed in the prophecies of scripture and all having a spiritual significance for his own time. This conclusive interpretation of the prophecies was dramatically conceived and beautifully preached; the conviction with which Edwards approached his own vision of the last days resonates throughout the climactic scenes depicting the arrival of God's glory. The gathered church of God's elect saints is brought forward to enjoy forever the beauty of redeemed creation in a period of perfect peace. According to Edwards, "Then shall the whole church be perfectly and forever delivered from this present evil world." The sense of religious community that has always characterized the Puritan vision of God's holy city echoes throughout his vision of the last days: "Now they shall all be gathered together, never to be separated any more. And not only shall all the members of the church now be gathered together, but all shall be gathered unto their Head, into His immediate glorious presence, never to be separated from him any more."[16] This millennial optimism contrasts sharply with his well-known Calvinist jeremiad, "Sinners in the Hands of an Angry God" (1732), which predicts a very different culmination of human time for the unregenerate.

Edwards's miscellany 262 (in "Miscellaneous Notebooks") declares, "The changing of the course of trade and the supplying of the world with its treasures from America is a type and forerunner of what is approaching in spiritual things, when the world shall be supplied with spiritual treasures from America."[17] His fusion of spiritual and secular forces anticipated the evangelical preaching of the Second Great Awakening because it forged a connection among reform, repentance, and spiritual regeneration and national progress. In this view, the long anticipated millennium would bring spiritual fulfillment to the faithful and national or communal blessings for the saints.

Edwards's anticipation of the millennium throughout his writing was accompanied by a reformer's emphasis on humanity's sinfulness and the need for repentance and regeneration in order for society to improve and avoid God's wrathful judgment. "Sinners in the Hands of an Angry God" anticipates some nineteenth-century evangelical preaching by stressing humankind's sinfulness and the punishment that waits the unregenerate while also urging repentance. Finney, the Beechers, and Stowe appropriated this language of the Puritan jeremiad when they begged listeners and readers to strive for benevolence and divine forgiveness. According to Finney, "there is in man a moral weakness that effectually shuts him off from salvation, save as God interposes with efficient help. Hence the salvation that meets him in this weakness and turns him effectually to love and to please God, must be intrinsically great. Again, it is because it delivers [him] from endless sinning and suffering."[18]

As Stowe did in *Uncle Tom's Cabin,* Finney amplified his prophetic pronouncement by shifting to a more optimistic vision of the last days: "Observe again, this salvation is not merely negative,—a salvation from sin and from suffering; it has a positive side. On this positive side, it includes perfect holiness and endless blessedness. It is not only deliverance from never-ending and ever-accumulating woe;—it is also endless bliss—exceeding in both kind and degree, all that we can conceive in this life."[19] This coupling of the jeremiad with blissful visions of the end of human time is prominent in the teachings in the books of Isaiah and Revelation. Ministers employed this rhetorical strategy throughout the Second Great Awakening, and it is also found throughout *Uncle Tom's Cabin.* The evangelical emphasis on covenant theology also closely resembles Emerson's view of progressive social reform—that the abolition of slavery, for example, could best be achieved through the reformation of individual souls, who, in turn, would transform the social order.

Stowe was well equipped to approach her era's spiritual arguments and contemporary debates about slavery. She lived just across the Ohio River from Kentucky and had interviewed escaped slaves as they made their way to depots on the Underground Railroad, one of which was Lane Seminary. Moreover, during a visit to Kentucky, she had witnessed a slave auction, which profoundly affected her views of the "peculiar institution." While her direct experience of the slave South was limited, she read widely in abolitionist literature, including Garrison's *Liberator,* the abolitionist newspaper he had founded in Boston in 1831, and Theodore Dwight Weld's *American Slavery as It Is* (1839), which contained many excerpts from newspapers advertising for the return of escaped slaves. Moreover, two of the other states where Stowe had lived—Massachusetts and Connecticut—had abolished slavery in the late eighteenth century, and another of her home states, Maine, had been admitted to the Union as a free state as part of the Missouri Compromise of 1820.

Stowe was steeped in evangelical preaching of the Second Great Awakening, as church attendance was virtually required in the Beecher family. While many pro-slavery sermons were preached north of the Mason-Dixon Line between 1830 and 1865, the rhetoric of abolitionism and its connection to the enthusiasm of the Awakening were regularly voiced in the sermons and lectures she heard. These sermons not only criticized mankind's inhumanity to his fellow man in chattel slavery but also associated postmillennial doctrines with the necessity for purifying the land of so egregious a sin in order to usher in the thousand-year reign of Christ, in spirit if not in person. As Finney often preached during revivals, the life eternal is a matter of personal choice, which in *The Great Salvation* he delineated as "woe" or "bliss":

> Before us, each and all, lies this eternal state of our being. We are all to live in this eternal state. There awaits us there either woe or bliss, without measure and beyond all our powers of computation. If woe, it will be greater than all finite minds can conceive. . . . Yet this infinite bliss and endless woe are the plain teaching of the Bible, and are in harmony with the decisive affirmations of the human reason. We know that if we continue to sin, the misery must come upon us;—if we live and die in holiness, the bliss will come.[20]

The choice for Finney, the abolitionist Beecher brothers, and other evangelical ministers of the Second Great Awakening was clear: rather than accepting the strict Calvinist belief in the divine predestination of all souls regardless of human action, they posited alternative modes of fulfillment for all in their congregations, elect and damned alike. Finney showed that the choice was clear: "In a converted state, the character is that of benevolence. . . . An individual who is converted is benevolent, and not supremely selfish. . . . It is the leading feature of his character, that he is seeking the happiness of others, and not his own happiness, as his supreme end."[21]

Finney was not a militant firebrand like Garrison was, who, at an 1854 Fourth of July celebration in Framingham, Massachusetts, publicly burned a copy of the Constitution, declaring it to be a "covenant with death" and an "agreement with hell."[22] But the Beechers and Finney were vocal antislavery advocates, and they specialized in evangelical Christian preaching that demanded conversion and obedience to the will of God (although few Finney pronouncements directly confronted the issue of chattel slavery). As evangelical reformers, they sought to transform society through the conversion of individual souls in large revival gatherings. In this respect, they were "equal opportunity" preachers of the gospel—that is, all persons were sinners and were justifiably condemned in the scheme of God's justice. However, repentance, forgiveness, mercy, and regeneration were available to individuals and societies alike. The evangelical message was easily joined to the progressive reform movements of the nineteenth century in order to bring about, in Lincoln's famous words, a "more perfect Union" and a "new birth of freedom" as the president would echo these sentiments in a political and social context, a vision long awaited by the antislavery evangelists not only as political freedom from chattel slavery but also as spiritual freedom from the most serious communal sin that mankind had ever committed.

Not all of Stowe's readers were exposed to antislavery rhetoric in evangelical sermons, but all were familiar with the rhetoric of the Bible. For example, when she delineated an obvious crucifixion scene as the dramatic conclusion for her intense narrative, many were moved not only because of the human tragedy the novel had developed but also because she was clearly linking the story of the Christ figure Tom with the larger sin of chattel slavery in American society. The dramatic energy of her characterization—for instance, the pitiable story of Cassy (an internal slave narrative that appears in chapter 34) or the auction scenes that recapitulate her experiences in Kentucky—is also displayed in a long, continuous account about man's inhumanity to man and the many evils of chattel slavery.

As Stowe made clear in her later book, *A Key to "Uncle Tom's Cabin"* (1853), she was not only keenly aware of the horrors of plantation slavery but also was familiar with slave narrative literature. She borrowed the character of Uncle Tom from Josiah Henson's slave narrative of

1842, and she had read Frederick Douglass's 1845 masterpiece *Narrative of the Life of Frederick Douglass, an American Slave, Written by Himself.* Her immersion in antislavery literature, her interviews with the few escaped slaves she had met in Cincinnati, and her awareness of progressive reform movements (for instance, temperance activism and utopian socialist communes such as George Ripley's Brook Farm in Roxbury, Massachusetts, and Bronson Alcott's Fruitlands in Harvard, Massachusetts) were coupled with her almost constant exposure to evangelical rhetorical strategies. In the "Concluding Remarks" of *Uncle Tom's Cabin,* she warned, "A mighty influence is abroad, surging and heaving in the world, as with an earthquake. And is America safe? Every nation that carries in its bosom great and unredressed injustice has the elements of this last convulsion."[23]

The novel, a response to the Fugitive Slave Act of 1850, was first published in serial form in 1851–52 in the *New Era,* a progressive reform journal. But Stowe's antislavery thinking had commenced much earlier, influenced by the turbulent antebellum slavery debate decades, the 1848 Paris commune uprising, and Elizabeth Cady Stanton's gathering of five hundred suffragettes at Seneca Falls, New York, to draft the Declaration of Sentiments and Resolutions, which borrowed the format of the Declaration of Independence to insist on equal rights for women. Margaret Fuller wrote regularly against male domination of women and in favor of equal rights for all people. The progressive reform movements addressed these injustices, and the utopian socialist communities that developed in New England and western New York State made efforts to rectify them; yet all were bound to obey federal and state laws.

In chapter 9 of *Uncle Tom's Cabin,* Stowe staged a debate between Senator John Bird and his wife, Mary, over the Fugitive Slave Act, which was an integral part of the Compromise of 1850. In the dramatic heat of this exchange, Stowe arranged for the runaway Eliza and her child Harry to arrive at the Bird door seeking refuge during their flight north. Senator Bird has advanced legalistic and rational arguments in his defense of the act, which are countered by his wife's moral, religious, and emotional views. Into this gendered division Stowe inserted Eliza and Harry, whose presence trumps the senator's rationalism, and the Birds decide to help Eliza escape to freedom. Throughout the novel, Stowe made her argument clear: that disenfranchised female northerners should use their moral "home and hearth" influence to convince their more politically powerful husbands of the wrongs of chattel slavery before it was too late to save the nation from eternal peril. The institution of slavery was, for her, always the "demonic other." Individual characters only represented aspects of this curse.

Chapter 9's debate between two free white Americans is balanced by chapter 33, in which Tom and Simon Legree, the incarnation of an evil slave master, debate the issue of slave-master obedience. Cassy has not picked her quota of cotton; and at the weighing ceremony at the end of the work day, she is sentenced to a flogging, which Tom is supposed to administer. He refuses and is sentenced to be flogged himself. In this dramatic scene, the moral authority of the Bible, represented by Tom's refusal to flog a helpless woman who is also ill, confronts a rational male argument for earthly law and marketplace economics. Christian charity and human sin emblematically challenge each other, just as Mary and John Bird debate the issue of slavery from a legal and Christian perspective and Shelby and Haley discuss the sale of Tom in chapter 1. The reader is not permitted to view Tom's flogging but is left to imagine the brutal scene.

Like an evangelical sermon, *Uncle Tom's Cabin* juxtaposes the moral authority of Christian doctrine to earthly sin and corruption so that the readers are placed between alternative modes of spiritual fulfillment, just as they were in the theology of Finney's evangelical sermons. The choices are simple and clearly delineated in both modes of discourse, the novel and the sermons. In fact, the novel concludes with one of the most serious antebellum sermonic warnings to appear in any literature of the period. Stowe clearly believed that slavery was so great a sin that it must be purged from the land, even with blood, if the nation was were to survive and prosper. She coupled the language of millennial discourse with the rhetoric of the jeremiad, and her book's final warning is clear: the United States is faced with a moral choice. Either there will be an improved, postmillennial-like social order of the postmillennial type suggested in the Book of Revelation, or the country will descend into the disunity, degradation, conflict, and chaos as predicted in prophecies of the Old Testament.

Stowe's warning anticipated the Civil War by only nine years, and immediately after the war, Congress made three amendments to the Constitution. In 1865, the Thirteenth Amendment abolished slavery in the United States; in 1867–68, the Fourteenth Amendment granted citizenship to the emancipated slaves; and in 1870, the Fifteenth Amendment granted the franchise to Negro male citizens, both former slaves and freedmen. Women would have to wait for the right to vote until passage of the Nineteenth Amendment in 1920. Stowe's dual purpose of calling attention to the pervasive evils of chattel slavery and alerting the nation to the pressing needs of women's rights were realized in these four amendments, although she did not live to witness passage of the last one. Appropriating her method of discourse in *Uncle Tom's Cabin* from Edwards and the sermon writers of the Second Great Awakening, she effectively coupled her antislavery message with evangelical rhetorical strategies to give the world a cast of characters and a moral argument concerning human dignity, justice, and freedom—an approach that subsequently resonated in twentieth-century civil rights discourse and in the rhetorical power of Martin Luther King, Jr. And, like David S. Reynolds's revolutionary methodology, the contextual influence of these evangelical writers and of Stowe's extraordinary novel will continue to influence American culture.

NOTES

1. David S. Reynolds, *Beneath the American Renaissance: The Subversive Imagination in the Age of Emerson and Melville* (Cambridge, Mass.: Harvard University Press, 1984), 3, 4. Also see F. O. Matthiessen, *American Renaissance* (Cambridge: Harvard University Press, 1940).
2. Nancy Koester, *Harriet Beecher Stowe: A Spiritual Life* (Grand Rapids, Mich.: Eerdmans, 2014), 359–60.
3. Claudia Stokes, *The Altar at Home: Sentimental Literature and Nineteenth-Century American Religion* (Philadelphia: University of Pennsylvania Press, 2014), 103–5.
4. Reynolds, *Beneath the American Renaissance*, 6–7.
5. Harold K. Bush, *American Declarations: Rebellion and Repentance in American Cultural History* (Urbana: University of Illinois Press, 1999), 2.
6. Harriet Beecher Stowe, *Uncle Tom's Cabin*, 2 vols. (Boston: Jewett, 1852), 2:268.
7. Ibid., 2:269.

8. Charles Grandison Finney, *The Doctrine of Election* (Oberlin, 1845).

9. Luke 13:1–9; Matthew 3:2; Mark 1:15, King James Version.

10. By the end of *Uncle Tom's Cabin*'s first week in print, the publisher had sold 10,000 copies in America. By the end of 1852 it had sold some 350,000 copies in English, and by 1860 it had sold 4.6 million copies in English and the book had been translated into sixteen languages, including Welsh and Bengali. See Mason I. Lowance, ed. *The Stowe Debate* (Amherst: University of Massachusetts Press, 1994), intro.

11. Philip Freneau, "The Rising Glory of America," in Mason I. Lowance, Jr., *The Language of Canaan: Metaphor and Symbol in New England from the Puritans to the Transcendentalists* (Cambridge, Mass.: Harvard University Press, 1980), 277–78.

12. Revelation 20:16.

13. Isaiah 65:17–25; Daniel 12:12–13; Revelation 20:1–3, 7.

14. Psalms 90:4, King James Version.

15. William Miller presented his views in *Evidence from Scripture History of the Second Coming of Christ about the Year 1843* (Troy, N.Y.: Kemble and Hooper, 1836); and *A Lecture on the Typical Sabbaths and Great Jubilee* (Boston: Himes, 1842).

16. Jonathan Edwards, *A History of the Work of Redemption*, ed. John Wilson (New Haven: Yale University Press, 1991), 44–45.

17. Jonathan Edwards, "Miscellaneous Notebooks," 62, in the archive of Beinecke Library, Yale University.

18. Charles Grandison Finney, "The Doom of Those Who Neglect the Great Salvation" (Oberlin, 1858), 2.

19. Finney, *The Great Salvation*, 4.

20. Ibid., 5.

21. Charles Grandison Finney, *True and False Conversion* (Oberlin, 1837), 3–4.

22. On Garrison's public destruction of a copy of the Constitution, see "William Lloyd Garrison," in *Dictionary of American Biography* (New York: Scribner, 1946–58), 168–75. See also William Lloyd Garrison and Wendell Phillips, "The Constitution a Proslavery Compact" (1845), in Mason I. Lowance, Jr., *A House Divided: The Antebellum Slavery Debates in America, 1776–1865* (Princeton: Princeton University Press, 2003), 335. A more detailed discussion of Garrison and the Constitution (and this incident) appears in Henry Mayer, *All on Fire: William Lloyd Garrison and the Abolition of Slavery* (New York: St. Martin's, 1998).

23. Stowe, *Uncle Tom's Cabin*, 2:269.

PART III

RECONSTRUCTING POPULAR RELIGION

CHAPTER II

HYMNS BY THE FIRESIDE
Religious Verse and the Rise and Fall of the Fireside Poets

Claudia Stokes

GIVEN THE recent religious turn of American literary studies, few writers are more deserving of a serious reappraisal than the Fireside Poets, a label commonly used to denote a group of popular nineteenth-century North Atlantic poets whose verses were for generations mainstays of the American classroom but who fell out of favor following World War I.[1] In a twentieth-century scholarly climate that privileged literary experimentation over piety and convention, the poems of Henry Wadsworth Longfellow and Oliver Wendell Holmes came to seem maudlin and moralistic alongside the esoteric difficulties of T. S. Eliot and Ezra Pound.[2] While the recent interest in poetry, transnationalism, and masculinity has yielded some important scholarship on the Fireside Poets, they remain on the fringes of current critical discourse because so much of their work is explicitly devout, a quality at odds with the twentieth-century predilection for skepticism and innovation.[3] Because their collections are filled with poems in praise of virtue and faith, these poets have been associated with stodgy traditionalism, and the metaphors that scholars have used to describe them reveal the influence of religion on this appraisal.[4] James Justus, for instance, has remarked that twentieth-century readers are "no longer able to read [the Fireside Poets'] works except as sacred texts"; in his view, their writings seemed to be impervious to interpretation and resistant to modern interpretive methods.[5] Kirsten Silva Gruesz similarly notes, "If the Firesiders have often been referred to as a self-proclaimed 'high priesthood' of literary culture in America, the nature of their priestly mediation is fundamentally parental: to select, to distill, and finally to offer for communal consumption a canon newly organized in meaningful ways."[6] She made a related observation in her analysis of Longfellow's lifelong work as a translator: "As translator, borrower, and reworker of those [Spanish-language literary] 'traditions' . . . Longfellow appointed himself the priest—not the minister—of American cultural life. Only a translator, after all, has access to the sacred texts of the 'originals'; only he can handle the vessels."[7]

As these examples attest, the literary authority of the Fireside Poets is often explicitly constituted in the language of clerical authority, a metaphor that has contributed to their classification as old-fashioned and unsophisticated. Though the poets in this group—which also included William Cullen Bryant, James Russell Lowell, and John Greenleaf Whittier—differed in their religious affiliations and practices, critics were fully justified in noting a ministerial quality in their work. This assessment typically derives from the Fireside Poets' pedigreed self-possession and explicit moralism, but it was also bolstered by their innumerable devotional poems, which offer counsel, engage scripture, and model religious piety. Holmes's 1858 poem "Mare Rubrum," for instance, begins as a nostalgic meditation on the passage of time, but its final stanza adopts a clerical tone:

> Nay, take the cup of blood-red wine,—
> Our hearts can boast a warmer glow,
> Filled from a vintage more divine
> . . . Rich as the priceless draught shall be
> That wet the bride of Cana's lip,—
> The wedding wine at Galilee![8]

Holmes here refers to the marriage at Cana, mentioned in the New Testament's Book of John, in which Christ miraculously transforms water into wine. But in inviting his audience to drink "divine" wine, Holmes also invokes the Eucharist, in which an ordained cleric similarly bids his congregants to drink consecrated wine and thus dramatizes another moment in the life of Christ, the Last Supper. Holmes concludes his poem by assuming priestly duties and positioning himself in a role of religious authority over his guest and the reader.

This ministerial self-presentation was by no means unusual among the Fireside Poets, who did not hesitate to use their poems to assume, albeit in text, some of the duties of the clergy. These priestly aspirations are most evident in their many hymn compositions. Indeed, the Fireside Poets were among the midcentury's most prolific hymn lyricists, collectively authoring hundreds of devotional poems that were set to music, included in worship services, and sung by congregations all over the Anglo-American world. In some instances, they intentionally composed hymns, which had often been commissioned to honor a special occasion or for inclusion in a volume, as with Longfellow's "Christ to the Young Man Said, 'Yet One Thing More'" (1848), composed in honor of his brother's ordination. In other instances, they wrote devotional poems using traditional hymn forms, as with Holmes's "Mare Rubrum," which he composed in the conventional hymn form of long meter. In employing hymn forms in devotional poems, the Fireside Poets courted the notice of hymn editors, who actively sought such works for inclusion in hymn collections and adapted hundreds of their poems for this use. In addition, the Fireside Poets gave dozens of their poems titles that expressly announced this generic affiliation—as with Bryant's "Hymn to the North Star" (1832) and Holmes's "A Hymn of Peace" (1869)—and that imparted a religious connotation to poems on a wide range of subjects. As these many poems attest, the hymn was among the Fireside Poets' signature poetic forms.

The relationship of the Fireside Poets to the hymn form is complex. Without question, they reaped considerable cultural capital from their many hymns, which contributed to their status as national icons of pious virtue and paternalistic benevolence. Hymns allowed them to extend their influence and reputation beyond the parameters of the literary public sphere and into the world of religious observance. Whereas poems such as "Mare Rubrum" merely simulated ministerial authority, hymns were a formal vehicle through which they could perform legitimate clerical duties within the worship service. Though these writers did not enter the pulpit or preach sermons, their hymns nevertheless instructed congregants in how to interpret scripture, comport themselves, and interpret the world around them. Thus, hymns allowed the Fireside Poets to achieve levels of influence unparalleled in American literary history. These benefits were reciprocal, for hymnody also profited from the sustained involvement of these poets.

Today, hymns are a conventional feature of congregational worship, but they were the subject of active controversy in the first half of the nineteenth century, becoming mainstream only in the 1850s. Hymns were for centuries regarded as suspect and even vulgar, but, in lending their prestige to this contentious form, the Fireside Poets helped allay the anxieties of critics and raised the form's quality and profile. In this way, they were instrumental in the history of American hymnody: they enabled a populist devotional form to achieve mainstream respectability and, in so doing, accrued immense moral authority. This contribution did not come without cost, however. The Fireside Poets came to seem old-fashioned to subsequent generations of critics, who expected poetry to challenge conventional beliefs and norms instead of reifying them. Though hymns enabled these poets to achieve religious and moral authority, they nevertheless also contributed to their decline in scholarly opinion.

As Christopher N. Phillips discusses in chapter 12 in this volume, hymns have long been employed for private reading and domestic worship. Yet even though they have a distinguished tradition among Catholics and Lutherans, they encountered resistance among Anglo-American Protestants who for centuries refused to permit hymns in public worship, insisting instead on psalmody, the metrical recitation of biblical devotional poems. Whereas psalms have the imprimatur of biblical authority, hymns may be authored by anyone—men or women, adults or children, clergy or laity, orthodox or heterodox—and they consequently caused widespread suspicion among clergy, who feared that such poems might circulate questionable doctrine and undermine clerical authority. The respectability of hymns was further complicated by their particular appeal to nonconformists, who saw them as a lyric platform for religious self-expression independent from the strictures of clerical authority and accepted doctrine. For this reason some of the earliest English-language hymnists—Philip Doddridge, Benjamin Keach, and Isaac Watts—were dissenters who used hymns to circumvent the established church and to propound an evangelical piety unmediated by clerical supervision. Hymns became immensely popular in the eighteenth century because of the avid promotion of John and Charles Wesley, the founders of Methodism. In their outreach to constituencies often underserved by the Anglican established church, the Wesleys used hymns to activate religious sentiment, attract followers, and circulate doctrine among the underclasses and the uneducated, who were often unable to pay the pew fees necessary for church attendance and who might also be unable to read scripture. For the unchurched and the illiterate, Methodist hymns served in place of the sermon and scripture, and they rendered clergy all but irrelevant. Methodism enabled congregational hymnody to acquire popularity despite its prohibition among mainline denominations, but at the same time Methodism's boisterous revival meetings and association with the underclasses—rural and frontier people, laborers, and slaves—marked hymnody as déclassé and contributed to mainline denominations' reluctance to adopt congregational hymnody. The sudden rise of Methodism in North America during the Second Great Awakening (1790–1840) put great pressure on mainline denominations, which found themselves losing both members and cultural relevance to this upstart sect.[9] They responded by electing to adopt some of the practices popularized by Methodists, hymnody among them, and the second quarter of the nineteenth century saw widespread efforts to produce mainline denominational hymnals that sought to impose clerical supervision, theological regularity, and aesthetic quality on this potentially subversive worship practice. The publication in the 1850s of two monumental hymn books, authored by mainline clergymen, signaled the new legitimacy of congregational hymnody: *The Plymouth Collection (1855)*, edited by Henry Ward Beecher, and *The Sabbath Hymn and Tune Book* (1859), spearheaded by Austin Phelps.

The history of hymnody impinged directly on William Cullen Bryant, whose career both indexed and contributed to the form's transformation in the nineteenth century. Born into a Calvinist family in 1794, at the beginning of the Second Great Awakening, Bryant personally experienced the era's revivalism and ardent religious fervor, and he vividly recalled these events in his memoir. As was typical of the era, hymns were not permitted in congregational worship during his childhood but were nevertheless an important fixture of his family's domestic worship, and Bryant acknowledged the centrality of hymns to his religious and literary development, noting the particular importance of Isaac Watts. "I may be said to have been nurtured on Watts's devotional poems," he wrote, observing elsewhere that he had been "a lad whose poetical diet had consisted mainly of the hymns of Dr. Watts."[10] Perhaps the most suggestive detail about this admission is Bryant's anecdote recounting how, as a young child, he frequently stood on a chair and declaimed Watts's hymns, an endeavor that his mother jokingly described as a childhood imitation of "preaching."[11] This early habit of hymn recitation was as an important starting point in Bryant's poetic career, for it enabled him to learn the workings of versification and prosody as well as the techniques of recitation. This story also offered a knowing wink to his contemporary readers, who would have been familiar with Bryant's renown as a public poet who habitually mounted a podium to recite poems or give addresses in honor of special occasions. (His death in 1878 followed one such event.) In telling this story of his childhood enthusiasms, Bryant suggested that this civic role began with his early predilection for robust hymn recitations, and he likewise suggested that his beginnings as a poet commenced with his childhood self-presentation as a hymnist.

However, there is more at work here in this anecdote, for it attests to the legitimacy of clerical anxieties about the populist leanings of the hymn. Clergy remained resistant to hymns for so long because these writings allowed laypeople to usurp ministerial duties, offer biblical exegesis and instruction, and teach readers and congregants what to believe or feel. Hymn authorship was completely open to the public. Many were written anonymously, and their pedigrees were untraceable: the writers might have been apostates or heretics who were working, some clerics feared, to spread heterodox doctrines to a receptive but unwitting congregation. Bryant's anecdote suggests that, even as a child, he was already aware of the insurrectionary uses of hymns, for he accessed the special moral authority of the hymnist by reciting lyrics as if he were a preacher or minister. Hymns enabled him to lecture to his own mother and temporarily fashion himself as an authority figure who literally towered over her, his elevated height signaling the special status he believed himself to acquire through the medium of hymnody. In this way, hymns briefly overturned the conventional hierarchy of his childhood household, and his anecdote substantiates the worries of mainline clergy that hymnody could impart ministerial authority to those who lacked the traditional qualifications.

In response to the popularity of Methodism, mainline denominations reluctantly sanctioned the inclusion of hymns in congregational worship, and the first decades of the nineteenth century saw widespread efforts to raise their profile, aesthetics, and class associations. Bryant's career began amid this endeavor, giving him an important professional opportunity. Following the 1817 publication of his celebrated poem "Thanatopsis," he spent several years away from poetry as he attempted to forge a career as a periodicals editor. In 1820, however, he was invited to contribute to Henry D. Sewall's *Collection of Psalms and Hymns, for Social and Private Worship*, an early example of mainline efforts to develop hymn books in order to compete with Methodism and remain viable. Critics have noted that this invitation ended Bryant's prolonged dry spell and sparked his most prolific period as a poet. The result was his 1821 collection *Thanatopsis and Other Poems*.[12] Hymnody thus launched Bryant's career while situating him at the center of mainline efforts to refine a populist, divisive devotional form.

In his preface to the hymn collection, Sewall openly acknowledged that he often found hymnody crude and vulgar, and he touted the book as an effort, in keeping with the era's mainline clerical practice, to elevate its aesthetic tone and caliber. He wrote, "It has been the principal object in this selection to combine taste with devotion. It is not meant that there is any natural repugnance between them; but perhaps there are few persons of cultivated mind, who have not had cause to lament their too frequent disunion."[13] To that end, he asked Catharine Maria Sedgwick to approach Bryant as a contributor, and in response the poet submitted six hymns that were clearly engineered for an elite audience, as evidenced by their careful prosody and elevated diction. For instance, the second stanza of "The Earth Is Full of Thy Riches" (1820) reads:

> For when this orb of sea and land
> Was moulded in thy forming hand,
> Thy calm, benignant smile impressed
> A beam of heaven upon its breast.[14]

Though Bryant's lines scan smoothly and use the elementary hymn form of long meter couplets, they also include such lofty words as "orb" and "benignant" that make the hymn unsuitable for the oral improvisation that was characteristic of revival hymnody. Instead, Bryant chose words that were more appropriate for the developed literacy of a sophisticated readership. His hymns satisfied Sewall's desire for refined, tasteful lyric, and they consequently found a receptive audience among readers and editors who shared those concerns. A century later, Bryant's hymns were still in common use and were anthologized in such important venues as the compilation *Lyra Sacra Americana* (1868) and James Martineau's *Hymns of Praise and Prayer* (1873).

Among his literary peers, Bryant was the first major figure to write hymns. For instance, in the Knickerbocker Group—which included Lydia Maria Child, Joseph Rodman Drake, Fitz-Greene Halleck, Washington Irving, and Robert Charles Sands—Bryant was the only writer to compose hymns. And among the Fireside Poets with which he was later associated, Bryant was also the first to write hymns. In this capacity, Bryant did a great deal to make this devotional form respectable and literary. Just by writing hymns, Bryant moved the form from the religious periphery to the lyric mainstream, positioning it as a legitimate poetic form deserving of attention and serious artistic engagement. Furthermore, the contents of his hymns often addressed criticisms and offered assurances of the form's respectability. For instance, his early hymn "The Lord Giveth Wisdom" (1820) counters criticisms of hymnody as emotionally overwrought, instead attesting to the form's restraint and intellectual value. To the dismay of mainline clergy, hymns often privileged the emotions as the seat of religious life, but Bryant's hymn focuses instead on the intellectual fruits of religious faith, praising the deity as a source of wisdom "whose beams alone / Light the mighty world of mind!"[15] Bryant here seeks to realign knowledge and piety, suggesting that the two need not be irreconcilable, but he also refashions the hymn from a medium of emotional expression to a medium of intellectual engagement. The hymn's stately trochaic quatrains attest to the form's compatibility with reasoned, temperate judgment, implicitly suggesting its suitability for a more educated, elite constituency.

In another poem, "The Aged Pastor" (1848), Bryant transformed the hymn from an agent of social and religious upheaval into an instrument of stability. The hymn describes the faithful stewardship of an aging minister in a changing world. Though "empires rose [and] . . . crumbled down," the pastor and his "flock" have "dwelt in peace and light . . . in perennial pastures led."[16] Though the hymn form had long been associated with social upheaval, this example offers assurances of religious constancy and longevity, allaying anxieties that hymns might undermine ministerial authority and religious traditionalism and linking them instead to stability and steady clerical leadership. Another hymn, "In Memoriam" (1856), depicts congregational song as a modest, wholesome expression of religious belief in keeping with conventional deportment and worship practice:

> Hymns on the ancient silence broke
> From hearts that faltered not,
> And undissembling lips that spoke
> The free and guileless thought.[17]

In Bryant's depiction, hymnody is not the raucous practice of an unlettered, unruly assembly but the unassuming expression of pious faith, a portrait in keeping with the newly mainstream status of hymnody in mainline congregations around the country.

In 1864, Bryant compiled and privately printed a small hymn collection, which included hymns he had composed throughout his life. This collection suggests that he deemed his hymn compositions to be among his most treasured, significant poems, worthy of preservation and circulation among those closest to him. By this time, he was by no means the only writer with an interest in hymns. All of the Fireside Poets were publishing them, though they began doing so decades after Bryant's 1820 beginnings and well after the form had become respectable. Among this cohort, only the youngest and most cynical, James Russell Lowell was uninterested in the form. He published just one, "A Winter-Evening Hymn to My Fire" (1854), which was a thoroughly irreligious poem more indebted to the ancient Greek version of the hymn, which typically offered praise to a pagan deity, than to the Christian devotional form. However, Oliver Wendell Holmes wrote many conventional hymns, among them poems composed in honor of such occasions as the 1864 Great Central Fair of Philadelphia and the 1865 Emancipation Proclamation. He also wrote innumerable devotional poems composed in hymn forms, often giving his poems titles that announced their reliance on this lyric genre, among them "Hymn of Trust" and "A Sunday Hymn," both of which he included in *Poems from the Professor at the Breakfast Table* (1858). His hymns became enormously popular and were included in hundreds of hymnbooks and hymn collections. John Greenleaf Whittier was also a prolific hymnist, writing almost two hundred of them, many of which are still fixtures of congregational song in the English-speaking world.[18] His hymns "Dear Lord and Father of Mankind" (1872), "Immortal Love, Forever Full" (1866), and "We May Not Climb the Heavenly Steeps" (1866) were reprinted and included in hundreds of hymnals and hymn collections. Yet he disavowed any identification or skill as a hymnist, perhaps because, as a Quaker, he did not feel an affinity for a devotional form that was traditionally excluded from Quaker worship. Whittier nevertheless actively employed the hymn in the service of his political activism, penning poems that grounded his political principles in scriptural precedent and the forms of congregational song. His 1834 antislavery poem "Hymn," for instance, uses the scriptural assertion that human beings are made in the image of the deity to advocate for the humanity of slaves:

> Thy children all, though hue and form
> Are varied in Thine own good will,
> With Thy own holy breathings warm,
> And fashioned in Thine image still.[19]

Another such poem, "Hymn for the Celebration of Emancipation at Newburyport" (1865), depicted abolition as divinely blessed.

It was Longfellow's blockbuster poem "A Psalm of Life," however, that made the biggest contribution to the burgeoning respectability of hymnody. Included in his collection *Voices of the Night* (1839), the poem became an instant sensation and was reprinted countless times, catapulting Longfellow into poetic superstardom.[20] Memorized and recited by generations of Americans, it had iconic status for 150 years, but today the poem has little cultural or academic standing and is discussed primarily as evidence either of Longfellow's sentimentality or tendency toward cliché.[21] Composed of nine quatrains of trochaic tetrameter, "A Psalm of Life" offers a rebuttal to the nihilist allegation that "Life is but an empty dream."[22] Longfellow responds by asserting that "Life is real! Life is earnest!" and the poem offers an uncynical defense of a life spent doing one's best, striving and "achieving," with "a heart for any fate." To modern eyes, the poem may seem unsophisticated, its modest quatrains reflecting the simplicity of its claims, as it places its trust in the value of a good day's work and a resilience in the face of grief. The poem's sentiments are generally recognized as utterly conventional, but analysis of the poem's conventionality typically overlooks the fact that the poem was composed as a hymn. It was written in trochaic long meter, a conventional hymn form, and, though it is not titled "Hymn of Life," a practice that would soon become common among the Fireside Poets, its reference to psalms makes that generic association implicit. The poem presents itself as a psalm, but a psalm is defined specifically by its inclusion in the Bible; by extension, a psalm-like devotional poem composed after the final redaction of the Bible is defined instead as a hymn: despite the title's claim to a biblical pedigree, the poem was a de facto hymn. In conformity with the conventions of the genre, the poem dispenses religious wisdom and advice, telling the reader how to understand life, approach suffering, and interact with others. For instance, the poem's third stanza asserts, "Not enjoyment, and not sorrow,/Is our destined end or way," a declaration that offers a theological position on life's purpose, which, the poem asserts, is continued productivity and endurance, despite life's inevitable challenges. In accordance with the potential heterodoxy of hymnody, this assertion diverges markedly from conventional Christian teachings about salvation or redemption and offers a secular belief in the importance of endeavor and resilience.

Longfellow's poem was so successful and popular in part because of the considerable contributions of hymnody. Though the poem was entirely irreligious and avoided mentioning either the deity or scripture, it was nevertheless promptly adapted into two different hymns, which, taken together, were included in nearly a hundred different collections in the nineteenth century, among them such august volumes as Beecher's *The Plymouth Collection* and *Lyra Sacra Americana*. The poem's wide circulation was thus not limited to the world of literary reprinting but included such extra-literary channels as the hymn book and congregational song. Critics have commented on its widespread oral circulation well into the twentieth century and its contributions of several phrases—such as "footprints on the sands of time"—to the popular lexicon.[23] Yet the poem's entrance into common parlance was strongly indebted to hymnody. The congregational performance of Longfellow's verses allowed it to reach constituencies that otherwise might not have encountered the poem in printed form. Thus, it is no accident that the poem had a long career as a spoken, recited lyric. Moreover, the very practice of memorizing and reciting moralistic verse, which for decades enabled "A Psalm of Life" to reverberate in everyday American life, was first popularized by advocates of hymnody, who strongly encouraged the memorization and recitation of hymns out of the belief that such works could shape character and foster piety.[24] A good hymn was supposed to deliver moral instruction in memorable, easily apprehensible phrasings, and, though "A Psalm of Life" would later receive criticism for these traits, it was successful precisely because it employed the qualities that made hymns successful. The poem's widespread oral circulation was animated by long-established practices of hymnody, and it may be the only poem in American literary history in which the common customs of hymnody carried over from the religious sphere into the literary public sphere.

Longfellow's "A Psalm of Life" did considerable work in establishing the mainstream respectability of hymns. In its promotion of normative views about hard work, patience, and endurance, the poem allayed concerns about hymns' capacity to upset the status quo, instead affirming that they could instill wholesome, conventional values. Hymnologists typically designate *The Plymouth Collection* as a marker of the form's ascent to legitimacy, but the immense popularity of "A Psalm of Life" fifteen years earlier pushed hymnody into the poetic mainstream and opened floodgates that could not be closed. Following the poem's success, Longfellow's peers quickly published dozens of similar works. Though many were successful, among them Whittier's suggestively titled poem "My Psalm" (1859), none received an equivalent public response.

Longfellow's poem left a discernible mark on the history of American hymnody. For instance, in 1858, the prolific hymnist John S. Adams published a hymn collection titled *The Psalms of Life,* thus proving that the poem had become a marquee name in the world of hymnody. Two years later, Austin Phelps hailed the poem as the gold standard of American hymnody. Phelps co-edited the 1859 *Sabbath Hymn and Tune Book,* which has long been regarded as an important indicator of mainline acceptance of hymnody, and in 1860 he published a manual, *Hymns and Choirs,* designed to instruct clergy in the proper selection and use of hymns. In that work, he asserted that the best hymns derive from the personal experiences of their writers: "Every true hymn is a 'Psalm of Life:' some soul has lived it."[25] For one of the chief architects of mainline hymnody, Longfellow's poem became the blueprint for the ideal American hymn.

With these resounding endorsements, the Fireside Poets successfully brought hymnody in line with conventional taste and sensibility, an endeavor with complex consequences. To be sure, they helped to neutralize a devotional form that had long been associated with religious populism and anticlerical insurgency. Their concessions to taste and aesthetics worked to reinstate hierarchical, elitist structures that hymnody had originally sought to dismantle.[26] In the hands of the Fireside Poets, hymnody was no longer the vehicle of anticlerical populism or the expression of ardent religious zeal. Instead, they reformed the hymn into a highly controlled, deeply aestheticized vehicle for religious sensibility. Even though poetic refinement disarmed the insurrectionary potential of hymnody, it didn't prevent mainline denominations from continuing to decline, losing ground first to Methodism and then later in the century to Catholicism. The primary beneficiaries of this enterprise were the Fireside Poets themselves, whose hymn compositions imparted considerable luster to their own public images and helped solidify their reputation for virtue. Ann Douglas has famously argued that the midcentury saw the reallocation of moral authority from the minister to the sentimental woman writer, but the history of American hymnody suggests that it was the Fireside Poets who most brazenly usurped that authority. Their poems not only performed clerical duties but also overrode long-standing ministerial objection and endorsed hymns as a valuable medium for moral instruction.[27] This consequence is patently evident in Longfellow's "A Psalm of Life," which not only made the poet an international celebrity but also implicitly situated him and his work within a sacred tradition.[28] The poem's titular reference to psalmody characterized the poem as a modern-day descendant of the biblical psalms, an assertion with some basis in historical fact: once hymnody became a customary feature of congregational worship, it effectively replaced psalmody, which receded from common use. At the same time, the poem's title positioned Longfellow as a successor of the psalmist, who, at the time of the poem's composition, was widely believed to be King David. The end result was the suggestion that Longfellow and his fellow hymnists were prophetic figures whose poems were divinely inspired sources of authority superior even to ordained clergy.

The authorizing power of the hymn did not last for long. By the mid-twentieth century, the Fireside Poets' commitment to such devotional forms contributed directly to their declining reputations, and in 1940 the critic F. O. Matthiessen disparaged Whittier as a "popular" poet who favored such "traditional popular forms" as "the ballad and hymns."[29] In juxtaposing Whittier's putative traditionalism with Walt Whitman's "determination to be new," Matthiessen interpreted Whittier's hymnody as evidence of his lesser status and relative unimportance, a judgment that he implicitly extended to the Fireside Poets as a whole, as evidenced by their near-total omission from his magisterial study of the American Renaissance. Since then, the Fireside Poets have steadily declined in scholarly opinion, their work occupying ever-dwindling space in literature anthologies and seldom entering the classroom. Though their hymns contributed to this decline, they nevertheless gave these poets a literary afterlife, as it were, for many of their hymns remain canonical fixtures of Anglo-American hymnody. Hymns such as Bryant's "Thou, Whose Unmeasured Temple Stands" (1820), Longfellow's "I Heard the Bells on Christmas Day" (1864), and Whittier's "Dear Lord and Father of Mankind" (1872) continue to be included in congregational hymnals. Though few schoolchildren now memorize and recite their poems, their hymns are still regularly performed in the domain of public worship, a setting that has vested these writers with more authority and influence than they ever would have achieved in the American classroom.

NOTES

1. Angela Sorby, *Schoolroom Poets: Childhood, Performance, and the Place of American Poetry, 1865–1917* (Durham: University of New Hampshire Press, 2005), xvii–xviii.

2. Dana Gioia, "Longfellow in the Aftermath of Modernism," in *The Columbia History of American Poetry*, ed. Jay Parini (New York: Columbia University Press, 1993), 80.

3. See, for instance, Kristen Silva Gruesz, "El Gran Poeta Longfellow and a Psalm of Exile," *American Literary History* 10 (Autumn 1998): 395–427; Eric L. Haralson, "Mars in Petticoats: Longfellow and Sentimental Masculinity," *Nineteenth-Century Literature* 51 (December 1996): 327–55; and Virginia Jackson, "Longfellow's Tradition; or, Picture-Writing a Nation," *Modern Language Quarterly* 59 (December 1998): 471–96.

4. Vernon Louis Parrington, for instance, asserted that Longfellow had "little creative originality" and "was the poet of an uncritical and unsophisticated generation" (*1800–1860: The Romantic Revolution in America*, vol. 2 of *Main Currents in American Thought* [1927; reprint, New York: Harcourt, Brace, 1954], 432).

5. James H. Justus, "The Fireside Poets: Hearthside Values and the Language of Care," in *Nineteenth-Century American Poetry*, ed. A. Robert Lee (London: Vision, 1985), 163.

6. Kirsten Silva Gruesz, "Feeling for the Fireside: Longfellow, Lynch, and the Topography of Poetic Power," in *Sentimental Men: Masculinity and the Politics of Affect in American Culture*, ed. Mary Chapman and Glenn Hendler (Berkeley: University of California Press, 1999), 53.

7. Gruesz, "El Gran Poeta Longfellow," 402.

8. Oliver Wendell Holmes, "Mare Rubrum," in *The Complete Poetical Works of Oliver Wendell Holmes* (Boston: Houghton Mifflin, 1923), 118.

9. Roger Finke and Rodney Stark have shown that, by 1850, Methodism was the nation's leading denomination, a development that caused a corresponding decline among mainline denominations. For instance, Congregationalists eroded from 20 percent of affiliated church members in 1776 to merely 4 percent in 1850 (*The Churching of America, 1776–2005: Winners and Losers in Our Religious Economy* [New Brunswick, N.J.: Rutgers University Press, 2005], 56).

10. Bryant's autobiographical reflections were composed in 1874–75 and were included in the biography written by his son-in-law. See Parke Godwin, *A Biography of William Cullen Bryant, with Extracts from His Private Correspondence*, 2 vols. (New York: Russell and Russell, 1883), 1:26. The latter quotation comes from the

reminiscences of John Bigelow, Bryant's colleague at the *Evening Post*, which Bryant edited for decades (*William Cullen Bryant* [1890; reprint, Detroit: Gale, 1970], 14).

11. His mother's remark appears in Charles H. Brown, *William Cullen Bryant* (New York: Scribner, 1971), 13.

12. Richard D. Birdsall, "William Cullen Bryant and Catherine Sedgwick—Their Debt to Berkshire," *New England Quarterly* 28 (September 1955): 360.

13. Henry D. Sewall, preface to *A Collection of Psalms and Hymns, for Social and Private Worship* (New York: Van Winkle, 1820), n.p.

14. William Cullen Bryant, *The Poetical Works of William Cullen Bryant* (1903; reprint, New York: AMS Press, 1972), 350.

15. Ibid., 353.

16. Ibid., 362.

17. Ibid., 363.

18. Samuel J. Rogal, *Congregational Hymns from the Poetry of John Greenleaf Whittier: A Comparative Study of the Sources and Final Works, with a Bibliographic Catalog of the Hymns* (Jefferson, N.C.: McFarland, 2010), 110–29.

19. John Greenleaf Whittier, *The Complete Poetical Works of John Greenleaf Whittier*, ed. Horace E. Scudder (Boston: Houghton Mifflin, 1894), 268.

20. Matthew Gartner, "Becoming Longfellow: Work, Manhood, and Poetry," *American Literature* 72 (March 2000): 72–73; Charles C. Calhoun, *Longfellow: A Rediscovered Life* (Boston: Beacon, 2004), 137.

21. See, for instance, Gioia, "Longfellow in the Aftermath of Modernism," 78–79.

22. Henry Wadsworth Longfellow, *Henry Wadsworth Longfellow: Poems and Other Writings* (New York: Library of America, 2000), 3.

23. Calhoun, *Longfellow*, ix.

24. Mary De Jong, "'Theirs the Sweetest Songs': Women Hymn Writers in the Nineteenth-Century United States," in *A Mighty Baptism: Race, Gender, and the Creation of American Protestantism*, ed. Susan Juster and Lisa MacFarlane (Ithaca: Cornell University Press, 1996), 141–42.

25. Austin Phelps, Edwards Park, and Daniel L. Furber, *Hymns and Choirs: or, The Matter and the Manner of the Service of Song in the House of the Lord* (Andover, Mass.: Draper, 1860), 6.

26. I have written about this extensively elsewhere. See Claudia Stokes, *The Altar at Home: Sentimental Literature and Nineteenth-Century American Religion* (Philadelphia: University of Pennsylvania Press, 2014), 67–102; and Claudia Stokes, "My Kingdom: Sentimentalism and the Refinement of Hymnody," *ESQ* 58, no. 3 (2012): 294–337.

27. Ann Douglas, *The Feminization of American Culture* (1977; reprint, New York: Anchor, 1988), 80–117.

28. Matthew Gartner makes a related clam ("Becoming Longfellow," 73–74).

29. F. O. Matthiessen, *American Renaissance: Art and Expression in the Age of Emerson and Whitman* (London: Oxford University Press, 1941), 557.

CHAPTER 12

KEEPING THE SABBATH AT HOME

Emily Dickinson and the Rise of Private Hymnody

Christopher N. Phillips

SCHOLARS RECOGNIZE that Emily Dickinson's poetry engages with the meters, imagery, and tone of hymnody, but few have considered that she might have actually written hymns. In her recent study of Dickinson and hymns, arguably the fullest treatment of the topic to date, Victoria N. Morgan emphasizes that she "does not aim to reclassify Dickinson's poems as hymns." Barton Levi St. Armand grandly (and imprecisely) claims that Dickinson converted "Puritan hymnology" into "a personal psalmody," while Martha Winburn England states that she "wrote nineteenth-century hymns."[1] England is closest to the mark, I believe, as her distinction hinges on the fact that the relative status of hymns and poems was in flux in the nineteenth century: a much wider range of form and subject matter was available to hymn writers in the 1850s than was the case in the 1750s or even the 1820s.[2] Hymns were indeed a part of what David S. Reynolds describes as the "dramatic shift in the rhetorical strategies of popular social texts" that helped to bring about the American Renaissance. They also shared in the specific shift of "popular religious discourse from the doctrinal to the imaginative" that he has articulated.[3] Reynolds's understanding of that style is focused on sermonic rhetoric, and his discussions of Dickinson in *Beneath the American Renaissance* focus on sermonic influences. The kind of fine-grained analysis that he has brought to bear on major authors' interactions with their cultural context has yet to be applied to hymns.[4] To understand Dickinson's relationship to hymnody requires a grasp of the dynamic history of hymns in the nineteenth century, careful attention to domestic space as a context for that history in Dickinson's own life, and a consideration of the poet's use of hymn language in her letters and poems.

The starting point for almost every discussion of Dickinson and hymns has been Isaac Watts, known as the father of English hymnody and the author of what he called the "System of Praise," including a volume of hymns (1707, revised 1709) and another of free psalm translations (1719).[5] More than sixty years ago, Thomas Johnson declared that nearly all of Dickinson's poems "employ meters derived from English hymnology" and that these meters were "familiar to her from childhood as the measure in which Watts's hymns were composed," and since then the equation of Watts and the hymn in Dickinson's world has gone virtually unquestioned.[6] Mary Loeffelholz has argued, "Background and foreground . . . remain stubbornly in their familiar places in Dickinson studies, with the background of nineteenth-century popular verse held artificially still as a uniform norm (sampled anywhere, it will be the same), the fixed target over which Dickinson's invention, experimentation, and subversion play."[7] With hymnody, the situation is even worse, as scholars fix the tradition not in its nineteenth-century heyday but at its symbolic origin: written by Watts, and always sung. The lyricization of Dickinson that Virginia Jackson has brought into view takes on an additional layer here, what we might call the liturgicization of the hymn, excluding the hymnic from other poetic registers, particularly those marked as private, personal, and literary. It requires little effort to imagine Dickinson as a private poet rejecting the values and demands of the publicly sung hymn, but as June Hadden Hobbs has argued, Dickinson's contemporaries "regarded hymns as devotional reading. . . . The main emphasis was on the printed page because hymns were primarily literary rather than oral expressions of personal faith."[8] Reading practices were at the heart of Dickinson's interaction with hymnody, and they shed light on her place within a larger print culture as well as spiritual culture.

Emily Dickinson did in fact write hymns, and hymns of her time. These were poetic texts meant to connect the human soul to God *and* to connect human souls to each other. She reached for the music of the spheres even as she found hymnody in housekeeping, as in Poem 891:

> I learned – at least – what Home could be –
> How ignorant I had been
> Of pretty ways of Covenant –
> How awkward at the Hymn
>
> Round our new Fireside.[9]

Hymnody had to be learned; and, until the twentieth century, it was learned first and foremost within the home. We must understand this literate, domestic hymnody if we are to recover a key dimension of Dickinson's world and work, and my work in this essay is meant to be a first step in understanding anew what her commitment to "keep[ing] the Sabbath . . . at home" entailed.[10]

Watts and Select: The Dickinsons' Hymns

Watts loomed large in Reformed church collections of Dickinson's time, but he was present in many forms. Emily Norcross's pre-marriage copy of his *Psalms and Hymns,* now at Harvard, was an 1810 imprint of "Barlow's Watts," an already-thirty-year-old revised edition that the Connecticut wit, Joel Barlow, made for his state's Congregationalists following independence. (For instance, he removed references to King George.) While the most famous Watts texts tended to remain the same across editions, over time they kept different company. First Church, Amherst, favored "Watts and Select" volumes containing most or all of the System of Praise plus an appendix of other hymns; both Samuel Worcester's *Psalms, Hymns, and Spiritual Songs* and Lowell Mason's *Church Psalmody* were of this variety. In her correspondence, Dickinson quotes hymn texts by James Montgomery, Saint Augustine, Anna Letitia Barbauld, William Cowper, and Watts, all available in *Church*

Psalmody, which First Church adopted in 1839.[11] The rapidly diversifying canon of hymnody in the mid-nineteenth century has received only glancing attention from scholars of the American Renaissance, but it is a crucial fact for understanding how writers such as Dickinson interacted with the hymnody available to them. Only after the dynamic history of hymns is in focus can we see her use of hymnody in light of Reynolds's assertion that the achievement of such writers "resulted not from a *rejection* of socioliterary context but rather from a full *assimilation* and *transformation*" of it.[12]

A similarly crucial issue is how the hymns would have been used. Watts was popular for devotional use in New England within a few years of the *Hymns'* initial publication, but he rose to prominence in American church services only in the late eighteenth century, following an initial wave of midcentury adoptions during the Great Awakening. Previously, American Protestants had sung only psalms in church, following John Calvin's teaching that only scriptural texts were appropriate for public worship (which is why Watts's *Psalms* were so frequently coupled with his *Hymns*).[13] And even after Watts was sung in public, not until the late nineteenth century did churches routinely provide hymnbooks in pew racks. The Dickinsons were typical of wealthy, pew-renting churchgoers of their time; they bought separate copies of their hymnbooks for home and church use. Other families opted to carry books between church and home, but private ownership was a shared reality among rich and poor. The books, generally small and without music, could be read as devotional poetry collections, even in church, and this affordance was of lasting importance to the Dickinson family.

Tunebooks and tune appendices were available starting in the late seventeenth century, but they were expensive to produce: copper printing plates were not durable enough for large print runs, and music type wore down quickly and was very difficult to set. Until about 1860 most tunebooks were used only by choirs and students in short-term singing schools taught by itinerant singing masters. First Church had sponsored several singing schools from the 1780s to as late as 1817, but from the 1820s onward church music was dominated by a choir and instrumental accompaniment, often professional. Emily Dickinson grew up in a church that had largely abandoned congregational singing in favor of congregants reading their books silently while designated musicians performed the texts.[14]

The Dickinsons took measures to preserve this arrangement. When First Church adopted *The Sabbath Hymn and Tune Book* (also called the Andover Collection) in 1860, the book was available in versions with and without printed tunes, as many worshippers resented having their reading practices disrupted by interlined music scores.[15] The Dickinsons were among this number; all the extant family copies are the words-only *Sabbath Hymn Book*. Even in the public space of the church pew, Edward Dickinson and his family preferred private textuality to public performance, using the hymnbook as both a badge of membership and a cone of silence within which to retreat. This sheds new light on Emily's confession to Susan Gilbert, her future sister-in-law, of rewriting a hymn in her head while the choir sang.[16] Scholars have read this as an early sign of rebellion that eventually resulted in Emily's withdrawal from church, but turning a sung worship text into a love poem was actually a practice for which the very arrangement of the service had allowed space. She was *supposed* to be alone with her book and her thoughts during the choir's performance of the song. Hymns provided a space for her poetic production precisely because they allowed for a privacy within public worship.

The Dickinsons were a musical family, and Emily's penchant for singing and piano is well documented.[17] Hymns were certainly sung and played in the home and in church; the poet told her Norcross cousins in a letter following her father's death that "almost the last tune he heard was, 'Rest from thy loved employ,'" likely a setting of James Montgomery's hymn "Servant of God, well done," played by the poet.[18] But it is easy, and unwise, to underestimate the degree to which hymns were experienced as *read* texts in Dickinson's world. They were read aloud from the pulpit, in the sermon and elsewhere in the service, as Dickinson alludes to in Poem 229. When she offers to send her brother a copy of *Village Hymns,* she does so in connection with his "meditat[ing] profoundly upon the Daily Food" (that is, the Bible) in his "closet."[19] And she told Susan to have one of her students read her a hymn as an antidote to reading about the poet's troubling feelings: "get some sweet little scholar to read a gentle hymn, about Bethleem [*sic*] and Mary, and you will sleep on sweetly and have as peaceful dreams, as if I had never written you all these ugly things."[20] While Dickinson probably heard, sang, and played hymns all her life, we cannot assume that singing was her default mode of experiencing hymn texts.

Even as families such as the Dickinsons resisted the innovation of hymnals with printed music, they readily consumed an emerging print genre, what I call the *private hymnbook*. These books often included many of the same texts as the church collections did, but they also ranged far more widely in including moral and nature poetry and texts from pre-Reformation Christian traditions (such as Catholicism and the Moravians)—and they were never intended for church use. These private hymnbooks were part of the explosion of the gift-book industry in the middle third of the nineteenth century and were predicated on practices of private and family reading of religious verse; they complemented the Dickinsons' preferred approach to their church hymnbooks. A closer examination of these books in the Dickinson homes sheds light on what hymnody and privacy may have meant to a poet too often branded a freethinking recluse.

Private Hymnbooks to Private Hymns

Starting in the 1820s, new hymn collections such as James Montgomery's *Christian Psalmist*, John Keble's *Christian Year*, and Reginald Heber's *Hymns* were designed to supply texts for worship but presented themselves as initially for private consumption, often in ornate gift-book presentations or with the generous white space of contemporary poetry books.[21] These books did feed hymnbooks, but they also fed other gift books, such as Rufus Griswold's 1848 *Sacred Poets of England and America*, a copy of which Susan Gilbert received from her classmates at Utica Female Academy, anticipating her collection of private hymnbooks that pushed the boundary between poetry and hymnody.

Susan's collection largely consisted of volumes compiled by Caroline Snowden Whitmarsh (later Guild), a Boston Unitarian whose early education at the Ursuline Academy in Charlestown probably influenced her ecumenical approach to religious verse. While male authors and compilers tended to dominate church collections, the most successful private hymnbooks of the 1850s and 1860s were edited by women, Whitmarsh foremost among them. Whitmarsh's first collection, *Hymns of the Ages* (1858), was an immediate success, even though she acknowledged reliance on antiquarian collections such as *Lyra Catholica* and *Lyra Germanica* at a moment of high anti-Catholic sentiment in America.[22] She sought to bring a wider range of Christian thought and spirituality to American Protestant readers, and her approach enjoyed sales good enough for her publisher, the elite firm Ticknor and Fields, to urge her to compile two further series of *Hymns of the Ages*. Susan Dickinson acquired copies of the first two series from her lifelong friend Frederic Dan Huntington, a Harvard professor and an Amherst College graduate, who had written laudatory prefaces for the first two volumes—which led to frequent attribution of the books to his editorship.

Hymns of the Ages was a popular gift book among highly educated and cultured adult readers, but Whitmarsh also produced another series for a decidedly younger audience: *Hymns for Mothers and Children* (1861). As she states in the preface, this was a very different project from the earlier one, due to the "sad lack of material." Her sources were not scholarly collections but small books she often had to borrow from the children who owned them; she also transcribed children's recitations, "for there are no Athenaeum libraries of children's books, and this [book] has literally been gathered 'out of the mouths of babes.'"[23] Yet for all its editorial difficulties, *Hymns for Mothers and Children* succeeded and extended into a second series four years later. Both books feature gilt bindings and numerous engravings, and the engraved title pages depict a mother reading to her children, but the construction of the collections makes it clear that children were meant to do their share of reading in the books. Sections for younger children and older children, poems voiced by children, and poems about play all invite a flesh-and-blood child speaker-reader. With many poems on moral topics, family milestones (births, birthdays, deaths), and natural scenery, the collection ranged far from content suited to church services—though the line between hymn and poem had always been more permeable in children's collections.

Susan Dickinson owned both series of *Hymns for Mothers and Children;* and while it is not known when she acquired them, it is plausible that the first series was a gift on the occasion of the birth of her first child, Ned Dickinson, in 1861. The ephemerality of the children's books that

Whitmarsh lamented reflects the general lack of recorded history of what passes between mother and child, from pregnancy and birth to care, early education, and the sharing of private reading from books such as Whitmarsh's. Such history went unrecorded in the Dickinson homes; not only is there no documentation directly linking Ned's birth and Susan's book, but there has been almost no commentary on the effect of becoming an aunt on the poet's development. Though Emily was close to all three of Susan's children, little if anything has been made of their births as inspiration for her works. Yet for a poet fascinated by not only children but also the power of hymns in their hands and mouths, a new child in her life just as her poetic production was rapidly accelerating could be expected to surface in her writing at some point.

This domestic, child-centered spirituality comes out forcefully in an early poem, one of the few that includes a named interlocutor—in this case, the Dickens-esque boy "Tim."[24] Poem 231 begins, "We dont cry – Tim and I – / We are far too grand – [.]" Tim and the speaker lock themselves away in fear of death, torn by a sense of helplessness and a longing for a final home, which leads to a crisis of fright:

> Then – we shake – Tim and I –
> And lest I – cry –
>
> Tim – reads a little Hymn –
> And we both pray,
> Please, Sir, I and Tim –
> Always lost the way![25]

The prayer is the expression of an orphan voice longing for comfort while fearing abandonment, and it comes after the turning point of the poem: hymn reading. At this point, actions of shutting in and out give place to reaching out into the unknown. While Tim reads the hymn merely to stave off tears, the reading inspires language, prayer, poetry—the connection between soul and God that hymns had been developed to foster. Yet this is not a binary scene; the close of Poem 231 is a prayer: "Take us simultaneous – Lord – / I – 'Tim' – and – me!"[26] For Dickinson, the hymn was always about greater connection, both horizontally and vertically.

"Clear[?] Strains of Hymn" in Dickinson's Writings

One source of confusion over Dickinson's deciding to call her own works hymns is that the poems she thus designated almost always take secular subjects: a hummingbird, the seasons, patriotism.[27] All of these topics feature in *Hymns for Mothers and Children,* with nature and patriotism boasting their own sections. But why call the poems hymns at all? Dickinson's letters suggest an answer: she apparently called poems hymns when her work was under threat of being cut short or misunderstood.

The most significant group of these works was a trio of pieces donated to an 1880 fundraiser at First Church's Mission Circle for children's missions abroad. In a letter to her future editor, Thomas Wentworth Higginson, Dickinson wondered "if they were faithful." He agreed to read the poems, and she sent him four, "lest one of them you might think profane."[28] She was concerned that her poems did not fit their new context, or might be judged not to fit, for she was offering them as commodities: they were gifts but were meant to fetch a price. Facing this sense of uncertainty about entering her poem-gifts into the marketplace, she decided to call her texts hymns as a way to claim a particular kind of social life for what critics have generally considered her private poetry. The connections to God and others would keep these poems "faithful," even as they moved out of old contexts and into something the poet could not foresee. She envisioned a hymn as a "letter to the world" that requires considerable doses of privacy to reach its public; yet as Dickinson repeatedly insisted, reaching their public is what hymns do.

Dickinson described one such public in a letter comforting her sister, Lavinia, after she kept vigil over the death of her aunt, Lavinia Norcross: "Well, she is safer now than 'we know or even think.' . . . Tuneful little aunt, singing, as we trust, hymns than which the robins have no sweeter ones."[29] This is the hymn of the faithful martyr, a music that stretches across the chasms of death, "Clear strains of Hymn / The River could not drown."[30] The strains stand out not for their content but for their supernatural beauty, outdoing the hymns that the robins sing.

For birds also sing hymns. In a famous letter, Dickinson shares an anecdote about finding a bird singing hidden in a bush: "wherefore sing, I said, since nobody *hears?* . . . '*My* business is to *sing*'—and away she rose! How do I know but cherubim, once, themselves, as patient, listened, and applauded her unnoticed hymn?"[31] The anecdote immediately follows the poet's declaration "*My* business is to love," emphasizing the parallels between poet and bird, loving and singing. The bird sings, despite a lack of visible audience, and rises to follow its song, which is (or may be) heard by angels. What Dickinson imagined her aunt doing in the heavenly presence of angels and a bird doing among the same angels on earth she also imagined herself doing. She understood the hymn as a form of hopeful communication, one in which lack of an evident audience is offset by faith in spiritual reception. Hymns are not simply poems that are spiritually received; the reception is what makes the hymn.

An episode of the Dickinson-Higginson correspondence dramatizes this hymning of a poem. In May 1874, Higginson sent Dickinson his Memorial Day poem, "Decoration," and she thanked him for the "Poem" that identifies the unmarked grave of a bereaved woman as that of the bravest soul in a soldiers' cemetery.[32] "Decoration" appeared in *Scribner's* in June; that same month, Dickinson's father, Edward, died suddenly. When she next wrote to Higginson in response to his condolences, she closed the letter with a new mention of "Decoration": "Your beautiful Hymn, was it not prophetic? It has assisted that Pause of Space which I call 'Father.'"[33] What had been a poem in May was now a hymn with "prophetic" importance, honoring a woman's bravery in the face of loss and negotiating the "Space" of an earthly father's absence and an ongoing struggle with a heavenly father. Higginson's sentimental occasional poem transformed through Dickinson's grief into a gateway to the luminous. It became a hymn in Dickinson's situated reading of it.

Dickinson imagined a similar, and gendered, power for hymns in Poem 454, which narrates how a presumably female speaker sustains a declining male character, beginning with these lines:

> I rose – because He sank –
> I thought it would be opposite –
> But when his power dropped –
> My Soul grew straight.[34]

This is one of Dickinson's most metrically complex poems, and several scholars have noted the broken quatrains and the inclusion of a pentameter line in the final stanza.[35] Yet little has been said about the "Hymn" that the speaker wields twice in the poem. In the second stanza, an incomplete verse relates the speaker's power: "I cheered my fainting Prince – / I sang firm – even – Chants – / I helped his Film – with Hymn." The chants' firmness and evenness have little to do with meter, though the dashes give a sense of restraint and measure to the line; the hymn's strength is not in its content or its form but lies deeper. The hymn that the speaker chants here is of death and the afterlife:

> I told him Best – must pass
> Through this low Arch of Flesh –
> No Casque so brave
> It spurn the Grave –
>
> I told him Worlds I knew
> Where Emperors grew –
> Who recollected us
> If we were true –

Death is inevitable but, as Dickinson continually insists, is not the end; if armor (the "Casque," or helmet) cannot ensure immortality, truth can. And this turns out to be a truth that surprises its teller, a truth not consciously known before it is voiced:

> And so with Thews of Hymn –
> And Sinew from within –
> And ways I knew not that I knew – till then –
> I lifted Him – [36]

While the male body and its armor both fail, "Hymn" has its own "Thews" and "Sinew"—this is brawn, but not male brawn, as Michael Manson points out. Nor is it strength that conquers another; instead, it sustains and connects. Manson reads the poem as setting the feminine power of the hymn stanza, or stave, above that of the traditionally male pentameter even while those powers fuse together in the closing stanza; the penultimate line is in iambic pentameter, and the stanza beginning "I told him Worlds I knew" scans as a heroic couplet.[37] While I find the gendered coding of the meters and stanzaic forms helpful in understanding this poem, the hymn that Dickinson's speaker wields here is not Watts's common-meter quatrain but the deeper spiritual power that animates that form. This power is not reducible to metrical form or propositional knowledge; the power and pleasure of the hymn does not inhere solely in the stanza. If it begins there—in the hymn heard in church, or read by a child at home or school, or recalled in mourning a loved one—it reaches beyond form into spirit and, in so doing, constitutes a peculiar interpersonal force that Dickinson acknowledged, celebrated, and wielded in her writings.

Yet Manson is right to insist that "Dickinson works mostly with meters that either realized or partially realized stanzaic form," a commitment that "suggests that something about the experience of this kind of rhythmic completion spoke to her."[38] Though the music she longed to listen to was "not Hymn from Pulpit read," reading from the pulpit, the classroom, or the closet could lead to such music.[39] The power of hymns for Dickinson was fundamentally spiritual, but it also had a certain embodiment—more precisely, an articulation. Her poems that deal directly with "Hymn" do not settle into regular metrical patterns, but a number of her other poems do; and when this regular metrics combines with theological subject matter, it can be difficult not to see her reaching back to Watts. Yet, as I have shown, Watts is hardly the whole story, or even the most relevant part of the story, when it comes to understanding Dickinson's relationship to hymnody. She engaged deeply with later hymnists, and she also reached back past Watts to older traditions, as her brother Austin did with his favorite "Jerusalem, my happy home," an English Renaissance translation of a text by Saint Augustine—and the only hymn Dickinson quotes more than once in her correspondence.

One final Dickinson piece highlights the range of her engagement with hymnody as well as its thematic importance to her work. Poem 598 is familiar to many students of the American Renaissance:

> The Brain – is wider than the Sky –
> For – put them side by side –
> The one the other will contain
> With ease – and You – beside –
>
> The Brain is deeper than the sea –
> For – hold them – Blue to Blue –

> The one the other will absorb –
> As Sponges – Buckets – do –
>
> The Brain is just the weight of God –
> For – Heft them – Pound for Pound –
> And they will differ – if they do –
> As Syllable from Sound – [40]

This vaunted celebration of the human intellect collapses the physical and the mental/spiritual, using the brain rather than the mind as God's great competitor. It also uses common meter, whose resonances go back to the earliest roots of American Puritanism. Poem 598 follows this long tradition in an imperative mode, demanding that the reader reflect, put, hold, heft, and learn of God and human infinity through experiments—at least ideal ones. The brain takes the mind's place, but the physical handling of God and brain together can only occur in imagination, creating a powerful example of what Sharon Cameron describes as Dickinson's "Choosing not choosing," of seeming to set up a forced dichotomy while not settling on either side of it.[41] Brain or mind? Body or spirit? Hymn or poem? Yes.

The perfect 8–6–8–6 common meter is unusual for Dickinson, who preferred to modify common and short meters. The thoughts in the stanzas are unusually complete, rounding off each quatrain, and the parallel structure across the three is also unusual for her. Few of her texts fit so well the formal criteria of hymnody, but the content of the poem is obviously not meant for church. When Johnson saw Dickinson vying with Watts, perhaps this juxtaposition of tight textual control and extravagant thought was what he had in mind; but by looking only to Watts, he distorted and misidentified her tradition. Watts was merely the most visible figure in a rich, complex mix of writers, and the dynamic world of hymnody in the mid-nineteenth century was clearly not lost on Dickinson. Indeed, works such as Poem 598 fit well, if surprisingly, into Anna Warner's description of the contents in her popular private hymnbook *Hymns of the Church Militant* (1858): "These are not assembly hymns, nor paraphrases, nor hymns written to order,—they are the living words of deep Christian experience."[42] Dickinson's experience was indeed deeply Christian, though with an unorthodox approach to church. Along with the cadences of Watts and others, she had absorbed a way of feeling and thinking in the world that drew on theology but expressed the spiritual through aesthetic effects. When we see hymns in her poems, we see something true, but not what we expected. We think we hear syllables when we actually hear sounds; and only in holding Dickinson's writings to hymns "Blue to Blue" can we discern what her project as a writer of hymns may in fact have been.

NOTES

1. Victoria N. Morgan, *Emily Dickinson and Hymn Culture: Tradition and Experience* (Burlington, Vt.: Ashgate, 2010), 5; Barton Levi St. Armand, *Emily Dickinson and Her Culture: The Soul's Society* (New York: Cambridge University Press, 1984), 37; Martha Winburn England and John Sparrow, *Hymns Unbidden: Donne, Herbert, Blake, Emily Dickinson, and the Hymnographers* (New York: New York Public Library, 1966), 119.

2. On the changing nature of hymnody in the mid-nineteenth century, see Claudia Stokes, *The Altar at Home: Sentimental Literature and Nineteenth-Century American Religion* (Philadelphia: University of Pennsylvania Press, 2014), chap. 2; as well as her chapter in this volume. Also see June Hadden Hobbs, *"I Sing for I Cannot Be Silent": The Feminization of American Hymnody, 1870–1920* (Pittsburgh: University of Pittsburgh Press, 1997), chap. 1. For larger overviews of the history of hymnody, the best sources are Lewis F. Benson, *The English Hymn: Its Development and Use in Worship* (New York: Doran, 1915); and, in an American context, Henry Wilder Foote, *Three Centuries of American Hymnody* (New York: Hymn Society of America, 1952).

3. David S. Reynolds, *Beneath the American Renaissance: The Subversive Imagination in the Age of Emerson and Melville* (1988; reprint, Cambridge, Mass.: Harvard University Press, 1989), 7, 15.

4. Claudia Stokes's essay on the Fireside Poets and hymns (chap. 11) represents an important contribution along these lines and speaks to how vibrant (and literary) hymn writing was in Dickinson's time.

5. Benson, *English Hymn*, 118–22.

6. Thomas H. Johnson, *Emily Dickinson: An Interpretive Biography* (1955; reprint, New York: Atheneum, 1972), 84. See also David T. Porter, *The Art of Emily Dickinson's Early Poetry* (Cambridge, Mass.: Harvard University Press, 1966), 55–62; and England and Sparrow, *Hymns Unbidden*, 121. For a definition of the hymn as a publicly sung form, see Morgan, *Dickinson and Hymn Culture*, chap. 2.

7. Mary Loeffelholz, "Really Indigenous Productions: Emily Dickinson, Josiah Holland, and Nineteenth-Century Popular Verse," in *A Companion to Emily Dickinson*, ed. Martha Nell Smith and Mary Loeffelholz (Malden, Mass.: Blackwell, 2008) 183–204, 192.

8. Hadden Hobbs, *I Sing*, 27.

9. Emily Dickinson, *The Poems of Emily Dickinson: Reading Edition*, ed. R. W. Franklin (Cambridge, Mass.: Harvard Univ. Press, 1998), 386. All cited poems refer to this edition; I follow Franklin's numbering style rather than the older style in Emily Dickinson, *The Complete Poems of Emily Dickinson*, ed. Thomas H. Johnson (Boston: Little, Brown, 1960).

10. Dickinson, Poem 236, 106.

11. Emily Dickinson, *The Letters of Emily Dickinson*, ed. Thomas H. Johnson, 3 vols. (Cambridge, Mass.: Belknap/Harvard Univ. Press, 1958), 1:111, 1:235, 1:217, 1:277. Morgan interprets Dickinson's quotation of "a Hymn they used to sing when I went to church" (2:593) as a revision of lines from Watts's "When I survey the wondrous cross" (*Dickinson and Hymn Culture*, 100). On First Church's adoption of *Church Psalmody*, see *250 Years at First Church in Amherst, 1739–1989* (Amherst, Mass.: First Congregational Church, 1990), 61.

12. Reynolds, *Beneath the American Renaissance*, 7.

13. For an overview of Watts's initial reception as a devotional writer, see Christopher N. Phillips, "Cotton Mather Brings Isaac Watts's Hymns to America; or, How to Perform a Hymn without Singing It," *New England Quarterly* 85 (June 2012): 203–21.

14. On First Church's singing schools and choir, see *250 Years*, 47, 49, 57–66. In 1883, the Parish Meeting voted to reject the music committee's suggestion that, following the resignation of the choir director, the church turn to "congregational singing for the present." In the early twentieth century, First Church's pastors were still trying, with little success, to get their congregation singing (88, 118). On the larger pattern in American churches of choirs inhibiting congregational singing, see Richard Crawford, introduction to Allen Perdue Britton, Irving Lowens, and Richard Crawford, *American Sacred Music Imprints, 1698–1810: A Bibliography* (Worcester, Mass.: American Antiquarian Society, 1990), 1–54, 20–21; and Benson, *English Hymn*, 387.

15. *250 Years at First Church*, 71. This was a typical reaction to the popular books introduced between 1850 and 1870, including Henry Ward Beecher's *The Plymouth Collection* (1855) and *Hymns Ancient and Modern* (1860). See Benson, *English Hymn*, 473–78; Susan Drain, *The Anglican Church in Nineteenth-Century Britain: "Hymns Ancient and Modern," 1860–1875* (Lewiston, N.Y.: Mellen, 1989).

16. Dickinson, *Letters*, 1:201.

17. See, for instance, Richard Sewall, *The Life of Emily Dickinson*, 2 vols. (New York: Farrar, Straus, and Giroux, 1974), 2:326, 407–8; and Roger Lundin, *Emily Dickinson and the Art of Belief* (Grand Rapids, Mich.: Eerdmans, 1998), 142–43.

18. Dickinson, *Letters*, 2:526.

19. Ibid., 1:234–35.

20. Ibid., 1:176.

21. Benson, *English Hymn*, 435–42.

22. On Protestant American attitudes toward Catholicism in the 1850s, see Jenny Franchot, *Roads to Rome: The Antebellum Protestant Encounter with Catholicism* (New York: Cambridge University Press, 1994).

23. Caroline Snowden Whitmarsh, ed., *Hymns for Mothers and Children*, 1st series (Boston, 1861), iii, iv.

24. On the Dickensian dimension of Tim and Dickinson's other alter ego character, Dollie, see Rise B. Axelrod and Steven Gould Axelrod, "Dickinson's Dickens: 'Tim' and 'Dollie,'" *Emily Dickinson Journal* 11, no. 1 (2002): 21–32.

25. Dickinson, Poem 231, 104–5.

26. Ibid., 105.

27. On the one exception, "The Savior must have been / A docile Gentleman" (Dickinson, Poem 1538, 571), Brenda Wineapple notes that the poem was once attached to a Christmas cake for the poet's niece and nephews and conjectures that this was probably the "profane" poem of the group sent to Higginson in 1880 (*White Heat: The Friendship of Emily Dickinson and Thomas Wentworth Higginson* [New York: Knopf, 2008], 228).

28. The titles she gave them were "Christ's Birthday," "Cupid's Sermon," "A Humming-Bird," and "My Country's Wardrobe" (Dickinson, *Letters*, 3:680, 3:681).

29. Ibid., 2:362.

30. Dickinson, Poem 323, 144.

31. Dickinson, *Letters*, 2:419.

32. Ibid., 2:525.

33. Ibid., 2:528.

34. Dickinson, Poem 454, 209.

35. Michael L. Manson, "'The Thews of Hymn': Dickinson's Metrical Grammar," in Smith and Loeffelholz, *A Companion to Emily Dickinson*, 368–90, 382–85; Annie Finch, *The Ghost of Meter: Culture and Prosody in American Free Verse* (Ann Arbor: University of Michigan Press, 1993), 26–27.

36. Dickinson, Poem 454, 210.

37. Manson, "Thews of Hymn," 384–85.

38. Ibid., 389–90.

39. Dickinson, Poem 229, 103.

40. Dickinson, Poem 598, 269.

41. Sharon Cameron, *Choosing Not Choosing: Dickinson's Fascicles* (Chicago: University of Chicago Press, 1992).

42. Anna Warner, *Hymns of the Church Militant* (New York, 1858), iv.

CHAPTER 13

"THE NEAREST DREAM RECEDES – UNREALIZED"

Emily Dickinson, Thomas Wentworth Higginson, and Fascicle 14

Vivian R. Pollak

IN MID-APRIL 1862, Thomas Wentworth Higginson went to the post office in Worcester, Massachusetts, where he was destined to receive a letter from a correspondent he had never met. It was Emily Dickinson, whose handwriting was unusual. He remembered it as peculiar and wholly unique, fossil-like, unworldly. It haunted him long after the event had passed. "Mr Higginson," she wrote,

> Are you too deeply occupied to say if my Verse is alive?
> The Mind is so near itself – it cannot see, distinctly – and I have none to ask –
> Should you think it breathed – and had you the leisure to tell me, I should feel quick gratitude –
> If I make the mistake – that you dared to tell me – would give me sincerer honor – toward you –
> I enclose my name – asking you, if you please – Sir – to tell me what is true?
> That you will not betray me – it is needless to ask – since Honor is it's own pawn – [1]

On separate sheets of notepaper, she included four untitled poems, among them "Safe in Their Alabaster Chambers," which had been published six weeks earlier by the *Springfield Republican* as "The Sleeping."[2] But it was another wholly unique poem that impressed him most deeply. "The nearest Dream recedes – unrealized" is the first poem in Fascicle 14, and Higginson identified with its schoolboy staring bewildered at a mocking sky.[3] With its elusive June bee, it provides an organizing metaphor for thinking further about what Dickinson wanted from Higginson at this point in her unorthodox literary career. For example, did she want him to help publish her poems? The short answer is yes and no. It depended. A contextualized reading of Fascicle 14 as an unfinished spiritual autobiography helps to explain why this matter of publication and audience is so difficult to resolve. Were her poems not filled with fantasies of fame, the story I tell would be simpler.

The person to whom our elusive poet was writing was an unchurched minister, a feminist abolitionist reviled in some quarters, revered in others. Higginson, who lost his father when he was ten, was closely identified with his mother Louisa, his sisters Susan and Anna, and his wife, Mary Elizabeth Channing, an invalid to whom he was devoted.[4] Throughout his career, he was empathic toward women; thus, a woman in trouble (for so Dickinson had presented herself) was all the more likely to attract his attention. His curiosity piqued about the person behind the unsigned poems who had enclosed her name in a separate envelope, he responded to her appeal by asking her to send more. Which she did, with a lag, apologizing for the delay and explaining that she had been ill and was still bedridden. Conflating her writing and her physical body, she thanked him for "the surgery ... not so painful as I supposed," mentioned that she had been reading his *Atlantic Monthly* essays, and, as she had done in her opening letter, referred to "honor," which she defined as not sparing her feelings by sugarcoating the truth. In essence, she was urging him to be frank.[5] Higginson now had seven poems, all but one of which she copied into booklets, or fascicles, which she bound with twine.[6]

Eventually, Dickinson sent Higginson more poems than she sent to any other correspondent, with the exception of her sister-in-law, Susan, yet she never confided in him about the fascicles she was constructing during her most driven years as a poet. Indeed, she explained to him in these opening days of their friendship and of his strange mentorship, "I had no Monarch in my life, and cannot rule myself, and when I try to organize – my little Force explodes – and leaves me bare and charred."[7] It is unlikely he ever understood the stages of her development as marked by the onset, flourish years, and decline of her fascicle project. The fascicles had already been taken apart by the time he and Mabel Loomis Todd began editing her manuscripts in 1889. It was Todd who called these groupings "fascicles," or "little volumes." In all probability, it was she who disassembled them.[8] Fortunately, she kept a record of their contents, aided by her astronomer husband David Peck Todd, which future editors have built on and refined.

In this essay, I argue that Higginson would have learned a lot about the kinds of organization that Emily Dickinson resisted had he been able to read Fascicle 14 in its entirety. He would have been able to see her nearest dreams as part of the episodic spiritual autobiography she was developing in which self-rule was a goal undermined by other currents of desire. The fascicle context helps to expose the rhythms of those contradictory desires, to make them more fully legible. In what follows, I will explore in some detail the development of Fascicle 14 in the hope that we may eventually experience the "steadfast Honey" that typically eludes the persona, to say nothing of readers who, like Higginson, are frustrated by the poet's seeming lack of clarity.[9] "I think you called me 'Wayward.' Will you help me improve?" she wrote, signing herself "Your Scholar."[10] "Are you perfectly powerful?" she asked mockingly.[11]

Common Day

Having sworn Higginson to secrecy in her very first letter—she made it a point of honor—Dickinson proceeded to tell him a lot about herself in what he experienced as her "abruptness and impulsiveness."[12] Hinting at a gender disturbance, she compared herself to "the Boy . . . by the Burying Ground," alluded to a "terror – since September," and confided, "I sing . . . because I am afraid."[13] She also misled him, stating disingenuously, "I made no verse – but one or two – until this winter – Sir." For a poet, Dickinson was no longer particularly young (she was thirty-one) and even more to the point, she had amassed hundreds of stunning poems she was organizing into fascicles which she kept to and for herself. In time, she addressed Higginson as "Master," an inappropriate form of address for someone who distrusted religious authority, never felt comfortable in the ministry, and believed that "the human soul, like any other noble vessel, was not built to be anchored, but to sail."[14] A freethinking Unitarian whose allegiances were ethical, social, and political rather than doctrinal, he sought to disseminate the "natural religion" he had absorbed from Ralph Waldo Emerson and other Transcendentalists.[15] Intriguingly, in June 1877, Dickinson wrote him, "I was told you were once a Clergyman," a statement that mystifies her knowledge of his life (the divinity school background, the Unitarian roots).[16] What else did she not know about the historical person with the appealing literary persona?[17]

In the spring of 1862, Higginson was frustrated by his inability to enlist in the army. His wife's illness constrained him. An effective popularizer, he was a nationally prominent figure who had proved too outspoken for his first congregation in Newburyport, Massachusetts, where he had used his pulpit to further a radical abolitionist agenda. Resigning from the pulpit before he was fired, he settled into the comparatively leisured life of a freelance intellectual before moving to Worcester in 1852, to the Free Church, which was "a seething centre of all reforms."[18] In 1854, he was part of a party that stormed a Boston courthouse in an unsuccessful attempt to free the fugitive slave Anthony Burns, but after nearly a year when the threat of imprisonment hung over him, the case was thrown out on a technicality and never came to trial. After a trip to the Azores in 1855 taken mainly to restore his wife's failing health, he was present in 1856 in Bleeding Kansas, glorying in his role as an unofficial warrior for the North. In 1857, he was a leader of the Worcester Disunion Convention, which urged the North to secede from the South. In 1858–59, he was an enthusiastic financial backer of John Brown's revolutionary raid on Harpers Ferry. Unlike his co-conspirators Franklin Sanborn, Samuel Gridley Howe, George Luther Stearns, Gerrit Smith, and Theodore Parker, Higginson stood his ground when Brown was captured, tried, and hanged.[19] In short, he was one of the North's most prominent abolitionists. To quote his friend Henry David Thoreau, Higginson was "the only Harvard Phi Beta Kappa, Unitarian minister, and master of seven languages who . . .

led a storming party against a federal bastion with a battering ram in his hands."[20] This, then, was the socially graceful reformer and serious amateur naturalist whose writings attracted Dickinson and to whom she turned as the professional critic she could trust. She said she had no one else to ask.

After the poet's death, her sister Lavinia burned Higginson's letters, an act she later came to regret. Fortunately, the mentor Dickinson addressed as friend, preceptor, and "Master" carefully preserved her letters to him.[21] Because her letters contain citations from his, we can go some distance toward recovering his language in the spring of 1862, when his praise affirmed her self-worth. He probably referred to her "genius," a word he favored in other writings and applied even to himself. By "genius," Higginson meant something like the "Inner Light" he celebrated in "The Sympathy of Religions," a noncontingent, essential self defined by a ruling passion. Potentially, everyone has such a genius, or guiding spirit, which is "not infallible though invaluable," although of course some writers are more interesting than others.[22] Dickinson, he thought, was more interesting than most contemporary poets. Because she was "wholly new and original," she satisfied his longing for novelty. On the subject of novelty, however, Higginson was conflicted. In some situations, he wanted to restrain genius and distrusted genius unalloyed. For example, he was no admirer of Whitman's sexually liberated antebellum persona, even if in the spring of 1862 he inquired whether she was familiar with Whitman's works.[23]

Whatever the nuances of the language, Higginson's praise overwhelmed her. "Your letter gave no Drunkenness, because I tasted Rum before," she explained to this well-known temperance advocate, "Domingo comes but once – yet I have had few pleasures so deep as your opinion, and if I tried to thank you, my tears would block my tongue."[24] Thus, while expressing gratitude for his support, she explained that she was keeping her wits about her: his praise wasn't making her giddy, and she enclosed no poems with this letter. Apparently Higginson then asked her for a photograph, and in July Dickinson told him she didn't have one to send. She painted a word portrait instead: "[I] am small, like the Wren, and my Hair is bold, like the Chestnut Bur – and my eyes, like the Sherry in the Glass, that the Guest leaves." She said her father was worried. He had photographs of the rest of the family, but not of her. What if she should die?[25] Perhaps her poems would outlive her – and so she enclosed four more. One of them described a dying soldier "On whose forbidden ear / The distant strains of Triumph / Burst – agonized – and Clear!"[26] Responding in August to his complaint that he was having trouble understanding her, she asked, "Are these more orderly?"[27] She enclosed two poems: "Before I got my eye put out" and "I cannot dance opon my Toes."[28] He may have wondered why thwarted ambitions were so much on her mind.

Meanwhile, Higginson was leading another life. He was longing for what he called "the tonic of war," a longing that was soon to be gratified.[29] His wife was better, his hunger for battle intense, and he enlisted. When Dickinson wrote to him in February 1863 that "War feels to me an oblique place," he seems not to have taken it upon himself to enlighten her. She expressed concern about his health and said that "when service is had in Church, for Our Arms, I include yourself."[30] Her own health was a continuing problem, and in 1864 and 1865 she moved into a boarding house in Cambridge to receive the eye treatments she needed. She also needed a break from the pressures of her home. The intervals between letters increased; years passed; he urged her to come to Boston to participate in the intellectual life to which he could introduce her. She wouldn't do it. He persisted, disbelieving: "You must come down to Boston sometimes? All ladies do."[31]

Finally, they met. Higginson's public life brought him to Amherst, where he had the chance to meet her face to face, twice. The first time, in 1870, he asked her if she never "felt want of employment, never going off the place & never seeing any visitor," to which she answered, "I never thought of conceiving that I could ever have the slightest approach to such a want in all future time," adding, "I feel that I have not expressed myself strongly enough."[32] Her intensity rattled him. He explained to his wife, "I never was with any one who drained my nerve power so much. Without touching her, she drew from me. I am glad not to live near her."[33] More than a hundred years later, we can read Higginson's visit in the context of Fascicle 14, one of the forty fascicles about which he knew nothing, although they organize more than eight hundred poems.[34] By concentrating my analysis of Dickinson's spiritual quest in a single fascicle, I am able to identify some structural elements that inform the fascicle project as a whole. I am not, however, arguing that the fascicle project is coherent in its progress toward a constant goal such as belief in a theocentric, Christian afterlife, or that Dickinson's metrics are derived exclusively from a single source such as hymns.[35] Rather, I want to focus on the poet's ability to extract what Higginson, in his most famous essay, called "motive power from the greatest obstacles."[36] That motive power drives us forward into the risks of a distinctly unorthodox style.

The Spiritual Integrity of Fascicle 14

Fascicle 14 has a unique distinction. Not only does it sound radically unfinished (in this it is not unique), but the material evidence indicates that it is missing its last poem or poems. Thus, whatever one thinks about the closural effect of the other fascicles, whether considered individually or collectively, Fascicle 14 throws into relief the problem of closure that haunts Dickinson studies and that haunted the poet. To quote R. W. Franklin, at some point in its complicated history Fascicle 14 became "a gathering place for wayward sheets" and did not recuperate its losses.[37] As the persona describes her ambitions and observations, facts and fictions mingle, blur, and clarify, but then something interrupts the flow of progressive thought and feeling. Contingency almost prevails.

Fascicle 14 alludes to friends and lovers who have let the persona down and to an inhibiting belief structure that includes the deity, whom she calls "The Weaver,"[38] to her own temperament, to nature, and to other antagonists beyond her power not only to tell but to define. When, for example, she writes of "the mocking sky" in what the fascicle calls the "maddest" dream, her sky trails clouds of theological and natural glory, but it has no heft.[39] As the poem begins to unravel in its last lines, the "sky" is not our still point in a turning world; rather, despite its initial promise, the sky reveals itself as just another victim in a cosmic drama of disappearances. It, too, is "Homesick for steadfast Honey."

The persona's fatalism is powerfully at play in other poems, including "'Heaven' – is what I cannot reach," which reiterates and redescribes the quest motif, tantalizing us with another incomplete revelation. Positioned as the fascicle's eighth poem, its tone is jaunty, self-satisfied. After so much confusion and aimless striving, the poet argues, it is good to be able to take the long view, if only to acknowledge one's limits.

> "Heaven" – is what I cannot reach!
> The Apple on the Tree –
> Provided it do hopeless – hang –
> That – "Heaven" is – to Me!
>
> The Color, on the cruising cloud –
> The interdicted Land –
> Behind the Hill – the House behind –
> There – Paradise – is found!
>
> Her teazing Purples – Afternoons –
> The credulous – decoy –
> Enamored – of the Conjuror –
> That spurned us – Yesterday![40]

The exclamation marks revivify an old story—the temptation in the Garden of Eden—and the hopelessly romantic persona is palpably exhilarated by her discovery. Oh of course, she says, silly me![41]

If we turn to Dickinson's use of exclamation marks in the rest of the fascicle, an interesting pattern emerges. Poems one through eight end with an exclamation. Poem nine does not. "The feet of people walking home," for which Dickinson used a loose leaf she had copied in 1858, probably in the late summer, ends with a period.[42] In Fascicle 1, the poem ends with an exclamation mark, intensifying a statement of faith in personal immortality. In Fascicle 14, the period breaks the pattern: the nine remaining poems end with dashes, with periods, or with a question mark ("A Toad, can die of Light").[43] In its new context, "The feet of people walking home / With gayer sandals go" reflects a desire to reclaim the intellectual and emotional confidence of an earlier time, the time when she began organizing her poetry in the belief that it might endure and, in enduring, confer personal immortality on her. Note that she saved the loose leaf she inserted into Fascicle 14. She was hoping to waste nothing.

After this surprising "Larceny" from her own "*Legacy*," the speaker emerges as less confident that "Death" is "but our rapt attention /

To Immortality."[44] Rather, the element of surprise is attenuated and the pace of the chase slows; the nearest dream, the anticipation of "steadfast Honey," recedes into the vast beyond. As Sharon Cameron observes in her wonderfully titled *Choosing Not Choosing*, poems often "repeat and modify aspects of each other" and may sometimes be seen as "variants" of each other.[45] Domhnall Mitchell agrees when he writes, "Poems in the fascicles endlessly revise each other."[46] Similarly, Alexandra Socarides describes some of the ways the fascicles "might be related to each other through repetition."[47] These are, however, repetitions with a difference. Yes, "The feet of people walking home" is a duplicate, but so is the third poem in Fascicle 14, "Ah, Moon – and Star," which Dickinson had carefully recopied in 1862.[48] Both duplicate poems mark her determination to waste nothing but do so in different ways. Dreaming of a heavenly home, the moon and star persona refers to herself as a space traveler who can borrow "a Bonnet – of the Lark – / And a Chamois' silver boot – / And a stirrup of an Antelope" but who is unable to close the gap between herself and someone who is "more than a firmament – from me."[49] Whoever this person is, she wants to speed her pace, to shed her pedestrian feet. Picturing herself in "The feet of people walking home" as a walker, a crocus, a vassal, a bargeman, a pearl fisherman, a thief, a peasant, and an angel, she turns to literature for guidance, but her "Classics vail their faces."[50] When we encounter this poem in Fascicle 1, the emphasis may fall on what happens next: "Such resurrection pours!" In Fascicle 14, however, the persona's visionary imagination is more hectic. Quoting herself is useful, and rereading the classics may be of some help, but time is running out. Although she would like to believe that "Death" is "but our rapt attention / To Immortality," the sands are threatening to bury her.

Fascicle 14 is replete with miraculous counterfactuals. I want to add another alternative history to its gay parade of bonnets and silver boots and stirrups and larks and chamois and antelopes and moons and stars.[51] Let us suppose that Higginson were reanimated and reading Fascicle 14 in its modern editions. He was a biographer and a historian. What might have been clarified for him? "Perhaps in time," he reminisced, "I could have got beyond that somewhat overstrained relation which not my will, but her needs, had forced upon us. Certainly I should have been most glad to bring it down to the level of simple truth and everyday comradeship; but it was not altogether easy."⁵² His language is compelling: something needed to be brought down, and it was not easy. What was it?

Higginson might have continued to believe that Dickinson's progress was wayward, her rhymes awkward, her meters halting, but he would have had a better understanding of the forces against which she was contending, given the many poems that describe incomplete friendships and unsatisfying loves or the positive and negative consequences of those frustrations. For example, the eleventh poem in the sequence is an elegy for someone who harbors "the Ethiop within" and who, in dying, wills his explosive energy to the tough-minded speaker.

> More Life – went out – when He went
> Than Ordinary Breath –
> Lit with a finer Phosphor –
> Requiring in the Quench –
>
> A Power of Renowned Cold,
> The Climate of the Grave
> A Temperature just adequate
> So Anthracite, to live –
>
> For some – an Ampler Zero –
> A Frost more needle keen
> Is nescessary, to reduce
> The Ethiop within.
>
> Others – extinguish easier –
> A Gnat's minutest Fan
> Sufficient to obliterate
> A Tract of Citizen –
>
> Whose Peat life – amply vivid –
> Ignores the solemn News
> That Popocatapel exists –
> Or Etna's Scarlets, Choose – ⁵³

In a famously grumpy essay, the New Critic R. P. Blackmur complained about the poem's difficulty. Writing in the *Southern Review* in 1937, he distinguished "a kind of repetitious fragmentariness" as "the characterizing fact of her sensibility." Parsing the imagery, he noted that "the word *anthracite* is the crux of the trouble," and then proceeded to explain, "Anthracite is coal, is hard, is black, gives heat, and has a rushing crisp sound."[54] Later criticism by Rebecca Patterson opened up the poem's geographical imagery and racial typology.[55] Yet if the poem's movement is in part recursive, and if Fascicle 14 moves forward into the heroisms of a fractured past, it advances in surprising directions, taking us into nooks and crannies of personal and national consciousness otherwise unexplored. That's one of the reasons Blackmur was so grumpy and Patterson open to its charms. Blackmur was looking for logical progression and linear development, whereas Patterson was eager to find correspondences between Dickinson's geographical imagination and her reading. When the day is done, though, *anthracite* remains a puzzling word because of the compression of the syntax, and the hunt for such sources continues, a contemporary favorite being Donald Grant Mitchell's *Reveries of a Bachelor*, which Dickinson is known to have enjoyed in 1852 and whose dreamy style she mimicked.[56]

The formidably well read Higginson would have enjoyed our energetic source hunting in Shakespeare, in the British romantic poets and Victorian novelists, and in antebellum popular culture, although Higginson being Higginson and curious about passion, he would remain eager to learn more about the intimate personal history that informs one of the best known poems in Fascicle 14, "Your Riches – taught me – Poverty," which Dickinson sent him in July 1862.[57] Comparing the fascicle version with the copy he received, Higginson would have noticed minor variations in stanza form, capitalization, punctuation, and diction. What stayed constant was Dickinson's faith in readers to fill in the blanks, even though, as she explained, feigning incredulity, when he complained about the obscurity of her style, "You say 'Beyond your knowledge.' You would not jest with me, because I believe you – but Preceptor – you cannot mean it? All men say 'What' to me, but I thought it a fashion."[58]

In real time, Higginson was leading another life. When he read "The nearest Dream recedes – unrealized," he was frustrated by his inability to volunteer for military action, a move that he believed would consolidate his career of useful public service. But his wife was ill and depended on his comforting presence. Private pressures prevailed. But during the late summer, Mary's health improved and he began recruiting a nine-months regiment. Several months later, Higginson at last found himself in South Carolina as the colonel of the first black regiment in either army, North or South. There was a break in the correspondence before Dickinson wrote again, in early February 1863, "War feels to me an oblique place."[59] She could follow his exploits in the *Springfield Republican* and had read his essay "The Procession of the Flowers" in the *Atlantic Monthly*.[60] She said that "though not reared to prayer – when service is had in Church, for Our Arms, I include yourself." It was not until early June 1864 that she wrote again, this time from a boarding house in Cambridge where she had been living since April and which she compared to a prison.[61] She was eager to hear from him, but Higginson was preoccupied; he had resigned his commission and did not respond. When she wrote again in January 1866, he took up the thread.[62] She asked him to instruct her, to keep her alive.[63] She measured degrees of aliveness acutely, and during the next twenty years, she continued to calibrate heroisms and disappointments, although not at the same inspired pace or in fascicles. She was making her peace with her dreams, asking what to make of a diminished thing.

Higginson Dreaming, Dickinson's Dreams

Several months after Dickinson's death in 1886, Higginson completed "The Monarch of Dreams," a long short story whose hero comes from a race of enthusiastic projectors and is suffering from a vaguely defined depression. The story is prefaced with an epigraph from Aeschylus's *Agamemnon*, which translates, "A ghost will seem to rule the house."[64] Higginson's quasi-autobiographical hero, Francis Ayrault, who has been unable to rescue a woman whom he loves, is unaware that he has been stifling feelings of sexualized aggression toward his dead wife. To move beyond this psychological impasse, he determines to control his dreams. At first, he succeeds. Then he begins to ignore his beloved little sister, his "sacred trust," his "Hart," who tells him he is "the kindest person in the whole world." He knows otherwise and is tempted to harm her.[65] Although Ayrault pulls back from the abyss, he remains haunted by his grotesque imaginings, and when the Civil War begins to roar through the real-time land from which his dreams protect him, he cannot rouse himself before the opportunity to reaffirm his manhood passes him by. In "The Monarch of Dreams," Higginson reveals long-smoldering antagonisms he usually repressed and that in his more lucid moments he viewed as unthinkable. Had he been privy to Fascicle 14, he would have seen that the opening line of the poem he remembered so vividly as "The nearest Dream" contains an important variant. It reads, "The *maddest* dream recedes – unrealized" (italics mine).[66] Dickinson's variant thus anticipates the moral of his story's conclusion: some dreams are unworthy of their dreamers; for the common good, they should not be realized. As to the fate of the story itself, it was to be expected; the literary powers-that-be were not interested, and when this "fairest child" of his invention was published as a free-standing booklet, it was at his own expense.[67]

To recapitulate. When Dickinson began explaining herself to Higginson in the spring of 1862, she told him, with some bitterness, "They are religious – except me – and address an Eclipse, every morning – whom they call their 'Father.'"[68] Dickinson was angry, but she was also anxious, and her religious anxieties were somewhat assuaged by Higginson, even as those angers and anxieties informed her basic rhythms and were constitutive of her art. An analogy may suffice. In 1860, when Higginson eulogized his favorite preacher, the heretical Theodore Parker, he recalled Parker's effect on him as primarily emotional. Parker, he explained, had a wonderful ability to reassure him.[69] Higginson had this calming effect on Dickinson, whether or not he encouraged her desire to enter the print public sphere, a desire about which she was deeply conflicted, given her temperament and the mixed messages she was receiving from her family and friends. The fact that he had once been a clergyman mattered to her, but Dickinson was unwilling to compromise her commitment to her own heretical experience of desire. To have done so would have been to destroy her genius, and she never forgot what he had done for her at the beginning of their correspondence. Whatever his limitations, he was her Theodore Parker. Quite simply, she felt that he had saved her writing life, but as she reminded him in 1869, after the psychic turmoil had abated, "Of our greatest acts we are ignorant."[70]

NOTES

1. Emily Dickinson, Letter 260, in *The Letters of Emily Dickinson*, ed. Thomas H. Johnson and Theodora Ward, 3 vols. (Cambridge, Mass.: Harvard University Press, 1958). Hereafter, letters will be cited by their numbers in this edition.

2. Emily Dickinson, Poem 124A, in *The Poems of Emily Dickinson*, ed. R. W. Franklin, 3 vols. (Cambridge, Mass.: Harvard University Press, 1998). Hereafter, poems will be cited by their numbers in this edition.

3. Dickinson, P 304B.

4. Higginson adored his wife, whose tart tongue and pithy sayings never ceased to amaze him. He quoted her in letters to family and friends, admired her values, and considered her brilliant. Nevertheless, her unwillingness or inability to bear a child troubled him, and following her death in 1877, his second marriage to Mary Potter Thacher was happier.

5. Dickinson, L 261.

6. The exception is a declaration of artistic maturity, "We play at Paste," P 282A. Perhaps Dickinson wrote it for the occasion.

7. Dickinson, L 271.

8. Mabel Loomis Todd, in Millicent Todd Bingham, *Ancestors' Brocades: The Literary Debut of Emily Dickinson* (New York: Harper, 1945), 17, 21. "Little" is Mabel Loomis Todd's, but "volumes" is Lavinia Dickinson's, who was Mabel's ally in editing until they quarreled. On their falling out, see Vivian R. Pollak, *Our Emily Dickinsons: American Women Poets and the Intimacies of Difference* (Philadelphia: University of Pennsylvania Press, 2016), chap. 2.

9. Dickinson, P 304B.

10. Dickinson, L 271.

11. Dickinson, L 268.

12. Thomas Wentworth Higginson, "Emily Dickinson's Letters," *Atlantic Monthly* 68 (October 1891): 446, reprinted in Willis J. Buckingham, ed., *Emily Dickinson's Reception in the 1890s: A Documentary History* (Pittsburgh: University of Pittsburgh Press, 1989), 182–97. Buckingham comments, "No other publication event gave Dickinson wider exposure in the nineties."

13. Dickinson, L 261.

14. Thomas Wentworth Higginson, "The Sympathy of Religions," in *The Magnificent Activist: The Writings of Thomas Wentworth Higginson (1823–1911)*, ed. Howard N. Meyer (Boston: Da Capo, 2000), 354.

15. See David M. Robinson, "'For Largest Liberty': Emerson, Natural Religion, and the Antislavery Crisis," *Religion and Literature* 41 (Spring 2009): 3–24.

16. Dickinson, L 503.

17. Dickinson liked celebrity ministers. In January 1854 she wrote to another Unitarian clergyman in Worcester, the Reverend Edward Everett Hale, inquiring about the last days of her friend Benjamin Franklin Newton. She wanted to know if poor Ben, who was only thirty-two years old when he lost his struggle with

tuberculosis, had been "content to die" (L 153). Hale reassured her, and in February she thanked him (Diana Wagner and Marcy Tanter, "New Dickinson Letter Clarifies Hale Correspondence," *Emily Dickinson Journal* 7 [Spring 1998]: 110–17). Several years later, she wrote to Hale reminding him of their earlier correspondence and in all probability attempted to interest him in her poetry. After that, the correspondence seems to have petered out. Higginson and Hale were good friends, having met as teenagers at Harvard College. When they were in Worcester together, they joked about starting a magazine for unfortunates. Here is Higginson memorializing his colleague: "The 'Unfortunates' . . . was to contain all the prose and verse sent to us by neighbors or strangers with request to get it published. I remember that we made out a title-page between us, with a table of contents, all genuine, for the imaginary first number." Higginson also wrote, "Probably no man in America, except [Henry Ward] Beecher, aroused and stimulated quite so many minds as Hale, and his personal popularity was unbounded" ("Edward Everett Hale," in *Carlyle's Laugh and Other Surprises* [Boston: Houghton Mifflin, 1909], 163, 159).

18. On the Free Church of Worcester as a seething center of all reforms, see Thomas Wentworth Higginson, "Cheerful Yesterdays," *Atlantic Monthly* 79 (January 1897): 53–64. On Higginson's liberal spirituality, see Leigh Eric Schmidt, *Restless Souls: The Making of American Spirituality from Emerson to Oprah* (San Francisco: HarperSanFrancisco, 2005), 106–41.

19. On Higginson and his co-conspirators, see David S. Reynolds, *John Brown Abolitionist: The Man Who Killed Slavery, Sparked the Civil War, and Seeded Civil Rights* (New York: Knopf, 2005). See also Tilden G. Edelstein, *Strange Enthusiasm: A Life of Thomas Wentworth Higginson* (New Haven: Yale University Press, 1968); and Edward J. Renehan, Jr., *The Secret Six: The True Tale of the Men Who Conspired with John Brown* (New York: Crown, 1995).

20. Henry David Thoreau, in Renehan, *The Secret Six*, 64–65. For Higginson's personal acquaintance with Thoreau, see Thomas Wentworth Higginson, *Short Studies of American Authors* (Boston: Lee and Shepard, 1880), 22–31. For Higginson's influence in shaping Thoreau's reputation, see Sandra Harbert Petrulionis, "'Beyond All Men of His Day': Thomas Wentworth Higginson and Thoreau's Legacy in Postbellum America," in *Thoreau at 200: Essays and Reassessments*, ed. Kristen Case and K. P. Van Anglen (New York: Cambridge University Press, 2016), 88–101.

21. For the "Master," see Dickinson, L 413, L 449, L 517, L 553, L 575. She never used this form of address to Higginson after his remarriage, which seems to have had a sobering effect on her.

22. Higginson, "The Sympathy of Religions," 354.

23. On Higginson's antagonism to Whitman, see Robert K. Nelson and Kenneth M. Price, "Debating Manliness: Thomas Wentworth Higginson, William Sloane Kennedy, and the Question of Whitman," *American Literature* 73 (September 2001): 497–524. On Dickinson's knowledge of Whitman and his reputation, see Vivian R. Pollak, *The Erotic Whitman* (Berkeley: University of California Press, 2000), xix, 187–88. I point out that even if Dickinson had never read Whitman's "book," she was

introduced to Whitman by the *Springfield Republican*, which published excerpts from *Leaves of Grass* and amplified her knowledge of his contemporary reputation.

24. Dickinson, L 265.
25. Dickinson, L 268.
26. Dickinson, P 112D.
27. Dickinson, L 271.
28. Dickinson, P 336A; P 381A.
29. Higginson, in Edelstein, *Strange Enthusiasm*, 245.
30. Dickinson, L 280.
31. Dickinson, L 330a.
32. Dickinson, L 342a.
33. Dickinson, L 342b. When Higginson visited Amherst in the summer of 1870, Dickinson was no longer transcribing poems onto unbound fascicle sheets, or "sets," a practice she abandoned in 1865 and resumed at a reduced pace in 1871–73. On the chronology of Dickinson's career, see Cristanne Miller, ed., *Emily Dickinson's Poems: As She Preserved Them* (Cambridge, Mass.: Harvard University Press, 2016). For a strong if not wholly persuasive challenge to the usual description of the sets as unbound fascicle sheets, see Alexandra Socarides, *Dickinson Unbound: Paper, Process, Poetics* (New York: Oxford University Press, 2012).
34. By Fascicle 5, these sequences begin to include tantalizing linguistic variants that open up one of the ways in which Dickinson cast anchoring doctrines to the wind. In Fascicle 5, for example, in a poem about female friendship, the line "Her heart is fit for rest" can also read "Her heart is fit for home" (P 121). In Fascicle 14, in a poem describing the difficulty of finding an emotionally talented friend sensitive to the persona's moods, whether that person be a man or a woman, "Hearts" yields to "Breasts" in the line "If Broadcloth Hearts are firmer" (P 306).
35. For a reading of Fascicle 40 as the triumphant conclusion of a Christian's progress, beginning with the first fascicle's first poem, see Dorothy Huff Oberhaus, *Emily Dickinson Fascicles: Method and Meaning* (University Park: Pennsylvania State University Press, 1995). I attend to a different form of spirituality, untethered from its institutional instantiation. In *Dickinson The Anxiety of Gender* (Ithaca: Cornell University Press, 1984), I refer to restless improvisations grounded in a hybrid form, the hymn-ballad quatrain. See also Cristanne Miller, "Hymn, the 'Ballad Wild,' and Free Verse," in *Reading in Time: Emily Dickinson in the Nineteenth Century* (Amherst: University of Massachusetts Press, 2012), 49–81.
36. Higginson, "The Sympathy of Religions," 354.
37. See R. W. Franklin, "The Dickinson Packet 14—and 20, 10, and 26," *Papers of the Bibliographical Society of America* 73 (January 1979): 349. Note that his language mimics Higginson's: "I think you called me 'wayward'" (Dickinson, L 271). Franklin confirms the missing sheet or sheets in his edition of *The Manuscript Books of Emily Dickinson*, 2 vols. (Cambridge, Mass.: Harvard University Press, 1981).
38. Dickinson, P 306A.
39. Dickinson, P 304A.

40. Dickinson, P 310A.

41. Critics who theorize Dickinson's dynamic punctuation include Kamilla Denman, who describes the poet's "transition from a dominant use of the exclamation mark to a preference for the dash" ("Emily Dickinson's Volcanic Punctuation," *Emily Dickinson Journal* 2 [Spring 1993]: 33). See also Susan Howe, "These Flames and Generosities of the Heart: Emily Dickinson and the Illogic of Sumptuary Values," in *The Birth-Mark: Unsettling the Wilderness in American Literary History* (Hanover, N.H.: University Press of New England, 1993): "In the early fascicles, Dickinson frequently uses exclamation marks. Around fascicles 6–12, as she begins to break her lines in a new way and to regularly insert variant words into the structure of her work, nervous and repetitive exclamation marks change to the more abstract and sweeping dash" (152). Whether we understand the marks as nervous and repetitive or as ejaculatory and outer-directed for dramatic effect, they complicate our understanding of the quest motif that organizes her religious imagination in Fascicle 14.

42. Dickinson, P 16B.

43. Dickinson, P 419A.

44. Dickinson, P 16B.

45. Sharon Cameron, *Choosing Not Choosing: Emily Dickinson's Fascicles* (Chicago: University of Chicago Press, 1992), 105, 5.

46. Domhnall Mitchell, *Emily Dickinson: Monarch of Perception* (Amherst: University of Massachusetts Press, 2000), 89.

47. Socarides, *Dickinson Unbound*, 87. See also Alexandra Socarides, "Managing Multiple Contexts: Dickinson, Genre, and the Circulation of Fascicle 1," in *Emily Dickinson's Fascicles: A Spectrum of Possibilities*, ed. Paul Crumbley and Eleanor Elson Heginbotham (Columbus: Ohio State University Press, 2014), 150–68.

48. Dickinson, P 16B; P 262B. Thirteen fascicles include duplicate poems. See Eleanor Elson Heginbotham, "Appendix B," *Reading the Fascicles of Emily Dickinson: Dwelling in Possibilities* (Columbus: Ohio State University Press, 2003), 155.

49. Dickinson, P 262B.

50. Dickinson, P 16B.

51. On the demonic end of the spectrum, the fascicle's lists include dreadful deaths, figured in one gruesome image as speaking with stirless lungs, "Among the cunning cells," P 308A.

52. Higginson, "The Letters of Emily Dickinson," 453.

53. Dickinson, P 415A.

54. R. P. Blackmur, "Emily Dickinson: Notes on Prejudice and Fact," *Southern Review* 3 (Fall 1937): 323, 339.

55. After the conquest of Mexico City in September 1847, U.S. soldiers explored the surrounding area. Among them was a Springfield, Massachusetts, native who sent an account of the "Expedition to the Summit of Popocatapetl [sic]" to the *Republican*. Dickinson, then a student at Mount Holyoke Female Seminary, was hungry for war news and probably read this article which misspells the volcano's name, as does her poem. On "the Ethiop within," see Rebecca Patterson, *Emily*

Dickinson's Imagery (Amherst: University of Massachusetts Press, 1979), 151–56. See also my essay "Dickinson and the Poetics of Whiteness," *Emily Dickinson Journal* 9 (Fall 2000): 84–95.

56. Dickinson, L 56.

57. She also sent "Your – Riches – taught me – poverty" as a letter-poem to "dear Sue," who helped to inspire it. See P 418A, L 258.

58. Dickinson, L 271.

59. Dickinson, L 280.

60. Thomas Wentworth Higginson, "The Procession of the Flowers," *Atlantic Monthly* 10 (December 1862): 42, 650–57. For a deft reading of Dickinson's response to Higginson's nature writings, see Brenda Wineapple, *White Heat: The Friendship of Emily Dickinson and Thomas Wentworth Higginson* (New York: Knopf, 2008), 96–98, 119, 146, 347n. For Higginson's influence on Thoreau's reputation as a naturist, see Lawrence Buell, *The Environmental Imagination: Thoreau, Nature Writing, and the Formation of American Culture* (Cambridge, Mass.: Harvard University Press, 1995), 322, 349, 354–57, 413.

61. Dickinson, L 290.

62. Dickinson, L 314.

63. Dickinson, L 316.

64. Aeschylus, *Agamemnon*, trans. and ed. Alan H. Sommerstein (Cambridge, Mass.: Harvard University Press, 2008), line 415.

65. On the controlling-dreams theme in Higginson's short story, see Caleb Crain, "The Monarch of Dreams," *New Republic*, May 28, 2001, 4–49. The quotations are from Thomas Wentworth Higginson, "The Monarch of Dreams," in *Writings*, 7 vols. (Cambridge, Mass.: Riverside, 1900), 5:244, 238.

66. Dickinson, P 304A.

67. On the "fairest child," see Thomas Wentworth Higginson, letter to Edmund Clarence Stedman, in Mary Thacher Higginson, ed., *Letters and Journals of Thomas Wentworth Higginson* (Boston: Houghton Mifflin, 1921), 335, in which Higginson suggests that rejection by the *Atlantic* increased the story's value in his eyes.

68. Dickinson, L 261.

69. Thomas Wentworth Higginson, "Theodore Parker," *Atlantic Monthly* 6 (October 1860): 449. See also Dickinson's positive references to Parker in 1859 and 1876 (L 213; L 449). In the first, she alludes to his toxic reputation, adding, "Then I like poison very well."

70. Dickinson, L 330.

CHAPTER 14

HARRIET BEECHER STOWE AND MARTYRDOM

Protestant Missions in Uncle Tom's Cabin *and* Uncle Tom's Cabin *in Protestant Missions*

Brian Yothers

TOPSY, THE mischievous but good-hearted slave girl redeemed by conversion to evangelical Christianity in Harriet Beecher Stowe's *Uncle Tom's Cabin,* has had a rich and varied afterlife in American literature and popular culture. One of her least likely reincarnations came in the form of a young girl in late nineteenth-century India. In Mary and Margaret W. Leitch's *Seven Years in Ceylon* (1890), the authors related the story of a young Indian girl whom missionaries called Topsy. For these missionaries, *Uncle Tom's Cabin* was a fertile source of tropes, particularly those related to people of color. Like her namesake, the Indian Topsy was, as the authors put it, "as full of mischief as an egg is of meat," and she also demonstrated the goodness of her heart in a conversion to Christianity, expressed in terms reminiscent of the nineteenth-century sentimental novel.[1] According to the Misses Leitch (as they were colloquially known), "One Sabbath, when the missionary was preaching of Christ's death on the cross for us, he noticed Topsy, usually so restless, sitting strangely quiet, and two great tears gathering in her lustrous eyes, which were fixed upon him."[2] Topsy had learned to "*feel right*," as Stowe wrote at the end of *Uncle Tom's Cabin*, and this affective response had led to her conversion to Christianity.[3]

Having converted, Topsy swiftly took on the role of the missionary for herself, in another recapitulation of the story of Stowe's Topsy, who "showed so much intelligence, activity, zeal, and desire to do good in the world, that she was at last recommended, and approved, as a missionary to one of the stations in Africa."[4] Finding a "fakir woman" in the streets who was giving voice to Hindu teachings, Topsy approached and, as a result of her "magic earnestness," drew the woman into the orbit of the missionaries. The "fakir woman" converted to Christianity, replacing her career of mendicant and itinerant Hindu preacher with that of a mendicant and itinerant Christian preacher, retracing her steps across India to undo her earlier efforts.[5]

Topsy's translation from an enslaved black American to a South Indian in a missionary school is characteristic of both the close links between the missionary movement and antislavery and Reconstruction in nineteenth-century America and the global impact of *Uncle Tom's Cabin*. Stowe's most famous novel had traveled around the globe and been translated into numerous European and Asian languages, and in its original English language form, it had accompanied American missionaries and traders as well as British colonialists.[6] Theatrical adaptations of the novel became a facet of popular culture around the world, not least in Asian societies colonized by or in contact with the British. Perhaps the most famous instance of this phenomenon appears in the story of Anna Leonowen, whose books *The English Governess at the Siamese Court: Being Recollections of Six Years at the Royal Palace in Bangkok* (1870) and *Siamese Harem Life* (1873) inspired Richard Rodgers's and Oscar Hammerstein's musical *The King and I*. It is hard to overstate the cultural importance of *Uncle Tom's Cabin*, which, as David S. Reynolds has recently pointed out, "was central to redefining American democracy on a more egalitarian basis."[7]

Yet we can only fully understand the complexity of the interaction between Stowe and missionary literary culture when we realize that she wrote from a cultural context in which missionaries and their narratives played a major role. Missionaries are one of the great overlooked presences in nineteenth-century American literary culture, and this is particularly true when we consider the work of an explicitly religious writer such as Stowe. In *Uncle Tom's Cabin,* which ranks with *Moby-Dick* as one of the most ambitious novels of the American Renaissance (and certainly the most popular), she makes use of motifs that would have been broadly familiar to her readers from missionary writings about women as such as Harriet Newell and Harriet Winslow, who were associated with the American Board of Commissioners for Foreign Missions (ABCFM) and died in the field in South Asia in the early nineteenth century. In developing Evangeline, Miss Ophelia, Topsy, Uncle Tom, George Harris, and others, Stowe drew on a rich body of figures related to missionaries, martyrdom, local clergy, and the confrontations among various religious and cultural traditions that took place on the mission field in the nineteenth century.

The writings of female missionaries were widely disseminated and highly visible during that century. Stowe had particular reason to be aware of Newell, whose story was told in numerous editions that circulated among most American Protestants (as Mary Kupiec Cayton has pointed out), and Winslow, who grew up as a Congregationalist in Stowe's native Litchfield, Connecticut.[8] Stowe's father, Lyman Beecher, was an officer in the American Tract Society, which published successive editions of Winslow's *Memoir.*[9] In one of her least well known works, *First Geography for Children* (1855), Stowe alluded specifically to the role of female education in Christian missions in South Asia, describing the efforts of "the missionaries in Hindostan" to "open a school for boys" and "teach the girls too" and explaining that this effort at female education initially drew criticism from local men.[10] The struggle for female education is a central strand of Winslow's *Memoir,* which recounts the writer's efforts "to obtain *girls* to attend the school" that she had founded as well as initial resistance to female education in the community.[11] While Stowe never directly cited Newell or Winslow, we can say with confidence that she was reading materials writing by missionaries in the 1850s and that she had ready access to texts by Congregationalist ABCFM missionaries in particular.[12]

Where do we find missionaries in *Uncle Tom's Cabin,* and where do we find *Uncle Tom's Cabin* in the later missionary movement? Missionaries provided models for the novel's characters and plotlines in several ways. First, the genre of the female missionary memoir was a source for Stowe's creation of Eva and her representation of the character's exemplary life and death. Second, the missionary goal of nurturing a "native clergy" provided a basis for Stowe's development of Uncle Tom, George Harris, and Topsy. Third, the antislavery and missionary movements shared common partners, notably the temperance movement. In the aftermath of the novel's massive publishing success, we can see how both these traits and the intersection of freedmen's education and the missionary movement after the Civil War made it a useful point of reference for missionaries who were describing their work to readers in the United States.

Martyrdom at Home and Abroad

On September 2, 1814, eighteen-year-old Harriet Lathrop, a cerebral and devout young woman living in New Haven, Connecticut, wrote the first of two letters that revealed the literary cultures that were to shape her future life. In this note to a friend, she included a lengthy explanation of her literary tastes, revealing her ambivalent admiration for the poetry of Lord Byron and her wholehearted enthusiasm for the work of William Cowper, Edward Young, Oliver Goldsmith, James Thomson, and William Shakespeare, whose "witches have always the power of bewitching me." Less than two weeks later, in a letter to her mother, Lathrop revealed that Shakespeare's tragedies and Young's *Night-Thoughts* were not the only sources of her meditations on mortality. She reflected on the fate of another young New England woman, Harriet Newell, who had died two years earlier off the coast of India: "I am almost ready to ask, Why was Harriet Newell taken from life, and a creature of so little worth as I am, continued here?"[13] Lathrop may have read about Newell in Leonard Woods's *A Sermon Preached at Haverhill (Mass.), in Remembrance of Mrs. Harriet Newell*, which had been published earlier in the year.[14] Newell had been a member of the first American mission to South Asia, and accounts of her saintly life and death were already attracting young women to missionary service in South Asia. Eventually, Lathrop married Reverend Miron Winslow (who became an important figure in the history of English-Tamil lexicography) and went as a missionary to Ceylon (today's Sri Lanka), where she died in 1833. Her grieving husband compiled her letters and diaries into *Memoir of Mrs. Harriet L. Winslow*, first published in 1837 and expanded in 1840, and the book inspired a new generation of potential missionaries and detailed the development of the American Mission in Jaffna, Ceylon. Winslow's *Memoir* consists of a large assortment of primary materials from her letters and diaries along with extensive commentary by her husband on her life and the progress of the American Mission in Ceylon, including numerous observations on the cultures of the island's Sinhalese and Tamil inhabitants. The 1840 edition concludes with a memorial poem by the popular poet Lydia Huntley Sigourney, also from Connecticut and a fellow Congregationalist, that praises Winslow as a heroine who had drawn other souls to heaven with her:

> Are not they there,—those infant souls,—
>   Are not they by thy side,—
> For whom thy sleepless prayer arose,
>   For whom thy Saviour died?
> . . . .
> Is it thy voice that makes response
>   In tone so sweet and free?
> Weep for yourselves, my dearest friends,
>   But weep no more for me.[15]

In this poem, Winslow emerges as a mirror of Christ; by dying as a missionary woman, she echoes his injunction to the women of Jerusalem, given on the way to his crucifixion. It is notable how enmeshed these Connecticut writers, Stowe and Sigourney, were with the lives of the missionary women who played such a substantial role in American religious publishing in the nineteenth century.

Newell and Winslow were emblematic of the figure of the dying missionary woman, which became a staple of the missionary publishing that expanded rapidly in the years after the establishment of the ABCFM in 1812. Missionary texts circulated broadly through magazines, sermons, and book-length texts such as Winslow's *Memoir,* and they served to recruit new missionaries and shape the self-understanding of nineteenth-century American Protestants. Moreover, despite their frequent religious chauvinism, they also helped to educate American Protestants about the varieties of religious and cultural difference around the globe.

In the mission field, Winslow made a major contribution to the history of women's education in Sri Lanka, founding the Female School at Oodooville (modern-day Uduvil). Moreover, she educated her students in both English and Tamil, a challenging second language to acquire and teach. As scholars such as Lisa Joy Pruitt and Dana Lee Robert have shown, the topic of American female education figures largely in both Harriets' posthumous reputations.[16] Mary Lyon's Mount Holyoke Female Seminary, for example, nurtured young women spiritually with missionary biographies such as Newell's and Winslow's yet also provided a rigorous secular education. The efforts of women in missions to create a sense of community and agency among women abroad was mirrored in how the texts that they created were used at home, and missionary narratives thus paralleled popular novels by women, not only Stowe's but also Susan Warner's *The Wide, Wide World*, Maria Susanna Cummins's *The Lamplighter* and *El Fureidis*, and Louisa May Alcott's *Little Women*.[17]

Both Newell and Winslow had their sanctity confirmed in widely circulated descriptions of their deaths. Newell, the first of many female missionary martyrs from the United States, received her apotheosis in Wood's sermon, which was broadly circulated and reprinted, and Winslow carried on Newell's legacy and created her own. Her death followed a longer stretch of service and therefore a larger record of accomplishment, but in both cases relatively young women became exemplary figures of suffering and heroism, and their examples recruited more women for the missionary movement and reinforced the role of women as moral exemplars operating in an increasingly public sphere.

There is a correlation to these saintly deaths in one of the most famous and frequently parodied portions of *Uncle Tom's Cabin*: Stowe's representation of the death of Eva, a missionary to both the enslaved and the enslavers in her family circle. Stowe describes Eva as "the little evangelist," and she shows her making conversions from her deathbed in a manner that parallels Sigourney's description of Winslow as having drawn "infant souls" to heaven with her: "'Amen,' was the murmured response of Tom and Mammy, and some of the elder ones, who belonged to the Methodist church. The younger and more thoughtless ones, for the time completely overcome, were sobbing, with their heads bowed upon their knees."[18] In other words, Eva comes to fill a similar role for readers of the novel that Winslow filled for readers of her memoir and that Newell filled for Winslow herself.

When crafting what would become one of the most influential, and one of the most praised and derided scenes in *Uncle Tom's Cabin,* the death of Eva, Stowe had an extensive vocabulary on which to draw relating to both the accomplishments of missionary women and the ways in which their deaths were represented and their memories mourned. As a Congregationalist from New England, she constituted a core part of the readership for the memoirs of female missionaries such as Newell and Winslow; and as we have seen, she referred directly to missionary accounts from South Asia in her textbook on geography. Eva had performed the role of the missionary woman well in *Uncle Tom's Cabin:* she had served as both an evangelist and an educator, and her success in the latter role had ensured her success in the former. Even Eva was not a more effective unofficial missionary than Uncle Tom was, a fact that points toward one of the more overlooked points of congruence between *Uncle Tom's Cabin* and the missionary movement.

Uncle Tom, George Harris, Topsy, Miss Ophelia, and the Quest for Indigenous Clergy

For modern readers, one of the more disturbing plot developments in *Uncle Tom's Cabin* is the ease with which Stowe ships George Harris off to serve as a missionary in Africa rather than allowing him to develop a life in the United States, the only home he has known. The novel's last-minute transformation into a colonizationist rather than abolitionist narrative seems to betray the egalitarian rhetoric that she uses elsewhere in the book. At the same time, Uncle Tom's martyrdom on Simon Legree's plantation seems to indicate that resistance to slavery is simply not allowable for characters of African descent. Meanwhile, Miss Ophelia's aversion to Topsy has been taken to reflect Stowe's own discomfort with black characters and individuals, in fiction and elsewhere. I believe, however, that we can arrive at a clearer vision of how Stowe presents each of these developments when we consider them in the context of the nineteenth-century overseas missionary endeavor, which betrayed an obsession with the necessity of identifying and promoting native clergy to minister to converts to Protestantism in their own homelands.

Nineteenth-century missionary texts repeatedly emphasize the need for indigenous clergy. In the *Memoir,* Winslow's husband wrote about this history:

> When, about three centuries since, the Portuguese formed their trading establishments in Jaffna, they attempted also to establish Romanism. They destroyed many heathen temples, built many temples and churches, and induced or compelled many of the natives nominally to embrace the Romish faith. When the Dutch followed them in 1656, they tried in a manner somewhat similar, by governmental influence, to introduce the Protestant faith. They did not allow the heathen temples to be rebuilt, forbade the public ceremonies of idolatry, made the profession of Christianity a requirement for all important offices.[19]

Several significant points emerge here. One is that the Portuguese, who introduced Catholicism, and the Dutch, who introduced Protestantism, are both distinguished from the present generation of missionaries by their use of coercion in matters of faith. Winslow was careful to point out that the British regime in Ceylon had withdrawn from state promotion of Christianity, and he regarded this as an opportunity to redeem the flawed legacy of the Dutch and Portuguese colonizers. Moreover, this attempt at redemption took place in a profoundly ambivalent context. When describing the country's current situation, Winslow noted that the Jaffna district was "like a country that had been overrun by fire, and in which a second growth of thorns and briars, and thick bushes, had grown up, more impenetrable than the primitive forest."[20] The earlier introduction of Christianity into Ceylon, then, was an obstacle for the incoming ABCFM missionaries, regardless of previous apparent successes. For these missionaries, as for Stowe in *Uncle Tom's Cabin,* the task at hand was not so much the introduction of Christianity as its proper definition.

Reverend Winslow's solution, as presented in the *Memoir,* was the establishment of a native leadership that would internalize the precepts of Christianity while maintaining roots in the indigenous culture of Ceylon. Using rhetoric paralleling that of British imperialism, with which the American missionaries had an ambivalent relationship, he wrote, "Native energies of mind, and native feelings, must be enlisted in the work. The extended provinces of Satan's empire must furnish materials to aid in their own subjection to Christ, as India has been subdued to a foreign power primarily by native troops."[21] On the one hand, then, he endorsed a kind of religious imperialism, which viewed the peoples of Ceylon as denizens of "Satan's empire" and drew a direct connection to British imperial policy in India. On the other hand, his call for "subjection to Christ" was equivocal with regard to political imperialism. He assumed that North American missionaries would ultimately make way for what he called *"native preachers"* rather than continuing indefinitely to exercise dominance over the Christians of the island.[22]

In the concluding chapter of *Uncle Tom's Cabin*, Stowe infamously presented colonization as a solution to the problem of slavery, and she has been justly criticized for a move that seemed to undermine the more strongly abolitionist aspects of much of the novel. Yet she framed this possibility within the context of Christian missionary endeavors rather than as a kind of deportation, which was often the form that colonizationist solutions to slavery took. Stowe contended, "Let the church of the north receive these poor sufferers in the spirit of Christ, receive them to the educating advantages of Christian republican society and schools."[23] Only then would the colonization process in Africa begin. Stowe walked a very fine line here: while she advocated sending formerly enslaved people to Liberia as missionaries, she used the idea that recently enslaved people could form the clergy of non-European countries to demonstrate their civic and intellectual potential. "The first desire of the emancipated slave, generally, is for *education*," she wrote. "There is nothing they are not willing to give or do to have their children instructed; and . . . they are remarkably intelligent and quick to learn."[24] Thus, her emphasis on the talent and industry of former slaves also established that they possessed the qualities for citizenship. In this way, she used the idea of a native clergy in relation to slavery to make a point that was, at its heart, abolitionist, even egalitarian, despite the fact that the surface argument was colonizationist.

Stowe's presentation of colonization as a response to slavery, then, was not merely a capitulation to the racism of even antislavery whites (although it almost certainly was that as well). Rather, it reflected the sense of transnational mission that Stowe shared with her contemporaries in the ABCFM and other missionary organizations. This argument for African American colonization as a variant on the call for indigenous clergy was of course highly problematic insofar as enslaved Americans were not in most cases indigenous to Africa and indeed, as Stowe herself acknowledged, had been present in North America for many generations. Many, like George Harris in *Uncle Tom's Cabin*, also shared European and African ancestry. Yet it is important to remember that Stowe was participating in a movement away from the assumption that North Americans of European descent constituted the natural leadership for churches in Asia and Africa. In other words, there was a countervailing and potentially antiracist tendency in her discussions of African missions that is easy to miss.

Temperance in the Ceylon Mission

Among other approaches, American missionaries meant to correct the missteps of their predecessors by introducing a vigorous and active temperance movement into colonial Ceylon. The interreligious implications of such a movement are curious: among adherents of Buddhism, Hinduism, and Islam in Ceylon, Christianity was not then (and has rarely been since) connected with the idea of abstention from alcohol. On the contrary, compared with the adherents of other religions, Christians, whether Catholic or Protestant, have been associated with greater tolerance for alcohol consumption. Helen I. Root's centennial history of the American mission in Ceylon makes this point clearly:

> An interesting development during those years was the growth of temperance sentiment. The missionaries in 1830 were using wine and beer, as so many Christian people had done at the time they left America, believing them essential to health and not realizing how great a stumbling block they were laying in the path of the native church. When the reinforcement of 1834 came fresh from the temperance agitation in the United States none of them used alcoholic drinks, and their example together with the conviction already growing in the minds of the senior missionaries led to the abandonment of their use

altogether. Dr. Scudder found his first temperance mass meeting so great a popular success as to convince him that the Mission ought to take a decided stand in the matter.[25]

As Root points out, American missionaries who embraced temperance and rejected alcohol were following a novel pattern in relation to the American context. Yet by taking that stand, they brought Christianity closer to the indigenous religious traditions of Ceylon. Perhaps this accounted for the popularity of temperance meetings, a popularity that helped to convince the early missionary Horace Scudder that temperance was an element of American evangelicalism that would translate well into the context of the mission field in Ceylon. Temperance was a revision of Christian practice that made it more, not less, congruent with historic cultural norms in Ceylon, a curious paradox for the missionaries, who noted that it had a positive effect on their standing with indigenous Sinhalese, Tamils, and Muslims. The situation demonstrates the complexity of the negotiations in which the ABCFM missionaries were engaged. They were carrying the gospel as understood by American Protestants to a multi-religious society that included Roman Catholics and Dutch Reformed Protestants alongside much larger populations of Hindus, Muslims, and Buddhists; and their own understanding of the demands of the gospel was being mediated by new developments in America as well as by their own observations on the mission field.

Reading *Uncle Tom's Cabin* in 1890s Ceylon

So we come full circle to the unlikely invocation of *Uncle Tom's Cabin* by two American missionaries in South Asia. When Margaret and Mary Leitch referred to Topsy in their discussion of indigenous clergy in *Seven Years in Ceylon,* they were drawing on a text with international resonance that would be familiar to potential supporters in both the United States and Great Britain. Indeed, they barely needed to set the scene at all when they invoked Topsy, merely referring to "the Topsy in 'Uncle Tom's Cabin'" as a shorthand for an array of characteristics that their readers, from whom they were soliciting funds for a medical school in northern Ceylon, would be certain to recognize from both Stowe's work and theatrical adaptations of the novel.

What made *Uncle Tom's Cabin* such a natural point of reference for the Leitch sisters was the way in which it combined some of the same strands in American culture that were becoming crucial to the missionary movement. Temperance and antislavery had often gone hand in hand in the early years of the republic, and Stowe had put a temperance sermon into Uncle Tom's mouth, presenting a circumstance in which Tom, a Christian of African descent, was evangelizing Augustine St. Clare, a lapsed Christian of European descent. The Leitch sisters were confronted by the fact that the Christian colonizers of the island had played the unsavory role of introducing hard liquor to adherents of three non-Christian religions that condemned its use: "The religions of the Hindus, Mohammedans, and Buddhists forbid the use of strong drink, and formerly the people of India and Ceylon were for the most part total abstainers."[26] Thus, the sisters found themselves in an unlikely alliance with Muslim, Hindu, and Buddhist clergy in protesting the sale of liquor by Christian colonizers in Ceylon. Moreover, they connected the traffic in liquor in northern Ceylon with the broader ambiguities of Christianity and colonialism in Asia, citing the British missionary to China, Hudson Taylor, on the debilitating effects of the opium trade. Thus, *Uncle Tom's Cabin*'s adoption of the rhetoric of the temperance movement to condemn the evils of slavery came full circle in the Leitch sisters' text: in their telling, the World's Women's Christian Temperance Union became the logical international successor to the international movement for the abolition of slavery. Stowe's interweaving of various elements of the nineteenth-century pursuit of moral reform drew upon an international temperance movement that served as both a model for antislavery activism early in the nineteenth century and as a successor to abolitionist moral passion in the later part of that century and, by doing so, contributed to the same ecosystem of moral reform and Christian proselytizing that took in missionaries such as Newell, Winslow, and the Leitch sisters.

Reynolds's early work in *Faith in Fiction* and *Beneath the American Renaissance* established close links between popular and religious literature of the nineteenth century and the literature that we presently consider canonical, including *Uncle Tom's Cabin*, a work that has required its own process of canonical recovery.[27] Yet missionary literature continues to receive scant attention as we seek to engage more profoundly with the intellectual world and the lived experience of nineteenth-century writers. Thus, finding Stowe in the mission field and the mission field in Stowe's most famous work can help us to recover sources of the nineteenth-century literary imagination in the United States. Reynolds has given us an admirable model for working with these texts, and the fact that much work remains to be done magnifies the scope of his accomplishment by showing us the way into it. American missionary literature, both for its own sake and for its relation to canonical American authors of the nineteenth century, provides literary scholars and critics with a world to explore that goes well beyond the boundaries of the nineteenth-century United States.

NOTES

1. Mary Leitch and Margaret W. Leitch, *Seven Years in Ceylon: Stories of Mission Life* (1890; reprint, New Delhi: Navrang, 1993), 123. For a brief biographical discussion of the Leitch sisters, see Ian Tyrell, *Reforming the World: The Creation of America's Moral Empire* (Princeton: Princeton University Press, 2010), 28–46.

2. Ibid., 124.

3. Harriet Beecher Stowe, *Uncle Tom's Cabin, Or, Life Among the Lowly* (1852; reprint, New York: Norton 2010), 404.

4. Ibid., 396.

5. Leitch and Leitch, *Seven Years in Ceylon*, 124–25.

6. See, for example, the list of translations in a biography of Stowe published around the same time as *Seven Years in Ceylon:* Florine Thayer-McCray, *The Life-Work of the Author of Uncle Tom's Cabin* (New York: Funk and Wagnalls, 1889), 112.

7. David S. Reynolds, *Mightier Than the Sword: "Uncle Tom's Cabin" and the Battle for America* (New York: Norton, 2011), xi.

8. Mary Cayton Kupiec, "The Canonization of Harriet Newell," in *Competing Kingdoms: Women, Mission, Nation, and the American Protestant Empire, 1812–1960*, ed. Barbara Reeves-Ellington, Kathryn Kish Sklar, and Connie A. Shemo (Durham, N.C.: Duke University Press, 2009), 69–93.

9. *Thirty-Eighth Annual Report of the American Tract Society, Boston, 1863* (New York: American Tract Society, 1863), 15, 181, 189.

10. Harriet Beecher Stowe, *First Geography for Children* (Boston: Phillips, Samson, 1855), 200.

11. Miron Winslow, *Memoir of Mrs. Harriet L. Winslow, Thirteen Years a Member of the American Mission in Ceylon* (1840; reprint, New Delhi: Asian Educational Services, 2003), 241.

12. Two excellent Stowe biographies are Joan Hedrick's magisterial *Harriet Beecher Stowe: A Life* (New York: Oxford University Press, 1994) and Nancy Koester's *Harriet Beecher Stowe: A Spiritual Life* (Grand Rapids, Mich.: Eerdmans, 2014). Neither deals with the question of possible influences on Stowe from foreign missions, but both point to how thoroughly enmeshed Stowe was in the wider currents of nineteenth-century evangelical Protestant culture.

13. Winslow, *Memoir*, 32, 34.

14. Leonard Woods, *A Sermon Preached at Haverhill (Mass.), in Remembrance of Mrs. Harriet Newell* (Boston: Armstrong, 1814). Woods's sermon on Newell was published repeatedly over the succeeding decades, both under its own name and as some variant on the title "A Memoir of Mrs. Harriet Newell," including in at least one edition published by the American Tract Society.

15. Winslow, *Memoir*, 480.

16. Lisa Joy Pruitt, *A Looking Glass for the Ladies: American Protestant Women and the Orient in the Nineteenth Century* (Macon, Ga.: Mercer University Press, 2005); Dana Lee Robert, *American Women in Mission: A Social History of their Thought and Practice* (Macon, Ga.: Mercer University Press, 1996).

17. Susan Warner, *The Wide, Wide World* (1850; reprint, New York: Feminist Press, 1986); Susanna Maria Cummins, *The Lamplighter* (Boston: Jewett, 1854); Susanna Maria Cummins, *El Fureidis* (Boston: Ticknor and Fields, 1860); Louisa May Alcott, *Little Women* (1868–69; reprint, New York: Norton, 2003).

18. Stowe, *Uncle Tom's Cabin*, 264.

19. Winslow, *Memoir*, 191.

20. Ibid., 100.

21. Ibid., 284.

22. Ibid., 283.

23. Stowe, *Uncle Tom's Cabin*, 405.

24. Ibid., 406.

25. Helen I. Root, *A Century in Ceylon: A Brief History of the Work of the American Board in Ceylon, 1816–1916* (1916; reprint, New Delhi: Asian Educational Services, 2004), 24.

26. Leitch and Leitch, *Seven Years in Ceylon*, 101.

27. David S. Reynolds, *Beneath the American Renaissance: The Subversive Imagination in the Age of Emerson and Melville* (Cambridge, Mass.: Harvard University Press, 1988); David S. Reynolds, *Faith in Fiction: The Emergence of Religious Literature in America* (Cambridge, Mass.: Harvard University Press, 1981).

CHAPTER 15

"GOD WILL GIVE HIM BLOOD TO DRINK"

Unholy Dying in The House of the Seven Gables

Jonathan A. Cook

ALTHOUGH HAWTHORNE considered *The House of the Seven Gables* to be a more "natural," "healthy," and "cheerful" product of his pen than *The Scarlet Letter*, it is still notable for its grotesque depiction of the deaths of two exemplary hypocrites and villains, the late seventeenth-century Puritan Colonel Pyncheon and his mid-nineteenth-century descendant and counterpart, Judge Jaffrey Pyncheon. In the cycle of hubris and nemesis that governs the novel's plot, the deaths of the two Pyncheon patriarchs initiate and terminate the curse on the family, which had been pronounced by the dying Matthew Maule on the Puritan usurper and is finally resolved by the judge's providential death. Given the Christian moralism that informs the narrative of *The House of the Seven Gables*, the bloody expirations of Colonel and Judge Pyncheon are graphic illustrations of what I call *unholy dying*, a notion based on a variety of contemporary religious and cultural practices as well as older Christian traditions. And while the extended portrait of Judge Pyncheon provides a striking example of a class of characters whom David S. Reynolds calls "oxymoronic oppressors," or pious hypocrites, found in antebellum popular fiction, his distinctive death, highlighted by the narrator's extraordinary verbal assault on his dead body in chapter 18, demonstrates Hawthorne's strategic adaptation of a broad range of Christian homiletics. *The House of the Seven Gables* may thus be said to qualify as an example of pre–Civil War American religious fiction—a genre for which Reynolds has provided the most complete guide—not because of any sectarian or tendentious aims but through its covert incorporation of key religious paradigms and biblical allusions.[1]

Largely set in the mid-nineteenth century, the novel draws on the American cultural traditions of death and dying influential at this time. An awareness of death was pervasive in antebellum America, where high childhood mortality, epidemic diseases, and antiquated medical practices limited average life expectancy to about age forty. In keeping with the ubiquitous culture of sentimentality that marked the era, death was idealized and sanitized to disguise its potential horrors, and a substantial literature of consolation emerged to assist the grieving. Evangelical models of a good or even beautiful death, which entailed loving family members surrounding the suitably prepared dying individual, were widely promulgated; and the deathbed scene was made to serve a didactic function, with special attention to the dying individual's last words, which might hint at a future state. Widespread theological speculation on the physical properties of heaven and the nature of reunion with loved ones went hand in hand with the so-called domestication of death, or the erasure of boundaries between earthly and heavenly homes. This connection was illustrated by the rural cemetery movement, beginning with the opening of Mount Auburn Cemetery in Cambridge, Massachusetts, in the early 1830s, and by the séances of the spiritualist movement, starting in the later 1840s.[2]

Even as death and dying were widely sentimentalized, their older moral associations with the terrifying potential for hell and damnation remained present for many individuals. Despite the emergence of liberal Protestant denominations such as the Unitarians and the Universalists, who denied the doctrine of eternal punishment, the evangelical revivalism of the Second Great Awakening continued to rely on the stark alternatives of damnation and salvation for persons undergoing the conversion experience. Representative here were the so-called "new measures" initiated by the Presbyterian-Congregational preacher Charles Grandison Finney, which included the use of an "anxious seat" for those under conviction of sin. And while threats of hellfire and damnation were not as pervasive as they had been a century earlier, many preachers like Finney still resorted to them as the ultimate rationale for spiritual regeneration. The Congregational church that dominated New England culture well into the nineteenth century officially maintained the Calvinist doctrines of innate depravity and predestination, and orthodox tradition going back to the Church Fathers highlighted the awful inevitability of death, judgment, heaven, and hell—the perennial "Four Last Things."[3]

By the second quarter of the nineteenth century, religious publishers and benevolent societies were circulating a massive number of Bibles, moral tracts, sermons, newspapers, periodicals, spiritual autobiographies, missionary memoirs, and older English devotional classics. Advances in print technologies facilitated the explosion of popular literature of all levels of sophistication and orthodoxy. The pervasive middle-class sentimental print culture of the era largely aimed at religious edification, and the many fictional, poetic, and homiletic descriptions of death and dying similarly reinforced the moral economies of Protestant Christianity. The vast corpus of sentimental literature for the grieving helped promote the Christian promise of spiritual immortality, just as popular religious classics such as John Bunyan's *Pilgrim's Progress,* Richard Baxter's *Call to the Unconverted,* and Philip Doddridge's *Rise and Progress of Religion in the Soul* taught contemporary Americans how to deal with the traditional challenges of both holy living and holy dying.[4]

As a product of this evangelical and homiletic middle-class culture, Hawthorne's *The House of the Seven Gables* inherited a complex array of religious influences. The motif of unholy dying in the novel begins with the shocking and suspicious death of Colonel Pyncheon in apparent fulfillment of Matthew Maule's dying curse on him: "God will give him blood to drink!" The colonel had punished the plebian Maule, sentencing him to death for alleged wizardry in order to obtain Maule's desirable property following years of unresolved legal dispute. After obtaining the land, the colonel builds a capacious mansion on the site in order to found a family dynasty, unpersuaded by the idea that a retributive evil spirit might haunt the house. Indeed, he is so convinced of the righteousness of his actions that he even hires his victim's son, Thomas, to build the residence. The colonel's death occurs on the day the new house is finished, when a "ceremony of consecration, festive, as well as religious, was now to be performed," along with a prayer and a sermon from the Reverend Higginson and a psalm sung by the community.[5]

Yet the colonel's manner of death manifestly negates and pollutes any attempt to consecrate the new house. For instead of experiencing a good death, with friends and family in attendance at the bedside, a conscience at rest, and the sharing of last words or signs indicating redemption in the afterlife, the colonel dies alone, except for the presence of a grandchild, "the only human being that ever dared to be familiar with him," who is the first to realize that the colonel is dead in his chair. Significantly, the dead man wears a look of dismay and shows signs of physical violence on his person. Earlier in the scene, the unexpected death of the colonel had inadvertently made his guests, including the lieutenant governor of the colony, rudely wait for his appearance; and when that eminent dignitary finally opens the door to the study, the crowd of guests discovers a scene of Gothic horror: the colonel with "a frown on his dark and massive countenance" and blood on his ruff, with his "hoary beard saturated with it." The narrator duly notes a local tradition holding that a voice resembling Matthew Maule's now repeats the wizard's dying words, with the verb changed from future to perfect tense: "God hath given him blood to drink!"[6]

Local doctors, after disputing over the cause of death, finally settle for apoplexy, a term then used to describe any effusion of blood, including pulmonary hemorrhage, as is likely the case here. Yet the primal horror of the colonel's bloody countenance seems to offer a deeper truth about his death, which includes rumors of retribution from Maule or his son. The signs of this were the alleged "marks of fingers on his throat, and the print of a bloody hand on his plaited ruff; and that his peaked beard was dishevelled, as if it had been fiercely clutched and pulled." To pull a man's beard at this time was, of course, the ultimate sign of disrespect. The narrator may dismiss these claims as rumors, along with another vague report of an open lattice window and a man "clambering over the garden-fence," but the grotesque circumstances show all the signs of an unredeemed, probably hell-bound sinner's egregiously unholy death.[7] Reinforcing this aura of moral corruption is the colonel's resemblance to an Old Testament prototype. As critics have noted, in his oppressive treatment of Matthew Maule and his retributive, blood-soaked death, the colonel reprises the tale in I Kings of the irreligious King Ahab, who coveted the commoner Naboth's vineyard, contrived his execution to gain the property, and eventually died from a bloody wound during battle with the Syrians. Throughout his unholy reign, Ahab had been opposed by the prophet Elijah, whose role in Hawthorne's novel is implicitly assumed by the mesmeric seer and moral commentator Holgrave.[8]

The first chapter of *The House of the Seven Gables* thus initiates a cycle of hubris and nemesis that will characterize the Pyncheon line as the events of the present-day narrative play themselves out. In addition to chronicling the origins of the historic Maule-Pyncheon feud, it sets the stage for the rest of the narrative in its mention of the "violent death—for so it was adjudged—of one member of the family, by a criminal act of another," which took place about three decades before the present time of the narrative.[9] Only at the end of the story do we learn the exact details of the putative "murder" of Jaffrey Pyncheon, for which his nephew Clifford was convicted and served thirty years in prison. In fact, the death (from an apoplectic attack, hastened by a fractured skull from a fall) was really the accidental result of the older Jaffrey's enraged discovery of the younger Jaffrey's attempt to rob him after the latter stole into his uncle's private chambers. Hawthorne loosely based this scene on a sensational 1830 Salem murder in which the enormously wealthy elderly shipping magnate Joseph White was killed by Richard Crowninshield. Like the younger Jaffrey, Crowninshield was the degenerate scion of a prominent family and had been hired by White's grandnephews, Frank and Joseph Knapp, who hoped to inherit part of their great-uncle's fortune.[10]

In Hawthorne's novel, the narrator notes that the older Jaffrey, a wealthy bachelor and antiquarian, had become convinced of the injustice of Colonel Pyncheon's actions, and he was on the verge of giving up the family mansion to a surviving Maule before his family stopped him. These details set the stage for the main plot of the novel involving Clifford's return home to live with his devoted elderly sister, Hepzibah, after three decades in prison and his ensuing persecution by the modern avatar of the iron-willed colonel, Judge Jaffrey Pyncheon, whose insensate greed likewise brings about his own demise. The secret Maule descendant Holgrave is a tenant in the house, and his daguerreotypist profession can be seen as a modern adaptation of the family's traditional mesmeric powers. Yet his inherited desire for the Pyncheon family's extinction is ultimately overcome by his love for the redemptive figure of Phoebe, whose name suggests the blessings of both sunlight and Christianity, based on Saint Paul's reference in Romans to "Phebe our sister" who is a "servant of the church" and "succourer of many."[11] Early in their acquaintance, Holgrave shows Phoebe a daguerreotype of the judge, which she mistakes for the portrait of the Puritan colonel in the parlor and which he himself sees as visible proof of the outwardly benignant judge's hypocrisy: "Here we have the man, sly, subtle, hard, imperious, and, withal, cold as ice." The psychological burden of his ancestral feud prompts Holgrave to denounce, in outspoken Jeffersonian and Emersonian terms, the dead weight of the past that "lies upon the Present like a giant's dead body" and controls its legal, cultural, medical, and religious traditions.[12]

The judge makes his first appearance in chapter 8, where his chief vices are immediately displayed to the reader. Especially notable are his inordinate greed and his strong fleshly desires, as indicated by his striking physical bulk and his oversexed attempt to kiss Phoebe: "The man, the sex, somehow or other, was entirely too prominent in the Judge's demonstrations of that sort."[13] As the chief villain of the narrative, he embodies the immorality that began with the colonel's selfish act of dispossession, but now the attempt to dispossess is directed at his cousin Clifford, whom the judge thinks has some knowledge of the large portion of the older Jaffrey's estate that he believes was never passed down to him as his uncle's sole heir. His gratuitous and delusive desire for an increase in his already substantial wealth is equivalent to the colonel's desire for the vast property in Maine that he was on the verge of obtaining before his death. Indeed, the legendary wealth that the judge believes is missing from his uncle's estate is that identical tract of land. (Holgrave later reveals the obsolete deed to the property moldering behind the picture of the original Pyncheon patriarch, hidden there by Thomas Maule.) As the judge tells Hepzibah in chapter 17, he had arranged Clifford's release from imprisonment solely to ferret out this information—an act of supreme hypocrisy and moral depravity because, as we discover in the last chapter, the judge himself was responsible for sending Clifford to prison to cover up his own crime.

In this meeting with Hepzibah, which takes place during the judge's second and last visit to the house, Phoebe is no longer present to act as a moderating influence on his behavior, and the judge becomes more intimidating, threatening to have Clifford institutionalized as revenge for withholding information about their uncle's estate, and revealing to Hepzibah that he has suborned a number of spies to report back about his cousin's eccentric behavior. Although she vigorously scolds him for desiring more money when he is already inordinately rich and for his ancestral "hard and grasping spirit," he insists on interviewing Clifford and goes to wait for him in the parlor chair where his ancestor was discovered with his bloody beard and ruff.[14] Here he falls victim to the hereditary apoplexy, suffering the same darkening of countenance and lethal hemorrhage as his Puritan ancestor did and thereby fulfilling the curse of the original Maule acting in the role of divine nemesis.

Chapter 18 of *The House of the Seven Gables,* in which the narrator relentlessly taunts the seated corpse of Judge Pyncheon, may invite contradictory responses from the reader. On one level, we relish the narrator's relentless exposure and verbal punishment of the novel's chief villain, whose ominous shadow has loomed over the Pyncheon residence from early in the narrative. On the other hand, the virtuosity of the narrator's detailed survey of the judge's worldly sins seems to be literary and moral overkill. What has been missing from analyses of the chapter, however, is awareness of the rich theological, homiletic, and moral texture of the narrator's scathing portrait of the dead judge.[15] For it is a virtuosic display of moralized rhetoric from the contemporary convention of the didactic death mixed with traditions of Puritan and evangelical sermonizing and a host of biblical proof texts and literary allusions. The chapter performs a scathing dissection of Judge Pyncheon's soul while celebrating the providential extinction of the novel's chief villain through an implied act of divine retribution.

The most striking fact here is that the judge's manner of death violates all of the desired features of the contemporary evangelical idea of a good or beautiful death. For he makes no preparation for mortality, has no family immediately present, receives no visit from the ministry, offers no confession of sins or preparation for the afterlife, and shares no memorably consolatory words or actions. His closest living relatives, Hepzibah and Clifford, flee from his hateful presence once they discover his body; in fact, the only living creatures that eventually appear are a mouse that momentarily "seems to meditate a journey of exploration over this great, black bulk" and a fly that "is creeping over the bridge of his nose, towards the would-be chief-magistrate's wide-open eyes!"[16] Instead of being surrounded by devoted family members or friends, his body is violated by common household pests—a graphic reminder of the traditional idea of death as the great leveler.

The judge's unholy death clearly invites us to picture his damnation, for the whole chapter is devoted to an elaborate demonstration that he has failed to do anything in his life to merit salvation. With his varied rhetorical devices, the narrator is implicitly simulating the role of a contemporary evangelical preacher attempting to convert a seasoned sinner who is sitting on the "anxious seat," except that this corpse will never rise from his ancestral chair to accept Christ into his life and avoid damnation. In addition, the narrator's tactical obliviousness to the truth of the judge's lifeless condition potentially parodies the era's sentimental denial of the ugly facts of human mortality, even as the traditional pious vigil over the corpse is replaced by a ghost-filled ritual of humiliation.

The narrator begins his remarks by assuming that the judge is merely asleep, an ironic strategy with a biblical prototype that allows the narrator to address the judge as a living individual. For a comparable insult to a hated enemy is evident in the story of the prophet Elijah's contest with King Ahab's 450 prophets of Baal on Mount Carmel, in which the Hebrew prophet challenges the prophets of the foreign god to send fire down from heaven to consume a sacrificed bullock. The Israelite prophet then taunts the inert foreign god who fails to respond to his prophets' appeal: "And it came to pass at noon, that Elijah mocked them, and said, Cry aloud: for he is a god; either he is talking, or he is pursuing, or he is in a journey, or peradventure he sleepeth, and must be awakened.[17]

As we read through the list of the various appointments that the judge is missing by sleeping in his chair, we increasingly understand that the narrator is tracking the ironic distance between the judge's moral laxity and the corrupt state of his soul. Many features of the narrator's exhortations recall key aspects of Christian tradition, especially its admonitions about the brevity and vanity of mortal life and its encouragement for Christians to shun the triple temptations of the world, the flesh, and the devil.[18] For instance, the narrator reports on the judge's confident projection of living for another two or three decades: "With his firm health, and the little inroad that age has made upon him, fifteen years, or twenty—yes, or perhaps five-and-twenty!—are no more than he may fairly call his own." The judge, according to the narrator, has assured himself that his recent signs of ill health are nothing to worry about: "A mere dimness of sight and dizziness of brain, was it?—or a disagreeable choking, or stifling, or gurgling, or bubbling, in the region of the thorax, as the anatomists say?" The judge would presumably merely laugh over "such trifles" with his doctor, but such dismissal fails to anticipate the mortal "crimson stain upon his shirt-bosom" that now marks his sinful inert body. The narrator also considers the well-known Christian theme of the vanity of life, as evident in the gradual disappearance of the dead man's face and body into the shades of night as the light fades from the window: "The features are all gone; there is only the paleness of them left. And how looks it now? There is no window! There is no face!"[19] The judge thus literally and figuratively has vanished into nothingness.

Resisting the varied powers of the "world" forms an integral part of evangelical Christian tradition, but here the narrator's representation of the deceased Judge Pyncheon exhibits not their resistance but their active promotion in his life.[20] Thus, we hear of the many appointments and activities that he had planned for the day, including a visit to an insurance office, a bank directors' meeting, a meeting with a State Street broker, a real estate auction, the purchase of a new horse, the meeting of a charitable society, the arrangement for an order of fruit trees, his donation to a political committee, and finally attendance at an elaborate political dinner that might lead to his nomination for governor. Making the judge into almost a caricature of Mammon, the narrator advises him to attend his bank directors' meeting: "Let him go thither, and loll at ease upon his money-bags! He has lounged long enough in the old chair."[21] The comment is a sardonic confirmation of what Christ taught in the Sermon on the Mount: "For where your treasure is, there will your heart be also."[22]

In Christian tradition, the believer is taught to mortify the desires of the flesh and live in the spirit.[23] But rather than fighting against carnal appetites, Judge Pyncheon seems to embody them: "It was he, you know, of whom it used to be said, in reference to his ogre-like appetite, that his Creator made him a great animal, but that the dinner-hour made him a great beast. Persons of his large sensual endowments must claim indulgence, at their feeding-time." As the narrator notes, by lingering in his chair, the judge is going to miss an important political dinner that will offer a host of delicious viands: "Real turtle, we understand, and salmon, tautog, canvass-backs, pig, English mutton, good roast-beef, or dainties of that serious kind, fit for substantial country-gentlemen, as these honorable persons mostly are." The word *substantial* here does double-duty, indicating both personal wealth and physical bulk. At the dinner, too, will be "a brand of old Madeira" that is "a glorious wine, fragrant, and full of gentle might; a bottled-up happiness, put by for use, a golden liquid, worth more than liquid gold; so rare and admirable, that veteran wine-bibbers count it among their epochs to have tasted it!" The wine is depicted as a kind of sacred elixir of life, as the narrator ironically implies: "It would all but revive a dead man! Would you like to sip it now, Judge Pyncheon?"[24]

The last of the trio of Christian moral prohibitions relates to the devil, an ironic figure in this case because the judge, being a "subtile, worldly, selfish, iron-hearted hypocrite," would seem to be already in the devil's grip.[25] The hellish Dantean atmosphere of the house, as the night darkens to blackness and the wind shrieks like the damned, clearly evokes the devil's domain, while the corpse seems to be under the influence of malign enchantment. Significantly, after the judge has declined to get out of his oaken chair, and after a parade of his ancestors has emerged in the moonlight before the portrait of the colonel, a mouse at the foot of his chair is scared away by the sudden appearance of a cat in the window: "This Grimalkin has a very ugly look. Is it a cat watching for a mouse, or the Devil for a human soul?" The ambiguity of the question hints that both possibilities may be true. Grimalkin was the nickname for an evil-looking female cat, often considered to be the demonic familiar of witches, a tradition originating in Scottish folklore. The name is invoked by one of the three witches in the first scene of *Macbeth,* and a few other traces of Shakespeare's Scottish tragedy relating to damnation can also be found in chapter 18 of Hawthorne's novel, as when the narrator says to the judge's body, echoing Macbeth's final despairing soliloquy on the meaningless of life: "You have lost a day. But tomorrow will be here anon. Will you rise, betimes, and make the most of it? Tomorrow! Tomorrow! Tomorrow!"[26] The ghostly procession of Judge Pyncheon's ancestors, with the ironic and mocking peripheral presence of the ghost of Thomas Maule, is also comparable to the ironic procession of eight kings, presented by the weird sisters and negating Macbeth's claim to the crown of Scotland. The judge's ancestors are associated with "the looking-glass, which, you are aware, is always a kind of window or doorway into the spiritual world"; likewise, in the "show" of eight kings, Banquo appears with a looking glass in his hand, a sign of his long and secure line of descent.[27] And just as Macbeth's overweening ambition to rule Scotland is now shown to be futile, so will Judge Pyncheon's family dynasty end with the death overseas of his only son, Jaffrey. Hence the judge's wealth will ironically revert to Clifford, Hepzibah, and Phoebe—another illustration of the traditional biblical theme, expounded by Ecclesiastes, of the vanity of human wishes.

It is thus appropriate that the narrator's earlier injunctions for the judge to get up out of his chair include a timely reminder of the Last Judgment: "We, that are alive, may rise betimes tomorrow. As for him that has died to-day, his tomorrow will be the resurrection-morn." The narrator in fact hints at the judge's hellish future: "An infinite, inscrutable blackness has annihilated sight! Where is our universe? All crumbled away from us; and we, adrift in chaos, may hearken to the gusts of homeless wind, that go sighing and murmuring about, in quest of what was once a world!" In this Dantean universe of chaotic wind and infernal night, as in the windy upper reaches of the *Inferno,* the soul and body of the judge seem to be entering "the blackness of darkness forever," as the text of Jude describes damnation. In the meantime, the subversive ticking of the judge's watch—"this little, quiet, never-ceasing throb of Time's pulse"—adds a Poe-like note of terror to the scene of gathering night.[28]

Before he has finished criticizing the judge and just as the morning sun enters the room, the narrator, in a series of pointed questions, makes a final appeal to the illustrious figure in the chair, asking, for example, whether he will "go forth a humbled and repentant man, sorrowful, gentle, seeking no profit, shrinking from worldly honor, hardly daring to love God, but bold to love his fellow-man, and to do him what good he may?"[29] The narrator's eloquent exhortations duplicate Saint Paul's well-known teachings in Romans to the early Christian community: "Love worketh no ill to his neighbor: therefore love is the fulfilling of the law. And that, knowing the time, that now it is high time to awake out of sleep: for now is our salvation nearer than when we believed. The night is far spent, the day is at hand: let us therefore cast off the works of darkness, and let us put on the armour of light."[30] Such an ideal of Christian behavior is obviously impossible in this case, and therefore the narrator's final injunction has a harsher, more aggressive tone: "Rise up, Judge Pyncheon! The morning sunshine glimmers through the foliage, and, beautiful and holy as it is, shuns not to kindle up your face. Rise up, thou subtile, worldly, selfish, iron-hearted hypocrite, and make thy choice, whether still to be subtile, worldly, selfish, iron-hearted, and hypocritical, or to tear these sins out of thy nature, though they bring the life-blood with them! The Avenger is upon thee! Rise up, before it be too late!"[31]

The narrator's sermonic appeal for a final deathbed conversion offers a stark choice between redemption and damnation, the latter hinted by the narrator's association of the word *subtile* with the judge, for it recalls the serpent of Eden, which "was more subtil than any beast of the field which the Lord God had made."[32] The verbal parallel confirms earlier diabolical associations with the judge, such as those found in chapter 8. He can hardly be expected to tear out the sins from his nature because he has shown no sign of repentance in his life and is obviously beyond hope. He has thus merited the avenging spirit of Christ as judge, as evoked by Saint Paul, who urged that "no man go beyond and defraud his brother in any matter: because that the Lord is the avenger of all such."[33] Judge Pyncheon has defrauded his cousin Clifford of thirty years of freedom and can expect the worst from Christ the avenger. Significantly, in the passage in Ephesians that originated the Christian idea of the need to oppose the unholy trinity of the world, the flesh, and the devil, Saint Paul similarly claimed that God's love enabled those who were "dead in sins" to be "quickened" and "raised" by Christ.[34] Judge Pyncheon, however, is both figuratively and literally "dead in sins" and will never be raised.

Following their discovery of the judge's death, Hepzibah and Clifford flee the house, for the latter is desperate to get away from the monstrous presence of the cousin who ruined his life. On the morning after they leave, readers witness the puzzlement of various members of the community as they discover that the house is empty and

Hepzibah's cent shop is closed. In a passage worthy of Flaubert, the narrator notes the ironic contrast between the mundane nature of the town's daily social and commercial activities and the terrifying existential abyss of death: "Had any observer of these proceedings been aware of the fearful secret, hidden within the house, it would have affected him with a singular shape and modification of horror, to see the current of human life making this small eddy hereabouts;—whirling sticks, straws, and all such trifles, round and round, right over the black depth where a dead corpse lay unseen."[35] Just as the local community was mystified and disturbed by the dead colonel's absence at the celebration of his new mansion (in chapter 1), their descendants—young Ned Higgins, the local butcher, and others—are bewildered and frustrated by the closed house. But when Phoebe returns that day from her summer sojourn with her family, a semblance of normal life returns to the mansion. After earlier taking a daguerreotype of the judge's corpse in the morning light of the parlor, Holgrave then shows her the image in order to apprize her of her relative's decease while clarifying for her the natural cause of death.

In the judge's constitutionally inherited apoplexy and its resemblance to his uncle's death three decades earlier, Holgrave sees indelible proof of Clifford's retroactive innocence. Morally, Holgrave is now free of the desire for revenge against the Pyncheon patriarch whose criminal family history has marginalized and then extinguished the rest of the Maule lineage, and he proposes to Phoebe, only later revealing his secret family identity in the final chapter. With her acceptance and the safe return of Hepzibah and Clifford, a new and redeemed Pyncheon family is now possible. The ancestral curse is lifted through the judge's grotesque and punitive death and Holgrave's spiritual redemption. The newly constituted family of four will remove itself from the ancestral house as an act of reparation to the ghost of Matthew Maule, and they will inherit the rest of Judge's Pyncheon's fortune (minus the delusive land claim in Maine), which represents legal restitution to Clifford as the original heir of the bachelor uncle and to Holgrave (via Phoebe) as the last living descendant of the legally oppressed Maules. The much-criticized conclusion of the novel is thus controlled by the logic of poetic justice and the conventions of comic reconciliation. Hence, the common critical predictions of inevitable troubles for the newly united Pyncheon-Maule family are needlessly churlish, notwithstanding the obligatory moralizing of Hawthorne's preface.[36]

In the novel's dénouement, Holgrave reveals the full truth behind the façade of the judge's reputation and his responsibility for inadvertently causing his uncle's death and then arranging matters so that Clifford took the blame. This truth then filters into the community, along with the ugly reality of the judge's manner of dying: "It is very singular, how the fact of a man's death often seems to give people a truer idea of his character, whether for good or evil, than they have ever possessed while he was living and acting among them."[37] The revelations bring out the truth of the judge's greed and hypocrisy, as in the antebellum tradition of the didactic death, which points to the individual's authentic moral nature and likely postmortem fate. From the perspective of the final chapter, we now know that the judge has richly merited the rhetorical assault he received in chapter 18, which has acted as the narrator's condign moral punishment and serves as a counterpart to the earlier exposure of the colonel's damnable sins. Part of our enjoyment of reading *The House of the Seven Gables* henceforth should be an appreciation of the author's employment of relevant biblical texts and Christian homiletic traditions manifested in the novel's two memorable scenes of unholy dying.

NOTES

1. Nathaniel Hawthorne, *The Letters, 1843–1853*, ed. Thomas Woodson, L. Neal Smith, and Norman Holmes Pearson (Columbus: Ohio State University Press, 1985), 421; David S. Reynolds, *Beneath the American Renaissance: The Subversive Imagination in the Age of Emerson and Melville* (New York: Knopf, 1988), 86–88, 126, 269–70; David S. Reynolds, *Faith in Fiction: The Emergence of Religious Literature in America* (Cambridge, Mass.: Harvard University Press, 1981). For overviews of the literary, historical, and biographical backgrounds of *The House of the Seven Gables*, see Peter Buitenhuis, *"The House of the Seven Gables": Severing Family and Colonial Ties* (Boston: Hall, 1991); Bernard Rosenthal, ed., *Critical Essays on "The House of the Seven Gables"* (Boston: Hall, 1995); and Jonathan A. Cook, "'The Most Satisfactory Villain That Ever Was': Charles W. Upham and *The House of the Seven Gables*," *New England Quarterly* 88 (June 2015): 252–85.

2. See David E. Stannard, ed., *Death in America* (Philadelphia: University of Pennsylvania Press, 1974); James J. Farrell, *Inventing the American Way of Death, 1830–1920* (Philadelphia: Temple University Press, 1980); and Gary Laderman, *The Sacred Remains: American Attitudes toward Death, 1799–1883* (New Haven: Yale University Press, 1996).

3. See Kathryn Gin Lum, *Damned Nation: Hell in America from the Revolution to Reconstruction* (New York: Oxford University Press, 2014), especially chap. 2; and Charles E. Hambrick-Stowe, *Charles G. Finney and the Spirit of American Evangelicalism* (Grand Rapids, Mich.: Eerdmans, 1996), especially chap. 5. On the "new measures" and "anxious seat," see Hambrick-Stowe, *Finney*, 38–39, 108–9. On the "Four Last Things," see Michael Wheeler, *Death and the Future Life in Victorian Literature and Theology* (New York: Cambridge University Press, 1990).

4. See David Paul Nord, *Faith in Reading: Religious Publishing and the Birth of Mass Media in America* (New York: Oxford University Press, 2004); Candy Gunther Brown, *The Word in the World: Evangelical Writing, Publishing, and Reading in America, 1789–1880* (Chapel Hill: University of North Carolina Press, 2004).

5. Nathaniel Hawthorne, *"The House of the Seven Gables,"* ed. Robert S. Levine (New York: Norton, 2006), 7, 8, 9.

6. Ibid., 13.

7. Ibid.

8. 1 Kings 17–22. Here and throughout, all biblical quotations refer to the King James Version. On *The House of the Seven Gables* and King Ahab, see Robert Clark, *History, Ideology, and Myth in American Fiction, 1823–1852* (London: Macmillan, 1984), 124–31; and Buitenhuis, "The House of the Seven Gables," 61.

9. Hawthorne, *The House of the Seven Gables*, 18.

10. On the Salem murder, see Robert Booth, *Death of an Empire: The Rise and Murderous Fall of Salem, America's Richest City* (New York: St. Martin's, 2011), chaps. 12–17. Also see John Cyril Barton, *Literary Executions: Capital Punishment and American Culture, 1820–1925* (Baltimore: Johns Hopkins University Press, 2014), chap. 4. Barton has analyzed Hawthorne's novel in relation to contemporary debates over the nature of evidence for the conviction of capital crimes, as illustrated by the Salem murder as well as the equally notorious 1850 Webster murder case in Boston. For more on Hawthorne's fictional use of the Salem murder, see Reynolds, *Beneath the American Renaissance*, 250–52; and Cook, "Most Satisfactory Villain," 279–80.

11. Romans 16:1–2.

12. Hawthorne, *The House of the Seven Gables*, 67, 130. On the role of the daguerreotype in the novel, see Alan Trachtenberg, "Seeing and Believing: Hawthorne's Reflections on the Daguerreotype in *The House of the Seven Gables*," *American Literary History* 9 (October 1997): 460–81; Michael C. Frank, "Photographing Ghosts: Ancestral Reproduction and Daguerreotypic Mimesis in Nathaniel Hawthorne's *The House of the Seven Gables*," *Literaria Pragensia* 17 (January 2007): 34–57; Stuart Burrows, *A Familiar Strangeness: American Fiction and the Language of Photography, 1839–1945* (Athens: University of Georgia Press, 2010), chap. 1; and Marcy J. Dinius, *The*

Camera and the Press: American Visual and Print Culture in the Age of the Daguerreotype (Philadelphia: University of Pennsylvania Press), chap. 2.

13. Hawthorne, *The House of the Seven Gables*, 85.
14. Ibid., 168.
15. See, for example, Peter J. Bellis, *Writing Revolution: Aesthetics and Politics in Hawthorne, Whitman, and Thoreau* (Athens: University of Georgia Press, 2003), 39–41; Roberta Weldon, *Hawthorne, Gender, and Death: Christianity and Its Discontents* (New York: Palgrave Macmillan, 2008), 74–78; Meredith McGill, *American Literature and the Culture of Reprinting, 1834–1853* (Philadelphia: University of Pennsylvania Press, 2007), 267–69; Barton, *Literary Executions*, 170–72; and Dinius, *Camera and Press*, 51–61.
16. Hawthorne, *The House of the Seven Gables*, 198, 200.
17. 1 Kings 18:27. Following Elijah's invocation to the Hebrew god, a divine fire consumes the sacrifice, and the prophets of Baal are all slain for their immoral imposture.
18. Psalms 39:5–16, 49:6–20, 90; Ecclesiastes 1, 2, 12; Ephesians 2:1–6; 1 John 2:15–16. For background, see Patrick Cullen, *Infernal Triad: The Flesh, the World, and the Devil in Spenser and Milton* (Princeton: Princeton University Press, 1974).
19. Hawthorne, *The House of the Seven Gables*, 190, 192, 194, 195.
20. John 17; Romans 12:2; 1 Corinthians 2:6–8; 1 Timothy 6:17–19; 1 John 2:15, 5:19.
21. Hawthorne, *The House of the Seven Gables*, 190.
22. Matthew 6:21.
23. Romans 8:5–13; Galatians 5:24–25; 1 Peter 1:24.
24. Hawthorne, *The House of the Seven Gables*, 194, 192–93.
25. Matthew 4:1–11; 2 Corinthians 2:11; Ephesians 6:12–17; James 4:7; 1 Peter 5:8–9; Hawthorne, *The House of the Seven Gables*, 199.
26. Hawthorne, *The House of the Seven Gables*, 198, 194.
27. Ibid., 198; William Shakespeare, *Macbeth*, in *The Riverside Shakespeare* (Boston: Houghton Mifflin, 1974), 4.1.119–20.
28. Hawthorne, *The House of the Seven Gables*, 194, 195.
29. Ibid., 199.
30. Romans 13:10–12.
31. Hawthorne, *The House of the Seven Gables*, 199.
32. Genesis 3:1.
33. 1 Thessalonians 4:6.
34. Ephesians 2:1–6.
35. Hawthorne, *The House of the Seven Gables*, 205.
36. For older but still relevant defenses of the artistic integrity of the novel and its conclusion, see Francis Joseph Battaglia, "*The House of the Seven Gables*: New Light on Old Problems," *PMLA* 82 (December 1967): 579–90; and Edwin G. Eigner, *The Metaphysical Novel in England and America: Dickens, Bulwer, Hawthorne, Melville* (Berkeley: University of California Press, 1978), 99–109.
37. Hawthorne, *The House of the Seven Gables*, 218.

AFTERWORD

GOD ABOVE, AMERICA BENEATH

Abraham Lincoln and Religion

David S. Reynolds

THE REMARKABLE variety of religious expression in pre–Civil War America revealed in this volume is a testament to what may be called the salient feature of American Protestantism: radical creativity fostered by religious freedom. The so-called *nova effect,* caused originally by the Protestant Reformation and seen worldwide in the explosion of religious and secular viewpoints, had some of its most diverse emanations in nineteenth-century America. Ralph Waldo Emerson caught the free religious spirit of the nation when he wrote, "The Protestant has his pew, which of course is only the first step to a church for every individual citizen—a church apiece."[1] He was pointing, albeit hyperbolically, to a very real phenomenon: America in the immediate aftermath of disestablishment witnessed numerous new denominations, sects, self-proclaimed prophets, religious communities, and spiritually tinged health fads, along with an avalanche of religious tracts, fiction, and poetry.[2] Alexis de Tocqueville noted in 1835, "In the United States there are an infinite variety of ceaselessly changing Christian sects."[3] Religion, in short, hit the fan. It grew increasingly more diverse and more culturally influential.

The multifarious religious attitudes and genres unleashed by the young democracy contributed to the polyvocality of both major and noncanonical American literature. This volume, as Harold K. Bush points out in the introduction, challenges the secularization thesis, which holds that religion faded as modernity approached. It also participates in the much-discussed religious turn in American studies by exploring *lived religion* of an especially rich variety. William James famously explored religion as it is experienced and acted out individually, with little emphasis on doctrines, philosophical concepts, or church history.[4] In examining how religion is manifested in American authors' lives and in the images, characters, and themes of their works, the contributors to this volume take an approach akin to James's experiential one. They treat religion as dialogic, affective, and phenomenological rather than as theological or abstract. Religion emerges in the interplay of personal emotion and metaphysical reflection, in the intersection of different cultural discourses, in the cross-fertilization of elite and popular cultures. This experiential imagining of antebellum religion is shown to have appeared variously in transcendentalism (chapters 1 and 2), in Nathaniel Hawthorne (chapters 3 and 15), in Herman Melville (chapters 5 and 7), in women's fiction (chapters 3, 6, 10, and 14), in the biblical novel (chapter 9), and in poetry (chapters 4, 8, 11, and 13).

The essays in these chapters are revelatory examples of what I term *reconstructive criticism,* which considers cross-influences and dynamics among major and popular authors, and its close relative *cultural biography,* which, as I've demonstrated in my books about Walt Whitman and John Brown, shows how cultural and social surroundings infiltrate the mind and shape behavior, motivation, and expression.[5] Every human life is culture- and time-specific. Outside influences saturate innermost thoughts. Neuroscience has found that, although all humans have virtually the same genome, gene *expression*—that is, the neurological activity of certain genes—can vary greatly from person to person, according to one's immediate cultural environment.[6] The cultural biographer's task is to describe that environment as fully as possible with the aim of revealing cross-influences between the individual and the outside world.

My current project, a cultural biography of Abraham Lincoln, has led me to rethink, among other matters, the relation between religion and America's greatest president. It is not generally known that Lincoln, a product of the same cultural forces that shaped the American Renaissance authors, was unusually inventive in religious expression in childhood and became uniquely so, among American political figures, in his later uses of religion. Lincoln's religious outlook was, to borrow Whitman's phrase, "the greatest of faiths and the least of faiths"— the greatest in his recognition of the importance of religion and the least in his adherence to particular creeds or denominations.[7] Lincoln once explained that he had never become a church member because he could not accept "the long, complicated statements of Christian doctrine which characterize . . . Articles of Belief and Confessions of Faith." He said that he would join a church that asked him simply to embrace Jesus' "condensed statement of the substance of both Law and Gospel, 'Thou shalt love the Lord thy God with all thy heart, and with all thy soul, and with all thy mind, and thy neighbor as myself.'"[8]

For Lincoln, it was essential for people to have a sense that God is above. But it was also essential that they did not act with the assurance that they knew God's intentions. He saw that America had produced a multitude of interpretations of God, many of them at loggerheads with each other. God, for Lincoln, must always be regarded as beyond human ken. Anything less would create narrowness, one-upmanship, and, at worst, war. When we look at his religious development in its cultural contexts, we see that his expansiveness came from his imaginative response to the religious and philosophical developments around him. His parents' Baptist faith was, among all American religions, the most varied in its manifestations.[9] No other religious body yielded so many different branches as the Baptists did. There were Primitive Baptists; Free-Will Baptists; Hard- and Soft-Shell Baptists; Particular Baptists; General Baptists; Six-Principle Baptists; Anti-Mission Baptists; Two-Seed-in-the-Spirit Baptists; German Seventh-Day Baptists; Close-Communion, General, Sabbatarian, and Foot-washing Baptists—all with different emphases in doctrine: so many, in fact, that a nineteenth-century historian of the religion remarked, "The term 'Baptist' has ceased to become a distinguishing name if used without a prefix."[10]

One Baptist offshoot was the Little Mount Church, the small church in Hardin County, Kentucky, whose members included Thomas and Nancy Hanks Lincoln, the future president's parents. This was a very special offshoot. The fifteen people who in 1809, the year of Lincoln's birth, broke from the Regular Baptist Church to form the Little Mount Church believed that the Bible stood opposed to slavery—a highly unusual view for that day, especially in Hardin County, where, in an adult population of some 2,600, nearly half were slaves. The Little Mount Church's minister, William Downs, whom Louis Warren calls "the first preacher whom Abraham Lincoln heard, and the preacher he heard most often in his childhood," was an ardent emancipationist, as was the church's other minister, David Elkin.[11] Lincoln would later declare that he could not remember a time when he did not loathe slavery. Today, such religious opposition to slavery may seem natural, but in the early nineteenth century it was not. Southern ministers were confident that the Bible supported slavery, and even in the North outspokenly abolitionist clergymen were sparse. It was extremely uncommon—a chance mutation—for a Kentucky church in a slaveholding area to organize on an antislavery basis. Lincoln's ethically based hatred of the South's peculiar institution, then, was nurtured by a rare, fortunate development in the metastasizing Baptist church.

If Lincoln's Baptist background opened the way to his antislavery convictions, it also cultivated creativity in religious matters. The splintering of the Baptists immersed him in an environment that was constantly engendering fresh faiths. A relative heard him say "that if he could take the best parts from all the churches, he could make a new church better than any of them."[12] During his youth, Lincoln was so taken by the colorful sermons he heard that he became an expert at imitating them. The Baptists and Methodists were the most influential denominations in popularizing what I've identified as the new religious style: a homiletics based not on the bygone Puritan tripartite division of text, exposition, and proof (or application) but on free-flowing, usually improvised sermons filled with lively images, anecdotes, vernacular speech, and sometimes humor.[13]

A historian of Kentucky religion explains that the Baptist preachers, unlearned but powerful, "mingled constantly with the masses of the people," "understood the force of their local dialect," and delivered "literally extemporaneous" sermons in which "they drew their illustrations from the daily habits of their hearers."[14] The Baptists' vivid sermons strongly affected Lincoln. John Locke Scripps, his earliest authorized biographer, wrote in 1860 that Lincoln had been shaped by "the early backwoods preachers" more than by schools or books. "Many of these early pioneer preachers," Scripps wrote, were "freed from conventional restraint" and "were gifted with a rare eloquence" that "wrought upon the imagination of their hearers."[15] Lincoln later told a friend, "I don't like to hear cut-and-dried sermons. No—when I hear a man preach, I like to see him act as if he were fighting bees!"[16]

The young Lincoln was so attracted to the new religious style that he imitated it whenever he could. Endowed with a wonderful memory, he would attend a service, go home, and regale others by repeating the sermon. Dennis Hanks recalled that Lincoln would stand "on a stump or log, . . . mimacing the Style & tone of the old Baptist preachers."[17] He said Lincoln would "repeat the sermin clean through from text to doxology. . . . I heerd him do it many a time."[18] Lincoln's stepsister, Matilda Johnson, reported that not only would he "repeat almost word for word the sermon he had heard the Sunday before," but, if he didn't attend church, "Abe would take down the bible, read a verse—give out a hymn—and we would sing—we were good singers . . .—he would preach & we would do the Crying—sometimes he would join the Chorus of Tears."[19]

Lincoln's sermonizing signified his strong penchant for performance. The religion of his youth and young manhood was, above everything, performative. So was virtually everything else he participated in. Many neighbors recalled his attending political speeches or trials and returning home, mounting a stump, and repeating what he had heard. The same applied to stories, jokes, or songs he learned: he loved to perform them in front of an audience. To call such behavior impersonation is not strong enough. Rather, it was a Whitmanesque, omnivorous absorption and recycling of cultural materials. Sermons, speeches, courtroom arguments, hymns, popular jokes, stories, and poems: Lincoln appreciated all of them for their performative value.

Lincoln's proclivity toward mimicry extended even to the Bible. Two of his earliest known writings, the poems "Adam and Eve's Wedding Song" (1825) and "The Chronicles of Reuben" (1829), are secular variations of Old Testament chapters that may be identified as harbingers of the cultural trend toward fictionalizing the Bible, a trend that eventually produced religious bestsellers such as *The Prince of the*

House of David, Ben-Hur, and *The Robe.* But whereas these inspirational novels were intended to buttress Christianity, Lincoln's biblical poems were jeux d'esprit that pointed Bible stories toward the sensual and the bawdy.

"Adam and Eve's Wedding Song," which the sixteen-year-old Lincoln adapted from a folk song when his sister, Sarah, married, Gentryville, Indiana, neighbor, Aaron Grigsby, emphasizes the somatic, not the sacred. The poem begins:

> When Adam was created
> He dwelt in Eden's shade,
> As Moses has recorded,
> And soon a bride was made.[20]

Lincoln goes on to say that God created woman out of Adam's underarm rib rather than out of another body part for good reason: the rib suggested the husband's duty to protect the wife, while the feet, for instance, would have symbolized his abuse of her, and the head would have led to her domination over him.

Besides directing the Eden story toward an earthy commentary on his sister's marriage, the wedding poem may have reflected Lincoln's doubts about the marriage (was Aaron Grigsby a wife abuser?). His feelings toward his brother-in-law became overtly hostile after Sarah died in childbirth in 1828. Lincoln reportedly accused Grigsby of tardiness in seeking medical help for Sarah while she was in labor. A feud arose between the Lincolns and the Grigsbys that led to Lincoln's next biblical narrative, "The Chronicles of Reuben," an acidic prose-poem that transformed an Old Testament story into an attack on the Grigsbys. The poem became so popular locally that it could be recited decades later by residents in the Gentryville area. Lincoln wrote it after he learned that he had not been invited to a party celebrating the dual marriages of the Grigsby brothers Reuben, Jr., and Charles. Written in a style that aped the cadences and imagery of the Bible, the poem describes a sexual mishap that occurs after the party, when the two grooms are led in the dark to the wrong rooms; each finds himself in bed with the other's wife. Based on the Old Testament story of the prophet Reuben, repudiated by his family for having slept with his father's concubine, Lincoln's coarse poem titillated some and outraged others, including a woman who called the poem "Smutty" and a twentieth-century Christian biographer of Lincoln who dismissed it as "a rude backwoods joke, written . . . in full accord with the standards of humor current in the time and general environment."[21]

Today what seems unorthodox about the poem is not its lewdness but its secularity. The poem shows that, by the age of twenty, Lincoln was thoroughly at ease in adapting the Bible for personal use—in this case, to pillory an unfriendly neighbor.

Behind Lincoln's youthful gamboling with sermons and the Bible lay a suspicion of organized religion, which also came through in his jokes and stories. He loved telling one about a Millerite couple who agree to share their secrets with each other in advance of ascending to heaven. The wife confesses that their son was sired by a one-eyed shoemaker in town. The husband, though outraged, says that at least their other children are his. The wife replies, "No, they belong to the neighborhood." The husband shouts, "I am ready to leave. *Gabriel, blow your horn!*"[22] Another Lincoln story involved a Baptist preacher who announces to his congregation, "I am the Christ whom I shall represent today." As he gives his sermon, a lizard runs up his pants, across his back, and onto his neck. The preacher flails wildly and disrobes, impelling a woman to stand up in her pew and cry, "Well, if you represent Christ, I am done believing in the Bible."[23] As president, Lincoln responded to a group of clergymen requesting better army chaplains by telling a story about a black boy he once met who was using street mud to build a miniature church, with steeple, pews, pulpit, and so on. When Lincoln asked the boy where the preacher was, the boy grinned and said, "Laws, I hain't got *mud* enough!"[24]

Lincoln's humorous and performative treatments of religion cloaked a struggle with doubt. In 1835, at the age of twenty-six, while living in New Salem, Illinois, he wrote what was known as a "little infidel book"—a slashing attack on the supernatural underpinnings of Christianity.[25] A friend who read the pamphlet tossed it into the fire, fearful that it might damage Lincoln's budding political reputation. The pamphlet bore evidence of his recent reading of freethinking texts such as Thomas Paine's *The Age of Reason* and Comte de Volney's *Ruins* along with antireligious poetry by the likes of Robert Burns and Lord Byron.

Those who knew Lincoln well reported that he kept his private views hidden. His secretary, John G. Nicolay, remarked of his religious opinions, "I do not know just what they were, never having heard him explain them in detail." David Davis, a longtime friend and advisor, used similar words: "I don't Know anything about Lincoln's Religion—don't think anybody Knew. The idea that Lincoln talked to a stranger about his religion or religious views—or made such speeches, remarks &c about it as published is absurd to me. . . . He was the most reticent—Secretive man I Ever Saw—or Expect to See."[26]

Lincoln's privacy in religious matters was doubtless linked to his veneration of America's founders—Thomas Jefferson, James Madison, George Washington, and others, who accepted the doctrine, inherited from Samuel von Pufendorf, that religion was a private matter between the individual and God. As Jefferson memorably put it in *Notes on the State of Virginia*, "it does me no injury for my neighbour to say there are twenty gods, or no god. It neither picks my pocket nor breaks my leg."[27]

This comment, while it had the positive effect of contributing to the separation of church and state, was disingenuous. Religion, of course, is not purely a private matter. It *can* pick one's pocket or break one's leg—or, to update the metaphor, fly jets into skyscrapers, cut off heads, or instigate ethnic cleansing. Its public dimension is also seen among evangelical voting blocs. Lincoln clearly understood the public uses of religion. Although he respected Jefferson, he departed from him in this case. Whatever Lincoln's private beliefs, he recognized the vital importance of religion for the nation. Jefferson, to safeguard the separation of church and state, issued no presidential proclamations regarding prayer, fasting, or thanksgiving. Lincoln, in the interest of saving the Union, not only issued nine such proclamations but also created the first national Thanksgiving, put "In God We Trust" on America's coins, and even entertained the idea of amending the Constitution so that it included a reference to God.

How did his bold public religious posture jibe with the furtiveness of his private religious expression? The answer seems to be that, in a very real sense, the private and the public Lincoln merged as time passed. On the religious level, Lincoln as president reached out to Catholics, Jews, and all kinds of Protestants. Whitman identified "UNIONISM, in its truest and amplest sense" as "the hard-pan of his character."[28] Lincoln himself wrote on the last day of his life that his goal was to create "a Union of hearts and hands as well as of States."[29] He saw that cultural union must undergird political union. And there was no more powerful impetus for cultural union than religion. America was increasingly a God-fearing, churchgoing, Bible-reading nation. This was the nation with which Lincoln came to identify, the one he tried to hold together with his repeated appeals to religion.

If we follow his career, we can trace his progress from a secular "political religion," as he called it, to a nondenominational civil religion that coupled biblical spirituality with natural law. In an 1836 address, he denounced the widespread "mobocratic spirit" and declared, "Let reverence for the laws . . . become the *political religion* of the nation."[30] But the laws, he found, could be appallingly unjust, as became clear with the succession of proslavery enactments of the 1850s, especially the Fugitive Slave Act, the Kansas Nebraska Act, and the Dred Scott decision. In an America controlled by proslavery politicians, human law proved to be egregiously flawed. Yet his respect for the founders would not allow him to follow the antislavery senator William Henry Seward, who declared in response to the Fugitive Slave Act that there was "a higher law" that Americans must obey, "the law of humanity, justice, equity, the law of nature and of nations."[31] Lincoln realized that to endorse openly the higher law doctrine was to head down a slippery slope—one that led, for example, to William Lloyd Garrison's 1854 public burning of the Constitution (which Garrison considered a proslavery document) and to John Brown's writing in 1858 of the Provisional Constitution and Ordinances for the People of the United States, a proposed antislavery substitute for the Constitution.[32]

Instead of taking such radical steps, Lincoln emphasized the founders' antislavery intentions and appealed to two ur texts cherished by Americans: the Declaration of Independence and the Bible. Without using the controversial phrase "the higher law," he invoked the Declaration's affirmation of human equality as his touchstone for opposing slavery, evidenced in many of his antislavery utterances, from the 1854 Peoria speech through the debates with Stephen Douglas to the Gettysburg Address.

But natural law, no matter how patriotically framed, did not have the weight or resonance of divine law. Therefore, Lincoln buttressed his stance on slavery with appeals to the Bible and the Judeo-Christian God. He quoted from both the Old and New Testaments frequently, as the occasion demanded. Jesus' declaration that "A house divided against itself cannot stand" provided him with his most memorable line about the disruptive effect of slavery.[33] All of his closest friends and advisors, with the exception of William Herndon, warned him against using the image, which, they said, was inflammatory and divisive.[34] But he understood better than they the powerful hold that the Bible held over the American people. The law of the Bible, he realized, was considered far higher than natural law; few Americans would dare to contravene it. The image provided him with an excellent weapon against Douglas. After the Little Giant objected when Lincoln said that a house divided cannot stand, Lincoln retorted, "Does the Judge [Douglas] say it *can* stand? [Laughter.] . . . If he does, then there is a question of veracity, not between him and me, but between the Judge and an authority of a somewhat higher character. [Laughter and applause.]"[35]

The Bible remained for Lincoln a powerful source of persuasion throughout the Civil War, right up to the Second Inaugural Address. A major point in the Second Inaugural—that both sides in the war read the same Bible and pray to the same God—reflects the unusual breadth of his religious vision. From the start of the war, Lincoln saw that religion could be twisted to defend any point of view, even the most ardently proslavery one. Confederates portrayed themselves as true Christians and their enemies as atheists or blasphemers; vice versa in the North. Few, in the North or South, were sufficiently detached from sectional loyalty to recognize the irony in the fact that American Christians, as they sent similar prayers heavenward, were at each other's throats. Lincoln, however, who had always been removed from narrow religious viewpoints, saw the irony clearly. He maintained that humans can worship, pray, and follow their conscience, but they must never assume complacently that they are following God's will, which remains ineffable.

This conviction comes through in Lincoln's most private revelation of faith, the so-called Meditation on the Divine Will, scribbled on a paper fragment. Written in early September 1862—a low point in the war, when the president, as his attorney general remarked, "seemed wrung by the bitterest anguish"—the Meditation begins, "The will of God prevails." Both the North and the South, it notes, claim the favor of God, who cannot be *"for and against* the same thing at the same time." But which side God favors cannot be fathomed. Lincoln wrote, "In the present civil war it is quite possible that God's purpose is something different from the purpose of either party." God could have prevented the war in the first place, he reflected, and he could stop the war at any time. The Meditation concludes with a laconic line: "Yet the contest proceeds."[36] As the most confidential surviving confession written in Lincoln's hand, the piece pays homage to God's omnipotence while discounting philistine, partial interpretations of God.

Lincoln's religion merged with his patriotism on the basis of national unity. For this reason, he took seriously a proposed Christian amendment to the Constitution. One of Jefferson Davis's first acts as Confederate president was to oversee the passage of a Constitution for the Confederacy whose opening paragraph mentioned God—a slap in the face for the North, which still maintained the godless Constitution of the founders. Lincoln felt pressure to summon God to the side of the United States as a nation. Calls for a religious amendment to the Constitution built in the North until 1863, when representatives of the National Reform Association, a group representing eleven Protestant denominations in the North, met with the president and urged him to push for an amendment that would add God and Jesus Christ to the preamble. Lincoln told the ministers, "The general aspect of your movement I cordially approve," though he added that "the work of amending the Constitution should not be done hastily."[37] If he sensed that Congress would object to this violation of the disestablishment clause, he was right. The amendment won approval from only a handful of legislators—including senators Charles Sumner, John Sherman, and B. Gratz Brown—and Lincoln dropped the idea. But the National Reform Association's mission was not lost, for in 1864 one of its members, James Pollock, the director of the U.S. Mint under Lincoln, persuaded Congress to put "In God We Trust" on an American coin—a motto that appeared on some currency until 1908–9 and since then has been a fixture on several coins.

Lincoln's public use of religion was visible in the rhetoric of his major speeches and his proclamations of prayer, fasting, or thanksgiving, which nationalized religion by putting the whole nation, North and South, under God. It was this nationalizing instinct that led him to add spontaneously the phrase "under God" after "this nation" as he delivered the Gettysburg Address and that impelled him to aver that both sides "pray to the same God" in the Second Inaugural.[38] Whereas Davis's religious proclamations asked God for Confederate victories and southern independence, Lincoln's religious proclamations were prayers for *all* Americans to come together in God's name. In various proclamations, he asked that "the united prayer of the nation [to] ascend to the Throne of Grace" to restore "law, order and peace, throughout the wide extent of our country" (August 12, 1861); that God spread "peace, harmony, and unity throughout our borders, and . . . the establishment of fraternal relations among all the countries of the earth (April 10, 1862); that God bring about "the restoration of our now divided and suffering Country, to its former happy condition of unity and peace" (March 30, 1863).[39] The religious spirit, which antebellum authors such as Emerson and Whitman saw as a common denominator among humans, was viewed similarly by Lincoln, who saw that cultural unity might best be achieved through religion.

It was for this reason that he instituted the first national Thanksgiving in 1863. Before then, thanksgiving celebrations were state affairs, held mainly in New England.[40] From the late 1830s onward, the author and editor Sara Josepha Hale led the effort to nationalize the holiday, but to some people nationalization seemed to be an undemocratic link between church and state. In September 1863, Hale wrote to Lincoln, requesting a proclamation that would make "the *day of our annual Thanksgiving . . . a National and fixed Union Festival.*"[41] As he proclaimed the last Thursday in November as "a day of Thanksgiving and Praise to our beneficent Father who dwelleth in the Heavens," Lincoln wrote that it is "fit and proper" that God's blessings should be "solemnly, reverently and gratefully acknowledged as with one heart and one voice by the whole American People . . . in every part of the United States."[42] This call for spiritual togetherness was fervent in its emphasis on national unity. Lincoln made a similar proclamation the next year, and the tradition was carried on under Andrew Johnson and later presidents, leading to the bill that Franklin D. Roosevelt signed in 1941 making the nationalization of Thanksgiving official.

All of Lincoln's religious influences came together in the Second Inaugural Address, which contains four biblical citations, three invocations of prayer, and fourteen mentions of God, all in the space of 701 words. The Second Inaugural reflected the pan-denomenationalism he had absorbed over his lifetime. Soaring above creeds and churches, the speech is unattached to a single religious viewpoint, which helps explain why it has had such broad appeal over the years, much like Whitman's religion-inflected *Leaves of Grass*, which is appreciated by people of all faiths and of no faith.

The address draws from the Bible to perform unifying cultural work. Lincoln challenged slaveholders by citing Genesis, "It may seem strange that any men should dare to ask a just God's assistance in wringing their bread from the sweat of other men's faces" but softened the critique by adding, after a semicolon, Jesus' command "but let us judge not that we be not judged."[43] He seemed to blast slavery again when he quotes another of Jesus' assertions: "Woe unto the world because of offences! for it must needs be that offences come; but woe to that man by whom the offence cometh!"[44] But instead of following the lead of ministers on both sides of slavery, who hurled barbs at each other, Lincoln tempered passion in his next sentence, which begins conditionally—"If we shall suppose that American Slavery is one of those offences which, in the providence of God, must needs come, but which, having continued through His appointed time, He now wills to remove"—and then identifies as "woe" this "terrible war" that God "gives to both North and South," leading to the question, "shall we discern therein any departure from those divine attributes which the believers in a Living God always ascribe to Him?" Lincoln here emphasized God's overwhelming power, above and beyond human understanding. We humans can only "suppose" that slavery is "one of those offences which, in the providence of God, must needs come" in "His appointed time." It was God who gave the war to the nation—"to both North and South"—and God alone could end the conflict.[45]

Lincoln concluded the address by balancing fate and free will as he laid out a plan of action that was both helpfully specific and inspiringly general: "With malice toward none; with charity for all; with firmness in the right, as God gives us to see the right, let us strive on to finish the work we are in; to bind up the nation's wounds; to care for him who shall have borne the battle, and for his widow, and his orphan—to do all which may achieve and cherish a just, and a lasting peace, among ourselves, and with all nations."[46] In other words, God is still in control here ("as God gives us to see the right") but humans have practical work ahead of them: they must shed malice, exercise charity, and work to bind the nation's wounds by assisting those who are the most helpless. The final phrase, which envisages peace and justice "among . . . all nations," universalizes the message of the speech and resoundingly proclaims unity.

It can be argued that the Second Inaugural imaginatively resolves some longstanding metaphysical issues of the American Renaissance. Since the New Criticism and poststructuralism, we associate Hawthorne, Melville, Poe, and Dickinson with ambiguity (or indeterminacy) and with a turn to art in the face of irresolvable metaphysical questions. We also suggest that Emerson, Thoreau, Whitman, and sometimes Dickinson turned ambiguity into mystery and a reveling in everyday miracles, a merging with the natural and spiritual environment. But, as Melville noted, merging with *"the all"* has a problem: How does "a fellow with a raging toothache" do it?[47]

America had a raging toothache: slavery. Lincoln felt the ache painfully and, alone among all American Renaissance figures, he did everything possible within the political system to cure it, including taking the risk of combining church and state with his religious proclamations, putting God on currency, and considering a religious amendment. He did so with full devotion to abolishing slavery but without animus against the South and without pretending to have a corner on God. His message in the Second Inaugural, as in the Meditation, was *ambiguity is all right*. In fact, he believed it was crucial for sustaining peace because conflict with others comes when we claim to have special knowledge of God's purposes. But we must pursue what our highest instincts call justice—not only for our group, our party, our race, but for all humans.

Tragically, the progress toward cultural unity that Lincoln sought to nurture came only through his assassination six weeks after the Second Inaugural Address. Whitman predicted that his murder would help unify a nation whose divisions had created unimaginable bloodshed and suffering. The death of America's "great Martyr Chief," Whitman wrote, provided "a cement to the whole people, subtler, more underlying, than anything in written constitution, or courts or armies"; it was the one thing needed only to "really, lastingly condense—a Nationality."[48] Time has proven Whitman right. Lincoln has remained one of the few constants amid shifting political winds and economic conditions—the most beloved of Americans among both northerners and southerners, both liberals and conservatives.

But Lincoln is not just a unifying national icon. He is a lasting example of the most desirable form of the higher law: that is, the principled pursuit of justice through a popularly elected government. He knew that even the most apparently virtuous aims, bolstered by religion, can be dangerous if they are not channeled through a democratically chosen government. Although we know that the electoral process doesn't always yield good results, we can accept his declaration that democracy remains "the last best hope of earth."[49]

Whitman noted that Lincoln's "invisible foundations" were "mystical, abstract, moral, spiritual, and his "religious nature" was "of the amplest, deepest-rooted, loftiest kind."[50] Through his visionary words, his principled actions, and his unmatched compassion, Abraham Lincoln can be said to have created a truly *American* religion—democratic in the broadest sense of the word.

NOTES

1. Ralph Waldo Emerson, *The Journals and Miscellaneous Notebooks of Ralph Waldo Emerson*, 16 vols. (Cambridge, Mass.: Harvard University Press, 1960–82), 10:178.

2. For a discussion of religious movements and health crazes, see David S. Reynolds, *Waking Giant: America in the Age of Jackson* (New York: HarperCollins, 2008), chaps. 4 and 5; and Alice Felt Tyler, *Freedom's Ferment: Phases of American Social History to 1860* (Minneapolis: University of Minnesota Press, 1944). On popular religious literature, see David S. Reynolds, *Faith in Fiction: The Emergence of Religious Literature in America* (Cambridge, Mass.: Harvard University Press, 1981).

3. Alexis de Tocqueville, *Democracy in America*, ed. J. P Mayer (Garden City, N.Y.: Doubleday, 1969), 432.

4. William James, *The Varieties of Religious Experience* (New York: Longmans, Green, 1902).

5. See David S. Reynolds, *Beneath the American Renaissance: The Subversive Imagination in the Age of Emerson and Melville* (New York: Knopf, 1988); David S. Reynolds, *Walt Whitman's America: A Cultural Biography* (New York: Knopf, 1995); and David S. Reynolds, *John Brown, Abolitionist: The Man Who Killed Slavery, Sparked the Civil War, and Seeded Civil Rights* (New York: Knopf, 2005).

6. See Joan Y. Chiao, Bobby K. Cheon, Narun Pornpattanangkul, Alyssa J. Mrazek, and Katherine D. Blizinsky, "Cultural Neuroscience: Progress and Promise," *Psychological Inquiry*, January 1, 2013, 1–19; Joan Y. Chiao, Bobby K. Cheon, Narun Pornpattananangkul, Alissa J. Mrazek, and Department of Psychology and Interdepartmental Neuroscience Program, Northwestern University, Evanston, Illinois Katherine D. Blizinsky (New York: Oxford University Press, 2014); and José Roberto Wajmas, Paulo Henrique, Ferreira Bertolucci, Letícia Lessa Mansur, and Serge Gauthier, "Culture as a Variable in Neuroscience and Clinical Neuropsychology: A Comprehensive Review," *Dementia and Neuropsychologia* 9 (September 2015): 203–18.

7. Walt Whitman, *Leaves of Grass* (Brooklyn, 1855), 48.

8. Francis B. Carpenter, *Six Months at the White House with Abraham Lincoln* (New York: Hurd and Houghton, 1866), 190.

9. Among the prominent studies of the diversification of American religion are Nathan O. Hatch, *The Democratization of American Christianity* (New Haven: Yale University Press, 1989); Jon Butler, *Awash in a Sea of Faith: Christianizing the American People* (Cambridge, Mass.: Harvard University Press, 1990); Christine Leigh Heyrman, *Southern Cross: The Beginnings of the Bible Belt* (New York: Knopf, 1997); and Mark A. Noll, *America's God: From Jonathan Edwards to Abraham Lincoln* (New York: Oxford University Press, 2002).

10. Louis A. Warren, *Lincoln's Parentage and Childhood* (New York: Century, 1926), 232.

11. Ibid., 244.

12. Dr. James LeGrande, paraphrasing remarks he heard from his mother, Sophie Hanks, undated interview with Arthur E. Morgan, Morgan Papers, Library of Congress.

13. Reynolds, *Beneath the American Renaissance*, chap. 1.

14. John H. Spencer, *A History of Kentucky Baptists, from 1769 to 1885*, 2 vols. (Cincinnati: Baumes, 1886), 1:493.

15. J. L. Scripps, *Life of Abraham Lincoln* (New York: [Horace Greeley, Tribune Tracts], 1860), 4.

16. Leonard W. Volk, "The Lincoln Life-Mask and How It Was Made," *Century* 23 (1881): 226.

17. Douglas L. Wilson, Rodney O. Davis, and Terry Wilson, eds., *Herndon's Informants: Letters, Interviews, and Statements about Abraham Lincoln* (Champaign: University of Illinois Press, 2007), 102.

18. Francis Fisher Browne, *The Every-day Life of Abraham Lincoln* (New York: Thompson, 1887), 54.

19. Wilson et al., *Herndon's Informants*, 109.

20. Ward Hill Lamon, *Recollections of Abraham Lincoln, 1847–1865* (Chicago: McClurg, 1895), 152.

21. Wilson et al., *Herndon's Informants*, 127; William Eleazer Barton, *The Soul of Abraham Lincoln* (New York: Doran, 1920), 81.

22. Wilson et al., *Herndon's Informants*, 172.

23. Paul M. Zall, ed., *Abe Lincoln's Legacy of Laughter: Humorous Stories by and about Abraham Lincoln* (Knoxville: University of Tennessee Press, 2007), 46.

24. Carpenter, *Six Months at the White House*, 277.

25. Douglas L. Wilson and Rodney O. Davis, eds., *Herndon on Lincoln: Letters* (Urbana: University of Illinois Press, 2016), 85.

26. Wilson et al., *Herndon's Informants*, 6, 348.

27. Thomas Jefferson, *Notes on the State of Virginia* (1782; reprint, New York: Harper and Row, 1964), 152.

28. Walt Whitman, *Prose Works, 1892*, ed. Floyd Stovall, 2 vols. (New York: New York University Press, 1963–64), 1:98

29. Abraham Lincoln, letter to James H. Van Alen, in Abraham Lincoln, *Collected Works*, ed. Roy B. Basler, Marion Dolores Pratt, and Lloyd A. Dunlap, 8 vols. (New Brunswick, N.J.: Rutgers University Press, 1953), 8:413.

30. Lincoln, *Collected Works*, 1:111–12.

31. William Henry Seward, "Freedom in the New Territories" (1850), in *The Senate, 1789–1989: Classic Speeches, 1830–1993*, ed. Robert C. Byrd (Washington, D.C.: Government Printing Office, 1994), 308.

32. Lincoln wrote in 1860, "I agree with Seward in his 'Irrepressible Conflict,' but I do not endorse his 'Higher Law' doctrine" (*Collected Works*, 4:50).

33. Ibid., 2:461.

34. David Herbert Donald, *Lincoln's Herndon* (New York: Knopf, 1948), 119.

35. Lincoln, *Collected Works*, 3:17.

36. Ibid., 5:404.

37. *Proceedings of the National Convention to Secure the Religious Amendment of the Constitution of the United States* (Philadelphia: Rodgers, 1872), viii.

38. The spontaneity of "under God" at Gettysburg can be gleaned from the fact that the phrase is absent from two drafts of the speech Lincoln wrote before November 19, 1863, but is included in three newspaper accounts written on the scene. See David S. Reynolds, ed., *Lincoln's Selected Writings* (New York: Norton, 2015), 329.

39. Lincoln, *Collected Works*, 4:482, 5:186, 6:156.

40. See Arlin M. Adams and Charles J. Emmerich, *A Nation Dedicated to Religious Liberty: The Constitutional Heritage of the Religion Clauses* (Philadelphia: University of Pennsylvania Press, 2015), 51.

41. Sarah J. Hale, letter to Abraham Lincoln, September 28, 1863, Abraham Lincoln Papers, Library of Congress.
42. Lincoln, *Collected Works*, 6:497.
43. Ibid., 8:333. The biblical references are to Genesis 3:19 and Matthew 7:1. Ibid.
44. The reference is to Matthew 18:7.
45. Ibid.
46. Ibid.
47. Herman Melville, letter to Nathaniel Hawthorne, June 1851, in Herman Melville, *Correspondence*, ed. Lynn Horth (Evanston, Ill.: Northwestern University Press, 1993), 193–94.
48. Whitman, *Prose Works, 1892*, 2:508.
49. Lincoln, *Collected Works*, 5:537.
50. Whitman, *Prose Works, 1892*, 2:602–3.

CONTRIBUTORS

JEFFREY BILBRO is associate professor of English at Spring Arbor University in southern Michigan. He has published over twenty peer-reviewed essays and two books: *Loving God's Wildness: The Christian Roots of Ecological Ethics in American Literature* (University of Alabama Press, 2015) and, co-authored with Jack Baker, *Wendell Berry and Higher Education: Cultivating Virtues of Place* (University Press of Kentucky, 2017).

HAROLD K. BUSH is professor of English at Saint Louis University and author of six books, including *Mark Twain and the Spiritual Crisis of His Age* (2007), *Lincoln in His Own Time* (2012), and most recently, *Continuing Bonds with the Dead: Parental Grief and Nineteenth-Century American Authors* (2016). He is lead editor of *The Letters of Mark Twain and Joseph H. Twichell* (2017) and his first novel, titled *The Hemingway Files*, was published in 2017.

DAWN COLEMAN is associate professor and director of graduate studies in English at the University of Tennessee. She is the author of *Preaching and the Rise of the American Novel* (The Ohio State University Press, 2013) and of numerous essays on nineteenth-century literature, religion, and secularity. She serves as the book review editor for *Leviathan: A Journal of Melville Studies* and is writing a book on narratives of religiously skeptical women in the nineteenth-century United States.

JONATHAN A. COOK is the author of *Inscrutable Malice: Theodicy, Eschatology, and the Biblical Sources of "Moby-Dick"* (Northern Illinois University Press, 2012) as well as many articles on Melville, Hawthorne, Poe, and others. His essay on Charles W. Upham and *The House of the Seven Gables* appeared in the June 2015 *New England Quarterly*. He is chair of the English Department at Middleburg Academy.

CONTRIBUTORS

TRACY FESSENDEN is Steve and Margaret Forster Professor in the School of Historical, Philosophical, and Religious Studies at Arizona State University. Her books include *Culture and Redemption: Religion, the Secular, and American Literature* (Princeton University Press, 2007) and *Religion around Billie Holiday* (Penn State University Press, 2018). She is at work on a book about photography.

ZACHARY MCLEOD HUTCHINS is assistant professor of English at Colorado State University and the author of *Inventing Eden: Primitivism, Millennialism, and the Making of New England* (Oxford University Press, 2014). Hutchins is also the editor of *Community Without Consent: New Perspectives on the Stamp Act* (Dartmouth College Press, 2016) and editor-in-chief of T.E.A.M.S., a scholarly collective digitizing early American sermons at earlyamericansermons.org.

RICHARD KOPLEY is Distinguished Professor of English, Emeritus, at Penn State DuBois. He is the author of *The Threads of The Scarlet Letter* (2003) and *Edgar Allan Poe and the Dupin Mysteries* (2008), an editor of *Resources for American Literary Study*, and an editor-in-chief of the American Literature module of Oxford Bibliographies Online. Recently Penn State University Press published his new edition of Ebenezer Wheelwright's 1842 novel *The Salem Belle*, a source for Nathaniel Hawthorne's novel *The Scarlet Letter*.

MASON I. LOWANCE, JR., is professor of English and American studies at the University of Massachusetts Amherst. He is a former NEH Fellow, Guggenheim Fellow, and is a life member of the American Antiquarian Society. His publications include *The Language of Canaan: Metaphor and Symbol in New England Writing from the Puritans to the Transcendentalists* (Harvard University Press); *The Typological Writings of Jonathan Edwards* (Yale University Press); and *A House Divided: The Slavery Debates in America, 1776–1865* (Princeton University Press).

JOHN MATTESON is Distinguished Professor of English at John Jay College of Criminal Justice in the City University of New York. He is the author of *The Lives of Margaret Fuller* and *Eden's Outcasts: The Story of Louisa May Alcott and Her Father*, which was awarded the 2008 Pulitzer Prize in Biography. His *Annotated Little Women* was published by W. W. Norton in 2015.

CHRISTOPHER N. PHILLIPS is associate professor of English at Lafayette College. He has written *Epic in American Culture, Settlement to Reconstruction* (Johns Hopkins University Press, 2012), *The Hymnal: A Reading History* (Johns Hopkins University Press, 2018), and edited *The Cambridge Companion to Literature of the American Renaissance* (2018). He is currently writing a study of the poetics of hymnody.

VIVIAN R. POLLAK is professor of English at Washington University in St. Louis, where she teaches courses in American literature and culture. Her most recent book is *Our Emily Dickinsons: American Women Poets and the Intimacies of Difference*. Her most recent article is "'Mrs. Morene of Mexico': A Todd-Johnson Misprint and Helen Hunt Jackson's *Ramona*," in the *Emily Dickinson Journal*. Her other books include *Dickinson: The Anxiety of Gender* and *The Erotic Whitman*. She serves on the board of *ESQ: A Journal of Nineteenth-Century American Literature and Culture*.

DAVID S. REYNOLDS is Distinguished Professor at the Graduate Center of the City University of New York. His books include *Beneath the American Renaissance*, *Walt Whitman's America*, *John Brown, Abolitionist*, *Waking Giant*, *Mightier than the Sword*, *George Lippard*, and *Faith in Fiction*. He is the editor or co-editor of seven books, including, most recently, *Lincoln's Selected Writings*. He is the winner of the Bancroft Prize, the Christian Gauss Award, the Ambassador Book Award, and was a finalist for the John Hope Franklin Publication Prize and the National Book Critics Circle Award.

MICHAEL ROBERTSON, professor of English at The College of New Jersey, is recipient of two National Endowment for the Humanities fellowships and author of three books, including *The Last Utopians* (Princeton University Press, 2018) and the award-winning *Worshipping Walt: The Whitman Disciples* (Princeton University Press, 2008). A member of the *Walt Whitman Quarterly Review* editorial board, he is co-editor of *Walt Whitman, Where the Future Becomes Present* (Iowa University Press, 2008).

GAIL K. SMITH taught American literature at Marquette University, Mississippi University for Women, and Birmingham-Southern College before moving to Vancouver, Bristish Columbia, where she is now an independent scholar. She has published on Harriet Beecher Stowe, Elizabeth Stuart Phelps, Louisa May Alcott, and others.

TIMOTHY SWEET is Eberly Family Distinguished Professor of American Literature at West Virginia University. His publications include *Traces of War: Poetry, Photography, and the Crisis of the Union* (Johns Hopkins University Press, 1990); *American Georgics: Economy and Environment in Early American Literature* (University of Pennsylvania Press, 2002); and the collection *Literary Cultures of the Civil War* (University of Georgia Press, 2016).

CLAUDIA STOKES is professor of English at Trinity University. She is the author of *Writers in Retrospect: The Rise of American Literary History, 1875–1910* (University of North Carolina Press, 2006) and *The Altar at Home: Sentimental Literature and Nineteenth-Century American Religion* (University of Pennsylvania Press, 2014). She is also co-editor, with Michael A. Elliott, of *American Literary Studies: A Methodological Reader* (New York University Press, 2002).

BRIAN YOTHERS is Frances Spatz Leighton Endowed Distinguished Professor of English at the University of Texas at El Paso. He is the author of *Reading Abolition* (2016), *Sacred Uncertainty* (2015), *Melville's Mirrors* (2011), and *The Romance of the Holy Land in American Travel Writing* (2007). He is co-editor with Jonathan Cook of *Visionary of the Word* (2017), editor of *Billy Budd: Critical Insights* (2017) and *The Scarlet Letter: Critical Insights* (2018), and associate editor of *Leviathan: A Journal of Melville Studies*.

INDEX

9/11 (September 11, 2001), 3, 25, 34

Adams, John S., 207
Adventists, 140, 143
Aeschylus, 238
Afghanistan, 25
Agamben, Giorgio, 88
Albanese, Catherine, 22, 28, 33–34
Alcott, Abba, 47
Alcott, Anna, 43
Alcott, Bronson, 37–38, 40–50, 189
Alcott, Louisa May, 38, 48, 53, 250
American Board of Commissioners of Foreign Missions (ABCFM), 247, 252–54, 256–57
Anderson, Benedict, 27
Aristotle, 59
Arnold, Matthew, 57
Atlantic Monthly, 238
Augustine, 213, 222

Bacon, Francis, 127
Baptists, 277, 278–79
Barbauld, Anna Letitia, 213
Barker, Joseph, 79
Barlow, Joel, 181, 184, 213
Baxter, Richard, 261
Bebbington, David W., 13
Beecher, Charles, 181
Beecher, Edward, 181

Beecher, Henry Ward, 109, 181, 199
Beecher, Lyman, 109, 181
Benjamin, Walter, 34–35
Benton, Thomas H., 72
Bercovitch, Sacvan, 5, 179
Bernhisel, John, 75
Bible, the Holy, 1, 8, 107–18, 140, 155, 157, 162, 179–80, 215, 284; King James Version of, 8
Bjerregaard, Carl H. A., 29–30
Blackmur, R. P., 236
Blake, Lillie Devereux, 53
Book of Mormon, 71, 141–57
Boston Journal, 167
Boston Traveller, 170
Bowles, M. E., 92
Branch, Lori, 6, 7
Breitwieser, Mitchell, 28
Brodhead, Richard, 141
Brontë, Charlotte, 59
Brown, B. Gratz, 285
Brown, John, 230, 283
Bryant, William Cullen, 196–97, 199–204, 208
Bucke, Richard Maurice, 144–45
Buddhism, 254
Bullard, Laura Curtis, 52
Bunyan, John, 261
Burns, Robert, 282
Bush, George W., 25

Bush, Harold K., 25, 116, 176, 178, 276
Bushman, Richard, 143–44, 150
Byron, George Gordon, Lord, 248, 282

Calvin, John, 128
Calvinism, 261
Candler, Peter, 132
Cary, Alice, 53
Caskey, Marie, 110
Catholicism, 21, 198, 207, 252
Cayton, Mary Kupiec, 247
Certeau, Michel de, 132
Ceylon (Sri Lanka), 245–57
Chambers, Robert, 96
Channing, Mary Elizabeth, 228, 238
Cheever, Henry T., 92–93
Chesebrough, Caroline, 54
Child, Lydia Maria, 202
Christianity, 3–5, 8, 13, 21, 29–30, 46, 115, 165, 252, 267–68, 281
Church of Jesus Christ of Latter-day Saints (LDS), 70–83, 140–57
Cicero, 115–16
Clark, Benjamin C., 169
Clark, Thomas M., 167
Clay, Henry, 72
Cole, Phyllis, 11
Coleridge, Samuel Taylor, 39, 60
Congregationalism, 166, 213, 247, 252, 261
Congregationalist, 171
Constitution, 77, 126, 129–31, 285–88
Cooper, James Fenimore, 94
I Corinthians, 8
Cowper, William, 213, 248
Cox, Harvey, 3
Creamer, Hannah Gardner, 52
Crevecouer, J. Hector St. John de, 90
Cross, Whitney R., 143
Crowninshield, Richard, 263
Cummins, Maria Susanna, 250

Dall, Caroline, 53
Darwin, Charles, 87
Davidson, Cathy, 129

Davis, Andrew Jackson, 22–23
Davis, David, 282
Dawson, Thomas, 166
Declaration of Independence, 1, 77, 189, 285–88
Disney World, 25
Derrida, Jacques, 3
Dickinson, Emily, 82, 211–24, 227–39
Dickinson, Lavinia, 231
Dickinson, Susan (Gilbert), 215–17, 228, 288
Dickinson, Ned, 217
Doddridge, Philip, 199, 261
Douglas, Ann, 207
Douglass, Frederick, 76, 79, 189
Downs, William, 278
Drake, Joseph Rodman, 202
Du Bois, W. E. B., 33
Dwight, Timothy, 181–82

Edwards, Jonathan, 184–86
Eichhorn, J. G., 108
Eliot, George, 54, 109
Eliot, T. S., 195
Emerson, Ellen, 21, 23, 29–30
Emerson, Ralph Waldo, 21, 23, 26–27, 29–33, 39, 50n9, 79, 96, 141, 168, 176, 178, 275
Emerson, Waldo, 23
England, Martha Winburn, 211
Eucharist, 21, 196
Evangelicalism, 179–91
Evans, Augusta Jane, 55; *Beulah*, 59–63

Farnham, Eliza, 55
Faust, Drew Gilpin, 28
Fern, Fanny, 53
Fessenden, Tracy, 4, 6
Finney, Charles Grandison, 143, 178–79, 186–88, 190, 260
Fireside Poets, 195–209
Fish, Stanley, 3
Fox-Genovese, Elizabeth, 68n20
Franchot, Jenny, 3
Freneau, Philip, 181

Friend, 93–94
Fuller, Margaret, 31–33, 189

Garrison, William Lloyd, 79, 182, 186
Genesis, Book of, 287
Givens, Terryl, 155–56
Goethe, Johann Wolfgang von, 60, 96
Goldfield, David, 11–12
Goldsmith, Oliver, 248
Goodman, Nan, 5
Greeley, Horace, 24
Grigsby, Charles, 280
Grigsby, Reuben, Jr., 280
Griswold, Rufus Wilmot, 216
Gruesz, Kirsten Silva, 196
Grow, Matthew J., 76

Haiti, 169–70
Halleck, Fitz-Greene, 202
Hanks, Dennis, 279
Hatch, Nathan O., 131
Hawthorne, Nathaniel, 12, 54, 82, 161–63, 176, 259–71, 276, 288; *The Blithedale Romance*, 8, 25, 54, 176; *The House of the Seven Gables*, 259–71; *The Scarlet Letter*, 54–59, 161–63, 176, 259
Heber, Reginald, 216
Hebrews (book of Bible), 8
Herald of Gospel Liberty, 164
Herder, Johann Gottfried von, 108, 110–11
Herndon, William, 284
Herod, 136
Higginson, Thomas Wentworth, 220, 227–39
Hinduism, 246, 254
Hobbs, June Hadden, 212
Hodge, Charles, 129
Holmes, Oliver Wendell, 195–97, 204
Homer, 108
Howe, Samuel Gridley, 230
Humphreys, David, 181
Hungerford, Amy, 5
Huntington, William, 166
hymns, 197–209, 211–24

Hymns for Mothers and Children, 217–19

Ingraham, J. H., 164
Iraq, 25
Irving, Washington, 69, 202
Islam, 254

Jackson, Virginia, 202
Jager, Colin, 56
James, William, 24, 276
Jay, William, 166
Jefferson, Thomas, 87, 94, 282
Jenkins, Philip, 6
jeremiad, 179–86
Jesus Christ, 116, 267, 270
John (apostle), 111
John, Gospel of, 21
John the Baptist, 38
Johnson, Matilda, 279
Jonah, Book of, 136
Judaism, 29
Justus, James, 195–96

Kabbalah, 29
Kane, Thomas, 75
Kauffman, Michael, 5
Kazin, Alfred, 3
Keach, Benjamin, 199
Keble, John, 216
King, Martin Luther, Jr., 191
Knapp, Frank, 263
Knapp, Joseph, 263
Koester, Nancy, 9, 176

Lamarck, Jean-Baptiste, 96
Lawrence, D. H., 97
Lehi, 148
Leitch, Mary, 245, 255–56
Leitch, Margaret W., 245, 255–56
Leonowen, Anna, 246
Levering, Miriam, 146
Levitt, Laura, 2
Lincoln, Abraham, 24, 276–89
Lincoln, Mary Todd, 24

Longfellow, Henry Wadsworth, 195–97, 204–9
Lowell, James Russell, 162, 196, 203–4
Lowth, Robert, 108
Luciano, Dana, 28
Lundin, Roger, 5
Luther, Martin, 118, 128
Lutherans, 198
Lyell, Charles, 88–90, 99

Madera, Judith, 12
Madison, James, 282
Madonna, the, 38
manifest destiny, 24, 29
Manson, Michael, 221–22
Mark, Gospel of, 180
Marshall, Megan, 10
Martineau, Harriet, 162–63
Martineau, James, 202
Mason, Lowell, 213
Matteson, John, 11
Matthew, Gospel of, 180
Matthews, Robert (Matthias), 143
Matthiessen, F. O., 10–11, 70, 175, 208
McClary, Susan, 14
McClure, John, 5
Melville, Herman, 12, 54, 87, 89–100, 125–36, 176, 276, 288; *Moby-Dick*, 8, 25, 54, 89–100, 125–36, 176, 247
Methodism, 199, 201, 207, 209n9, 250
Michaelis, J. D., 108
millennialism, 179–91
Miller, William, 143, 179
Millerites, 179, 183, 281
Milton, John, 77
missionaries, 245–57
Mitchell, Donald Grant, 237
Modern, John, 5, 55
Montgomery, James, 92–93, 213, 215, 216
Morgan, Victoria N., 211
Mormons, 70–83, 140
Moroni, 146, 155
Muslims, 78, 254–55

National Era, 76, 117
Nephi, 147–48, 154
Nephites, 147–54
New Americanists, 2
Newell, Harriet, 247–50
New Testament, 1, 8, 165, 196
Nichols, Mary Gove, 54–55
Nicolay, John G., 282
Noyes, John Humphrey, 143

Old Testament, 262
Oneida Perfectionists, 140, 143
Ong, Walter, 127–28, 131
Orsi, Robert, 5

Paine, Thomas, 149, 281
Panoplist, 171
Parker, Theodore, 230, 239
Paul (apostle), 8, 264, 269–70
Peabody, Andrew Preston, 163
Peter (apostle), 111
Phelps, Austin, 199, 207
Phelps, Elizabeth Stuart, 25
Phillips, Christopher N., 198
Phillips, Wendell, 79
photography, 24
Pickard, Samuel T., 69
Plato, 30
Poe, Edgar Allan, 8–9, 25, 54, 60, 161, 288
Pollock, James, 285
Pound, Ezra, 195
Pratt, Orson, 79
Protestantism, 126, 128, 198, 217, 252, 254, 275
Psalms, Book of, 183
Psyche, 49–50
Pufendorf, Samuel von, 282
Puritanism, 183–84

Quakers, 70

Reese, David Meredith, 71–72
Revelation, Book of, 179
Reynolds, David S., 2, 7, 9–15, 22, 40, 52–53, 69, 107, 119, 126, 130–31, 140, 161,

171, 175, 176, 177–78, 191, 211–12, 214, 246, 256–57, 259
Richards, Maria T., 164
Richardson, Robert D., 23
Ripley, George, 189
Root, Helen I., 254–55

Sabbath Hymn Book, 215
Sanborn, Franklin, 230
Sands, Robert Charles, 202
Sargent, M. H., 164
Schmidt, Leigh Eric, 4, 22, 26, 29–31
Scoresby, William, 91–92
Scripps, John Locke, 278–79
Sebold, Alice, 25
Second Great Awakening, 175–91, 260
secularization thesis, 5
Sedgwick, Catharine Maria, 201
Sewall, Henry D., 201
Shakers, 140
Shakespeare, William, 75, 80–81, 108, 237, 248, 268–69
Shelley, Mary, 96
Sherman, John, 285
Sigourney, Lydia Huntley, 249
Smith, Adam, 111
Smith, Gerrit, 230
Smith, Joseph, 72–74, 81, 140–57
Socrates, 38
Southern Literary Messenger, 117
Spiritualism, 25
Spirituals, 182
Springfield Republican, 53, 228, 238
Stanton, Elizabeth Cady, 189
St. Armand, Barton Levi, 211
Stearns, George Luther, 230
Stewart, Dugald, 111
Stoddard, Elizabeth, 53, 54; *The Morgesons*, 63–66
Stokes, Claudia, 177
Stowe, Calvin, 108–12, 181
Stowe, Harriet Beecher, 24, 107–19, 176–91, 245–57; *Uncle Tom's Cabin*, 8, 25, 52, 107–19, 176, 178–91, 245–57

Strauss, David F., 108
Stuart, Moses, 109
Sufism, 29
Sumner, Charles, 79, 285
Swedenborg, Emanuel, 72
Swedenborgianism, 72

Talmud, 110
Taylor, Charles, 4, 6, 55
Taylor, Edward, 9
Taylor, Hudson, 256
Thomson, James, 248
Thompson, George, 80
Thoreau, Henry David, 39, 82, 176, 230; *Walden*, 8
Tocqueville, Alexis de, 275
Todd, David Peck, 229
Todd, Mabel Loomis, 229
Transcendentalism, 29
Traubel, Horace, 142
Trump, Donald, 6

Unitarianism, 230

Vermont Chronicle, 168
Village Hymns, 215

Wallace, Lew, 171
Warner, Anna, 223
Warner, Susan, 52, 250
War on Terror, 3
Washington, George, 282
Watts, Isaac, 199–200, 212–14
Weber, Max, 149
Weiss, John, 31
Weld, Theodore Dwight, 186
Wellmon, Chad, 127–28
Wesley, Charles, 199
Wesley, John, 199
Wette, W. M. L. de, 108, 110
Wheelwright, Ebenezer, 161–71; *The Salem Belle*, 163, 166; *Traditions of Palestine*, 163–71
White, Hayden, 13
White, Joseph, 263

Whitman, Walt, 12, 24, 82, 140–57, 277, 283, 288–89; *Leaves of Grass*, 140–57
Whitmarsh, Caroline Snowden, 216–18
Whittier, John Greenleaf, 69–83, 196, 204, 208
Wilentz, Sean, 9
Winslow, Harriet Lathrop, 247–50, 252
Winslow, Miron, 248, 252–53

Worcester, Samuel, 213

Yothers, Brian, 7
Young, Brigham, 80
Young, Edward, 248

Zion's Herald and Wesleyan Journal, 169
Zoroastrianism, 29

www.ingramcontent.com/pod-product-compliance
Lightning Source LLC
Chambersburg PA
CBHW020638230426
43665CB00008B/224